D1282975

The Making of the Modern English State, 1460–1660

British Studies Series

General Editor JEREMY BLACK

Published

John Charmley **A History of Conservative Politics, 1900–1996**
David Childs **Britain since 1939**
John Davis **A History of Britain, 1885–1939**
David Eastwood **Government and Community in the English Provinces, 1700–1870**
Philip Edwards **The Making of the Modern English State, 1460–1660**
W. H. Fraser **A History of British Trade Unionism, 1700–1998**
Brian Hill **The Early Parties and Politics in Britain, 1688–1832**
Katrina Honeyman **Women, Gender and Industrialisation in England, 1700–1870**
Kevin Jefferys **Retreat from New Jerusalem: British Politics, 1951–1964**
David Loades **Power in Tudor England**
Alexander Murdoch **British History, 1660–1832: National Identity and Local Culture**
Anthony Musson and W. M. Ormrod **The Evolution of English Justice: Law, Politics and Society in the Fourteenth Century**
Murray G. H. Pittock **Inventing and Resisting Britain: Cultural Identities in Britain and Ireland, 1685–1789**
Nick Smart **The National Government, 1931–40**
Andrew Thorpe **A History of the British Labour Party**

British Studies Series
Series Standing Order
ISBN 0–333–71691–4 hardcover
ISBN 0–333–69332–9 paperback
(*outside North America only*)

You can receive future titles in this series as they are published by placing a standing order. Please contact your bookseller or, in case of difficulty, write to us at the address below with your name and address, the title of the series and the ISBN quoted above.

Customer Services Department, Macmillan Distribution Ltd
Houndmills, Basingstoke, Hampshire RG21 6XS, England

The Making of the Modern English State, 1460–1660

Philip Edwards

palgrave

First published 2001 by
PALGRAVE
Houndmills, Basingstoke, Hampshire RG21 6XS and
175 Fifth Avenue, New York, N.Y. 10010
Companies and representatives throughout the world

PALGRAVE is the new global academic imprint of
St. Martin's Press LLC Scholarly and Reference Division and
Palgrave Publishers Ltd (formerly Macmillan Press Ltd).

Outside North America
ISBN 0–333–69835–5 hardback
ISBN 0–333–69836–3 paperback

In North America
ISBN 0–312–23613–1 hardback
ISBN 0–312–23614–X paperback

This book is printed on paper suitable for recycling and
made from fully managed and sustained forest sources.

A catalogue record for this book is available
from the British Library.

Library of Congress Cataloging-in-Publication Data
Edwards, Philip, 1944–
      The making of the modern English state, 1460–1660 /
      Philip Edwards.
          p. cm. — (British studies series)
      Includes bibliographical references (p.) and index.
      ISBN 0–312–23613–1 — ISBN 0–312–23614–X (pbk.)
        1. Great Britain—Politics and government—1485–1603.
      2. Great Britain—Politics and government—1603–1714.
      3. Great Britain—Politics and government—1461–1483.
      I. Title. II. Series.

DA300.E39 2000
942—dc21
                                                    00–030888

10   9   8   7   6   5   4   3   2   1
10   09   08   07   06   05   04   03   02   01

Printed in China

Genealogy

Contents

Prologue

In the period covered by this book, 1460–1660, the kingdom of England underwent dramatic and formative changes that led to the creation of the true modern English state, a state quite distinct from the more cosmopolitan and foreign-dominated one of the Middle Ages. There was no sharp break, of course, between the more European past and the nationalist future, but on the contrary much continuity, especially in the area of the constitution. However, it was not until the early fifteenth century, just before our period begins, that the line of foreign rulers over England finally embraced English as their daily tongue, the symbol of their unalloyed alliance with the English people: Henry V (1413–22) was actually the first English king after the Norman Conquest habitually to speak English, rather than a dialect of French. Medieval England had been ruled by two lines of French kings, the Normans and the Angevins (also known as Plantagenets). Accordingly much of the work of government in the early fifteenth century still continued to be written in Norman-French, but what becomes evident by the second half of the fifteenth century is the increasing use of the English language in government. Richard III (1483–5), for example, was the first English king to take his coronation oath in English. But this fifteenth-century English was still embryonic and stiff, and would need another century and indeed the 'Elizabethan Renaissance' to turn it into the marvellously flexible language that we know today.

In 1460, despite its memories of great glories in the past, England was merely a second-rate power on the edge of Europe, seemingly all set for further decline into the anarchy of civil war. Yet by 1660 England was a power to be reckoned with, boasting an enormous cultural achievement, and well on its way to commercial and imperial glory that would make it the leading European and indeed world power in the eighteenth and nineteenth centuries. The 200 years between the two civil wars covered in this book can be viewed as having a creative unity all of their own. They constituted above all the last great age of personal

1

monarchy in England, and, if we also allow in Henry V, the only period of truly *English* personal monarchy, even though ironically none of the three dynasties involved – Plantagenets, Tudors and Stuarts – had English roots. After 1660, the constitutional nature of the later Stuarts is contentious and they cannot be unequivocally counted as personal monarchs; indeed their foolhardy attempts to revive personal monarchy after the traumas of the Great Civil War led swiftly to the establishment in 1689 of true constitutional monarchy after the 'Glorious Revolution', which would lead to a new chapter in English (and indeed British) history. The period is also bounded by a crisis of political authority – in both the 1450s and the 1650s – caused by the absence of a true monarch: an inane king in the 1450s and no king at all in the 1650s.

The evolution of England by 1460: the monarchy

Throughout the Middle Ages, and through most of the period covered by this book, ending with the creation of the Republic in 1649, England was a personal monarchy, where the monarch both ruled and reigned. The personality, and indeed the health, of the sovereign had enormous consequences on the history and well-being of the state. The medieval English monarchy had emerged as one of the most powerful in Europe, in the sense of the king's ability to enforce his will on his subjects and gain obedience, as well as in the sophistication of his administration. The political development of England was indeed precocious – as far back as the original English state of the Anglo-Saxons (409–1066). By the tenth and eleventh centuries the Old English state was administratively the most sophisticated in Europe and had taken massive strides towards national unification. Unfortunately, the growth of this first national state was to be impeded by foreign invasion in the eleventh century, first by the Danes and then by Duke William of Normandy.

After the Norman Conquest, kings of England increased their power, while Henry II (1154–89), the first of the Plantagenets, was also the richest king of his age. Yet despite this England was never to develop into an absolutist state of the type that became common in Europe in the sixteenth and seventeenth centuries.

Why did England differ from continental trends towards absolute monarchy in the period covered by this book? The answer lies in England's medieval development.

In the mid-fifteenth century the greatest English lawyer of his day, Sir John Fortescue, expressed his views on the nature of the English monarchy in his *De Laudibus Legum Anglie* (In Praise of the Laws of England). This treatise, written in the 1460s in the form of a dialogue between Fortescue himself, the chancellor in the exiled Lancastrian court sheltering in France during the Wars of the Roses, and the young Prince Edward of Lancaster, was intended to teach the prince about the rights and duties of an English king. According to Fortescue, the king was the source and fountain of all justice and law, but he was not to follow the precepts of Roman law to be found in many places in Europe – especially not its famous principle of 'what pleases the prince has the force of law'. Instead, the king was to study and maintain the laws of England. Fortescue was here consciously contrasting English and continental (especially French) political practice. The French monarchy, he says, was a 'dominium regale' (a royal domain), wherein all power resided in the Crown; but England, on the other hand, was a 'dominium politicum et regale' (a political and royal domain), where power was shared between the king and his leading subjects. For example, the English monarch could not impose laws or taxes without the consent of Parliament. The (admittedly idealised) constitutional system that Fortescue was outlining was the fruit of the struggle against the growth of royal power in England during previous centuries.

Monarchical power had indeed waxed from William the Conqueror to Henry II, becoming arbitrary and authoritarian, but eventually it provoked opposition from the barons. Such resistance began in the reign of Henry II's son, King John (1199–1215) against whom there arose the first of a long series of attempts by the barons to control the Crown. Their first major achievement in imposing a constitutional check on the king was Magna Carta (1215). Three provisions of this great charter stand out as having particular significance: first, that no free man could be imprisoned or lose his lands without due process of law; second, that kings could not deny or sell justice; and third, that taxation needed the consent of the leading men of the realm, the tenants-in-chief (that is the great lords who held land directly from the king in the feudal system). Although at first Magna Carta applied only to the minority of freemen, with the disappearance of servility by the end of the Middle Ages its significance became widespread.

A similar struggle developed under Henry III (1216–72) and the institution of Parliament was born as a result, which in time would become the most effective curb on royal power. Tensions between monarch and barons continued under Edward I (1272–1307) because of his demands for increased taxation; landowners, merchants and clergy were all indignant and pointed to Magna Carta as their defence against unjust taxation. Throughout the fourteenth century the financial pressures of war would engender tensions and evoke a wider opposition to arbitrary monarchy. The fourteenth century indeed saw the quarrel between monarchy and baronage climax with two royal abdications and murders – an amazing trend emulated nowhere else in Europe.

Edward II (1307–27) tried to rule in an arbitrary fashion, and finally was forced to abdicate, being imprisoned and then gruesomely murdered. Richard II (1377–99) was the second royal sacrifice. He had ruled absolutely, levying taxes without parliamentary authority and ignoring the laws of England. His arbitrariness climaxed when he attempted to prevent the greatest magnate in the realm, Henry Bolingbroke, from succeeding his father John of Gaunt as Duke of Lancaster, and instead ordered Bolingbroke banished for life. Such autocratic behaviour and interference in the rights of property inheritance united the landowning classes against Richard, so that when Bolingbroke returned in July 1399 he was warmly welcomed by his fellow magnates. Bolingbroke succeeded because of Richard's unpopularity and because of the perceived need for a leading magnate to take control of the realm and remove hated royal favourites. It is less clear whether people were actually supporting Bolingbroke as a new candidate for the throne, while Richard believed that he would himself remain king but within parliamentary limits. However, flushed with success, Bolingbroke seized his opportunity and announced that Richard had abdicated. As Richard was childless, Bolingbroke claimed the throne by right of blood, being descended from Henry III's supposedly eldest son Edmund Crouchback. Of course, Henry III's eldest son had really been King Edward I, but the fiction was maintained that Edmund had been the eldest although set aside because of physical deformity. There being initially no opposition to the seizure of the throne, Henry Bolingbroke, claiming divine sanction for his actions, became King Henry IV, the first ruler of the House of Lancaster, while Richard was soon put to death in secret.

The history of the House of Lancaster forms the prelude to the period covered by this book. Because they were usurpers, the Lancastrians were a weak dynasty, susceptible to the demands of both the lords and the Parliament to oversee the government. The seeming modernity of the use of frequent, indeed annual, Parliaments made this a period of 'Lancastrian constitutionalism' in the eyes of Victorian historians. In reality, it signified weak monarchy. Henry IV had rebellions to face, one of which would have destroyed the unity of England had it been successful: that of the Earl of Northumberland and his son Henry Percy (Hotspur) with the Welsh rebel Owain Glyndwr and his son-in-law Sir Edmund Mortimer. By the Tripartite Indenture of 1405 these confederate rebels aimed to divide England into three separate zones. The rebellions failed and Henry IV was able to bequeath the realm to his son Henry V, who tried to divert the energies of the nobles into another bout of foreign war with France. However, before embarking at Southampton in 1415 Henry V had first to quash the plot led by Richard Earl of Cambridge, grandfather of the Yorkist monarch Edward IV (1461–83). Fortunately for the Lancastrians this phase of the Hundred Years War would be a glorious one for England and the victory at Agincourt (1415) its crowning achievement. Henry V's victories in France seemed to give the divine seal of approval at last to the usurping Lancastrians, and the new dynasty could then settle down amidst general approval – and no more plots. So that when this great warrior king died, still young, in 1422, the kingdom was transferred peacefully to a baby, one who would, however, grow up into a weak and unstable, and at times insane, king. It was the problems posed by the weak monarchy of Henry VI, rather than those engendered by the earlier usurpation of 1399, which would lead eventually to the Wars of the Roses.

The ideal of kingship – the belief that the king was a man set apart by God with special powers conferred on him – survived even these two royal murders. From the reign of Henry I

(1100–35) onwards kings had claimed certain healing powers, especially concerning the disease of scrofula (a lymphatic condition); this act of healing was known as 'touching for the king's evil', and would be practised right down to the end of the seventeenth century. From the time of Edward II there had grown up the belief in the miraculous power of the coronation oil. The king was 'the Lord's anointed', 'the vicar of God in the kingdom'. Despite, or more probably because of, the sordid reality of royal murders the semi-divine nature of the monarchic ideal continued to be emphasised, while the aloofness and importance of monarchy as an institution were stressed by the growth of the royal Court in the later Middle Ages. Edward II and Richard II both enlarged the royal Court and made ceremonial there more elaborate. Yorkists and Tudors were to go even further in this direction of courtly magnificence because they were adamant that the Court should constitute the only political centre of the state. The magnificence of the Court was meant to emulate the wonder of Heaven, further underlining the general belief that royal power came from God, and that any challenge to it was both a crime and a sin. The words of address to a king became more elaborate in the later Middle Ages: he was now saluted as 'our most sovereign and gracious lord', 'your highness' and 'your majesty', whereas in earlier times he was simply addressed as 'my lord the king'. Richard II also began the tradition of claiming to be an 'emperor' in his realm.

The monarchy was also becoming more *English* by the end of the Middle Ages, and this was certainly a new development. After 1066 the kings of England were foreigners, who spoke a dialect of the French language, with England being simply part of a wider empire – first the Norman Empire (of Normandy and Maine) and then the much greater Angevin Empire that was brought together on the marriage of Henry II to the heiress Eleanor of Aquitaine. The Angevin Empire included Anjou, Normandy, Poitou, Guyenne, Gascony and other territories stretching right down through western France to the Pyrenees. This huge Angevin Empire began to break up under King John – casualties of an expanding France. In 1259 Henry III (1216–72) formally surrendered any rights to Normandy, Anjou and Poitou, and agreed to keep Gascony and other territories only as feudal dependencies of France, and to do homage to the French

Crown for them. With the loss of these continental possessions England itself became increasingly important to these Plantagenet kings and indeed the focal point of their inheritance. Edward III disliked doing homage to the French king, and went as far as to put forward his own claim to the throne of France (through his mother) when it became vacant on the death of the last Capetian, and thus he initiated the Hundred Years War (1338–1453). However, the nobles of England were worried that if Edward were to be successful in his claim to the French throne then England would be swallowed up in a larger French empire. Edward III had therefore to soothe such fears in his Parliament of 1340.

The point here, of course, is that no one thought automatically in terms of a greater England; the threat was of a greater France, where the English nobles would lose out. There was no guarantee of an independent history for England. But the Hundred Years War would be a real spur to the growth of English national feeling that penetrated the upper and lower orders, coinciding with the emergence for the first time in the late fourteenth century of court patronage for English-language writers, such as Geoffrey Chaucer. Surviving English-language works before this period tend to come from the periphery of England, but now under the impetus of war one sees the emergence of English literature at a bilingual Court. As mentioned earlier, Henry V was the first English king whose native tongue was English, but as so much administration was still done in French, the scene in Shakespeare's *Henry V* in which the conqueror finds it difficult to converse with Princess Catherine of Valois because of his ignorance of French is quite false and anachronistic.

Although Henry V was a military genius his enormous success was mainly due to divisions within the French ruling house, and after his death the war went badly. By its end in 1453 only the port of Calais remained in English hands, but this would act as the inspiration for continued European ambitions for over a century. The emergence of a true English monarchy did not automatically entail the abandonment of such medieval ambitions. Thus when Henry VIII (1509–47) at the start of his reign was intent on invading France to claim the throne he was continuing a long late-medieval tradition: Henry VIII saw himself above all as a new Henry V. England was not to reconcile itself to being just an island kingdom until the reign of Elizabeth (1558–1603), who would positively reject territorial aggrandisement in Europe; the loss of Calais in 1558 would eventually lead to expansion westwards and to colonial ambitions in America. England after 1558 felt impelled to carve out a new identity for itself, as little enmeshed with Europe as possible, even though (for annoyance value mainly) English monarchs went on claiming officially to be kings of France right down to 1802.

English society

We need first to bear in mind the population figures for England in the Middle Ages and in the Tudor and early Stuart periods:

1066   1.2–1.6 million
1300   3.75 million
1430   2.1 million
1525   2.3 million
1545   2.8 million
1603   4.3 million
1650   5.2 million

There had been a steady growth in the English population after 1066, and there now seems general agreement that the population figure reached by 1300 was too large for the agriculture of the day to support. In 1300 there was the spectre of land hunger, low wages, starvation, even cannibalism. In the first half of the fourteenth century one discerns a weakened and malnourished population that was unable to withstand the calamity of the Black Death, which struck Europe as a whole in the years 1348–50; like most of Europe England lost about one-third of its people. The Black Death was a pandemic of the plague, a disease caused by rat fleas. The most common form was bubonic plague, named after the swellings (or *buboes*) that appeared in the groin (from a flea-bite in the leg), in the armpits (from a bite on the arm) or on the neck (from a bite on the face). Bubonic plague broke out in the summer months in towns and cities because of insanitary conditions, when the warm temperatures were ideal for the multiplication of these fleas. Death would come after some five days, and the mortality rate for bubonic plague was between 60 and 85 per cent. The Black Death of the fourteenth century had involved more than just bubonic plague: also the more deadly pneumonic and septicaemic forms. The bubonic form of the plague was to remain a major feature of the life in England until the last famous outbreak in 1665. England was a permanently enzootic area, which meant that there was no need for any new importation of infected rats to keep the disease rampant. In the reign of Charles I, in September 1625, there was the famous incident at Malpas in Cheshire where everyone in the village died of the plague, and the last full-grown man to get the disease actually dug his own grave in the yard and buried himself in it. He seems to have taken this strange action because he was certain he was about to die and knew that the remaining servant-girl and a boy would not be able to get his body out of the house.[1]

Although clearly a horrible experience for those who lived through the Black Death in the fourteenth century, one can say that its effects were in many ways good for the tough people who survived unscathed. Those effects included an increase in wages as labour was now in short supply; indeed wages doubled in the period 1350–1415. There was also a fall in land prices because of the surplus of land on the market. And the servile status of the peasantry was lifted with the decline of feudalism that was hastened by the population disaster. Of course, feudalism was already dying out before the great mortality because of its own economic success in creating surpluses. Feudalism was meant to be a static system, but once it started producing surpluses for investment it led on inexorably to the beginning of capitalism.

The population catastrophe in the mid-fourteenth century helped the changeover by landlords from direct demesne farming to leasing out their demesnes to prosperous peasants (because this was cheaper than paying the peasants higher wages); and these successful peasants took full advantage of the new economic and social environment to better themselves and rise up in the world. Under the newly emerging system servile peasants were transformed into freeholders, copyholders and leaseholders, with labour services being commuted to money rents. So, the demographic reverse and the decline of classical feudalism led to the growth of personal freedom among the peasantry. However, this was not granted to them overnight or without resistance on the part of the ruling landed class. One of the main demands of the Peasants' Revolt of 1381 was the abolition of feudal servility. The Peasants' Revolt was a failure, but the lot of the peasants would indeed improve because of impersonal economic forces, especially the scarcity of labour. The smaller labour force could demand higher wages and free itself from its servile status, and while the ruling group might try to thwart the majority it eventually was forced to make concessions. Thus whereas most peasants had been servile in 1300, the vast majority were legally free by 1500. The later Middle Ages indeed saw much social mobility. Many of the great Tudor families owed their initial rise to shrewd deals made by their peasant ancestors from the late fourteenth century onwards. For example, the Spencers of Althorp (Northamptonshire) emerged as successful yeomen graziers by the end of the fifteenth century, solid gentry in the sixteenth and nobility in the seventeenth century. A similar story can be told of the great Cecil family of the Elizabethan period: in the fifteenth century they had been yeomanry from the Welsh border, going by the name of Seisyll.

Except for Marxist historians, for whom all history is dominated by class conflict, there seems general agreement that the idea of class is an inappropriate one with which to analyse early modern Europe. To speak of classes is anachronistic because most people did not have class consciousness, a prerequisite for the existence of true class differentiation. There were too many local, vertical barriers to the development of class consciousness; people felt loyalty to their local superiors rather than to people of their own social or economic status further afield. It was status groups rather than classes that made up early modern English society. Peter Laslett has argued that only one true class existed in early modern England, that of the gentry, the ruling landowning class because they alone had a consciousness of forming a national class, whose members intermarried on a nationwide basis. Even Marxist historians, who still argue for the existence of classes below that of the gentry, recognise that class consciousness was diluted and blunted at this time.

As for the ruling class, the gentry made up about 1 per cent of the population in the fifteenth century, rising to about 2 per cent at the beginning of the seventeenth. At the top were the nobles, who were certainly a separate legal entity, but not a separate class, simply the richest and most successful members of the landowning gentry. They sat in the House of Lords but their sons could sit in the House of Commons. The nobles were originally the military companions of the king, and throughout our period would remain great military figures in their localities. The two original noble titles were the (Anglo-Saxon) earl and the (Norman) baron, but in the late Middle Ages new distinctions were formulated between members of the nobility: at the very top were (non-royal) dukes, then came marquises (both created by Richard II), viscounts (from 1440), as well as the old earls and barons (or lords). These refinements and gradations were the result of the growth of Parliament, and the need to specify who exactly was eligible to attend the House of Lords by writs of summons. For most of our period before the great creation of new peerages by James I (1603–25) there were some 60 nobles at any time summoned to the Lords. Below the nobility came the gentry proper, the most distinguished being designated knight, then esquire and finally at the bottom gentleman (the last title a recent fifteenth-century one). The lowliest gentry title of 'gentleman' marked the crucial dividing line in a pre-industrial society without machines: the gentleman did not work with his hands, unlike the vast majority of mankind. The exception to this rule was military service, the only form of manual work that was appropriate to the gentry's concept of honour. In the reign of Elizabeth a gentleman would be defined by William Harrison in his *Description of England* as one 'who can live idly and without manual labour, and thereto is able and will bear the port, charge and countenance of a gentleman, he shall be called master, which is the title that men give to esquires and gentlemen, and reputed for a gentleman'.

The gentry ruled an agrarian society. The vast majority of people lived and worked on the land. Below the gentry came the yeomanry (the affluent tenant-farmers), cottagers, copyholders and finally the growing band of landless labourers. As for the towns, they remained fairly small, and were home to about 6 per cent of the population in 1500, but rising to about 10 per cent thereafter. Nevertheless, town-dwellers were very important economically. Towns were regional centres as well as the springboards for overseas trade; they were also the centres of the professions and the trade guilds. There were no real urban dynasties in England unlike in many European cities (such as Venice or Amsterdam): instead rich English merchants bought land in the countryside and became gentry, loosening their ties with trade. Only London was a big city, with about 45 000 people in 1460, rising to 200 000 in 1600 and 400 000 by 1650. All other towns remained small in comparison: in 1460 Norwich and Bristol had about 10 000 inhabitants apiece, Coventry some 6000 and York about 7000 citizens, and the rises thereafter were modest. Norwich had about 15 000 in 1600, and Bristol about 12 000.[2] Most towns were still much involved in local rural life, but even so one should not forget that towns were essentially non-feudal and largely self-governing, with a greater independence and sense of freedom than in the countryside. Most of the larger towns still had their walls to delineate their special status. Social mobility too was much easier in the towns and cities, where even poor boys could do well. The pantomime story of Dick Whittington, which was first narrated in 1605, and which seems to have had little to do with the real Sir Richard Whittington, lord mayor of London (*d.* 1423), kept alive the eternal hope of social mobility, especially that poor boys coming to London could find wealth and fame.

How long could people expect to live in the period 1460–1660? To answer this question we must first bear in mind that as late as the 1690s, the government statistician Gregory King suggested that the average life expectancy in his day was only 32 years. This was, of course, a statistical average based on the huge prevailing infant mortality rate. According to King, life expectancy in England was similar to what could be expected elsewhere in western Europe. Certainly life expectancy was much different from what we are experiencing now at the beginning of the twenty-first century (where it is about 75 years), but King's figure is too general. There was a wide variation, with some areas experiencing an average of nearly 50 with other areas (mainly towns) experiencing nearer the European average of 30. What we do know for certain is that England (like elsewhere) was overwhelmingly a young society, and that despite the huge infant mortality rate and the high vulnerablity of children the largest group in society was that aged between birth and nine, the second largest that between 10 and 20 years. Probably half the population in the late fifteenth and sixteenth centuries was aged under 20. There were no national censuses of the population in our period, and our knowledge of demographic trends is based on extrapolation from a variety of sources. One local census, that of the township of Ealing near London in 1599, is probably typical: here nearly 50 per cent of inhabitants were under 20 years of age; 20 per cent were 20 to 40 years; 24.5 per cent were over 50; and only 7 per cent were aged 60 or more. Thus old people were a small minority in early modern England; indeed the same proportion of old people would continue down to 1900, whereas today some 16 per cent of the population are above 60. However, it would not really be true to say that people are living longer today in the sense of pushing back the frontiers of longevity. The idea of old age has remained constant from biblical times: old age is 'three score years and ten'. Today most people reach old age; very few did so in our period. However, we do find examples of really old people at this time – great exceptions who prove the rule – and we shall look at two of them. The most famous old person in English history lived through a large span of our period: William Parr may have been born in 1483, when Richard III seized the throne, and he died in 1635, during the personal rule of Charles I. If these dates are correct then he reached the age of 151 or 152, and had lived through some of the greatest changes in English life. He became a great celebrity in his last years, having been 'discovered' and paraded around the fairs as a curiosity. It seems that he married for the first time at the age of 80 in the early years of Elizabeth's reign, and that the Armada year of 1588 (when he was 105) was especially memorable if only because he had to do public penance for getting a spinster pregnant! He was very proud of this achievement and boasted of it to an embarrassed Charles I. Another, but less famous, great survivor of our period – whose life achievements were thankfully recorded for us – was the Welshman Gwilym ap Hywel ap Dafydd of Anglesey in north Wales, who died in March 1581 at the age of 105. He had been three times married and had lived with two other women. By his first wife he had had 22 children, by the second ten, and by the third four; with seven illegitimate children he had fathered a grand total of 43 children, the eldest of whom in 1581 was a man aged 84, and the youngest a boy of two-and-a-half!

Some aspects of the English economy, 1460–1660

The economy remained pre-industrial throughout our period. This does not mean that there were no industries at all, but that agriculture still dominated the scene and the livelihood of people. There was little in the way of mechanisation or investment in fixed capital equipment that would increase productivity significantly, and there were few technological improvements. Early modern industries involved the production of basic human needs, such as food, clothing and housing; and there were few industrial workers who did not also work in agriculture. At the base of the industrial pyramid were the traditional handcraft industries of the towns working on basic raw materials, such as carpentry, barrel-making, plumbing, etc. These handcraft industries were usually grouped into guilds which maintained quality control and regulated entry to the crafts. These traditional associations of workers began to decline in the Tudor period. Unlike in some European states, the English government did nothing to protect the guilds but rather allowed new industries to flourish outside of them, especially the mining ventures of the Elizabethan period.

Above the guilds came the more commercialised 'domestic' or 'putting-out' system of industry, especially for textiles. This was very much a rural industry, with cottagers being employed at home to spin wool or yarn. Merchant entrepreneurs would supply the raw material to the workers in their homes and collect the semi-finished product, to be finished off elsewhere by fullers and dyers. There were no factories in this system, with the exception of two early Tudor clothiers who maintained large numbers of workers at the same spot, namely John Winchecombe (alias Jack of Newbury), who employed about 500 workers, and William Stumpe, who made a spinning 'factory' out of some outbuildings of the dissolved Malmesbury Abbey. But these men were the great exceptions to the dispersed domestic production system, and any tendency to a factory system was frustrated by the Act of 1555 which prevented the accumulation of more than two looms. Because of local demand from an increasing population and by increased overseas orders the production of woollen cloth increased tenfold in our period, with diversification in the kinds of cloths produced. The major development was the production of lighter cloths, called the 'new draperies' in the early seventeenth century under the impetus of foreign Protestant refugee cloth workers. The only major technological innovation in this sector of industry was the invention of the 'stocking-frame' to replace hand knitting in the 1590s by William Lee, which, after initially being discouraged by the government, was hired by domestic workers and helped the hosiery industry to expand in the seventeenth century.

More 'modern' forms of production were those centralised undertakings with fixed capital equipment, such as blast furnaces, watermills and windmills, as well as mining ventures and shipbuilding yards. Although these concerns involved aspects of an assembly line, few were really large-scale industries or employed many permanent workers. Some extravagant claims have been made for an early industrial revolution in this period but they have found few supporters. Certainly there was progress. Iron production more than doubled in the sixteenth and early seventeenth centuries, and coal production tripled. Coal remained largely a domestic fuel rather than an industrial one before 1660, with charcoal being preferred for firing blast furnaces. Nevertheless coal was being experimented with as an industrial fuel by the early seventeenth century for such things as salt evaporation and soap-boiling.

The overwhelming majority of English people lived by agriculture, which over our two centuries made substantial progress and improvement, so that while malnutrition remained a bugbear for a large part of the population, famine disappeared, except for some rare occurrences in the 1590s in the far north, whereas famines remained a regular nightmare on the European scene down to the early eighteenth century. The reason for England's better performance was the replacement of peasant subsistence farming by the increasing commercialisation of agriculture, with large farms, capitalist methods and investment, and much regional specialisation. The old view that medieval farming methods remained unreformed until the 'agricultural revolution' of the late eighteenth century has been disproved in the last 50 years. The alternative extreme hypothesis of an agricultural revolution in the sixteenth and seventeenth centuries, as proposed by Eric Kerridge in 1967,[3] has not found widespread acceptance although it has focused attention on the significant improvements of this period. Historians of agriculture differ widely in their judgements, although the general consensus is that the years 1460–1660 witnessed substantial agricultural growth, but with much regional diversity, so that innovations of one region might take another two centuries to become generally known. There was certainly an increase in the area of cultivation in our period – perhaps by as much as 25 per cent. Forest and park were enclosed for tillage, fertile marshland and fen were reclaimed, and the thin soils of chalk and limestone uplands were cultivated. There was a substantial increase in production through the enclosure of the former great open fields, which allowed the farmer greater freedom to organise, to innovate and to specialise for the growing market.[4] Perhaps as much as 45 per cent of land was already enclosed for tillage by 1500, slowly reaching about 47 per cent by 1600 but then skyrocketing to 71 per cent by 1700 and at least 75 per cent by 1750. Besides enclosures, from the early seventeenth century there was considerable reclamation of fens, swamps and marshes, especially with the importation of foreign engineers and the infusion of capital. By the General Drainage Act of 1600 land could be given to those with the necessary capital to drain it.

Productivity was also raised by improved methods, such as the development after 1550 of what is termed alternate (or convertible or 'up and down') husbandry – that is, the alternation of tillage with pasture on the same fields. In the early Tudor period alternate husbandry was mainly confined to the north-west, but after 1560, and especially after 1590, it spread to half the farm lands, replacing the old system of permanent tillage or pasture. Fields were put to crops for three or four years in succession, and then laid with legumes and grasses. Closes began to be broken up for short tillage intervals, followed by leys of 6–20 years long. This large use of grass improved the feeding of livestock and the greater production of manure, in turn leading to greater production of cereals. Kerridge has made much of the growth of alternate husbandry for his interpretation of a revolution in agriculture. Another innovation in our period which Kerridge emphasised was the floating water meadow – a method to improve the productivity of the chalk downlands. This was probably first employed in Herefordshire late in Elizabeth's reign.[5] The floating water meadow was an irrigational device, diverting stream water to cover a meadow. The chalk and other minerals in the water were useful as a fertiliser, and the water itself protected the soil from frost. The result was lush grass in spring and summer and larger flocks of sheep. However, while an important innovation, the floating water meadow was probably not as widespread or as efficient as Kerridge believed. Just as our period was closing, some new fodder crops were being introduced, such as clover and turnips, especially owing to the influence of Dutch Protestant refugees. More printed works about farming appeared in our period, such as Mr Fitzherbert's *Boke of Husbandrye*, and Gervase Markham's many books on horse breeding, husbandry and home economy. However, it is difficult to know how widely these books were read. Nevertheless it is clear that all together the innovations of the years 1460–1660 improved productivity and laid the essential basis for the expansion of agriculture from the late eighteenth century onwards.

The major incentive for agricultural improvement was the population growth that reached 5.2 million by 1650 and the consequent price rise, but these two necessary conditions cannot have been a full and sufficient cause of progress in agriculture because they also existed in Europe, which nevertheless did not witness great improvements and where famines still regularly occurred down to the eighteenth century. England must have had peculiarities of its own which aided its development. These may be sought in the greater individualism which Alan Macfarlane has discerned in the English, compared to the Europeans, stretching way back into the Middle Ages,[6] the opening up of the land market in the 1530s with the dissolution of the monasteries, and the high degree of internal peace and freedom from foreign invasion which the Tudor regime offered and which was eagerly sought by the growing landowning elite.

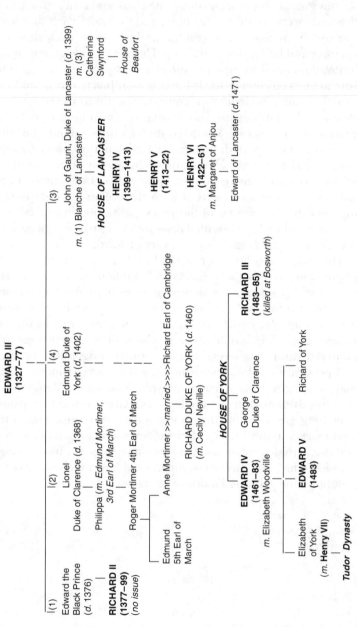

THE HOUSES OF LANCASTER AND YORK

EDWARD III
(1327–77)

(1) Edward the Black Prince (d. 1376)
— RICHARD II (1377–99) (no issue)

(2) Lionel Duke of Clarence (d. 1368)
— Philippa (m. Edmund Mortimer, 3rd Earl of March)
— Roger Mortimer 4th Earl of March
— Edmund 5th Earl of March

Anne Mortimer >>married.>>>> Richard Earl of Cambridge
— RICHARD DUKE OF YORK (d. 1460) (m. Cecily Neville)

HOUSE OF YORK

EDWARD IV (1461–83) m. Elizabeth Woodville

George Duke of Clarence

RICHARD III (1483–85) (killed at Bosworth)

EDWARD V (1483)

Richard of York

Elizabeth of York (m. Henry VII)

Tudor Dynasty

(3) John of Gaunt, Duke of Lancaster (d. 1399)
m. (1) Blanche of Lancaster
m. (3) Catherine Swynford
— House of Beaufort

HOUSE OF LANCASTER

HENRY IV (1399–1413)

HENRY V (1413–22)

HENRY VI (1422–61) m. Margaret of Anjou

Edward of Lancaster (d. 1471)

(4) Edmund Duke of York (d. 1402)

1 The Wars of the Roses

The term 'Wars of the Roses' is the traditional title given to a complex and protracted, but not continuous, conflict among the political elite in England in the second half of the fifteenth century. The Crown changed hands violently five times between 1461 and 1485. The ruling Plantagenets became divided into Yorkist and Lancastrian parties striving for the throne. Finally after the elimination of most claimants the Plantagenets found themselves swept from power with the arrival of a new dynasty in the person of Henry Tudor, victor of the battle of Bosworth (22 August 1485). Henry Tudor had only the flimsiest claim to the Crown of England, and his success was due solely to the events of a single day: the very future of England hung on the outcome of a battle, just as it had back in 1066. There was nothing inevitable about the accession of the Tudors: far from it, their advent was one of the flukes of a very confused period of English history; and it is more true to say that Richard III, the last of the Yorkist branch of the Plantagenets, lost Bosworth than that Henry Tudor positively won it. The crucial point is that so much in the history of this period depended on personalities and accidents. And the final victors who were to emphasise their very Englishness in the sixteenth century were in reality descendants of an obscure Welsh family who had been involved in the great Welsh rebellion against Henry IV in the early fifteenth century. Such were the most unexpected results of this amazingly dramatic age.

The normal dating of the Wars of the Roses is from 1455 (with the first battle at St Albans) to 1485 (and the battle of Bosworth). However, both the significance and the duration of the wars became subjects of dispute among historians in the twentieth century. It may be wiser to argue that, in terms of a crisis occasioned by competing claims to the English throne, the wars really began in 1460, when Richard Duke of York presented for the first time his formal claim to the throne, and ended in 1487 when the new Tudor dynasty was made secure by its victory at the battle of Stoke against the last Yorkist remnants in England. As no clear dynastic issue was raised before 1460 perhaps the period from 1455 to 1459 (i.e. between the first battle of St Albans and the flight of the Yorkist leaders from England) should be seen only as prelude to the wars, rather than as an integral part. One should also remember that the battles came in clusters, with long periods of peace for most people in between: these years of battles were 1459–61, 1469–71 and 1483–7.

The term 'Wars of the Roses'

Although this has become a popular term, it must be remembered that those actually involved in the fighting were not aware of the name 'Wars of the Roses'. No one at the time could say that he was fighting in the 'Wars of the Roses', in the way that in the twentieth century combatants were conscious of participating in the Second World War or the Gulf War (to use the popular title). The colourful and romantic name of the 'Wars of the Roses' is not contemporary to the fifteenth century. Rather, the idea, though not the exact term, was born in the sixteenth century and was the product of Tudor propaganda. Indeed, it is important to grasp that we still today see so much of the fifteenth century through the eyes of Tudor writers. The great Tudor intellectual Sir Thomas Smith in 1561 referred to 'the striving of the two roses', and this notion was popularised in the history plays of William Shakespeare written in the 1590s. In the same vein the diarist Sir John Oglander in 1646 referred to 'the quarrel of the warring roses'. A century later, the Scottish philosopher and historian David Hume in his *History of England* (1761) also referred to rose emblems in a serious work of history, when he used the phrase 'the wars between the two roses'. However, the exact term 'Wars of the Roses' was first coined by the novelist Sir Walter Scott on page 1 of his novel *Ivanhoe* of 1820. Since Scott's time that term has been in common use to epitomise the political upheaval of the late fifteenth century. Thus the phrase 'Wars of the Roses' has a long history. It is nevertheless a term which many modern historians have criticised, and some have been eager to disparage and condemn it as hopelessly distorting the reality of the conflict and to urge its complete removal. To S. B. Chrimes, the term represented 'a figment of retrospective imagination';[1] to R. L. Storey, 'the title is misconceived'.

As a historical concept the term 'Wars of the Roses' contains three interpretative ideas, which have not found many defenders among scholars of late. The first of these is that there were two clearly delineated sides or parties involved in the fighting, who wore emblems of different coloured roses: white roses for the House of York, and red roses for the House of Lancaster. The second inbuilt idea is that all the warfare of the period had a causal link: that is, that the battles were not separate or isolated events but the the result of one major problem or cause, namely the usurpation of the Crown by the House of Lancaster back in 1399 and the subsequent dynastic problem raised. Indeed, the Tudor myth of 'the striving of the two roses' was that the whole period from 1399 to 1485 represented a disastrous unity brought on by an act of wickedness. Who was the real, legitimate King of England? The head of the House of Lancaster, or the head of the House of York? The third idea involved in the term 'Wars of the Roses' is that as 'wars' they were truly disruptive and divisive, and a major wound in English social life that took a long time to heal – this was the 'anarchy' propaganda view of the Tudors.

Modern historians tend to dislike the term 'Wars of the Roses' as a serious description of the conflict because it is misleading and anachronistic. To start with, on the pedantic point of rose emblems as the badges of both sides, were there in fact two sides each with a clear rose emblem? The answer is no. The general issue of the usage of emblems in the period is not clear at all. While it is true that coloured roses were important emblems, among many others, on both sides (especially the Yorkist) they were not the most important badge of either side. Neither side was exclusively recognised by a rose emblem. Henry VI of Lancaster never used the red rose at all; his personal badge, worn by his immediate followers, was that of a swan and antelope. His queen, Margaret of Anjou, used the white swan as an emblem; their son, Prince Edward of Lancaster, was represented by the swan and ostrich feather. As for the Yorkists, their leader at the beginning of the conflict, Richard Duke of York, was better known by the badge of a falcon and fetterlock, although it must be admitted that he was addressed in a political poem of 1458 as 'the rose', while his son Edward Earl of March was normally symbolised by the badge of a sunburst, still to be seen in St George's Chapel, Windsor. Like his father, Edward could be recognised by a rose emblem, and he was called 'the rose of Rouen' after his place of birth. The Yorkist Richard III's premier emblem was a seated boar. But it is not just the pedantic accuracy in regard to emblems that is important. The significant point is that the term 'Wars of the Roses' suggests clearer parties and more unity and purpose on both sides than actually existed. In this sense it does indeed distort the truth.

The idea of two rival factions each with a rose emblem goes back to the Tudor period rather than to the age of the warfare itself. Henry VII, founder of the Tudor dynasty, immediately encouraged the notion of unity symbolised by the new double Tudor rose. In the pageant put on for his visit to the city of York in March 1486, a spectacle portraying the joining of 'a rich white rose' to 'a royal rich red rose' was mounted in honour of Henry's marriage to Elizabeth of York. The Tudor rose is almost certainly the one meant in the very earliest reference to rose emblems in relation to the politics of the 1480s. According to the Crowland Chronicle (written in 1486), the defeat of Richard III by Henry Tudor was viewed in this light:

> the Boar's tusks quailed
> And to avenge the White the Red Rose bloomed.

It may well be that the Tudors were more enthusiastic for the red rose emblem than the Lancastrians had ever been, and there is some evidence of their use of it before the battle of Bosworth. During Henry Tudor's exile the Welsh poet Robyn Ddu had envisaged a time when 'red roses will rule in splendour'.

As for the second built-in idea, the essential unity of the conflict, the traditional view was that the Wars of the Roses were in origin a dynastic contest for the throne between the two rival royal houses. The Yorkists, it used to be claimed, could never forgive the Lancastrians for their usurpation of the throne back in 1399. Certainly, this was the official basis of Edward IV's claim in 1461. The parliamentary declaration of the new king's title categorically claimed that the deposition of the true king, Richard II, had been 'against God's law' and that 'persecution, punishment and tribulation' had been visited on the realm by

God's command. This was the beginning of the myth of continuous dynastic rivalry between 1399 and 1461, and continuing down to 1485. However, almost all modern historians are eager to deny the dynastic element in the origins of the political quarrel. They claim that the dynastic element became important only with the return of Richard Duke of York in September 1460; when he was killed in the following December, his son Edward Earl of March was forced into claiming the throne simply in order to save his own life.

As for the third ingredient in the term, namely that these were true, destructive wars, this was very much a Tudor myth used as a warning against anarchy, and this 'disaster' view was certainly perpetuated by nineteenth-century historians. Today the current view is that the battles were small-scale affairs which impinged little on daily life or on the economy. In no sense can they be compared in their destructiveness with the Hundred Years War, the Great Civil War of the seventeenth century or with civil wars of the twentieth-century variety.

The origins of war: the 1450s

The Wars really began with the political crisis of 1460. What had caused this crisis? Any informed observers of the political scene at the beginning of 1460 would, in reviewing the previous decade, certainly have debated the faults and deficiencies of King Henry VI. Aged 38, he was the son of that great warrior king, Henry V, and the fruit of his father's conquest of France, for one of the prizes had been marriage to Princess Catherine of Valois, daughter of Charles VI of France. The couple married in June 1420, and Prince Henry of Lancaster was born a year later. By the Treaty of Troyes (1420) the Dauphin had been disinherited, and Henry V became recognised as the heir to the French throne, and he was to act as regent during the remainder of Charles VI's lifetime. This arrangement was not destined to last, because Henry V died in 1422 and Charles VI followed him to the grave shortly afterwards. These two deaths meant officially that the infant Henry VI succeeded to both kingdoms, and young Henry was to be crowned at Notre Dame in Paris. Until Henry came of age in 1437 a Regency Council governed

England quite effectively on his behalf.[2] But in that year Henry declared himself of age, at the age of 16, and that was when the trouble began. Henry VI had a mental weakness which he had probably inherited from his French grandfather. None of this became apparent until the 1440s, but in that decade his rule became a dismal tale of corruption in government and of a complete lack of leadership. Henry VI developed into an unstable and unmilitary king; he was the complete opposite of the medieval ideal of kingship. A king in the fifteenth century was not just a figurehead: he was meant to rule and lead in battle, and also to inspire both fear and loyalty. Henry VI was a great failure in these regards, and never led his troops into battle. On the credit side he was extremely religious and pious, even more than his father had been, but he was unable to combine these fine qualities with any semblance of royal leadership. Henry was also by this time a most unimpressive figure, especially to regular observers in the capital. Instead of stunning his subjects with magnificent regal garb, the king wore the same old drab clothes. The magic of monarchy was disappearing fast.

Another factor which brought shame on the monarchy was the recent loss of England's French possessions, during the last stages of the Hundred Years War. Historians have generally considered that the attempts of successive English kings to maintain their possessions and titles in France were doomed to failure. But, of course, English people of the time did not see it that way. Whether inevitable or not, England's withdrawal from France was complete by 1450, save for the port of Calais which England would hang on to for another 100 years. Anyone associated with the final withdrawal earned the contempt of the ordinary English person. It was all a great blow to national pride and a very unsettling factor in English domestic politics. However, in no sense did the loss of France lead directly to civil war in England.

As for the internal government of England, there was great concern about the increase in lawlessness and the general lack of effective government. The feeble-minded king had simply lost control over the nobility, who had become a law unto themselves in their own localities. His tendency to grant pardons, even to those guilty of murder and treason, in the hope of their rehabilitation was laudable, but in the context of an already violent age this policy only made the situation worse. Between 1448 and 1455 some one-sixth of the nobles found themselves in gaol for violent activities. Although it is true that almost any period of later medieval England can be viewed as fairly lawless, it remains clear that disorder had become rampant.

The nobility (and gentry) traditionally looked to a powerful king as an arbiter, but Henry VI had seemingly become too dependent on a small court clique, who exploited their favoured position by using justice for their own ends, by raiding the royal treasury and by securing for themselves grants of land from the royal domains. So as government degenerated into a free-for-all among a small group of courtiers, those excluded from this governing clique lost confidence in the government's ability to arbitrate, and instead took to settling disputes among themselves by armed force. The country was rapidly disintegrating into a jigsaw of independent territories under lords with their own small private armies based on indentured retainers and tenants. For example, the mighty Percy family in the north displayed an army of just over 700 men in 1454 in order to carry out a private vendetta.

Some historians have painted a picture of the origins of the Wars of the Roses as lying in that system called 'bastard feudalism', a pejorative term invented in the Victorian era by the Reverend Charles Plummer, by which is meant the system of more fluid relationships based on money and personal service that emerged in the later Middle Ages to replace the earlier forms of classical feudalism, where the permanent relationship between lord and bonded tenant had been based on residence and service on the lord's manor. The basis of military service was no longer land but money. Now we see lords offering money, livery and maintenance to their followers, whether household or domestic servants, tenants and dependants or soldiers recruited by indenture (by which is meant an indented agreement or contract); to all of these lords offered their protection. They could all wear the lord's *livery* (or badge of allegiance, which might possibly involve a full uniform), and in return the lord would *maintain* them at law (i.e. support them in legal actions). The lord might go so far as to browbeat a jury to give a verdict in his retainer's favour; this action by the lord was known as 'embracery' and was a major problem at the time. The existence of these rival armed bands led to the growth of violence as a means of settling disputes, especially with the decline in regard for the impartial authority of the royal legal system. One need not envisage such armed bands as being enormous to appreciate the damage they might inflict. The numbers of indentured retainers were never gigantic: few lords had more than about 80 soldiers in their pay, but the ranks could easily be swelled by other dependants into troublesome forces.

Throughout the length and breadth of England there was much local feuding as the great magnates in particular had recourse to violence to settle their disputes. Did all this local feuding (interlinked with more powerful groups above) simply snowball into the upheaval known as the Wars of the Roses?[3] That was an attractive idea at one time, but while one cannot deny the possible disruptive consequences of 'bastard feudalism' historians today do not present it as the primary cause of the Wars of the Roses. In itself 'bastard feudalism' was neither good nor bad; what made it bad was royal weakness.

Any observer of the scene at the beginning of 1460 would certainly have been familiar with the tales of armed combat between rival noble armies in recent years – for example, in the north of England the great enmity and feuding between the two leading families of Neville and Percy, in the south-west between the Bonvilles and the Courtenays. Politics and social life were extremely violent. People remembered the death in mysterious circumstances back in 1447 of Humphrey Duke of Gloucester, the king's uncle and the brother of Henry V. Gloucester had been the leading opponent of the group then in power, and the general suspicions were that they had got rid of him. Gloucester's death was probably natural, but belief in his murder was widely voiced.

Then came the crisis year of 1450. Whether this crisis was mainly the result of the deep rivalry within the nobility or the loss of France remains problematic. The very first member of the ruling clique to be murdered in 1450 had been a churchman, Adam Moleyns; he was murdered in January at Portsmouth by mutinous soldiers because of the loss of Normandy as well as because of grievances over their pay. Then the leading member of the government, William de la Pole, Duke of Suffolk was murdered – in May 1450. He had been accused of treason by the House of Commons and also of mismanaging the war with

France. Suffolk fled into exile, but *en route* for Calais his ship was intercepted, and after an on-board 'trial' the duke was beheaded, and his naked, headless corpse was dumped on the beach at Dover.

But the major event of that same year was Jack Cade's rebellion in Kent, which broke out in May because of the fear of retribution by the king against Kentishmen for Suffolk's murder. The leader claimed to belong to the Mortimer family (the family of the Duke of York). This was essentially a popular rebellion which demanded political reforms, especially the overthrow of hated officials (by which they meant followers of Suffolk) and their replacement by lords of the 'true blood from his royal realm, that is to say, the high and mighty prince, the Duke of York, exiled from our sovereign lord's person by the suggestions of those false traitors the Duke of Suffolk and his affinity'. The rebellion grew violent when Cade and his followers invaded the City of London by threatening to burn down London Bridge. The rebels condemned 'extortioners and traitors', and Lord Saye and Sele, the treasurer, was put on trial and beheaded. When rebellion spread to Wiltshire, Bishop Ayscough, a supporter of the hated Suffolk, was dragged from his church and beheaded by the mob. The event, and its savage repression, left a legacy of bitterness in the south-east of England, with no serious attempt being made to remedy most of the grievances of the insurgents; the longer-term consequence of this for us was that in 1460 the Yorkists were almost guaranteed support in Kent and the surrounding counties.

Richard Duke of York and the dynastic issue

Mention of York's name brings us to a crucial figure in the story. He was the central figure in the decade of the 1450s. York was the richest and most powerful magnate in the realm with a claim to the throne that some people thought was better than that of the current occupier. York had fought in France, which had left him out of pocket because of arrears of pay: then he found himself appointed lieutenant of Ireland. York returned to England in late August 1450, in the midst of a crisis but personally untainted by the calamitous loss of France. Those disillusioned with the governing clique could look to York as their saviour now. He came as a reformer and to neutralise the threat posed by the return from France of his arch-rival Edmund Duke of Somerset, whom he blamed for the loss of Normandy.

Let us now look at the dynastic issue involved at this time. Richard Duke of York was descended from Philippa, daughter of Edward III's second son, Lionel Duke of Clarence. Richard was also descended from Edward III's fourth son, Edmund Duke of York, whose son Richard Earl of Cambridge had married Anne Mortimer, granddaughter of the same Philippa. But that was a good claim only if the crown of England could descend through a female – through Philippa (known as the *heir general*). Henry VI of Lancaster claimed descent through the *heir male* of Edward III, through the line of Edward's third son, John of Gaunt. The question of the succession had not been formally determined in the Middle Ages. The Crown normally went to the eldest son, but there was no legal prohibition on descent through a female (as there was in neighbouring France with its Salic law). Lawyers had been reluctant to meddle in politics and give a firm decision. So if there was no son to succeed, should the throne descend through a *senior female line* or through a *junior male line*? The Lancastrians had used force to gain the throne in 1399, not legal arguments. There had been some Yorkist opposition in the years before 1415, it is true, but from 1415 onwards the Yorkist claim to the throne had lain dormant. There had certainly been no Yorkist challenge to Henry VI when he was an infant, which would have been the best time to have mounted a challenge. The Lancastrians seem to have been fully accepted by the nobility at large as the true kings of England. Also, the fact that the treaty of Troyes had vested the throne of France in the heirs of the Lancastrian Henry V had certainly buttressed the claims of his family to the English throne. Indeed there was no overt Yorkist opposition to the Lancastrian claim to the throne between 1415 and 1460, when the Yorkists were forced to take up arms to defend themselves, and in so doing had need to resurrect their old dynastic claim.

It is clear that when Duke Richard returned to Court from Ireland in 1450 his aim was not to claim the throne for the Yorkists, but to gain control over the existing king because the country was in a state of great confusion. In 1450 Henry VI was still childless, although for five years or so he had been married to the French princess, Margaret of Anjou. The chances were that no heir would ever be born of this marriage. So York's plan was for his family to succeed to the throne on the death of the childless Henry. Duke Richard was now both *heir general* and *heir male* of Edward III. York's policy in 1450–1 was to use constitutional means to force himself on the government and to remove his arch-enemy Somerset, whom he suspected of wishing to become Henry's designated heir. York also needed to break into the government circle simply to get paid for his war service in France. Richard had a party of supporters in the House of Commons, and one of them proposed that York should now be made the king's heir. In his so-called 'constitutional opposition', which involved an attempt to gain the election of supporters to Parliament, York was unsuccessful; and he thereupon retired to his Welsh estates, until finally in 1452 he organised an armed rebellion, not against the king, but against the ruling clique led by Somerset. This show of force (but no battle) at Dartmouth and Blackheath failed, and York had to grovel before the king and take a humiliating oath for future good behaviour. Thus, even though Richard of York was next in line to the throne and had justifiable complaints, because he had taken up arms against his anointed king he lost the support of the nobility, who remained solidly behind King Henry. The nobles were certainly not itching to fight. While York had advocated reform the nobles had offered him support, but now he seemed entirely outcast. The nobility had acted responsibly, and this fact has suggested to most historians that the origins of the Wars of the Roses are not in fact to be found in the lawlessness and disorder associated with 'bastard feudalism'.

Yet this was not to be the end of Duke Richard's story, because he was to be brought out of disgrace and isolation by two events: the first was the overt bout of insanity of the king between August 1453 and December 1454; the second was the very unexpected birth of an heir to the throne in December 1453. With Henry VI now insane, York as the magnate nearest the Crown was made 'protector and defender' of the realm in April 1454 by the lords of the council (27 March). The first protectorate (3 April 1454– January 1455) was ratified by Parliament and lasted until Henry regained his sanity. In gaining the position of lord protector for himself, York had been opposed by Queen Margaret, who had wanted herself made regent in the French fashion. Although she had been instrumental in Henry's return of the county of Maine to France back in 1448, Margaret had previously taken no part in domestic politics; but now, it seems, she had woken up to the danger presented to the dynasty. In an age of high infant mortality the presence of one vulnerable infant did not rule out a future Yorkist succession. Still there is no clear evidence that at this stage York wanted the Crown either for himself or for his family at the expense of the existing monarch. York probably just wanted a greater say in the government as befitted the premier nobleman of the realm. The protectorate had been gained for Richard partly through the support of his new ally Richard Neville, Earl of Salisbury, who became lord chancellor. The Duke of Somerset had earlier been deprived of his offices and imprisoned in the Tower (23 November 1453), and attempts were made to make him stand trial for treason for misdeeds in both France and England. Yet York's supremacy and his enemy's discomfiture could last only as long as the king remained incapacitated; and Henry would soon regain his sanity. Indeed on the king's regaining his health, Somerset was declared innocent of any criminal charge, while arbitrators were to examine issues of contention between York and Somerset.

With the ending of the first protectorate and his consequent relegation to more ordinary status, York was now seriously threatened by the vengeful attitude of Queen Margaret and her ally Somerset, who had been swiftly restored to power. Punishment seemed imminent when a meeting of the Great Council was summoned to be held at Leicester in the Midlands, the heart of Lancastrian power. York's aim was to prevent this Council meeting because it would result in his political overthrow and ensconce his opponents in power. At least, this is probably what he thought. Fearing the worst, York, Salisbury and his son Warwick armed themselves, and they clashed with a royalist army (*en route* to Leicester) at St Albans, to the north of London, on 22 May. Probably no more than 60 men were killed in this engagement, fought within the town square and centre. It was a victory for the larger Yorkist force certainly (perhaps 3000 men to the royalists' 2000), but in the Yorkists' eyes it was a 'battle' fought for self-protection; and one must agree with Storey's verdict that 'it is

absurd to suggest that the logical conclusion to their victory
would have been a change of dynasty. So drastic a measure was
out of the question.'[4] And that has been the general opinion of
historians in denying the dynastic ingredient in the politics of the
1450s. Indeed, the king was treated with great respect, and York
was to lead the nobles in offering pledges of loyalty to him. The
main results of the first battle of St Albans were the capture of the
king, the killing of Edmund Duke of Somerset and Henry second
Earl of Northumberland, and the establishment (for political
reasons rather than owing to the state of the king's health) of
the short *second protectorate* (19 November 1455–25 February
1456). The House of Commons had demanded a protectorate,
and the agreement for one specified that it would be terminated
at a convenient time by the king with the advice of the lords. The
lords, clearly, were to have the determining role.

   We now come to the period after the ending of the second
protectorate. For most of this time, ever since the king regained
his sanity, there had been peace – but a very tense one. However,
it is important to realise that few people wanted war. The nobles
remained loyal to their anointed king; all blame for previous
instability had been laid at the feet of the now dead Somerset.
Henry VI himself made a huge effort to support peace and
reconciliation, but all his good offices were to be undone by his
wife, Queen Margaret, under whose influence he increasingly
fell. The queen dominated these last years of peace, with the
king a very passive figure. It was Margaret who urged the king
to move his Court in September 1456 to Coventry in the Midlands, to the lands of the duchy of Lancaster and the earldom of
Chester where she could build up an armed opposition party to
the Yorkists. This retreat to the Midlands resulted in 'a period of
administrative difficulty, governmental paralysis, and intensified
political faction'.[5] A war of words ensued with increasing criticism
being voiced by the Court against the Yorkists, who were made to
feel isolated and vulnerable. One last attempt was made by the
king at reconciliation during a Great Council called in Westminster, the ambitious 'Loveday' in March 1458 when both parties
pledged themselves in St Paul's Cathedral to keep the peace and
thereupon paraded arm in arm. Henry himself revisited the
battlefield at St Albans in a spirit of drawing a curtain across
that episode. However the reality was that young Lancastrians

were itching for revenge, especially those who had lost a father at St Albans, and general lawlessness continued unabated. The Earl of Warwick was a particular target for the plots of Lancastrian nobles, but luckily he was able to foil them. A political poem of the time warned the Yorkists (signified by their emblems) to beware the plotting of their enemies:[6]

> But pray we all to god that died on a spear
> To save the rose, the lion, the eagle and the bear

A Great Council was called to meet at Coventry in June 1459, but York and his party either were not invited or decided not to go. Fearing action being plotted against them by Margaret's clique, the Yorkists tried to organise themselves and made for Worcester. However Salisbury's path was impeded on 23 September at Blore Heath (Shropshire) by a larger royalist force under the elderly Lord Audley. Perhaps some 2000 men, including Audley himself, were slain at Blore Heath in a four-hour fight. Nevertheless Salisbury pressed on to Worcester where he met up with York and Warwick, and sent an appeal to the king. The Yorkists then retreated towards Ludlow on the advance of a larger royalist army containing the king, who offered a pardon to all save Salisbury (because of his role in Audley's death). There was a clear reluctance on the part of the Yorkist rank and file to fight the king, and the (treasonable) rumour was spread that the king was already dead in order to encourage them to attack the royalist force. Thus at the 'rout of Ludford Bridge' (near Ludlow) on 12 October 1459 the Yorkist army disintegrated, and their leaders were forced to flee in different directions. Richard of York escaped into Wales and back to Ireland, while his son Edward Earl of March, together with Warwick and his father Salisbury, fled in the other direction, to Calais. 'The engagements at Blore Heath and Ludford Bridge', writes Professor Griffiths, 'were the culmination of three years of political and military planning by Queen Margaret and the court she dominated.'[7]

Between those two battles writs went out for a new Parliament to meet at Coventry on 20 November. This proved to be a very partisan assembly indeed, the elections having been organised by biased sheriffs. This 'Parliament of Devils', as it became known, passed Acts of Attainder against the fleeing Yorkists. This was a major blunder on the part of the Court because it involved the extinction of titles to land and the confiscation of lands. This was seen as an attack on private property and thus a major threat to the ruling class. Similar behaviour by Richard II back in 1399 had provoked the Lancastrian usurpation of the throne. The Yorkists clearly would not remain passive exiles; to return and reclaim their inheritance would necessitate the use of armed force. Although the Lords of the Parliament swore in December 1459 to remain faithful to King Henry, this action of attainting the Yorkists does seem to have been a turning-point in York's ability to attract supporters.

The campaigns of 1460–4

The Wars of the Roses truly got under way in the year 1460, especially from September with the return from Ireland of Richard Duke of York. For the first time the dynastic element became clear because now York had the definite aim to seize the throne for himself and the Yorkists. At least it was clear in the mind of Duke Richard, although his supporters may not have concurred with him on this. The evidence suggests that while York coveted the throne, the other Yorkists simply wanted, as in the past, to control Henry VI. The first of the Yorkists to return to England in 1460 were Edward Earl of March and the two Nevilles, Salisbury and Warwick; before they left Calais they prepared the way with a propaganda campaign which claimed that Henry VI himself was innocent but that he had fallen into the hands of wicked counsellors who oppressed the land. The king was hailed as 'noble ... virtuous, righteous, and blessed of disposition'. March, Warwick and Salisbury landed at Sandwich (Kent) in June. With no show of opposition they soon reached London, which for some time had sympathised with the Yorkist point of view, partly because of London's heavy investment in Yorkist-held Calais, and partly because of opposition to the government's favouring of foreign merchants. Even so, the City opened its gates only reluctantly to the Yorkist earls on 2 July. At this stage the Lancastrian Court was still in the Midlands, and the few loyal soldiers left in the capital could not withstand the Yorkist force outside or the City authorities within. Thus London fell to the Yorkists. Next, a royalist army clashed with the Yorkists under March and Warwick at Northampton (10 July), and the Yorkists, through the desertion of Lord Grey, were able to capture the king, who was escorted back to London but still very much treated with the full respect due to the legitimate sovereign. March and Warwick had achieved their objective – control of the king. They went on to swear in St Paul's Cathedral that they meant no harm to King Henry.

However, Richard Duke of York, following news of the events from Ireland, wanted more than this; and he returned to England in September only after the real danger had passed. He now came specifically to claim the throne. The duke made his way to the Palace of Westminster with trumpeters preceding him, bearing royal banners and with his sword being borne upright in the manner of a king. York clearly expected acclamation from the lords assembled in the Parliament Chamber in his overt bid for the throne. But his ceremonial entry was received in stony silence. It was a humiliating blow. There was no general demand for the removal of Henry VI. There was no support forthcoming for York. Even March and Warwick were angry, it appears, at York's presumptuous behaviour. Nevertheless, nothing would deter York from going ahead and laying a formal claim to the throne. He argued before the lords that 'though right rest for a time and be put in silence, yet it does not rot nor shall it perish'. A compromise was eventually struck mainly because of the absence of most of the fervent Lancastrians and the exhortations of the new chancellor George Neville, Bishop of Exeter, who browbeat the majority of neutralist lords into taking sides. Under the resulting Act of Accord (10 October 1460) Henry VI was to remain king for his lifetime, but his son Prince Edward was disinherited, and the succession was vested in the House of York. The precedent for this seems to have been the treaty of Troyes. In the meantime York would act as lord protector for a third time.

However, this plan was to be thwarted by the hatred felt by Queen Margaret, who was naturally enough jealous for the rights of her young son. She had fled into Wales after the battle of Northampton, and then made her way to the Midlands and the north where she began collecting an army. In retaliation York also began recruiting forces and made his way northwards into Yorkshire. War was now about to break out again, but for the first time with a clear dynastic motivation on both sides. At the very end of the year (30 December) York left the safety of his castle of Sandal, near Wakefield, and led out an army which was considerably smaller than it should have been (because many of his men were out on foraging patrols) in a bid to attack the royalists. According to one source, York was lured out of the castle by enemies masquerading as allies. The battle of Wakefield was a great disaster for the Yorkists. York himself and Richard Earl of Salisbury were both killed, and their heads placed on spikes above the gates of the city of York. Richard's head was given a paper crown.

The royalist forces under Queen Margaret then marched south, but they earned hatred all the way by their constant plunder and violence, which they engaged in mainly because of unpaid wages. The queen met Warwick at the second battle of St Albans (17 February 1461), and partly owing to desertion by his troops the earl lost this battle. Also his Burgundian mercenaries with their novel multiple-barrel guns tended to kill themselves rather than the enemy as these guns often malfunctioned and shot backwards. This royalist victory resulted in Margaret's regaining her husband, who it seems according to one source had been only vaguely aware of the fighting, having spent most of his time singing and laughing while seated under a tree well away from the battle zone. Although defeated, Warwick engineered his escape from the field and managed to get back to London. When Margaret reached London, the City refused to open its gates to her army until it received assurances that there would be no violent retribution. Southern hatred for northerners was a potent factor which could be employed to help the Yorkists; and while the warfare overall should not be seen as a north versus south conflict, nevertheless there were times when traditional north–south hostility played a vital and determining role. One such moment was now in 1461. While negotiations were being carried on, Margaret withdrew her army to Dunstable, near St Albans. The reason for this was probably to allay the Londoners' fears about plundering, but in hindsight it was a foolish move that gave time to the Yorkists to regroup and replan.

But if York was dead and Warwick defeated, Edward Earl of March was still on the loose and on the move towards the capital, and he had already gained a notable victory in the west of England at Mortimer's Cross (Herefordshire) over the Lancastrian Earl of Wiltshire and Jasper Tudor, Earl of Pembroke. These two men succeeded in escaping, but one of the significant Lancastrian casualties at Mortimer's Cross was Pembroke's father Owen Tudor, grandfather of the future Henry VII. Victorious in the field, Edward, who was joined by Warwick in Oxfordshire, then rushed to London, which admitted them both on 27 February.

A group of nobles and clerics joined them there, including Archbishop Bourchier, who then agreed to proclaim him in Westminster Abbey on 4 March as King Edward IV. Edward had not supported his father's bid for the throne, but York's death and the tactics of Queen Margaret in making the Yorkists into outlaws had changed all that. The papal nuncio Coppini wrote exaggeratedly to the Duke of Milan that 'my lord of Warwick...has made a new king of the son of the Duke of York'. Unfortunately and erroneously, that was also how Warwick himself seemed to sum up the situation – with dire consequences for the future.

Thus Edward became king at the age of 19, but only a small group of nobles had been present at his acclamation. Permanence on the throne (and a full coronation) could be assured only by military victory over Margaret's main army; and this was to be achieved on Palm Sunday 1461 (29 March) at Towton in the north of England, when the Lancastrian nobility was all but wiped out. The great northern families who had remained so loyal to Lancaster had taken a beating, and the great Earl of Northumberland lay dead. Those left alive tried to make their peace with the young Edward. It appears that some 19 peers had fought on the Lancastrian side at Towton, compared with only around nine for Edward. This was without doubt the biggest battle of the wars, with perhaps some 50 000 men involved, a slight majority fighting for the Lancastrians. The savagery of this battle has very recently been confirmed by the discovery of some 29 skeletons of foot soldiers who had been viciously and repeatedly battered in the engagement.[8] Henry VI, Prince Edward of Lancaster and Queen Margaret were not present at Towton, having already fled to Scotland, to be joined later there by survivors Somerset and Exeter.

Edward IV soon made his will felt throughout the kingdom. Lancastrian resistance persisted only in Wales and in the north-east of England where the still free Henry VI and Queen Margaret received help from the Scots. In Wales Jasper Earl of Pembroke, Henry Duke of Exeter and Henry Duke of Somerset were making nuisances of themselves through their possession of a number of castles. Lord Herbert successfully captured Pembroke Castle in July 1461 and then defeated the Lancastrians in north Wales. As the Welsh castles fell to the Yorkists, that mighty fortress at Harlech remained a lonely bastion of the Lancastrian cause in Wales for the next seven years. Although Harlech was potentially very dangerous as an invasion point, it seemed to Edward that it was not worth the effort to reduce it now. The resistance in the north-east seemed more worrying, but Edward's initial policy was naïvely optimistic in allowing Lancastrians who surrendered to reoccupy their posts. Edward also pardoned the Duke of Somerset on his capture in December 1462 – an action he lived to regret. Edward's problem in the far north was that Scotland offered refuge for his opponents. Furthermore, through Queen Margaret's visit to the French Court an agreement was made between Henry VI and Louis XI of France (June 1462), by which Calais was surrendered to France in return for money and men; and in July 1463, with a Scottish army led in person by the 12-year-old King James III, a Lancastrian force invaded from Scotland and besieged Norham Castle. Henry VI was physically present, along with Queen Margaret. This invasion failed miserably, however, and Warwick and his brother John Lord Montague answered it with a vicious campaign of retaliation and reprisals over the Scottish border.

Queen Margaret sailed for France in August 1463, leaving her husband in the care of the Bishop of St Andrews; she would never see King Henry again. Edward worked to counter any future Franco-Scottish aid to the Lancastrians by concluding an agreement with France (October 1463), and then with Scotland (December 1463), thereby cutting off help to Henry VI, who was transferred over the border into England to survive the best he could at Bamburgh Castle. Although neutralising the Scottish threat, Edward was to be frustrated by the flight of the Duke of

Somerset, whom he had unsuccessfully tried to win over to the Yorkist cause by pardon, restoration and favours (including allowing him the signal honour of sharing his bed). The ungrateful Somerset joined Henry's band of adherents around Bamburgh Castle and acted as a magnet for Lancastrian remnants, whose control of the area to the north of Newcastle was jeopardising Edward's negotiations with the Scots. Edward's major permanent activist in the north-east, Lord Montague, defeated Lancastrian forces led by Somerset at both Hedgeley Moor and Hexham in April and May 1464. Somerset and over 30 other Lancastrian notables were then executed. For services rendered, Montague was rewarded with the earldom of Northumberland, with the lands formerly owned by the Percy family. The deposed Henry VI, who had not been present in those recent battles, was recaptured after a year on the run in Lancashire in July 1465 and brought south to the Tower of London. The Lancastrian threat to Edward IV was clearly now over; and only in far west Wales did the Lancastrians still show the flag, in the long siege of Harlech Castle, which ended in August 1468.

Renewal of war and the Readeption[9] of Henry VI

The subjugation of the north should have been the end of the so-called 'Wars of the Roses'. The Lancastrians were thoroughly beaten and most of their leaders dead, while the Yorkists were now firmly ensconced. But the story was not over: the fighting was to flare up again owing mainly to personal factors, above all by the overriding ambition of one of Edward's closest allies, Richard Neville, Earl of Warwick, known to history as 'Warwick the kingmaker'. So we turn now to the divisions within the victorious Yorkist camp. The Neville clan had been allied with the Yorkists since 1455, and they had been rewarded with the Northumberland estates of the defeated Lancastrian Percies. Richard Neville himself had gained immensely from Edward's victory in 1461; his brother George had become Archbishop of York and lord chancellor. So great was the earl's power that many contemporaries regarded him as the real power behind the throne, with Edward as just a puppet. This was not, however, the case: the reins of power always remained in Edward's hands, and in time he asserted his supremacy. Then in May 1464 Edward secretly married a not very rich widow whose maiden name was Elizabeth Woodville. This marriage was kept a secret because she was hardly a good catch or match for the King of England. Edward himself realised that this was an inappropriate union because it was kept a secret until the following September. If Elizabeth Woodville's beauty was the major reason for the king's ardour, this does not communicate to us today through the oldest surviving portrait of her.[10] Yet there can be no doubt that Edward had fallen in love with her and was obsessed with her. For her part, Elizabeth refused to give in to his pleas for sexual satisfaction because she did not wish to end up as one of his discarded mistresses: she would consent only if she were to be queen. It was indeed usual in the later Middle Ages for an English monarch to marry into one of the great royal houses of Europe; Elizabeth Woodville was the first English-born consort since King John married Isabella of Gloucester, and to make matters worse she was not a great heiress but a widow with children. The marriage had also gone counter to Warwick's plan for Edward to marry a French princess to cement an alliance with the old enemy. Furthermore, Elizabeth Woodville had a large and rather impecunious family who now expected to be taken care of. And taken care of they certainly were – too well in Warwick's opinion! Elizabeth Woodville already had two sons by her first husband, and she also had five sisters and five brothers; and these were married off now into powerful families, old and new, of the Yorkist regime. Warwick was extremely annoyed when one of the queen's brothers (John Woodville), who was still only a teenager, was married off to the 67-year-old Catherine Neville, Duchess of Norfolk, the earl's aunt. Especially irritating to Warwick was that the marriage-pool in the upper classes had now evaporated, but the sonless earl was still seeking suitable husbands for his two daughters, Isabella and Anne, who would eventually inherit their father's vast estates. There was simply no one in their class bracket available for them to marry, apart from Edward's own two brothers, George Duke of Clarence and Richard Duke of Gloucester; and Edward had consistently refused to allow Warwick's family to unite with his own. Under the protection of the king the Woodvilles created a party at Court which looked only to King Edward and which excluded the

Nevilles. In March 1466 the queen's father Earl Rivers became lord treasurer. By 1467 Edward signalled his alienation from Warwick when he sacked Archbishop George Neville as lord chancellor. In the same year the king made a further breach with the earl over foreign policy. Warwick wanted an alliance with France, whereas the king wanted an alliance with Burgundy (as the Netherlands were called at this time). In 1467 a political and economic agreement was reached with Burgundy, and in 1468 it was sealed by the marriage of Edward's sister Margaret to Archduke Charles the Bold of Burgundy in one of the most lavish wedding celebrations of the age.

Warwick's ascendancy was manifestly at an end, although he was by no means disgraced – just put in his rightful, subordinate place. However, this demotion he could not stomach and, along with his brother the archbishop, he entered into a conspiracy with Clarence, but being suspected of intrigue they all made their flight to Calais in 1469, where on 11 July, Clarence married Isabella Neville, with the archbishop officiating. Just before these events transpired, a rebellion secretly initiated by Warwick and led by someone calling himself Robin of Redesdale broke out in Yorkshire, gained strength and moved south. Using the pseudonym from the Robin Hood myth, the rebellion aimed to exploit social discontent, but the rebels' main demands were political, calling for the overthrow of unpopular favourites, such as the Woodvilles and the new earls of Pembroke and Devon, who were compared to the favourites employed by Edward II, Richard II and Henry VI – all kings who had in fact been forced to abdicate. Edward seems to have found it hard to believe that his brother and the earl could be guilty of such treason, hence he reacted slowly to the danger. Warwick and Clarence soon returned from Calais to London, and then headed an army to join up with the Robin of Redesdale rebels to march against the king, who remained seemingly paralysed at Nottingham – in fact he was waiting for Devon and Pembroke to join him with their forces at Northampton. The rebels on their march south avoided Nottingham and made towards London to rendezvous with Warwick. Unfortunately for the king the separate forces of Devon and Pembroke did not join together, either because of error or probably because the two earls quarrelled, and Devon with his archers was away from the scene when battle commenced. When news finally reached the Earl of Devon that fighting had commenced, he calculated that his chances of victory were much too slim and so withdrew his men, leaving Pembroke in the lurch. The battle of Edgecote, near Banbury, on 26 July 1469 ended up as a victory for Warwick, who exploited the occasion to execute his enemies, the Earl of Pembroke and his brother Sir Richard Herbert. Shortly afterwards Edward IV himself was taken prisoner on his way to Northampton by Archbishop Neville. As for the absent Humphrey Earl of Devon, he was later caught and executed by the common people. The queen's father Earl Rivers and her brother Sir John Woodville were also subsequently caught and put to death.

With the king in Warwick's clutches the earl aimed, at least at first, not to depose Edward but to rule through him as a puppet king. However, Warwick isolated himself because he could find little general support from the nobles for such a policy which violated the sanctity of kingship. Edward had not broken the conventions of kingly rule simply by falling out with Warwick. Moreover, most of the lords were still dependent on Edward for their position; even the commons who had participated in the rebellion had done so not to capture the king but solely to remove 'wicked ministers'. There was also an escalation of lawlessness and disorder resulting from the crisis at the centre and the loss of confidence in the monarchy of the absent Edward IV. Warwick was forced to release Edward in September on the news of a Lancastrian rebellion on the Scottish border. Edward pretended to fall in line with Warwick's plans to be the real power behind the throne and returned to London, but in reality he bided his time and built up his power base against 'the Kingmaker'.

Edward struck back in 1470 as a result of yet another rebellion blowing up, this time in Lincolnshire, which began as a local quarrel but was subsequently fanned up by Warwick and Clarence to challenge the king. Possibly Warwick was now thinking of deposing Edward and replacing him with brother Clarence. This time, however, Edward gained the upper hand, and on 12 March the rebels were scattered at Lose-Cote Field (near Stamford in Lincolnshire), so called because the rebels lost their protective clothes in flight after the battle. Warwick's and Clarence's machinations were now obvious to all, and despite offers of clemency by the king the two conspirators decided to flee the realm, taking with them their wives and daughters. They made for Calais but, being refused entry and shot at by the garrison, the rebels eventually put in at Honfleur, Normandy. The nobility had disliked Warwick's plan and had not supported him in the rebellion; even his brother, John Neville, Earl of Northumberland, remained loyal to the king at this stage.

The last act in the drama was an amazing one, and quite impossible to have predicted. In France Warwick was persuaded by King Louis XI to make common cause with the old enemy, Margaret of Anjou, and work for the restoration of the House of Lancaster. Prince Edward of Lancaster was to marry Anne Neville, who would thus become queen if the enterprise went well. However, this deal between former antagonists left Clarence rather out in the cold, and so his mind began to prepare itself for an eventual *rapprochement* with his brother, especially when Edward wooed him over by a secret messenger. Anyhow, with French help an invasion force was prepared that would land in the west of England at a time when internal rebellions led by Warwick's family supporters had already broken out in support. Queen Margaret and her son Prince Edward would stay in France and not return until the country was quiet and obedient. Accordingly rebellions broke out in Yorkshire and Cumberland led by Warwick's supporters. Edward's policy was to prevent Warwick leaving port by blockading it with the support of Burgundian vessels. But the king's luck ran out when storm-winds scattered the besieging vessels and allowed Warwick's band to leave port unmolested on 9 September.

Warwick's fleet landed near Exeter on the Devon coast, and with the king still away in the north after putting down the rebellions there, the invaders were able to seize power in the south. Warwick, Clarence, Oxford and Jasper Tudor led the invaders, and were joined on land by Shrewsbury and Lord Stanley. All but Jasper (who went into Wales) marched northwards, gathering a sizeable army as they went. How they acquired such a large force – perhaps 30 000 – is a mystery, but if true it is eloquent testimony to the changeability of large sections of the population. People now seemed genuinely confused in their loyalties and wanted the return of stability – no matter from whom. King Edward seemed not overperturbed by the invasion until the surprise defection of John Neville, Marquis Montague. He was clearly unhappy with the loss of the earldom of Northumberland, now restored by Edward to Henry Percy and not even the acquisition, by way of compensation, of the lands of the late Earl of Devon, the elevation to a marquisate and the possibility of his infant son (betrothed to Princess Elizabeth) one day being king could bind him indissolubly to Edward. Luckily Edward had just enough warning of Montague's treason to make good his own escape, along with his brother Richard of Gloucester, to Burgundy. In London Henry VI was restored to his throne – the period of the *Readeption* – on 6 October 1470.

The situation in England was tense with the return of the House of Lancaster, because the surviving Lancastrian nobles wanted to regain those lands that had been confiscated from them and given to the Yorkists. But this was now difficult, and there were no obvious victims whose lands could be seized and used as rewards. Warwick himself, with good reason, was hated by the Lancastrian magnates. Louis XI of France now demanded payment for his assistance to the rebel cause: England was to declare war on his enemy Burgundy. This, of course, gave Burgundy good reason to support Edward IV, and the archduke supplied both financial and military assistance. Edward was really lucky that Louis was so belligerent towards Burgundy; otherwise even the fact that the archduchess was his sister probably would not have been enough to gain Burgundy's help.

In March 1471 Edward with a fleet of 36 ships and about 1500 supporters landed in Yorkshire, at Ravenspur on the Humber, at the same place where Bolingbroke had landed back in 1399. There was no great force of opposition to prevent his march south, but no great welcome either. He had to defuse what opposition there was by claiming, as had Bolingbroke, that he was returning only to claim his duchy and not the throne. People in the north were reluctant to help, and he entered the city of York only by voicing loyalty to Henry VI. Edward was very fortunate that neither Northumberland nor Montague organised against him on his march south. This was probably because it was hard for them to recruit a force against him when he was not overtly claiming the throne but demanding only what was rightly his. Edward had to wait until he reached Nottingham in the Midlands before he won 600 recruits, while at Leicester he gained another 3000, thanks mainly to the influence in that region of his comrade-in-arms, William Lord Hastings. Warwick meanwhile was waiting at Coventry with a large force, which he expected to be further augmented by troops under Oxford, Exeter, Montague and Clarence. However, at this juncture Clarence decided to embrace his brother's cause and went over with some 4000 men to join up with him near the town of Warwick, where he begged his elder brother's forgiveness. By this time Edward had revealed his true hand by reclaiming the throne. The three brothers – Edward, Clarence and Gloucester – now made for London rather than attacking the Earl of Warwick. Possession of London had been an important boon in 1461, and the psychological advantage was deemed to be necessary now. The City fathers were perplexed at what to do: defend Henry VI who was already there, or open the gates to welcome Edward IV? They opted for Edward, partly because the Yorkist army was not recruited from the northerners whom they loathed and partly because those Lancastrians left in London, notably the Duke of Somerset, thought it wise to depart to greet Queen Margaret and Prince Edward, who were about to land. Only Archbishop Neville attempted to rally support for the Lancastrian cause, but his determination wilted on the news of Edward's approach, and he sent word that he wished to submit.

On 11 April Edward re-entered London in style and sought out his wife and children then in sanctuary in Westminster Abbey. Henry VI was taken and again incarcerated in the Tower of London. Two days later, Edward led out his army in search of Warwick; both rivals saw the need for a quick victory to save their skins. Two battles decided the issue once and for all. On Easter Sunday (14 April) in a thick mist before dawn, Edward launched a surprise attack against Warwick's larger force at Barnet. The numerical superiority of Warwick's side was cancelled by a number of major mistakes they made because of mutual suspiciousness and the lack of visibility (such as Warwick's attack – or 'friendly fire' – on his ally Oxford). There were heavy casualties on both sides in this three-hour ordeal, but Edward managed to win the day, while both Warwick and his brother Montague were killed. The same day that Barnet was fought saw the landing of Queen Margaret and her son in the south-west at Weymouth (Dorset). Receiving the bad news, they and the Duke of Somerset

made for Exeter in the West Country and aimed to meet up with
Jasper Tudor and his Welsh recruits. Edward was not sure which
way Margaret would move but made his way down to the south-
west to prevent the enemy crossing the Severn estuary and
reaching the Marches of Wales. On 3 May the Yorkists caught
up with the Lancastrians at Tewkesbury (Gloucestershire) late in
the afternoon, and on the following day battle commenced.
Prince Edward of Lancaster and the Earl of Devon were both
killed on the battlefield; afterwards the Duke of Somerset was
executed. Queen Margaret became Edward's prisoner. Incipient
rebellions in the north in Margaret's favour fizzled out on news of
Tewkesbury. Only one aftershock was still to register, namely the
attack on London by Warwick's kinsman Thomas the Bastard of
Fauconberg on 12 May. The Bastard, as he was known, collected
support from Calais and Kent, including the mayor of Canterbury, as well as from the sailors who had served under him and
demanded entry into London. But, encouraged by reports of
Tewkesbury, Londoners refused his demand. Fauconberg, like
Cade in 1450, tried to gain entry by destroying the southern gate
of London bridge, but this manoeuvre failed, and he tried to
blast his way in with cannon-fire and by using his ships to transport men to the north side of the Thames. For some days the
assault continued, but eventually a counter-attack by the Londoners sent the Bastard's men fleeing.

Edward IV returned to London on 21 May and was then
accepted once more by the vast majority of nobles as the true
king. Henry VI was quietly murdered in the Tower of London
that same night (21/22 May), and so there was no longer a viable
Lancastrian claimant to the throne. Officially, it was claimed that
the former king had died of melancholy. The dynastic element,
which first made its appearance in 1460, was over by 1471. The
vast majority of lords thought that the conflict was all over and
pledged their loyalty to the restored Yorkists. It was only because
of very special circumstances, namely the split within the House
of York occasioned by the usurpation of Richard III, that the war
revived between 1483 and 1485, when a new dynasty would seize
the opportunity offered to take over the state. Henry Tudor at
Bosworth would win the day not just for the Lancastrians, with
whom he had a tenuous link, but also for the alienated Yorkists
who had rallied to him in their hatred of King Richard. The

battle of Bosworth was, therefore, not a simple struggle between York and Lancaster. The term 'Wars of the Roses' fails yet again to encapsulate the historical situation.

The wars and society

The political upheaval in England in the mid-fifteenth century underlines the fragility of elite politics; problems at the centre could lead to the collapse of the whole dynastic system. It will be quite apparent that these were not ideological wars in any way, and this lack of ideology is what distinguishes the Wars of the Roses from the Great Civil War of the mid-seventeenth century. The Wars of the Roses were primarily a contest for the throne occasioned by the incompetence of Henry VI, a fact that undermined the whole basis of later medieval politics, which depended on a strong, impartial monarch at the centre. The king was expected to provide 'good lordship', and it was this that was seriously absent. There was a split within the very top ranks of the ruling class, with groups lower down being sucked in because of the system of 'bastard feudalism', which was thus a secondary, rather than a primary, cause of the conflict.

While many historians view the Great Civil War as a 'revolution', this word cannot seriously be applied to the 'Wars of the Roses', although Professor Charles Ross tried to use it in this context.[11] Indeed Professor Ross tried to argue that this was 'the first truly revolutionary period in English history' in the sense that opposition groups made it their main objective to overthrow the king himself, not just to replace the king's ministers. However, even if one concedes that there was a new political situation involved, nevertheless the term 'revolution' suggests much wider changes in politics and society; and the criterion for a revolution is normally that a very different society emerges as a result. Nothing of the sort happened in fifteenth-century England. If anything monarchic power was strengthened to combat the fear of anarchy, and the same aristocratic society continued on, even if, as we shall see, the political power of the nobility was to be reduced. Furthermore, how 'new' was this situation really? One cannot forget the civil war back in the mid-twelfth century between the supporters of Stephen and those of Matilda on the death of Henry I; and the removal of Edward II and Richard II proves that plans to dethrone existing monarchs were hardly novel. The final removal of Henry VI in 1471 was to be achieved in a thoroughly medieval and secretive way. What we have is drama at the top, but the life of society carried on in its customary way. No 'revolution' had occurred.

How much of a turning-point in English history were the wars? Recent scholarship has overturned the views of many contemporaries, and also the judgement of the nineteenth century, that the wars amounted to a complete disaster and the ruination of later medieval England. It is true that the Crowland Chronicle relates that 'the slaughter of men was immense: for besides the dukes, earls, barons and distinguished warriors who were cruelly slain, multitudes almost innumerable of the common people died of their wounds. Such was the kingdom for nearly ten years.' The chronicler John Warkworth emphasised the financial suffering of the common people through exactions to pay for the warfare. However, while such a general impression of upheaval and misery must have seemed true to many contemporaries, there is now general agreement that their woes were exaggerated and cannot be verified by surviving evidence. Although, it must be confessed, we do not know much about the details of the battles or the actual numbers involved, we can say with confidence that contemporary estimates of fighting men and casualties were grossly inflated. Armies were small, consisting of lords, their retainers, those brought by the retainers, tenants as well as the shire and town levies (or militia); and the duration of the fighting was short. Most battles lasted about three hours or so, one of the main reasons being that the heavily armoured knights, wearing the novel complete head-to-foot armour of the fifteenth century, tired so fast, especially as they tended to dismount from their horses – which could easily be shot from under them by archers with longbows – and fight on the ground with flails and maces. The longest and biggest battle, the only one to last all day, was Towton in 1461. It is possible that some 50 000 men fought there, and one contemporary view that some 28 000 men died on that day may very well be close to the truth. On the other hand, another contemporary writer puts the number of dead at Towton at only 9000. These wide variations in estimates prohibit any definitive judgements on the scale of the fighting. But there is no doubt that Towton represented the biggest ordeal. All the other battles were much smaller affairs, often mere skirmishes. Apart from timing and choice of location, there was no real battle strategy involved: once action commenced it became a chaotic series of hand-to-hand encounters.

J. R. Lander has argued that between 1450 and 1485 the total length of the *actual fighting* was less than 12 or 13 weeks.[12] That may be true, but if one calculates, as did Anthony Goodman, the total amount of *campaigning* that adds up to the bigger figure of at least some 428 days service.[13] A. J. Pollard adds other episodes, such as the Lancastrian siege of Yorkist Calais and other episodes in Wales and the north, to give a figure of well in excess of 700 days.[14] Frequent military activity and preparedness for conflict thus made it more of an upheaval, perhaps, than historians like Lander thought. Yet there is still no comparison to be made with the Hundred Years War in either duration of campaigning or devastation wreaked on civilians. There was no scorched-earth policy, as in France, and there is little doubt that the English economy was affected in only a small way by the political troubles.[15] The only time the civilian population was sorely tested by plundering and destruction by disorderly soldiery was during Queen Margaret's advance southwards towards London in 1461. The worst social effect was that it exacerbated the pre-existing condition of lawlessness in society. John Gillingham makes the telling point that 'more British were killed in a single day at the Somme [in the First World War] than in the whole of the Wars of the Roses'.[16]

Who exactly was engaged in the fighting? The class most directly involved was, of course, the nobility, the warrior class. They might have wanted to stay outside the conflict and sit on the fence, but they found this impossible. Of the 70 peers alive at the beginning of the wars a high proportion (56/70) took part in the conflict in the first stage between 1460 and 1461. Something like 75 per cent of the nobility fought at Towton. As to the numbers involved in the next major flare-up, between 1469 and 1471, estimates vary from about 40 to 70 per cent. But by the last stage, in the years 1483–7 the preparedness of the nobles to join in was to decline sharply because there was simply too much to lose. Sitting on the fence now seemed by far the better alternative; apathy or circumspection was to be the major characteristic of the last phase of the conflict. When the nobles did participate, local feuding might be a major factor in deciding which party a noble fought for, but there was also much changing of sides for both personal reasons and judgement on what was good for the realm – which claimant would restore or maintain the peace better; and one must not forget the nucleus of men who showed continuous loyalty to the Lancastrian king. Before 1460 the nobility had shown little inclination to oppose Henry VI by supporting the Yorkists, who had managed to gain only two converts in 1459. Noble involvement came only after the Lancastrians' clearly unfair treatment of the Yorkists. The biggest problem in deciding the extent of noble participation lies with the contemporary sources, which are often so vague. The fact that an account of a battle does not mention a particular nobleman does not necessarily mean that he was not there, and it certainly does not necessarily follow that absentees from a battle regarded themselves as neutral. Sometimes partisans simply could not get to the field of battle to play their part. Consider, for example, the absence of that stalwart Lancastrian Jasper Tudor from both Barnet and Tewkesbury.

Defeated noblemen caught on the battlefield could expect only execution; but if they escaped from the field they had a good chance of being left alone. Between 1455 and 1487, 38 peers were killed in the fighting, the overwhelming majority of them in the 1460s. So many noble deaths in a short period of time must have left a heavy scar on the consciousness of the nobility.[17] It used to be claimed that the Wars of the Roses wiped out the old nobility for good; but this was certainly not the case. In the later Middle Ages it was usual for about 27 per cent of noble families to die out simply by failure to produce adult male heirs in the normal course of nature. Between 1450 and 1500 some 38 families died out, but only 12 of these did so through violence of some kind; and only seven families became extinct with the wars as the main reason. Most nobles killed on the battlefield had heirs to keep the family name going. K. B. McFarlane showed that indeed fewer noble families died out in the second half of the fifteenth century than was normal in the later Middle Ages generally.[18]

Yet the wars did have important consequences for the nobility. The major change for them was psychological and political.

Those worst affected by the slaughter were those 'overmighty subjects' (as Sir John Fortescue called them), those great lords with political ambitions, such as 'Warwick the Kingmaker'. The revival of monarchy following the wars was to see the eclipse of such 'overmighty subjects'. Taming the nobility was to be a major and consistent Tudor policy. By the end of Henry VII's reign only two really powerful magnates had survived, and one of these would be executed in 1521.[19] The Tudors were to be very suspicious of any overmighty traits in their subjects.

Who else fought? The nobles could call upon their indentured retainers and tenants. The numbers of military retainers were not as large as once thought, but they formed the kernel of a lord's fighting force: the Earl of Salisbury had 140 in 1454, while the Duke of Buckingham had 90 at first St Albans. So clearly the majority of soldiers were untrained tenants. Of course, the more nobles involved the larger the general participation, but even less information is available on the commoners than for nobles. Apart from some individuals being named for rewards or condemnation, little record remains of the extent of positive gentry sympathies. While they must have been involved, most have left little mark in the records. K. B. McFarlane argued that while the gentry followed their noble lords, they did not do so in a slavish way; rather, 'they freely chose their part',[20] perhaps preferring the overriding claims of the king to those of a hostile local lord. Certainly indentured retainers could make use of the clause in their contract which gave primary allegiance to the king. There were many occasions where seemingly large numbers of gentry were engaged. The bulk of all fighting forces, however, must have been the ordinary tenants who were dragged along. We have evidence from the beginning of the Great Civil War in 1642 of lords and gentry simply marching their tenants to battle on pain of eviction or death, so if we accept that evidence of coercion two centuries later there can be little doubt over how these armies in the Wars of the Roses were recruited. As it was these local men and clients who made up a lord's army, armies remained small, and kept in being for only a short time since it was difficult for any lord to keep his clients and tenants together for long away from home. Because the bulk of combatants were untrained tenants they also tended to desert or flee the battle at the first opportunity. However, the north of England had a tradition of supplying men to fight the Scots, and these northern tenants probably proved more trustworthy for battle than their southern counterparts. It was an accepted idea of the time that while defeated nobles should be put to the sword on the battle-field, the vanquished peasants should be spared; and with some exceptions this rule seems to have been followed. Although there were few sieges of towns and cities, there were occasions when townsmen were called upon to defend their homes against in-vaders. In 1471, for example, the citizens of London put up a sturdy defence of the capital against the Lancastrian Bastard of Fauconberg. Also some townsmen are individually mentioned as being present in the great battles of the wars, such as the recor-der of Bristol, who fell at Tewkesbury.

The material damage of the Wars of the Roses proved to be not very great or lasting. Psychological damage proved more impor-tant and permanent. The myth was promulgated by the Tudors, and the fear of the evils of civil war allowed the Tudors to push through major and unnerving changes without great protests. At the beginning of the Great Civil War of the seventeenth century men were restudying the Wars of the Roses for lessons for their own times.

2 The Restored Monarchy 1461–1509: Edward IV, Richard III and Henry VII

The fear of anarchy generated during the period of the Wars of the Roses led to the revival of monarchy as the only institution capable of maintaining order, and even though the wars, as one historian has written, 'came close to destroying the hereditary basis of the English monarchy',[1] the long-term result into the sixteenth century was to strengthen the claims of legitimacy. None of this could be foreseen at the time, and indeed one must stress the critical nature of this period in the development of the English state. The fifteenth century, which had begun with a rebellion which threatened to dismember the English state, would also witness a threat to monarchy towards its close. Three usurpers, all claiming both legitimacy and divine approval, ruled England in the years 1461–1509: the two Yorkist brothers Edward IV and Richard III, and the first Tudor monarch Henry VII.

Edward IV (1461–83)

Well over six foot tall, the charismatic Edward IV was all that Henry VI had not been: physically at least, he seemed the ideal king. Commentators close to the king's own day praised Edward for his industry, impartiality, popularity with the people and his restoration of prosperity after the civil wars. That Edward was a womaniser cannot be doubted; as the contemporary Italian visitor to England, Dominic Mancini, put it:

> he was licentious in the extreme.... He pursued with no discrimination the married and the unmarried, the noble and the lowly: however, he took none by force.

With all of this licentiousness, however, Edward combined a serious devotion to his kingly duties; and his achievement was to breathe new life into traditional medieval monarchy. In the late nineteenth century J. R. Green surmised that the restoration of royal power, first under the Yorkists, and then under the early Tudors, amounted to the creation of an absolutist 'New Monarchy'. Green thought that the king's 'indolence and gaiety were mere veils beneath which Edward shrouded a profound political ability'. The notion of a 'New Monarchy' was roundly attacked in the twentieth century as a myth. It is now claimed that there was nothing really new about the Yorkist or early Tudor monarchy; it was extremely traditional, if not in some respects even rather primitive, being so dependent on household government. If 'New Monarchy' suggests the origins of political absolutism then such ideas must certainly be rejected. Yet it must be conceded that England did partake in the general growth of monarchic power in Europe at the expense of the nobility, and both the growing centralisation of the state and the increased propaganda and iconography of monarchy suggest elements of novelty that should not be forgotten in a chorus of denunciation of the term 'New Monarchy'; indeed recently attempts have been made to justify it by Anthony Goodman[2] and John Watts.[3] While it was not really 'new' or absolutist, it was not simply 'old' either. What we have, of course, is a combination of traditional and groundbreaking, with the old framework still predominating. Medieval monarchy was always evolving.

The reign of Edward IV is notable for the monarch's close attention to business – in great contrast to his predecessor. In his first Parliament, in the first ever recorded speech from the throne, Edward vowed to restore law and order and the authority of the Crown. And in the years to come Edward was to show his personal interest in all aspects of life, from commercial affairs to impartial justice. In doing all this he created no new institutions, but simply revived traditional methods and brought in new men: members of his family principally, but he was prepared to use anyone who demonstrated loyalty. Historians have pointed to the frequent use of the royal signature on documents to prove his keen devotion to business. On the patent roll of 1461 one-third of all grants were authorised 'by the King' or 'the King by word of mouth'; also evident is the increased use of the signet ring for sealing correspondence and authenticating warrants. The officer responsible for application of the signet, the royal secretary, became a much more important official than ever before. Indeed, the foundations of the important Tudor office of principal secretary were laid by Edward IV.[4]

The king's council also shows clearly a revival of the monarchy. Weak monarchy might mean either a large council divided into competing factions or no real council at all but a small number of councillors making all the decisions themselves and alienating everyone else. Strong monarchy at this time was characterised by a small obedient council, answerable directly to the king and serving solely during the royal pleasure and with no claim to automatic membership through birth. Under Edward IV there was a core of 9–12 regular councillors, although occasionally the full sworn council of 25 might meet. Edward himself presided over council meetings in the Star Chamber at Westminster. The council took over many of the routine burdens that would otherwise have fallen to the king and dealt with administrative matters large and small, as well as acting as an intermediary body between the king and his nobles, and between the centre and the localities.

What kind of men did Edward rely on as his councillors? In the first part of the reign – during the 1460s – he relied on the established nobility to make up his council, but after the Readeption, with his position more securely established, he promoted in the 1470s men of humbler origins, men of his own creation whom he could thoroughly trust, such as Bishop Morton. Increasing numbers of councillors after 1471 were new men: some 23 councillors from the gentry are known from the years after 1471. It was not that Edward had an animus against the nobility, but they had proved that they could not always be trusted and the crisis of 1469–71 had made him seek new sources of support.

The growth of royal power in the state was mirrored in the growth of the Court. Increasingly the royal Court replaced the local courts of the great nobles as the one true centre of power, influence and patronage. If a man of ambition wanted to get on in the world he would need court connections; he would need the patronage of great courtiers to advance his cause with the king. Indeed the very term 'courtier' first appears in Edward's reign. Politics in the late fifteenth and early sixteenth centuries would increasingly be based on the Court, where political conflicts would now be fought, rather than on the battlefield. The monarch consciously fostered the growth of the Court as a manifestation of his greatness. Sir John Fortescue advised a monarch to spend lavishly, for miserliness was a characteristic disliked in a king, who should always epitomise generosity. Even when short of money, Edward never economised on public splendour because he realised its propaganda value. He spent a fortune on jewels and furniture. He was also a collector of manuscript books, and can be considered as the official founder of the royal library. He was a leading patron of architects, sculptors, glaziers and goldsmiths. Edward's greatest monument was St George's Chapel, Windsor.

The king's privileged servants at Court were the men through whom the king's personal rule of the land was exercised. The Court was becoming the undisputed political centre of the realm, and was crucial in cementing allegiances between the king and the localities. High-born household servants were the links between the monarchy and the great landed families of the counties. Leading families increasingly sent their sons and daughters to Court to be apprenticed as members of the ruling elite. This was the way for families to get on and make a good marriage.

Edward and the nobility

In this period of revived monarchy, what was Edward's attitude towards the nobles as a group? Did he plan to diminish their authority? As a medieval king, of course, he survived or fell by the way he treated his nobles. The nobility expected 'good lordship' from their king; in return the king needed their unswerving loyalty since he had no standing army or police force of his own to keep order in the realm. Without their support in the provinces the king would have no throne. What Edward needed to do was to reduce the excessive power of the nobles that had been such a destabilising factor in the time of Henry VI. Some historians have seen Edward as a successful king in taming his nobles and reducing the scourge of the 'overmighty subject'. This has been reiterated recently by Christine Carpenter, who claims that Edward was 'one of the most effective managers of the nobility ever to have ruled England'.[5] However, others have denied that Edward was in any sense master of the situation, allowing too many powerful nobles to thrive unchecked and being himself too dependent on one noble faction, the Woodvilles.[6]

In the 1460s Edward depended on a group of the old nobility, together with those members of the gentry whom he had newly ennobled. He confined his patronage to a small group of powerful men to whom he entrusted the running of their own localities: Warwick and his younger brother John Neville in the north of England; Hastings in the Midlands; the Earl of Devon in the south and west; and the Earl of Pembroke in Wales and the Marches. But these magnates were resentful of each other. In his second reign after 1471 Edward preferred the regions to be mainly in the (supposedly) safer hands of members of the royal family. The king's brothers Clarence and Gloucester divided among themselves the lands and affinity of the late Earl of Warwick in the north, while young Prince Edward was sent with a council to Ludlow to supervise Wales and the Marches. The king's second son, Richard of Shrewsbury, had lands settled on him in the Midlands, where the trusted Hastings was also prominent. Elsewhere, lands and power were granted to members of the queen's family, especially to Thomas Grey, first Marquis of Dorset and Richard Grey, the queen's sons by her first marriage. The rapacity shown by the queen, and her bending of the inheritance laws in gaining lands for her family, made the Woodvilles the object of hatred among the great landowning class. While thus preferring to make 'over-mighty subjects' of members of the royal family, Edward was still prepared to make 'over-mighty subjects' out of some non-royal individuals, such as with the restoration of the Percies to the earldom of Northumberland.

Edward had no plan to tame the nobles by reducing their numbers, but created one duke, eight earls and six barons in the first decade; and in the whole reign there were 32 new peerage creations. He was also generous in his disposal of royal patronage. This was especially true of the way in which he dispersed the great prizes that had come to him as a result of victory in 1461 to a small number of nobles whom he thereby made even more powerful. This was an odd way of going about things if his policy had really been to get rid of 'over-mighty subjects'. It appears that Edward did not spread his patronage very widely, and that too many of the nobles and gentry felt excluded.[7] However, Christine Carpenter has recently argued for the notion of the successful absorption of most lords into Edward's system.[8] No definite answer is possible. Essentially, one's judgement on Edward's relations with his nobles is coloured by one's interpretation of the usurpation of 1483: was this crisis fuelled by noble rivalries generated by Edward's failings or was it something completely unexpected that Edward could not have foreseen?

Edward seemingly accepted the traditional powers of the nobles, and 'bastard feudalism' was not seriously attacked. True, there was an Act passed in 1468 against the keeping of retainers by the nobility, but this specifically excluded those domestic servants, legal experts or other retainers kept on 'for lawful service to be done'. In other words, a loophole was made which allowed retaining of any sort of which the king approved. This meant in effect that loyal peers could keep their private armies, but the gentry were not to be allowed this privilege.

Edward's financial achievement

Perhaps Edward's greatest achievement as king lay in the realm of finance, because after a long period of royal indebtedness he restored the solvency of the Crown. He was the first king since Henry II to die unencumbered by debt. Fortescue in his *The Governance of England* pinpointed the restoration of the finances, along with a more efficient royal council, as the key to national recovery. Although earlier medieval kings had obtained money from a variety of sources, including parliamentary taxation, there had been a growing resistance from the 1380s onwards to financing the Crown through parliamentary taxation. Instead the king was now expected to 'live of his own', and Edward certainly aimed to do this. He had no wish to go cap in hand to Parliament, but instead wanted to be master in his own house.

Being expected now not to ask Parliament for money except in extraordinary circumstances (such as wartime), Edward could expect ordinary revenue from four sources: customs duties, the profits of justice, the profits of feudalism, and the crown lands. The biggest source of ordinary revenues came from the king's right to collect customs duties, known as tunnage and poundage. Trade was depressed in the first decade, bringing in only some £25 000 per annum, but in the second part of the reign trade and customs dues greatly expanded; and commercial treaties were signed with France, Burgundy and the Hanseatic League. After 1471 new officials, called the surveyors of customs, were introduced to tighten up the collection, and with such improved efficiency some £34 000 a year was netted. The profits of justice were those resulting from fines levied for breaches of penal statutes, and an increase was seen from this quarter with the greater attention which Edward gave to the maintenance of law and order. The profits of feudalism were those incomes deriving from the king as feudal overlord; all of his tenants-in-chief holding by knight service were required to pay the king such dues as relief, wardship or escheat on the change of owner. Although these sources also yielded greater rewards, Edward did not have the stomach to demand his full feudal rights from the nobles, and he allowed them to evade much inheritance tax. Instead, Edward came to rely on a renewed exploitation of the royal estates. The Yorkists were the first English rulers to depend on them so heavily, and such exploitation was to bring in some £22 000 per annum. The main reason for this greater exploitation was the use of the chamber of the household as the main financial centre of the kingdom, in preference to that department of state, the Exchequer. This 'chamber finance' meant the reversion to a more primitive administrative system in one sense, but coupled with the most recent methods of estate management.

Edward IV's personal financial management greatly boosted his revenues. By 1475 he could pay off his debts and be solvent. After that date a fortune began to be accumulated, helped along by such things as the French pension of 50 000 gold crowns a year granted him by the French king for aborting his invasion of that country (Treaty of Pécquigny 1475), as well as such arbitrary devices as benevolences (or gifts in lieu of military service) and the ransom money for Margaret of Anjou. The king was also (and unusually) personally involved in trade, making numerous foreign commercial treaties, and as a result of all this he was enjoying revenues of about £70 000 a year towards the end.

Law enforcement

Edward IV also made a determined, though limited, effort to restore law and order to a lawless generation. Violence was endemic throughout the Middle Ages, to a degree that we would find appalling today. Without the king's authority local magnates had a free hand in their areas. Edward IV made a real assault on the worst excesses of lawlessness. He himself was always on the move, going in person to dispense justice in the localities. Or else he sent commissions of *oyer and terminer* made up of 20–30 commissioners, normally under a great nobleman. These commissions were Edward's major instrument for reducing crime, and they suppressed the worst examples of disturbance of the peace. However, he was not fully consistent in his policies. Above all, he was too free with pardons: people with influence who committed crimes, even murder, found pardons easy to obtain. In this he was really only slightly less generous than Henry VI. Edward especially turned a blind eye towards lawlessness by those nobles who were not deemed to be a direct threat to the Crown. The king accepted the accustomed violence of society, and aggression to settle scores between individuals continued unabated; any improvement was only marginal. Greater success came with the campaign against violence which threatened the interests and revenues of the Crown, and a more determined effort was made to suppress treason, rebellion and piracy.

Divisions within the House of York

The second decade of Edward's reign was complicated by divisions within the royal family itself, especially by the foolish behaviour of George Duke of Clarence. To start with, there was the quarrel between Clarence and Gloucester over the estates of their late father-in-law, Warwick. Clarence, who had married Isabella Neville, wanted to get them all, and so he bitterly opposed the marriage in 1472 of his brother Gloucester to Anne Neville, widow of Prince Edward of Lancaster. Clarence was so hostile to this marriage that, it seems, he had Anne abducted and hidden away to prevent his brother finding her. The land settlement, involving the carving up of the Neville estates and the extinguishment of the claims of Warwick's widow, was a truly sordid affair, but it ended very much in Clarence's favour, mainly thanks to the king's preparedness to placate him. Edward further appeased the ungrateful Clarence by granting him certain honours initially intended for Gloucester. But Clarence remained dissatisfied, and he seems to have become involved in a conspiracy with his wife's uncle Archbishop George Neville to gain the throne. Clarence may also have been involved in an abortive rebellion in May 1473 involving the Earl of Oxford. Thus Clarence was very much a thorn in Edward's side; even so, the king kept on forgiving his errant brother until finally Edward came to realise that Clarence's intrigues would end only by his removal from this world. When his wife Isabella died in 1476, Clarence wished to marry Mary of Burgundy, the daughter of Archduke Charles by Isabella of Bourbon. Now Mary was already betrothed to Maximilian of Habsburg (the future emperor), and Clarence's actions might well have sparked off a war. Edward was understandably furious with Clarence over this. He also feared that such an ambitious match was designed to challenge his own position as king. It is very likely that Clarence still had not given up his desire for the throne. According to Mancini, it was the Woodvilles who most desired Clarence's death because the queen thought that Clarence would not allow her young son Prince Edward to succeed to the throne. Mancini also mentioned the rumour that Clarence had been employing magic spells to destroy his brother the king. There was also the rumour that Clarence knew of an alleged pre-contract of marriage between the king and Lady Eleanor Butler; and this pre-contract could be seen as invalidating his marriage to Elizabeth Woodville and thus bastardising his children by her. This was an issue that was to come to light later, in the usurpation crisis of 1483. Besides dabbling in treason – he may also have been a conspirator in an obscure uprising in May and June 1477 – Clarence was acting in a very arrogant manner, even taking the law into his own hands by summary executions. Eventually he was condemned to death by parliamentary attainder in 1478, assuredly helped by the many Woodville supporters sitting in this Parliament. Perhaps between one-third and one-half of the Commons were ardent supporters of the Court, the government having intervened directly in elections to ensure Clarence's sentence. The indictment claims that Henry VI had made Clarence his heir, but there is no independent evidence for this assertion. Although Clarence was openly condemned, he was not publicly executed, but killed secretly in the Tower of London, probably, as Mancini relates, in 'a jar of sweet wine'. Shakespeare elaborated this early tradition by specifying the instrument of death as a butt of Malmsey wine. Whatever the exact truth Clarence seems to have come to a deservedly sticky end!

Edward IV died unexpectedly on 9 April 1483 – possibly a stroke or pleurisy – at the relatively young age of 40. He had been a successful warrior king, even if he had lost prestige by not prosecuting the invasion of France in 1475; nevertheless his authority was proved by the almost universal turnout of the nobility in crossing the Channel with him. Despite this undoubted ascendancy Edward failed the crucial final kingly act of peacefully transferring his throne to his son. Edward died a wealthy and powerful king with two sons to succeed him, and the House of York seemed invincible and permanent; yet just over two years later the Yorkist regime was to be swept away for good. In the meantime Edward's two young sons had disappeared, presumed murdered, and the throne had been taken over by the Duke of Gloucester, who ruled for a short time as the last Yorkist king, Richard III.

The enigma of Richard III (1483–5)

Why did Richard of Gloucester, the boy-king's uncle, decide to disinherit Edward V? Was it the product of a long-laid scheme or an act of impetuosity after his brother's death? Unless Richard had been planning to murder his brother Edward IV one cannot see any logic in the Tudor–Shakespearean story that Richard had been coveting the Crown for many years. Edward's early death came as a surprise to everyone, and Richard, unlike Clarence, had been exceedingly loyal to him. Nevertheless, out of the untimely death of Edward IV there would unfold a drama of intrigue and conspiracy, of murder and the vanishing of innocent princes which would capture the imagination of generations of people thereafter and which would give birth to the perpetual enigma of King Richard III.

The story of the high political drama of the year 1483 – an unprecedented series of sharp and brutal events – will never be related to everyone's satisfaction, simply because the surviving evidence for what went on in the corridors of power is scanty, unreliable and contradictory. Although many of the impersonal records of governmental administration survive, they throw only indirect light on the otherwise murky world of conspiracy at Court. Most historians agree that the best contemporary source for the facts, though not always for the interpretation of them, is a document known as the Crowland Continuation, which is an addition to the chronicle of Crowland Abbey (near Peterborough); the section relating the years 1470–85 was written at Crowland in 1486 by a visitor there – a man who had been at Court and had sat in on council meetings, and was thus generally well informed, although not privy to the very highest politics. The second contemporary source is the account by the Italian visitor Dominic Mancini of the last years of Edward IV's reign and the seizure of power by Richard III. Mancini was present in England as Edward's reign drew to a close and through until early July; he wrote down his account in France for his patron, and was completed by 1 December 1483. It is thus an independent and contemporary account (indeed the earliest) by someone without any axe to grind. Both the Crowland Continuation and Mancini's narrative were the products of new Renaissance history, with a genuine attempt to set out the perceived facts. The major problem with Mancini as a source is that his evidence is mainly second-hand: what people had told him. He is therefore a purveyor of rumour, and because he could not speak English he was even more at the mercy of his informants. However, as rumours are potent spurs to action in history, Mancini's account is crucial for an understanding of the way so many people understood the events of the time. But it should not be taken on trust, and on some issues he was plainly wrong.

For the historian of the usurpation of 1483 the problems and contradictions of the evidence begin straightaway with the death of Edward IV. Following Mancini, modern historians have generally pointed to a rift within the royal family between the Woodville faction and Richard of Gloucester. Richard, in Mancini's version, had kept himself far away in the north because of fear of the Woodvilles, especially after the elimination of his brother

Clarence. There was also apparently a mortal feud between Hastings and the Woodvilles. The initial crisis was thus due to these rifts and tensions at the top. If there is any truth in this then Edward IV himself must take much of the blame for the chaos that ensued on his death, even though, as Mancini relates, he had tried to reconcile Hastings and the Marquis of Dorset. Not long before he died, Edward gave added honours to the Woodville family. On 8 March 1483 Anthony second Earl Rivers, the queen's brother, who was with Prince Edward and his council at Ludlow, had been given authority to raise troops along the Welsh border, while her other brother, Sir Edward Woodville, had been put in charge of Edward's navy. The queen's son Dorset was given command of the Tower of London, with the royal treasure stored there. Everything suggested that effective power would go to the Woodvilles on the king's death. But, of course, in making these appointments Edward did not expect to die! When he shortly realised he was about to depart this world, he made a new will with new executors. This final will no longer survives, and what the changes amounted to is uncertain; but they either arranged for his brother Richard to be made protector or else established the council as a group to be the government of the realm until the boy came of age. The earliest evidence for Edward's choosing a protectorate under his brother is Mancini, and later Polydore Vergil, the early Tudor historian, also fully accepted the story; but the Crowland Continuation makes no mention of it, and thus silently denies it. If true the clause establishing the protectorate essentially undid Edward's work in favour of the Woodvilles. The will, therefore, on this scenario, far from easing the tense situation, would have made matters worse and made a political crisis almost inevitable. Edward may well have hoped that the two sides of the family would be reconciled, but, if so, such thinking would have been naïve and wishful. Richard as protector would be in control and would inevitably seek support from leading nobles who had been alienated by the king or by Woodville arrogance. Furthermore, both Richard and the Woodvilles were in possession of considerable armed forces.

The above argument presupposes that Richard and the Woodvilles really did form competing, hostile factions; but this no longer seems to be securely established. Recently it has been denied that there was any Woodville faction in existence for Richard to fear, and that all signs were of their cooperation, not of any conflict.[9] Indeed Richard had just acted as arbiter in a dispute affecting the Woodvilles – hardly a good choice had they been enemies. Mancini's account that Richard had been hiding away in the north seems very suspect, and the main flaw lies in his belief that Richard blamed the Woodvilles for the death of Clarence. It seems clear that Clarence deserved his fate and that Richard had agreed with his brother the king on the necessity of the matter. If there was no basis to the rivalry between Richard and the Woodvilles before April 1483 then Mancini must have got this story from Richard's supporters eager to find reasons to justify his subsequent behaviour.

If Edward IV really wished to make his brother protector then the majority of the council certainly broke the will by deciding on a conciliar form of government with Richard as leading councillor, but not with the full authority of a protector. Mancini says that this breaking of the will was made to prevent Richard becoming too powerful. Mancini's account gives the impression that the majority of the council were in league with the Woodvilles and their ambitions to take over the state; a minority of councillors wanted to make no move until Richard's arrival. Mancini cites Dorset as boasting: 'We are so important that even without the king's uncle we can make and enforce these decisions.' On this scenario Richard might well have been fearful of what the Woodvilles had in store for him. This was certainly to be the propaganda case that Richard was soon to employ to justify his swift actions.

Despite the recent claims that the Woodvilles did not constitute an ambitious faction that needed to be feared, Crowland states that the 'wiser' councillors thought that the Woodville relatives of the young king should not have control of him and should not bring him to London amidst a huge armed force. Thus one section of the council does seem to have regarded the Woodvilles as a *potentially* over-powerful clique which needed to be controlled. One such councillor was Lord Hastings, a devoted servant to Edward IV but an enemy of the queen and her family. The council stated its desire for a peaceful accession of Edward V, but this fact alone indicates the existence of tension and doubt about the matter. Hastings demanded that Edward V's return to

London should not be in the midst of an enormous Woodville army, and it was finally agreed that no more than 2000 men (which was still a huge number) should accompany the new king back to London. This compromise pleased Hastings, who felt that the imminent arrival of his allies Gloucester and Buckingham would establish a balance of forces.

Richard was at the time of his brother's death still serving in the north of England. According to Mancini, Hastings urged Richard to return to the capital as soon as possible to prevent a Woodville take-over of the state and to avenge the insults done to him. The Woodvilles, for their part, wanted the return of the boy-king to London for an early coronation, but there is no evidence of overdue haste on their part. Furthermore, Rivers agreed to meet up with Richard and Buckingham on their way south, and for them all to enter London together. This meeting had been suggested by Richard, who had enquired of the prince's route to the capital. There seemed no reason for the Woodvilles to suspect Richard, who had already made the Yorkshire gentry swear an oath of loyalty to Edward V.

Accordingly Rivers left the royal party at Stony Stratford and went to meet Gloucester and Buckingham at Northampton, where the three men had a pleasant dinner on the evening of 29 April. But at dawn the following morning Rivers was immediately arrested. Richard then caught up with Edward V's entourage at Stony Stratford, where he seized the person of the king and also arrested Sir Richard Grey and the Edwardian loyalist Sir Thomas Vaughan; these three men were then sent up north. According to Crowland, Richard claimed he did this only to protect himself because 'he knew for certain that there were men close to the king who had sworn to destroy his honour and his life'. It is impossible from this distance to say whether these fears were grounded or groundless. The way that Rivers went to meet the two dukes and was not heavily protected, and was indeed caught off guard, suggests that these were mere excuses. Did the events of 30 April mean that as early as this date Richard had decided to usurp the throne? Publicly he offered only reverence to Edward V, but it is noteworthy that on 2 May the coronation was postponed. Although Mancini depicts the seizure of the boy-king as a form of self-defence on

Richard's part, it looks more like a clearing of the decks for further action.

News of these disturbing events reached London late the same day; and the queen with her daughters and younger son Richard immediately fled into sanctuary in Westminster Abbey. Her brother Sir Edward Woodville escaped to sea with the fleet – and more of the royal treasure. On 4 May Edward V and his uncle Richard entered London to great cheering and rejoicing, along with four cartloads of arms bearing Woodville emblems to 'prove' the existence of a plot against his life. The boy-king was sent to reside in the royal apartments of the Tower of London in preparation, as was customary, for his ceremonial procession through the City of London to Westminster for his coronation. At a council meeting on 10 May two decisions were made: for the coronation date to be fixed, and for Richard to be accepted as protector. Richard thus had the support of the council as long as he was working on behalf of the true king. Richard was to act as protector only until the coronation, but there is some evidence that he wanted it prolonged a few more years until the king was declared of age (when Edward was 15 or 16).

At what stage did Richard go beyond wanting an extended protectorate to plotting to seize the Crown itself? Mancini suggests some date in May 1483, but few people could have perceived this because the general appearance in May was one of harmony; the Yorkist establishment, including Lord Hastings, seemed to be thoroughly pleased with the turn of events. Rosemary Horrox argues that from mid-May onwards Gloucester's position as Protector was secure, buttressed by his brother's supporters; therefore 'it is difficult to argue that he was panicked into seizing the throne . . . it was Gloucester who chose to put an end to it'.[10]

Seemingly harmonious government can be traced down to the council meeting of 9 June and its discussion of arrangements for Edward V's coronation. However, on 10 June Richard wrote to the city of York, asking for military support for himself and Buckingham to counteract the Woodville faction ('the Queen, her blood, adherents and affinity'), who he claimed were out to murder them. This notion of a Woodville conspiracy seems hard to accept especially as they had earlier failed to organise any plot against Gloucester. And if by some miracle they were now a threat to Richard it is hard to see how his appeal to the north could have helped in the short term because of the time it would take to organise such a force to come south. The appeal to the north makes sense only if Richard were thinking in the longer term.

But how could the Woodvilles now represent a threat to the protector? One traditional explanation has been to cite the role of Lord Hastings in turning against Richard and making common cause with the queen. In this scenario, Richard found himself once more surrounded by enemies and had to strike back at them. Gloucester does not in fact mention Hastings as an enemy in his letter of 10 June to the city of York, and neither Crowland nor Mancini shows any knowledge of a possible *rapprochement* or alliance between Hastings and the Woodvilles. Such a conspiratorial alliance between the queen and Hastings seems intrinsically unlikely, but it is given in some detail by Vergil, and some modern historians have also given it credence.[11] Vergil claimed that Hastings turned against Richard straightaway after the seizures at Northampton and Stony Stratford, and that at an early date he entered into a conspiracy with his erstwhile foe Dorset. Thus Vergil completely contradicts Crowland, who contrasts the pleasure Hastings obtained from Richard's superseding the Woodvilles in power with his subsequent grisly end at Richard's hands. Mancini reports the belief that Richard saw Hastings as a barrier to his assumption of the throne. If Hastings was really involved in any conspiracy then he allowed himself quite amazingly to be taken by surprise by Richard in the council chamber at the Tower of London on 13 June.

The crucial date on Richard's path to the throne seems to have been Friday 13 June, when in a spectacular scene Lord Hastings was arrested at a council meeting and summarily dragged out and beheaded by the protector's authority on Tower Green. Three other councillors were arrested at the same time. The Crowland account is sparse on detail, but Mancini relates that:

> the Protector, as pre-arranged, cried out that an ambush had been prepared for him, and that they had come with hidden arms, that they might be first to open the attack.

The element of surprise appears very much on the same lines as at Northampton and Stony Stratford.

If Hastings was not involved in any conspiracy, why did Richard not wait longer to strike him down – for example, until the arrival of his northern supporters? Crowland and Mancini both report the belief that Richard had to remove him if he were to proceed with usurpation because he knew that Hastings was loyal to Edward IV and Edward V. Crowland makes the telling point that after Hastings' death and the removal of the other councillors Richard and Buckingham could then do what they liked. Killing Hastings meant removing the head of the old Edwardian loyalist establishment. Mancini thought that Hastings was killed 'by a friend whom he had never doubted' and that the idea of a 'plot had been feigned by the duke so as to escape the odium of such a crime'.

Of Hastings' supporters on the council who had also been arrested at the same time – Archbishop Rotherham, Lord Stanley and Bishop Morton – the first two later made their peace with Richard and were readmitted to the council, but Morton was sent to Brecon Castle in south Wales with Buckingham as his gaoler. The execution of Hastings meant that no further opposition could be expected from the council.

The next event was that Prince Richard was forced out of sanctuary on Monday 16 June into the arms of the protector. Both Crowland and Mancini emphasise Gloucester's threat to use force and his employment of Archbishop Bourchier to persuade the queen to give her son up. Crowland says that the archbishop relayed the protector's wish that the younger boy should comfort his brother the king, and that the queen willingly agreed to let go of him, while Mancini reports that Richard ostensibly wanted the younger boy available for the coronation ceremony. If that was indeed the tale, it was soon belied because immediately Richard postponed the coronation until November, and the Parliament summoned for 25 June was also delayed.

Richard then moved speedily to assert his own claim to the throne. This was first voiced by the priest Father Ralph Shaw on Sunday 22 June in an open-air sermon. The basis of the claim was that Edward IV's children by Elizabeth Woodville were illegitimate because of Edward's pre-contract of marriage with Lady Eleanor Butler. Under church law it could be argued that this pre-contract rendered Edward's marriage in 1464 to Elizabeth

Woodville invalid, especially as that marriage had been celebrated in secret and not publicly in church, and with no banns having been read out; thus all their children were bastards. Edward V, on this reasoning, was no true king; and since Clarence had been attainted, his son the Earl of Warwick was also ineligible for the throne because an attainder meant the legal death of the whole family. This left only Duke Richard as the genuine claimant. Historians sympathetic to Richard can therefore argue that Richard was not a usurper at all but the true king.[12] Despite the claim that the pre-contract, if true, affected the legitimacy only of Edward's eldest daughter, Elizabeth of York (born 1465), not that of the two princes (born in 1470 and 1472) because Eleanor Butler had died in 1468, it now seems definite that under canon law unless fresh vows had been taken by Edward and Elizabeth after Dame Eleanor's death the marriage remained invalid and any later children were still to be regarded as bastards.[13] We have no knowledge of any such fresh vows being taken. As Edward had almost certainly enjoyed sexual relations with Dame Eleanor it appears that any pre-contract with her was absolutely binding on him. Edward V stood a better chance at common law than in canon law, because in the common law of property descent an heir accepted as such at his father's death (even if he were a bastard by another father) was still to be accepted as the legitimate heir. Edward V was certainly and publicly accepted as the heir of Edward IV on 9 April 1483, and on this reasoning his claim to the throne should not have been challenged. The problem was that the Crown of England was never regarded as just another piece of property, subject to property law, but as something special, in a class of its own; and no one was clear how the descent should be judged. Factors other than purely strict heredity in the royal succession had counted in the past, and with such grave doubts Richard should really have passed the matter over to both the spiritual courts and Parliament for resolution – which of course he signally failed to do. All that one can say is that if the pre-contract was true Richard had a good claim to the throne. But was it true? Historians have differed, and at present there is no way of knowing.

The pre-contract, if genuine, was apparently known only to Bishop Stillington; and in June 1483 the good bishop is supposed to have revealed the fact to Richard, who recovering from the shock felt compelled to put himself forward for the throne. It has been argued that the pre-contract was true and that it was because of Clarence's knowledge of it that he had been eliminated. Richard's claim was repeated by Buckingham on 24 June to the mayor and aldermen of the City of London, and the following day to an assembly of lords and gentry who had assembled for the summoned Parliament. All these groups now implored Richard to assume the throne. Whether Richard's claims to the throne were accepted out of fear or out of conviction it is hard to say. Probably the overriding concern for most people was the need for continued stability whatever the rights and wrongs of the situation. A deputation led by Buckingham ostentatiously went to implore Richard to accept the Crown. He did so and took his place on the marble chair in Westminster Hall, and the official date of Richard's accession was set at 26 June. Richard's trusted servants were rewarded: William Catesby was made chancellor of the Exchequer, while John Howard became Duke of Norfolk. Soon Richard's northern forces (perhaps 4000) arrived on the northern outskirts of the City, led by the Earl of Northumberland.

The coronation ceremony was quickly arranged for Sunday 6 July in Westminster Abbey. Richard was crowned in a ceremony of unprecedented magnificence, being the first king to take the coronation oath in English. The overwhelming majority of nobles attended the event, as did a large number of knights formerly in his brother's service, so that whatever private fears people might have harboured there can no doubt that Richard was initially accepted by the Yorkist establishment. The coronation was a resounding success and augured well for the future.

The coronation jubilantly accomplished, Richard then set out on a royal progress through the Midlands into the north of England in order to advertise his kingship and win support by making grants to towns and religious establishments on the way. But Richard was soon to be in for a rude shock. While staying at the home of his leading supporter Francis Lord Lovell the king was informed of serious trouble back in London. Writing by signet letter from Minster Lovell on 29 July to Lord Chancellor Russell, Richard referred to news 'that certain persons of such as of late had taken upon them the fact of an enterprise, as we doubt not you have heard, be attached, and in ward'. The lord chancellor was to proceed against these unnamed arrested malefactors. This seems to relate to conspiracies to free the two princes mentioned by Crowland, who also related a rumour:

> that those men who had fled to sanctuaries had advised that some of the King's [Edward IV's] daughters should leave Westminster in disguise and go overseas so that if any human fate, inside the Tower, were to befall the male children, nevertheless through the saving of the persons of the daughters the kingdom might some day return to the rightful heirs.

This led to Richard ordering the complete encirclement of the sanctuary at Westminster to prevent the flight of the Woodville girls. If one accepts the view that Richard was responsible for the imminent disappearance of the princes, then it is very likely it was these reports that triggered Richard's determination to get rid of them. Meanwhile, Richard continued on his progress north which had as high points the investiture of his son Edward as Prince of Wales at Nottingham (24 August) and a repeat of the coronation ceremony at York Minster (8 September). On his way back south in October he was to hear of another rebellion against him.

The princes in the Tower

The fact that Richard had assumed the throne by disinheriting his nephews did not necessarily mean that he had to go on and murder them. After all, Henry VI had been kept alive throughout the first decade of Edward IV's reign. Perhaps the continued use of Henry VI as a focal point for rebellion made Richard decide that he had to eliminate the threat now posed by the boys. There was obviously some logic in this, but even in the violent world of the fifteenth century the murder of two innocent children would not have been regarded as acceptable political behaviour. Edward V had not shown himself to be an incompetent king or one who had broken the conventions of good lordship. All this, of course, assumes that Richard was indeed behind the murder of the two boys, and that the two boys were murdered at all – both still very contentious issues.

When Richard took the throne, the two princes were moved within the Tower of London, from the royal apartments (which no longer exist today, but were just to the south of the White Tower) into the Garden Tower (which is known today as the Bloody Tower). The Great Chronicle of London relates that when Sir Edmund Shaw was lord mayor of the City (i.e. before 29 October 1483) 'the children of King Edward were seen shooting and playing in the garden of the Tower, by sundry times'. They were later moved into what Mancini refers to as the 'inner apartments' of the Tower, which must mean into the central White Tower. This idea is strengthened by the fact that two skeletons, presumed to be of two teenage boys, were indeed found just outside the White Tower in 1674. Mancini also relates that the boys were seen more and more rarely until at last they disappeared for ever. According to Mancini's informants: 'The physician Argentine, the last of his attendants whose services the King enjoyed, reported that the young King, like a victim prepared for sacrifice, sought remission of his sins by daily confession and penance, because he believed that death was facing him.' Mancini includes a crucial emotional point that needs to be borne in mind in any discussion on the 'heartless politics' of the period: 'I have seen many men burst forth into tears and lamentations when mention was made of him after his removal from men's sight; and already there was a suspicion that he had been done away with.' Here we have Mancini as a real eyewitness to the grief felt.

Did Richard murder the princes in the Tower? That is one of the great historical mysteries that, barring a near-miraculous documentary discovery, will always remain unsolved. If Richard did not kill them, then who else might have been guilty? The names that have been put forward include Buckingham, Norfolk and Henry VII (after he became king). The chances of the two princes living to the accession of Henry VII were reduced by the findings of the scientific investigation of the sets of bones in 1933, which argued that the skeletons dug up in 1674 were those of two boys aged 9–11 and 12–13, not at least 13 and 15 which they would have had to have been if Henry VII had murdered them. Although these scientific findings have been criticised and challenged over the years by Ricardians, recent studies of the dental data have tended to support the identity of the boys and their murder in the reign of Richard III. The teeth show ages of children 9–10 and 12–14. Also the skeletons are related: they both show a rare condition known as hypodontia, which means that they had permanently missing teeth. This condition the skeletons shared with a cousin of the two princes, Lady Anne Mowbray, who had been betrothed to Prince Richard, and who died in 1481 at the age of nearly nine. Anne's skeleton was discovered during excavations in the City of London in the 1960s and examined scientifically. Although many people remain highly sceptical, it does look as though we have the evidence of the boys' murder before 1485. However, to convince those doubters who claim that the bones could come from almost any century what is needed is a radiocarbon dating to establish definitely their fifteenth-century origins, as well as the application of new scientific techniques to establish their sex. If we can believe those who observed the discovery in 1674 in their assertion that the bones had 'pieces of rag and velvet about them' this would almost clinch the matter since velvet was a recent invention from Renaissance Italy, affordable only to the very richest people.[14] However, no pieces of velvet had survived in 1933 to corroborate this point. Proof that these are indeed the remains of the two princes is not, of course, the same as saying that Richard definitely murdered them. The case against Henry VII is a non-starter, especially as none of the rebels against him ever accused him of their murder.

There now seems little reason to doubt that the death of the two boys occurred sometime between the very end of July and October 1483 while they were still prisoners in the Tower. Crowland states a belief in their death at this time, and Mancini thought that the princes were dead by July 1483. Buckingham, during the rebellion of October 1483, also claimed that the boys were dead. If the boys were still alive in October why did Richard not show them to the London public to scotch such dangerous rumours? Richard's silence at this crucial time was deafening.

Buckingham's rebellion, 1483

The disappearance of the two princes was certainly the major reason for the rebellion that sprang up in October 1483 in the southern and western counties of England, misleadingly known to history as 'Buckingham's rebellion', because although Buckingham joined in the uprising he certainly did not start it. Between early October and the first week of November many leading gentry in all of the counties of southern and south-western England rose in revolt. Although the different uprisings were to be quashed, and there was to be no major battle, the rebellion was not doomed to failure. It was a much more serious affair than the way Richard's government painted it in the subsequent Act of Attainder of January 1484, which minimised both the geographical and the chronological extent of the risings. The Act of Attainder also tried to label Buckingham as the organiser and ringleader. However, his role now appears to be marginal, and he attracted very few supporters to his side in Wales and the Marches. Why Buckingham should have changed sides is yet another frustrating mystery of this very enigmatic period. He was probably persuaded by Bishop Morton, his prisoner at Brecon Castle, to revolt against his erstwhile ally. Yet Buckingham's motivation is not clear. The most likely reason for Buckingham's treachery was that he became convinced that the rebellion being hatched would indeed prosper and that Richard's days were numbered; he therefore had to save his own skin.

It has been shown that only a minority of the rebels can be classified as having been narrow Woodville adherents, ex-Lancastrians or self-seekers; the overwhelming majority were former servants and supporters of Edward IV who were now infuriated by Richard's abysmal treatment of the princes.[15] Nor was it a question of 'outs' versus 'ins', because many of the rebels were in service to King Richard, including five yeomen from the royal household. What is evident is a definite split in the Yorkist establishment, with a minority daring to sacrifice everything to get rid of Richard. However, what began as a loyalist rebellion to secure the release of the princes soon turned into a movement to place Henry Tudor on the throne. Tudor's mother, Lady Margaret Beaufort, may have been involved in the plot against Richard from early on, before any news of the boys' death, probably with a view to gaining her son's restoration at the hands of the Woodvilles. Now that the princes were gone, she and Elizabeth Woodville reached an agreement for Henry to marry

Elizabeth of York. This agreement indicates clearly that Elizabeth Woodville strongly believed that her two sons were already dead.

This was, therefore, a rebellion of loyalists, which Buckingham for his own reasons joined. His optimism regarding its outcome is a key indicator that the rebellion initially had a great chance of success, and that Richard was lucky to have survived. Indeed one reason for the rebellion's failure was Buckingham's very participation, because few lords or gentlemen in Wales or the Marches were prepared to join up with him, so very loathed was he; another reason was Buckingham's inability to cross the flooded river Severn into England owing to terrible storms. Buckingham was then betrayed in Shropshire and executed at Salisbury. These same storms also prevented the landing of Henry Tudor, who had to remain waiting off Plymouth (or Poole), before returning to his base in Brittany empty-handed.

There were two major consequences of 'Buckingham's rebellion': there was now a clear opposition party in exile, and at home Richard was forced drastically to remodel the base of his support. The rebellion had certainly transformed the prospects of the exiled Welsh Lancastrian Henry Tudor, who now had allies in all those who had taken up arms or who had been forced to flee the realm. Henry Tudor was one of the few remaining Lancastrian partisans, but he now had Yorkist supporters also; and on Christmas day 1483, in order to seal an alliance with the Woodvilles and other Yorkists, he made a promise at Rennes Cathedral in Brittany to marry Elizabeth of York once he had defeated the usurper.

Within England itself Richard was forced to abandon his previous policy of continuity with the Yorkist establishment. He now brought some of his key northern supporters down to the south to take over the lands and positions of the rebels. Although huge numbers were not involved, certainly not more than 30, they were enough to cause much resentment in the south, especially if one remembers the groups of retainers that accompanied them. The hatred of northerners by southerners was compounded by the fact that the newcomers were generally socially inferior, not being great landowners themselves in the north, but younger sons who depended almost entirely on Richard for their prosperity. In time this policy of bringing in new men would assuredly have worked, but Richard was not destined to have time on his side, and in the short term this policy created much bitterness in the south. Also the fact that Richard redistributed the confiscated lands to his supporters before Parliament could pass an Act of Attainder gave a tyrannical taste to the whole transfer. Richard was once again bypassing the niceties of the law.

Over 100 people were attainted by Richard III in his only Parliament of January–April 1484, and although a third of these later successfully petitioned for a pardon and received some of their lands back, they were never employed by Richard again; and a legacy of bitterness remained in southern England. It is important to remember that the picture of the tyrannical Richard was manufactured in the south; the north remained loyal and well disposed towards him.

In the immediate aftermath of the failed rebellion Richard enjoyed a period of calm, when he aimed to win over the nation by the exercise of good kingship. Parliament confirmed Richard's title to the throne on the grounds of Edward V's illegitimacy caused by his father's pre-contract, and also legitimised Richard's attainders and arbitrary confiscations. Furthermore, Parliament was also to be used to make the regime popular. Richard agreed to a series of reforms, including the promise to ban forced gifts or 'benevolences', and much is made of this by modern Ricardians.

The situation seemed to improve for the king when in March 1484 Elizabeth Woodville was persuaded to allow her five daughters to leave sanctuary and return to Court, an event which Ricardians have interpreted as proving the king's innocence of child murder. Yet perhaps what is more significant is that Richard had publicly to guarantee their safety and to promise not to 'imprison [them] within the Tower of London' – which strongly suggests that their brothers had not prospered there. Few people, it seems, had much faith in Richard, and his luck really deserted him with the death of his only legitimate son Prince Edward on 9 April 1484 (exactly one year since the death of Edward IV). The Crowland chronicler, no friend to Richard, relates how the king and queen were distraught by their son's death and comforted each other.

Then on 16 March 1485, Queen Anne died of (probably) tuberculosis, aged less than 30. If Anne had not died by the hand of God (itself seen as a judgement against Richard, especially as it occurred on a day when there was an eclipse of the sun) then many people at the time believed that Richard had poisoned her in order to marry his niece Elizabeth of York because of his eagerness to beget a male successor, and also to prevent any political capital being made from Tudor's claim on her. So low had Richard's reputation fallen that he had to deny publicly that he intended marrying his niece.

It was now only a matter of time before Henry Tudor chanced a second invasion, while Richard was fast losing support. Richard and his cronies appeared as alien outsiders in southern England, seemingly out of touch with public opinion generally. One hostile activist, William Collingbourne of Wiltshire, wrote a number of doggerel verses which he pinned up in various places in July 1484 around the City of London, the most famous of which attacked the slender basis of the king's rule, with Richard's only true friends being Ratcliffe, Catesby and Lovell (which was almost, but not quite, correct):

> The Cat, the Rat, and Lovell our Dog
> Ruling all England under an Hog.

References are to Lovell's and Richard's emblems of a silver wolf and a boar, and Catesby's of a white cat.

The king's only serious hope was to capture Tudor, and to this end in June 1484 Richard succeeded in reaching an agreement with the treasurer of the duchy of Brittany, where Henry had his court in exile. The duke, who had allowed Tudor to stay there so long, was temporarily out of action in September through illness; hence Richard's success with the treasurer. However, being warned in time by Bishop Morton, who had got wind of the conspiracy while in Flanders, Henry was able to flee in disguise to neighbouring France, where he was welcomed by Charles VIII, who agreed in November to provide him with money for men and arms to mount an invasion of England. As Brittany and France were enemies, Richard's deal with the Bretons had given Charles VIII good cause to plot against England. French support also encouraged small outbreaks of resistance in England – especially in Essex and Hertfordshire. There was also disaffection in the Calais region, where the garrison at Hammes guarding the

Lancastrian Earl of Oxford allowed him to escape and indeed joined him in his flight to Tudor's side. The worrying thing for Richard was that some of the new rebels had been his servants. Dr Horrox's conclusion is that 'Richard's inability as king to retain the loyalties of his own servants is a damning indictment of his regime.'[16] Richard made his headquarters at Nottingham in the very centre of England and awaited the arrival of Tudor's force. Richard made complex arrangements to defeat him, but he could not depend on the loyalty of the men he put in charge. Elaborate and expensive defence mechanisms were put in place, and despite his assurances to Parliament Richard asked the gentry for benevolences. Yet few paid up. According to an old prophecy an invasion force would land at Milford; but which Milford – Milford Haven in west Wales, or Milford near Southampton?

The emergence of Henry Tudor

But for the mistakes of Richard III there would have been no Tudor accession. Henry Tudor's story really begins with his Welsh grandfather Owen Tudor, who married in secret the widow of Henry V, Catherine of Valois. Owen Tudor sprang from an old Welsh family that had served the princes of Gwynedd in the thirteenth century and subsequently the English monarch in north Wales. However, the family had fallen from grace by supporting the rebellion of Owain Glyndwr against Henry IV, and so how exactly Owen made his way to the English Court remains something of a mystery. He somehow obtained a post in the dowager queen's household. Owen and Catherine certainly fell in love and married in secret, around the year 1432. When Catherine died in 1437, Owen found himself persecuted for his effrontery in marrying the former queen. But eventually, in November 1439, Owen received a pardon and a position in the household of his stepson Henry VI. Catherine gave birth to four children by Owen; of the three boys one became a monk, but the other two were befriended by the king and ennobled in 1452: Edmund Tudor became Earl of Richmond, and Jasper Tudor Earl of Pembroke, with precedence above all other nobles except for dukes. Edmund Tudor went on to marry Lady Margaret Beaufort, the leading member of her family and thus a very wealthy lady. The Beauforts were of illegitimate royal descent (from John of Gaunt, Duke of Lancaster by his mistress and last wife, Catherine Swynford) and although later legitimated were specifically barred from the throne. Margaret gave birth to her son Henry Tudor on 28 January 1457 at Pembroke Castle in west Wales when she was still only 14 years of age. However, she had already become a widow, for her husband Edmund had died, probably of the plague. The infant Henry was then put in the charge of his uncle Jasper, while his mother went off and married again. Henry remained with his uncle until the Yorkists captured Pembroke Castle in 1461. In the new Yorkist regime Henry Tudor became the ward of William Herbert, the new Earl of Pembroke. At this time Henry was nowhere near the throne, and Herbert's aim was to turn Tudor into a good Yorkist and marry him to his daughter. However, Herbert's death at Edgecote (1469) and the renewal of war completely changed Henry Tudor's life story. His uncle Jasper regained possession of the boy during the Readeption, and on the return of Edward IV Jasper took his nephew into exile. Still there was no question at this early date of his being an alternative to the Yorkists even though Henry VI and his son were dead. His chance came only with the division of the Yorkists occasioned by the usurpation of Richard III. In Brittany and then in France, he could pose as an alternative king of England; and the discontented certainly did assemble under his banner in exile – men like Morton, Richard Foxe, Edward Poynings and the Earl of Oxford. Despite this inflow of talent, Henry's chances still did not appear good. Thus he could not delay his invasion too long lest Richard should strengthen his position.

The battle of Bosworth, 1485

On Sunday 7 August Henry's little fleet landed at Milford Haven in far west Wales with an army of about 4000 men, made up of between 400 and 500 English exiles, some 1000 members of the *Garde Écossaise* (the elite Scots Guard of the French king) and the rest mainly Norman mercenaries. Richard expected Tudor's small forces to be contained in Wales by Sir Walter Herbert and

Rhys ap Thomas, who instead, after much hesitation, eventually went over to the invader. Henry Tudor met no opposition at all through Wales or the English Midlands until he got to Bosworth field. Even so, this was not enough to win the day, and Henry hoped to gain the support of his stepfather Lord Stanley. However, Stanley wanted to be sure of being on the winning side and refused to show his cards. The fateful battle took place on 22 August, but little is known for certain about its details; surviving accounts are meagre in the extreme. The only contemporary records are the Crowland Chronicle, Polydore Vergil, the London 'Great Chronicle' and the 'Stanley ballads', and none contains an eyewitness account. Even the exact location of the battlefield is not crystal clear. According to recent research, the fighting took place further south than the traditional site of Ambien Hill – nearer to Dadlington than to Market Bosworth.[17] At the battle Henry Tudor had about 5000 men, while Richard probably had between 8000 and 10 000 men, possibly even reaching 15 000. Thus Richard with his numerical superiority should have won the day – and he nearly did. Richard decided to leave the main body of the royal army and attack Henry and his immediate followers directly as they moved towards the Stanley contingent in an effort to persuade them to desert Richard. Henry was nearly killed (indeed his standard-bearer was slain by Richard), but was saved at the last minute by the decision of the Stanley brothers, Lord Thomas and Sir William Stanley, to throw in their lot with the invader; and it was Sir William Stanley's men who actually saved Henry Tudor at that crucial moment. Also helpful was the treason, or tardiness, of Henry Percy, fourth Earl of Northumberland. Whether Richard's rash dash was a fatal tactical blunder or a recognition that the battle was already going badly for him it is impossible to tell. Richard undoubtedly fought bravely, hoping to clinch victory by personal combat with his arch foe, but was struck down by a Welsh pikeman. Somewhere his gold circlet was discovered on the field, according to legend on a hawthorn bush – which legend must surely be true because of the motif of thorns and crowns in Henry VII's chapel in Westminster Abbey – and his stepfather Lord Stanley crowned Henry with it. Richard was only 32 years of age when died; he was the first English king since 1066 to lose his life on the battlefield.

Henry VII and the Tudor triumph

No one in 1485 could have predicted that the victor of Bosworth would establish a dynasty that would last for well over 100 years and be one of the most celebrated royal lines in the whole of English history. Despite this victory, it would be quite some time before the Tudors could feel that they had come to stay. And if there is a common theme to the whole Tudor dynasty it was their fear that their hold on the throne was never fully secure.

Despite all the problems of 1485, Henry VII behaved like a king from the very start. He was helped, of course, by the fact that there was no viable alternative claimant to the throne. Richard's designated heir, his nephew John de la Pole, Earl of Lincoln, professed loyalty to the new dynasty, while Edward Earl of Warwick was a prisoner in the Tower. At the first Parliament of the reign (in November 1485) an Act of Attainder was passed against some 30 supporters of Richard III. By dating his reign one day before Bosworth, Henry could claim that Richard and his party were in arms against the lawful ruler, and that thus their lands were forfeit. But neither in this Parliament nor later was the honour, or the legality of the rule, of Edward IV ever besmirched. After all, Henry was soon to marry Edward's daughter, Elizabeth of York. Moreover, Henry's victory had not been a narrow Lancastrian one but a joint one with disaffected, or 'loyalist', Yorkists, and there was no attempt to exclude them from his new government. Henry's first two lord chancellors were former servants of Edward IV: Archbishop Rotherham and Bishop Alcock. Bishop Courtenay was Henry's first lord privy seal: he had served both Henry VI and Edward IV but had fled as an alienated Yorkist to Tudor's side in 1483. Henry's supporters in exile were naturally well rewarded, especially his uncle Jasper, who became Duke of Bedford.

Continuing opposition

Yet opposition was still alive, and the Wars of the Roses in a sense continued for another two years after Bosworth. Although there was no viable claimant to the throne the forces of discontent were still able to give Henry's heart a flutter. There were some minor problems in 1486, with Lord Lovell's attempt to ambush the king in Yorkshire, and the small-scale rebellion of Humphrey Stafford in Warwickshire. Then in 1487 a serious rebellion flared up in support of the Earl of Warwick. The genuine earl was locked up in the Tower, but a young boy named Lambert Simnel had been coached to play the part. Simnel was taken to Ireland, where he was recognised as 'Edward VI' by the Yorkist Earl of Kildare, lord lieutenant of Ireland. Henry displayed the real Warwick to the London crowds, but this did nothing to disperse the gathering clouds of rebellion. Simnel fled to Burgundy, where Lincoln joined him. Margaret of Burgundy gave her support and blessing to the plot, even though she must have known that Simnel was an impostor. She supplied 2000 German mercenaries for Simnel's return to Ireland, where he was crowned king in Dublin Cathedral. An army of invasion from Ireland under Lincoln was easily quashed by Henry's superior numbers at Stoke, which can be regarded as the last battle in the Wars of the Roses. Lincoln himself was killed, and Lovell disappeared from view after the event. Simnel was, amazingly, pardoned by Henry, and given a job in the royal kitchens.

The second major rebellion of the reign was that named after Perkin Warbeck, a Flemish youth, the servant of a Breton clothes merchant. While showing off fine clothes in Cork, Ireland, in 1491 some obscure conspirators persuaded him to impersonate Richard of York, the younger of the two dead princes in the Tower. Warbeck thus became the stooge of the remnants of the Yorkist party in exile. He was also given foreign aid. At first Charles VIII of France supported him (until 1492); then he was taken to Burgundy where Margaret gave him help and hospitality. Henry VII replied to this Burgundian threat with a trade boycott against Flanders (1493–5), which paid off, and Warbeck moved on to Vienna where the Emperor Maximilian recognised him as 'Richard IV'; in return Maximilian was recognised as his heir should he succeed in his enterprise but die childless.

Back in England, Warbeck started gaining allies here too, notably – and surprisingly – Sir William Stanley, brother of the king's stepfather. Sir William, whose judgement had proved correct at Bosworth, dreadfully miscalculated now; he probably thought that Warbeck would succeed because of imperial support. Stanley's plotting was denounced by an informer; he was found guilty and executed in 1495, and his lands in north-east

Wales were confiscated by the Crown. Warbeck failed to land in England or get support in Ireland, so hoped for better luck in Scotland, where indeed James IV made him welcome and provided him with an aristocratic wife. An initial Scottish raid into the north of England was a failure, but a year later in 1497 Warbeck saw a golden opportunity to be exploited in the Cornish peasant rebellion, which was directed principally against new taxation measures. Warbeck landed in Cornwall and soon gained some 8000 recruits to his cause. But on the approach of the royal army under Lord Daubeney, Warbeck and some leading supporters lost their nerve and deserted their Cornish followers. Warbeck surrendered on the promise of a pardon, and confessed all. As a foreigner, Warbeck was not technically a traitor, and he was for a while kept at Court, but after an attempted escape he was imprisoned in the Tower. On the pretext of a conspiracy with the Earl of Warwick, who was still held there, they were both put to death in 1499: Warbeck was hanged as a commoner, while Warwick suffered a noble beheading. Warwick was probably sacrificed to appease the Spaniards, who in the negotiations over the marriage of Prince Arthur to Catherine of Aragon, made it clear that they wanted no possible rivals left alive.

Thus it was only by 1500, some 15 years after Bosworth, that Henry could feel that his throne was safe. In 1496 one Florentine observer had claimed that the king was not liked because of his avarice and that if a new claimant emerged everyone would abandon Henry. Then there was the reported conversation at Calais in either 1499 or 1503 on the subject of the succession: apparently the soldiers involved wanted the third Duke of Buckingham or Edmund de la Pole as king, should Henry die, as seemed possible because of the king's ill health. No one present mentioned the actual heir, Prince Arthur or Prince Henry! It is hard to gauge how typical these sentiments were, but it is indicative that some 15 years or more after Bosworth there was still no solid feeling that the Tudors had come to stay.

The kingship of Henry VII, 1485–1509

The traditional picture of Henry VII was that of 'a wonder for wise men', 'a wise and watchful king': he was 'the Solomon of

England'. These phrases come from Francis Bacon's *History of the Reign of King Henry VII* (1622) – although Catherine of Aragon had earlier referred to him as 'a second Solomon' – and this generally laudatory view[18] has been repeated down the ages. Henry has been seen as a modern king who solved the problems posed by the Wars of the Roses, and revamped English government. Again, according to the old view (mainly of the late nineteenth century), he aimed to eliminate the nobility and rule through the 'middle classes'. More recent evaluations, however, tend to reduce Henry's achievement, and emphasise his medieval characteristics rather than what was new.[19] And he is no longer viewed as being so hostile to the nobility despite his undoubted suspiciousness of them. Of course, in 1485 Henry Tudor was untutored in the art of governing a realm. He had visited London only once (if at all) and been in exile for 14 years; his inexperience and uncertainty are thus very evident in his early years on the throne.

According to Polydore Vergil, Henry was slender in build but strong, with above average height and white, thin hair; his teeth were poor and black. After 1500 we know that his sight was deteriorating. Visually, we have the terracotta bust of the king made in his later years (1508–9) by Pietro Torrigiano, which shows him in the way his propaganda machine wanted him to be regarded: the all-wise and just father of his people. An earlier painting by Michael Sittow from 1505, however, gives a more psychologically realistic depiction of a mean, penny-pinching, suspicious Henry, who seems to be nervously tapping his fingers. Henry is generally remembered only as a serious, sober king: a no-fun accountant. He certainly took his royal duties seriously, but he was still the centre of a world of courtly pleasures and entertainments. He was cheerful in conversation and liked games, including tennis, for which he set a fashion, and he enjoyed a bet. He was also very pious, attending two or three (very short) masses every day, and the Court was made to follow rigorously the Church's rules on fasting. Henry founded the famous chapel named after him at Westminster Abbey, and he completed the chapels at Windsor and King's College, Cambridge. He was in no way lecherous like his predecessor or successor, remaining a faithful husband to his queen.

Despite his many gifts and outstanding achievements Henry VII was never to become a greatly loved king. He was certainly not the populist like Edward IV. Although not personally charismatic, Henry realised the glamour of monarchy to be an essential ingredient in political stability, and so he never stinted on spectacle and pageantry; it was all there to emphasise the dignity of monarchy and of the divine permanence of the system, theoretically aping the magnificence and unchanging nature of heaven. Indeed the reign of Henry VII brought in a new period of political imagery as expressed in public ceremony and spectacle, in emulation of the court of Burgundy. The dignity of the monarchy was also to be reinforced by emphasis on the royal prerogative; Henry was more determined than Edward IV had been to increase, or at least clearly to restate, the theoretical powers of monarchy. To this end a new departure was signalled by the eight readings that were given at Lincoln's Inn in 1495 on the fourteenth-century compilation *Prerogativa Regis* (the King's Prerogatives). He was also the first to employ the arched imperial crown on coins.

Henry and the nobility

Henry VII has often been painted as a king who was anti-noble. This is patently not true. Henry was a nobleman himself, with the same class interests. Like Edward IV before him, but much more successfully – *pace* Carpenter – he wanted to tame them and make them serve the monarchy. Luckily, through accident of natural wastage and the inheritance laws, Henry had far fewer 'overmighty subjects' to deal with than had his Yorkist and Lancastrian predecessors. There was no duke of York, no duke of Lancaster or earl of March to contend with: Henry was all of these himself now. He had no brothers to rival him in the new royal family. His only blood uncle, Jasper Duke of Bedford, was extremely loyal. There was no Warwick, no Norfolk; the new Duke of Buckingham was only an infant. The only two other great nobles, Northumberland (who was killed in 1489 leaving a minor to succeed him) and Dorset, were carefully watched. Thus Henry found himself in a much more stable situation, and he was especially fortunate in his first decade when he had not yet fully secured his throne. Henry was to show himself extremely mindful of the need to control all members of the nobility, both inside and outside the royal family. Although his uncle Bedford and his stepfather Derby (Stanley) were well rewarded, the prizes were not as lavish as those bestowed by Edward IV on his two brothers. And he never allowed his younger son Henry Duke of York to rival his heir Prince Arthur by ensuring that the income from Prince Henry's estates remained within the king's control.

Henry VII was determined to tame the aristocracy, and he used the instrument of attainder as a well-thought-out threat to keep them in line. Whereas Edward IV's attainders had come in bunches in 1461 and 1471, and then decreased, Henry VII's attainders grew in volume as the reign progressed, with most attainders being passed in the Parliament of 1504; only the Parliament of 1497 saw no attainders at all. This trend was partly due to the fact that Henry suffered rebellions in bits and pieces at least down to 1497, whereas Edward IV had known peace after 1471. However, the increase as Henry's reign wore on was, above all, due to a different policy on the use of attainders: they were being employed not just to punish but also to control. Henry was prepared to reverse attainders, but only at a price and only by slow stages – to prove the good faith of the recipient. The Howards of Norfolk, for example, took 19 years to get their lands and their ducal title back after the death of John Howard at Bosworth. It was rare for a restored family to get all of its lands back, and one should bear in mind that the majority of Henry's attainders stood unreversed – 86 out of 139. He also used a number of threats and penalties to keep the nobles in line: fines for breaches of the law (or sales of pardons); bonds and recognisances; and the exploitation of royal feudal rights. As for bonds and recognisances (financial penalties for disloyalty), they were now employed systematically and ruthlessly after 1502, so that between 36 and 46 of the 62 noble families were financially yoked to Henry by such means.

Unlike Edward IV who more than replenished the losses sustained among the nobles during the Wars of the Roses, Henry VII reduced the peerage overall by some 25 per cent; and whereas there were 20 high noble families in 1489, there were only to be ten in 1509. There were merely nine new creations to the peerage, and really just three of these were entirely new, the rest comprising men with old claims to their titles now being summoned to the Lords. Nor did Henry give crown lands away to build up potential 'overmighty subjects'. It seems that few nobles, apart from Bedford and Oxford, could exercise much influence over him.

Henry VII abandoned Edward IV's policy of governing the country through potentially over-mighty subjects (either from the nobility or from the royal family). The only exception was the power which he conferred on his son Prince Arthur, who was sent to rule Wales and the Marches with the re-establishment of the council in the Marches at Ludlow. Henry VII's policy was also to gain possession of most of the major castles and fortresses of the realm, and to a large degree he succeeded. Such castles were turned into royal residences for royal progresses around the country. As the years passed by, the Tudor nobility, although still militarily important in their localities, would become increasingly a courtier nobility.

Law and order

Francis Bacon said of Henry VII that he was the best lawgiver since Edward I. Undoubtedly, Henry made a more impressive attack on lawlessness than had Edward IV, but modern historians are generally unprepared to endorse Bacon's fulsome praise: indeed Professor Chrimes sums up the modern attitude in his verdict that his enactments 'are hardly of sufficient novelty or substance to confer upon Henry VII any great reputation as a legislator'.[20] Certainly, Bacon's claim that Henry made England orderly and quiet almost overnight must be rejected. A large degree of lawlessness would always remain as just part of the system. Nevertheless, a certain degree of tightening up can be detected by the king in his tackling of the problem. Then later, in 1504, there was an act against livery and maintenance which on paper seemed a serious attempt to abolish the practice. Only domestic servants, lawyers and officials could be retained – but no armed followers, unless a placard (or licence) had been obtained. Very few prosecutions are known under this statute, and they were mainly directed against the gentry rather than at the nobility. The only case against a peer is the celebrated one of

1507 against George Neville, Lord Abergavenny, who was officially fined £70 000 in King's Bench for unlawful retaining. But with sureties from his friends and his own recognisance for £100 000 he actually paid the king only a much smaller sum of £500 a year, and was later licensed to keep retainers. Very probably, Abergavenny was made an example of because it seems that for a time Henry suspected him of conniving with the Cornish rebels back in 1497 and more recently of having dealings with Edmund de la Pole, Earl of Suffolk. Henry realised perfectly well that he needed the local nobles to retain their private armies to maintain the peace for him at home as well as to fight abroad when called upon. Law and order were significantly improved only in the area of trade and customs duties, where the royal purse was affected.

Henry VII's council

The king's council was, of course, the focus of decision-making, the nerve centre of policy; and like Edward IV's council, it was fluid and flexible. Members were appointed solely by the king and were directly answerable to him; like his predecessor he chose men of experience from whatever origins, and no matter what their past political loyalties had been – so long as they were faithful now. It seems that the core of Henry's council was formed in exile in 1484, and consisted of those most loyal to him; but as king he also welcomed former Yorkists of proven ability. There was a high degree of continuity with at least 10, if not 35, councillors of Edward IV finding seats on Henry's council; indeed 20 had served Richard III. As for the status of the 227 councillors known for Henry's reign, 43 were peers; and about two-thirds of the peerage attended at least one council meeting; 45 councillors were courtiers, 61 were churchmen, 27 lawyers and 49 bureaucrats and officials. Henry thus depended on no single group, but he was clearly not anti-magnate. Nevertheless, 'the numerical importance of both the peerage and the ecclesiastical group shows a decline as against the rise of the legal element'.[21] Henry also came increasingly to depend on a small number of household officers who dominated the council in the years after 1500: men like Sir Thomas Lovell, Sir Richard

Guildford, Sir Edward Poynings, Lord Daubeney and Sir Reginald Bray.

The council was there to give advice, to administer and to deal with judicial work. Henry VII normally attended the meetings unless only routine work was being despatched. A fuller council met during the 16 weeks of the legal terms in the Star Chamber. There could be present on such occasions between 40 and 60 councillors, but it was more usual to have an attendance of about 30. However, out of term time the king went on progress, and he took with him a smaller number of councillors – known as the council attendant, comprising about 16 men, of whom a smaller number of 4–11 members would sit around the table together.

A parallel body, with administrative, advisory and judicial duties, was the council in the Marches of Wales at Ludlow. Originally created by Edward IV for his son Prince Edward, it was revived in 1501 by Henry VII for Prince Arthur; but after the latter's death in went into abeyance until its revival in 1525. A less formalised council under wardens-general was used to police the north of England.

Henry VII's income

Like Edward IV, Henry VII was expected to 'live of his own'; that is, to survive on those incomes that were his by law on a permanent basis: crown lands, fiscal feudalism, the profits of the legal system and customs duties. All these – apart from customs dues which went to the Exchequer – were paid into the the royal chamber, so that chamber finance was the main distinguishing feature of Henry's reign, as it had been of Edward IV's. Fines for breaches of the law were more efficiently recovered, and Henry obtained in his first Parliament the life grant of the customs duties (tunnage and poundage) following the precedent of Richard III's Parliament of 1484. Customs duties once again brought in the largest single amount, but the crown lands and fiscal feudalism were enormously exploited by Henry VII.

Henry followed Edward IV in the revival of the crown lands as a major source of income. Because of his victory at Bosworth Henry found himself possessed of huge landed wealth. At first Henry's inexperience was manifest: in 1485 the new king was

receiving only £11 700 p.a. compared to the £25 000 p.a. collected by Richard III from the royal estates. But by 1502 he was
raking in some £40 000 p.a., an increase over Edward IV's
£22 000 p.a., owing to greater exploitation of the lands and to
better methods of estate management on Edward's model. Both
kings took an interest personally in the accounting of this revenue, which came in directly to the king's chamber of the household, bypassing the slower course of the Exchequer, which in any
case was not geared to the supervision of landed estates.

The major reason for the greater yield from the royal estates
under Henry VII was that he was much more efficient than
Edward IV had been in trying to recover all those royal rights
and payments which were due to the king as feudal overlord
from his tenants: that is, the emphasis on fiscal feudalism.
Although feudalism proper no longer existed, the legal forms
of feudalism remained. If the king could prove that land was held
from him by a chief or capital tenure then he could extract
important feudal payments from his tenant. The most lucrative
were relief, wardship and escheat; one of these was bound to
operate when a tenant-in-chief died. If such a landowner was
succeeded by an adult heir (aged over 21), then the new tenant
was bound to pay the king a *relief*. If that heir was a minor, then
he or she would become a ward of the king, which meant that
during the period of the minority the king could administer the
ward's lands to his own benefit and profit. The king could also
arrange for the marriage of his ward. It was common for the king
to sell these wardships to other members of the landowning class
who could exploit the lands; these purchasers of course had an
eye on the marriage of the heir, because the purchase of a wardship was an ideal way to augment landed estates, especially
through the marriage of an heiress to the guardian's son. The
traffic in wardships would remain a big money-spinner right
down to the 1640s. Henry VII first appointed a surveyor of the
king's wards in 1503 to bring more organisation to the business.
If a family died out, and there was no heir, then the lands
reverted or *escheated* back to the Crown.

Henry VII was determined to recover lost feudal income, and
his main instrument for this work was the investigation known as
the *inquisition post mortem*, which was a commission to investigate
the extent, value and tenure of these lands, and to determine

whether or not there was an heir. Under Henry VII almost any pretext was used to request such an investigation if there was the slightest hope that land had been held by knight service in chief. From 1491 onwards Henry also began a series of special commissions of investigation into concealed lands. A popular device that had been used by landowners to avoid paying the feudal dues had been the so-called *enfeoffment to uses*. This was an attempt to prevent lands descending from tenant to heir, thus bypassing all payments. The person who enjoyed the use of the land (the landowner in reality) was termed (in Norman French) the *cestui que use*; he had all the benefits of the lands, but the ownership in law was granted to a number of *feoffees to uses*, i.e. joint tenants, who as a legal entity or body would never die but carry on for ever, since although individual feoffees would die they would be replaced. This legal body never dying, feudal payments did not have to be made. It was a device that could be used to bequeath lands by will or for ignoring the rights of heiresses. Henry VII made an attempt to curb the practice, but he did not get very far. An Act of Parliament was passed in 1489 'against fraudulent feoffments to deprive the king of his wards', but it was limited to those who died intestate, and it seemed resigned to accepting the notion of bequest of land by will. Thus the problem was nowhere near to solution. Later, Henry VIII's government would try its hand at solving the problem by the Statute of Uses in 1536, which tried to turn the *cestui que use* into the legal owner; but the uproar from the landowning classes was so great that the government would have to climb down in the Statute of Wills in 1540, which allowed the landowners to bequeath two-thirds of their estates by will, thus avoiding feudal dues on most of their estates.

In his later years Henry VII undoubtedly gained a reputation for avarice. A Florentine visitor to England reported in 1496: 'The King is feared rather than loved, and this is due to his avarice.' Henry was very efficient by the standards of the day in building up his finances, but did he go beyond simple efficiency and become rapacious? Did he start treating the monarchy like a business? It was one thing to rescue the Crown from insolvency, but quite another for the king to lack generosity. Most historians have followed contemporary sources, such as the Great Chronicle and Polydore Vergil, in accepting Henry's descent into unkingly avarice in his later years. Despite some controversy over this, it now seems clear that the traditional verdict seems proved by the great outburst against the king's policies on his death, when the late king's two chief ministers, Sir Richard Empson and Edmund Dudley, were both executed by the young Henry VIII as a sop to popular feeling or vested interests. Dudley indeed left a confession regarding unjust exactions. Henry's fiscal demands seem to have alienated the nobility and gentry, and he can be accused of lacking that key ingredient of kingly success, namely 'good lordship'.

Henry VII's foreign policy

Henry's foreign policy, it is generally agreed, was largely geared to maintaining internal peace and thus aimed to avoid aggressive, ambitious and expensive projects. However, recently this consensus was queried by John Currin, whose study of the Treaty of Redon of 1489 with Brittany against France revealed Henry's desire to reclaim the old Plantagenet territories of Gascony and Normandy as well as the Crown of France itself.[22] Nevertheless, such claims must be seen as only a diplomatic smokescreen or else as early thoughts on securing the new dynasty at home by a patriotic war in the manner of Henry V: but they were certainly not followed up later. Henry VII's foreign-policy aims were to gain international recognition of his dynasty and to prevent foreign support for Yorkist pretenders, and also to contain the growth of France by preventing its absorption of the two independent duchies situated directly opposite England, namely Brittany and Burgundy.

The annexation of Brittany by France was accounted a hostile act, and Henry prepared for war: in 1489 he signed both the Treaty of Redon with the Bretons and the more celebrated Treaty of Medina del Campo of 1489 with Spain, by the terms of which Prince Arthur was betrothed to Catherine of Aragon, daughter of the Spanish rulers Ferdinand of Aragon and Isabella of Castile, while Spain agreed not to succour Yorkist pretenders and pledged to go to war with France over the future of Brittany. This Spanish treaty was a major feather in Henry's cap. Parliament did its part by paying £100 000 to the king to help him in his task of war with France. In 1492 Henry VII claimed the throne of France and mounted a large invasion with an army of some 12 000 men, besieging the town of Boulogne. However, Henry had no real aim of conquest, unlike his predecessor Edward IV in 1475, and he was there only reluctantly because of commitments to his allies and he had gambled in advance on being bought off by the French king. France kept Brittany but paid Henry in instalments the sum of £159 000 and agreed not to help a Yorkist pretender. Henry was well pleased with the cash, but there was much indignation back home at the terms of the Treaty of Étaples (1492), which could hardly be accounted a diplomatic victory. Thereafter Henry wished to stay on good terms with France, and refused later urgings to attack her.

Burgundy too had to be kept free from French ambitions, but Burgundy had shown itself a Yorkist stronghold. Despite Burgundy's economic importance to England, Henry was prepared to damage both the English and the Burgundian economy by forbidding exports there (especially raw wool). Burgundy was so badly affected by Henry's trade boycott that in 1496 the differences were patched up and trade resumed by an agreement wherein both sides vowed not to harbour the other's enemies. Thus both France and Burgundy had now agreed to remain on good terms with Tudor England. This left only Scotland as the focal point for opposition. However, a truce with Scotland in 1497 – the first such since 1328 – was followed by a full treaty later (1502), which was to include the marriage of Henry's daughter Margaret to King James IV. This laid the basis for a possible new beginning in Anglo-Scottish relations and was pregnant with a future dynasty to replace the Tudors in England almost exactly a century later.

Yet this fine diplomatic web of alliances, so carefully and painstakingly spun by Henry, was soon to be torn down because of the deaths of some of the leading participants. Prince Arthur's death in 1502 upset the alliance with Spain; it also meant that the continuance of the Tudor dynasty depended on the life of young Prince Henry. But Spain was eager to keep the English alliance alive, so Catherine was now intended for Prince Henry instead. The death of Elizabeth of York in 1503 led to the king having to contemplate his own remarriage to ensure another male heir.

Henry's alliance with Spain was ruined by the death of Isabella of Castile, which led to a serious split within the Spanish royal house. But he maintained his links to Burgundy, with a treaty in 1506 by which Edmund de la Pole would be handed over to Henry. This left only Richard de la Pole still at liberty in Europe to wave the White Rose banner. However, this major prop of Henry's diplomatic stage collapsed with the sudden death of Philip of Burgundy, and the Emperor Maximilian took over Burgundy on behalf of his infant grandson, the Archduke Charles. Although by this time Henry appeared very vulnerable on the international chessboard, with only one ally – the very unreliable Maximilian – the reality of the situation was not so dismal. In 1507 Henry's daughter Mary was betrothed to the Habsburg heir Archduke Charles of Burgundy, which was a great vote of confidence in the new English dynasty. Thus a great prospect seemed to be opening up for the Tudors.

Despite much ill health Henry VII's death came suddenly on 21 April 1509 at the age of 52, after nearly a quarter of a century on the throne. Of his eight children, only three survived him: his son Henry, and his daughters Margaret and Mary. Historians are still divided on his achievement: T. B. Pugh referred in 1992 to Henry's 'remarkably successful reign' and his 'masterful exercise of royal authority',[23] while Christine Carpenter in 1995 condemned Henry's rule as 'not a type of kingship appropriate to late-medieval England'[24] because of his alienation of the nobility. In general Henry has been more praised by Tudor specialists than by medievalists, but even the medievalist Pugh regards his financial achievement as commendable, and praises 'the wise and judicious precautions' taken over the succession.[25] Perhaps Henry was lucky to have survived without facing a baronial rebellion for his lack of 'good lordship'.[26] It was indeed a major achievement for Henry just to have remained in power and to have bequeathed a peaceful succession. He died a rich, but not popular, king. As far as we know, there were no factions in his Court: he ruled in isolation and sought solitude in the newly created privy chamber. He may have left £500 000 in plate and jewellery; certainly there were no financial problems in the first decade of his successor's reign. Indeed his sober and unspectacular rule supplied the essential basis for a century or so of Tudor rule. And although he in no sense planned it, or was even conscious of it, he helped in the foundation of a future Great Britain by introducing Welsh blood and loyalty into the dynasty and by marrying his daughter into the Scottish royal house of Stewart. No mean achievement.

THE TUDOR DYNASTY (1485–1603)

Tudur ap Goronwy (d. 1367)
|
Mareduld ap Tudur
|
Owain ap Mareduld m. Catherine of Valois (widow of **Henry V**)
(*Owen Tudor*) |

Edmund Tudor m. Margaret Beaufort (great-great-granddaughter of **Edward III**)
(*Earl of Richmond*) |

HENRY VII m. Elizabeth of York (daughter of **Edward IV**)
(1485–1509) |

Henry VIII m. 1) Catherine of Aragon 1509
(1509–47)

m. 2) Anne Boleyn 1533

m. 3) Jane Seymour 1536

m. 4) Anne of Cleves 1540 (*no issue*)
m. 5) Catherine Howard 1540 (*no issue*)
m. 6) Catherine Parr 1543 (*no issue*)

MARY I m. *Philip of Spain*
(1553–58)   (*no issue*)

ELIZABETH I
(1558–1603)

EDWARD VI
(1547–53)

3 The Reign of Henry VIII, 1509–47

Henry VIII was not quite 18 years of age when he became king in April 1509 – the first peaceful accession of a monarch since 1422. The contrast between father and son has been noted by most historians: the serious, hard-working Henry VII was succeeded by a young man who seemingly sought only pleasure and military glory. Young Henry had not been educated in the arts of government as his elder brother Arthur had been. The death of the elder prince had made Henry VII overprotective of his only remaining son, who was kept isolated for fear of getting a fatal disease. Henry VIII had grown into a handsome prince over six feet tall, excelling at sport and also with intellectual tastes. He was a skilled linguist, with a fluency in French, Spanish, Italian and Latin, and a competent musician (the song 'Pastime with good company' was certainly written by him) as well as a fine dancer; he was thus a good example of the 'universal man' beloved in the Renaissance.

We may well believe that we can draw much closer to the political world of Henry VIII than to the more obscure world of the fifteenth century on account of the novel prevalence of realistic paintings and drawings of those who thronged the Court. A whole gallery of true-to-life pictures of courtiers great and small, particularly those painted in the 1530s by the visiting artist Hans Holbein, passes before our eyes. But are we being misled by the realism of the artwork? Historians today are completely divided on the way politics worked in this reign and on the personality of the king himself. Henry VIII's large frame and terrifying gaze in the portraits suggest that he was completely in charge of policy and dominant at Court. But was he dominant, or instead largely passive? Was he the master puppeteer fully in command, or merely the puppet of factions who really controlled the direction of policy? There is simply no agreement on this among modern historians.

The reign of Henry VIII seems to fall into three distinct periods: the first from 1509 to 1529 is characterised by an initial reaction against the policies of Henry VII ('the aristocratic reaction'), preparation for war with France, and the rise and consequent dominance of Thomas Cardinal Wolsey. The second period, 1530–40, was a decade of enormous change and reform, encompassing the Anglican Reformation and engineered by that skilled bureaucrat, Thomas Cromwell. The last period from Cromwell's execution in July 1540 to the king's own death in January 1547 was notable for the absence of a clear first minister and for a return to war and consequent economic hardship: a dismal period of decline that has been condemned as 'puerile and fatuous compared to the giant strides and historic achievements of the middle years of his reign'.[1] The reign of Henry VIII ended as it had begun – in warfare against the medieval enemy, France.

The 'aristocratic reaction' and the rise of Thomas Wolsey

The start of the new reign witnessed what is termed 'an aristocratic reaction' to the policies of Henry VII. The new king turned his back on his father's regime and the latter's attempt to browbeat the nobility into subjection. One of Henry VIII's first acts was to allow the execution of Empson and Dudley as a sop to the nobles. Henry VIII was clearly making a bid for popularity as well as, be it noted, demonstrating a very cruel, ruthless streak right at the start despite his youth. Whether these executions show him determined to be master in his own house or weakly giving in to the baying of the noble hounds is impossible to say. What we can see is the nobility once again prominent in the royal council, and surrounding the king at Court, where his daily companions were the younger brothers, sons and sons-in-law of peers. It may well be that Henry was consciously striving for noble support for the first great ambition of his reign – war with France. Such a war may well have been part of the reasoning behind his decision to marry Catherine of Aragon, namely to get Spanish support. Henry VIII modelled himself on that great winner of battles, Henry V, who had ascended the throne almost 100 years previously, and who had made the Lancastrian regime strong by foreign conquests after the unpopular usurper Henry IV. Attacking the unpopular policies of Henry VII and embarking on a successful policy of war would solidify the hold of the Tudor dynasty on England.

There has been a general tendency to regard Henry VIII as a playboy king for most of the first 20-year period, finding the daily attention to business too irksome, especially 'because writing to me is somewhat tedious' as Henry confessed in a famous letter of *c*. 1518; he looked to others to do the dreary work for him. This view of the king allows for the rise to power of Thomas Wolsey, an extremely hard-working cleric who promised to release Henry from the daily grind which his father had undertaken; it also allows for the general belief that Wolsey was the real maker of policy between 1515 and 1529, with the king taking a keen interest only in warfare. The picture thus emerges of an arrogant, pompous and ostentatious Wolsey who forgot he was merely a royal servant and regarded himself as an 'alter rex' (a second king), outshining the real one. Much of this was dependent on the hostile comments of the poet John Skelton, who berated the cardinal for his desire 'To rule king and Kaiser'.

> Why come ye not to court?
> To which court?
> To the King's Court? –
> Nay, to Hampton Court:
> The King's Court
> Should have the excellence;
> But Hampton Court
> Hath the preeminence

However, it now seems evident that Skelton's picture is a distorted one, and should be jettisoned as a guide to Wolsey's role at the time. Most historians have regarded the king as virtually absent from policy-making in this first period. But this conventional interpretation is now seriously under challenge. Peter Gwyn has portrayed Henry as being in command from the start, indeed using Wolsey as an instrument of the royal will, while Sybil Jack has drawn attention to Henry's personal supervision of his finances.[2] Inherent in Gwyn's revisionism is his scepticism of the role of faction in the politics of the period and thus of much recent writing on the reign of Henry VIII which tries to make sense of Henrician politics by applying the 'faction model'.

According to many writers old and new, factional politics returned in the early years of Henry VIII. A clerical faction led by Archbishop Warham and Bishop Foxe has been discerned, and an opposing aristocratic one led by Thomas Howard, Earl of Surrey. The clerics seemingly supported peace while the nobles were itching for war. According to the factional interpretation, Wolsey's entry into politics was as a member of this 'peace' party through the patronage of Foxe; later, however, Wolsey because of ambition would abandon the 'peace' party to support the war-mongers. The notion of Wolsey's sinister entry into politics certainly goes back to the early sixteenth century itself. The cardinal had many enemies, who immortalised their grievances against him in their writings. Polydore Vergil is one source for the view that Henry was bewitched by Wolsey, who came to power through Foxe's patronage only to abandon him later. But a rereading of the evidence suggests that there may have been no war or peace parties as such.[3] The argument too that Wolsey treacherously forced Foxe out of politics has also been challenged by Gwyn, who presents evidence to show a harmonious working relationship as well as Foxe's clear wish to retire from the hurly-burly of court life, for both spiritual and health reasons. Gwyn thus wishes to remove the spectre of faction from the workings of the early Henrician Court. From the beginning Henry was completely in charge.

In the period of the 'aristocratic reaction' it comes initially as a surprise that the politician who emerged as the king's leading man came from very humble origins, the son of a butcher and cattle-dealer from Suffolk. Yet from such inauspicious beginnings Wolsey made a career in the Church that would eventually take him to the top in both Church and state. He made his way through the patronage of clergy who valued his intellectual gifts. He held many livings in the Church, often at the same time, and although such pluralism was common in the contemporary European Church it was extremely unusual for England; indeed the large scale of his pluralism makes Wolsey unique in English history. In 1515 he became lord chancellor (the last such to rule England) and Henry obtained a cardinal's hat for him from Rome. In 1518 Wolsey became papal legate *a latere*, confirmed as a life grant in 1524, which made him superior to the Archbishop of Canterbury and thus primate of England. Henry had initially chosen Wolsey because of his administrative gifts displayed in the equipping of the invasion force for France in 1513, but he may well have continued reposing his trust in him as a counterweight to the re-emergent nobles. If Gwyn is correct about Henry's overall control from the start then it made good sense to entrust power to an outsider who would be completely dependent on the king. The same letter wherein Henry confessed his dislike of writing also instructed Wolsey: 'I would you should make good watch on the Duke of Suffolk, on the Duke of Buckingham, on my lord of Northumberland, on my lord of Derby, on my lord of Wiltshire and on others which you think suspect to see what they do with this news.' Like his father, the new king remained very suspicious of his nobles even though his monarchy needed them to maintain order. The Duke of Buckingham would be executed in 1521 on hearsay evidence rather than an overt deed; Henry was worried that the duke would repeat the actions of his father.

The Court and government under Wolsey

In many ways the rule of Wolsey can be seen as perpetuating the traditions established by Henry VII of centralising the state with the royal Court as its firm focus. There can be no doubt either that factions were banished from Court in Wolsey's period of power. David Starkey has argued for the emergence of anti-Wolsey elements in the king's privy chamber, that most private suite of rooms where the king ate, slept, dressed and relieved himself. This last activity was not entirely private but watched over by the head of the privy chamber, the groom of the stool. Unlike the aloof Henry VII, the new boisterous fun-loving king used his privy chamber increasingly to surround himself (especially after 1515) with athletic young friends, his boon companions or 'minions', of higher social status than his father's colourless body servants. Thus during the first decade the character of the privy chamber changed, and historians such as Starkey and Ives have argued that it became the cockpit of faction politics because these well-born young men who attended to all the king's most private needs could influence him with requests or suggestions, being close to the king's ear (or any other part of him for that matter!). Henry VIII's first groom of the stool was his boyhood friend William Compton, who soon became a favourite, something not seen under the old king. According to one report, the best time to approach Henry if one wanted one's request granted was 'when he [the king] had gone largely to the stool, for then he used to be very pleasant'. No wonder that by 1511 it was thought that Compton was the man to lobby if one looked for royal favour.

According to Starkey, the politicisation of the privy chamber really began when, in imitation of the French model, the members of the privy chamber were elevated to the status of gentlemen of the privy chamber in September 1518, and then their influence became so great and such a threat to the cardinal that he had to undertake a purge of the privy chamber in May 1519. The Venetian ambassador reported home that the 'minions' had become 'so intimate with the King that in the course of time they might have ousted him [Wolsey] from the government'. Instead, Wolsey now replaced possible rivals by his own 'creatures'.[4] However, recent studies of this event by Greg Walker and Peter Gwyn have scotched this interpretation of bitter rivalry and purging.[5] Wolsey himself seems not to have been involved in the change of personnel: he was absent at the critical time with dysentery, and those excluded were in no way punished or demoted. The real reason for the expulsion of the minions was the feeling of the more conservative councillors that the young men of the privy chamber had imbibed too many 'French vices and brags' from their visit to France, and were too familiar with the king.

Possessed of so much power, how did Wolsey exercise it? On balance historical opinion has not been very flattering to Wolsey. Liberal Protestant historians have seen embodied in him all the vices of the later medieval Roman Church, while modern Catholics have blamed him for letting the side down and giving substance to the complaints of the reformers, especially with his two bastard children by one Mistress Lark. Among modern commentators, G. R. Elton tried to belittle his achievement, mainly to contrast him with his hero the very professional Thomas Cromwell. Elton claims that Wolsey was only a gifted amateur who 'lacked intellectual foundations, larger beliefs and bureaucratic expertise . . . an uncomplicated activist untroubled by speculative thought or spiritual reservations'.[6] Nevertheless the modern Catholic historian J. J. Scarisbrick has taken a more appreciative view of Wolsey, discerning 'something lofty and great about him'.[7] And whatever he might have lacked by training he certainly made up for by sheer hard work. He was a great enthusiast who learnt the skills on the job; and he was not an amateur in the sense of being inefficient, although admittedly he never finished many of the tasks which he so zestfully embarked upon.

Wolsey's work as a judge was probably his greatest achievement, being the founder of that great Tudor law court, the court of Star Chamber.[8] On 5 May 1516 at a council meeting Wolsey talked about the degree of lawlessness and disorder prevailing in the realm and that he would teach offenders 'the law of Star Chamber'. By this he meant the full judicial force of the king's council sitting in the Star Chamber as a regular court of law. The royal council, of course, had always exercised judicial functions, having been petitioned for redress of grievances, but its judicial work had always been mixed up with its other administrative and executive functions in a haphazard way, judicial matters normally being relegated to last item of business. This was hardly ideal for suitors to the court. Wolsey's innovation was that by October 1518 he had set aside two whole days in the week just for legal business: Wednesdays and Fridays – a routine which remained in force right down to 1641. The court consisted of the councillors together with the justices of King's Bench and Common Pleas. This settled court became very popular in the Tudor period, with 120 cases a year on average, compared to only 12.5 in the undifferentiated system under Henry VII. If the name 'Star Chamber' today conjures up something sinister in the mind, the fault was mainly due to its employment by Charles I a century later against opponents of his regime. Under the Tudors it was a popular court responding to the huge demand for litigation in a society that was increasingly resorting to the law to settle its disputes. People were turning to conciliar justice mainly because of the problems of the common-law courts of the time, the inflexibility of the common law and the many technicalities that could be placed in the way of a speedy resolution of issues. Another problem with the common-law courts was the presence of a jury which was still open to partisanship or intimidation.

There was no jury in the Star Chamber, only the councillors and their assistant judges using their common sense. What the court of the Star Chamber brought to criminal actions was the principle of equity (or fairness), and followed the procedure of the written 'English bill' in gathering evidence. Officially, matters for the Star Chamber had to have involved the use of force, such as in riots or trespass, even if the issue really concerned landownership, and its punishments consisted of fines and imprisonment. Disputes where force was not cited had to go to the lord chancellor's court of Chancery, where business remained at the same rate as previously. Later, in 1525 Wolsey would establish parallel bodies to the Star Chamber with the re-creation in 1525 of the council in the Marches of Wales with Princess Mary at Ludlow and the council of the north with the king's illegitimate son Henry Fitzroy, Duke of Richmond at York, exercising both conciliar and common-law jurisdictions. Besides the administrative needs involved in these two bodies, there were also dynastic considerations in giving the king's only surviving children government experience at a time when it seemed that he would have no more heirs. Wolsey was also innovative in sowing the seeds for the creation of the later court of Requests, a kind of Star Chamber for poorer petitioners. This innovation grew out of the judicial functions of the council attendant, that is those councillors who were always with the king on his travels around the realm as distinct from those with Wolsey in the Star Chamber. In 1519 Wolsey appointed a number of former attendant councillors who were specialists in justice to a new committee to meet at Westminster during the legal terms, and these men only rarely rejoined the council attendant out of term time, so that in effect they left the king's council.

Wolsey thus had a real interest in making justice more widely and readily available, and in the history of the development of the English state this deserves recognition. He was also concerned to discipline sheriffs and make them less corrupt. His genuine sympathy for the poor can be seen in his attempt to curb enclosures for sheep farming. Like most Tudor contemporaries his diagnosis of social ills was false; sheep farming was not the major reason for the perceived economic ills of the time. There were few such enclosures after 1500, and they were not the cause of economic woes. However, contemporaries were convinced of the evils of sheep farming in causing depopulation and unemployment, and Wolsey was eager to respond to their call for reform. Wolsey's zeal can be seen in his establishing a major inquiry into the extent of the problem, which yielded the first real information on the subject.[9] J. J. Scarisbrick emphasises Wolsey's concern with social stability as his main motivation, but possibly he also thought in terms of hurting his rich opponents.

Unlike his protégé Thomas Cromwell, Wolsey was certainly not a great parliamentary manager and he had little legislation to put before Parliament. In 1523 he tried to browbeat Parliament to increase the rate of tax to pay for his foreign policy, and breached the convention of the Commons by appearing there in person. More positively, he can be credited with the origins of the Tudor subsidy, the graduated income tax that became the basis of Tudor taxation.

Wolsey and the Church

Wolsey was more of a priest than has often been supposed; he did not have the mind of a layman. Although he had no genuine religious vocation he was not simply masquerading as a priest. He became a churchman with a conventional piety, who said mass and the divine office daily. Traditionally he has been seen as a worldly and ambitious ecclesiastic who took advantage of the king's laziness to take control of the government of the realm. In this old view his arrogation of power merely underlined the dangerous independent power of the Church and its allegiance to a foreign ruler. His legateship was regarded as manifesting the unpleasant realities of papal power. However, this view ignores the extent to which the English Church was already subject to the state, with its bishops as long-time royal servants. Indeed the notion that Henry unwittingly allowed Wolsey to use papal power in the Church to take over secular government indicts the king of gross negligence and dereliction of duty. Nevertheless the argument has persisted that Wolsey based his power on the Church and that his great ambition was to become pope. Today such a view is difficult to justify. Wolsey certainly had no wish to be pope, except at the very end in 1529 when he needed the office to gain the king's marital objectives. Wolsey realised only too well that his power base was in England, not in Rome. Indeed Peter Gwyn sees Wolsey as a loyal royal servant, not as any kind of 'second king'.

In Gwyn's view, Henry wanted to control the Church from the very start; and Henry's procurement of Wolsey's papal legate-ship, unifying the English Church under him, was a step towards this. How far this was a clear policy on the part of the king or simply some kind of instinct, and how far Wolsey was consciously playing along must remain points of contention. Wolsey appears to have had a divided loyalty, rather than being a slavish hench-man of the king. Most medieval churchmen had such divided loyalties. Wolsey's colleagues, it must be remembered, although royal servants, did not acquiesce easily in the surrender of eccle-siastical jurisdiction in the 1530s. That Wolsey certainly de-veloped a care for the Church is revealed in the small but very significant episode known as the 'Matter of Wilton' in 1528. On this occasion a new abbess was required for a Benedictine nun-nery in Wiltshire, and the election was entrusted to Wolsey. At first the king supported Anne Boleyn's nominee (the sister of her brother-in-law), but it was soon revealed that this lady was of lax morals, being guilty of fornication with two priests and a layman. On being told of this Henry refused his support, but instead of then supporting Wolsey's excellent candidate he suggested a third. The king was adamant for his new nominee, but Wolsey simply ignored three royal letters and succeeded in getting his own candidate elected. What does this small incident, as late as 1528, reveal? It certainly shows Wolsey being eager for the health and welfare of the Church, even being prepared to ignore his master the king. Whether it shows Wolsey as an arrogant 'alter rex' forgetting his place is also quite possible. The exact nature of the relationship between the king and the cardinal is still hard to pin down.

How significant was Wolsey's rule of the Church to the coming Reformation? Did his 'failure' to undertake reform make it inevitable? Wolsey was no great reformer, that is clear enough. His attempted reforms, in the legatine consitutions of 1518, apparently added up to little more than restating earlier rules for clerical conduct. But at least he did see the need for some reform, however modest. It has been claimed that his sweeping legatine powers added up to an 'ecclesiastical despotism'. This seems an exaggeration. Certainly he used his powers to invade the jurisdiction of his episcopal colleagues, and they must have baulked at paying him for exercising their jurisdiction which had previously been free for them: now they had to pay on average a quarter of their income from fees (but not from their lands) to the papal legate. Wolsey made Warham agree to share the work and fines emanating from wills which covered more than one diocese in a new legatine court. It used to be thought that Wolsey was hated for this by his colleagues, but apart from inevitable grumbling they seem on the whole to have put up with the new system. Nor should one think in terms of a personal 'despotism' being exercised by Wolsey. He is known to have influenced the choice of only two or three bishops (out of seven) elected during his years in power. The claim that he interfered in monastic elections is answered by the fact that the great majority (18 out of 20) were entrusted to him by the monasteries involved. What Wolsey's legatine power did achieve was to allow a personal unity to the English Church: either Henry had intended this all along, or he had simply learned from Wolsey's experiment. Whichever way, the most important aspect of Wolsey's rule over the English Church was governmental unity: only in this sense, although Wolsey himself had no inkling of it, did he foretell the future religious history of England with its national Church.

Wolsey and foreign policy

Henry VIII saw himself as the embodiment of England's honour as expressed in military glory. The king's honour and reputation meant his standing in the international club of rulers. He desired to re-enact the great victories of his predecessor Henry V in his campaign for the throne of France; and this reign sees the last military attempts to that end. Almost as soon as he became king Henry initiated activities directed towards war with France: Calais was strengthened, the navy was built up, and negotiations were opened with foreign allies. Foreign policy was seen by both king and cardinal as by far the most important category of business. The foreign policy pursued in the years of Wolsey's presence at Court is complex, full of reversals of policy, yet it is central to understanding the early Henrician regime, as well as being the last example of a truly medieval-type foreign policy with the invasion of France as a main objective.

One can distinguish four main periods in terms of foreign policy between 1509 and 1529. In the first (1509–14) Henry embarked on a war with France as a member of an alliance forged in 1511 called the 'Holy League', because it included the pope, and also Venice, Spain and the Holy Roman Empire. Henry VIII himself led an army of invasion into France and captured Thérouanne and Tournai, while Surrey defeated the Scots at Flodden. However, with these successes behind him Henry agreed to a diplomatic revolution, making peace with the French in 1514. By this peace treaty England would keep Tournai, and Henry's sister Princess Mary would marry the aged Louis XII of France. There was a measure of glory for England in this, but it fell far short of the English claim to France.

The second period (1515–18) is characterised by the coming to power in France of a young, brash monarch in the form of Francis I, who was dissatisfied with the arrangements of his predecessor and who wanted a great victory in northern Italy: his gaining this victory at the battle of Marignano in 1515 made France supreme in northern Italy. This dashing success by the new French king meant, as far as England was concerned, that the glory of 1514 had evaporated and that the international situation was wide open again. Eventually both France and England saw the sense of making peace, and what had begun as a Franco-English treaty blossomed into the first major non-aggression pact in European history, the Treaty of London (1518), whereby more than 20 states agreed to come to the aid of a victim of aggression.

The Treaty of London, which was a diplomatic coup in itself getting as it did so many diplomats on English soil, inaugurated phase three (1518–25). The treaty stole, and enlarged on, an original idea of the pope for a general European peace. England in 1518–20 was seemingly acting as an honest broker in the maintenance of peace;[10] but this peace was not destined to last. France attacked the Imperialists in Navarre, and England joined with the Emperor Charles V against what seemed to be French aggression in violation of the Treaty of London. Once again England appeared set on invading France, and the 'Great Enterprise' was planned in 1523; however, what eventuated was little more than an abortive march on Paris by the Duke of Suffolk. Yet, despite prospects of Imperial success, negotiations were opened up in 1524 between England and France. Imperial success came in a devastating way with the defeat, and indeed capture, of Francis I at Pavia, in northern Italy, in February 1525. This victory should have pleased England as the emperor's ally, yet in August 1525 France and England signed the Treaty of the More, followed in 1526 by England's membership of the League of Cognac with France and the papacy, directed towards pushing the dominant Imperialists out of northern Italy (phase four, 1526–9). This seemed an impossible task, however; and the pope himself became a prisoner of the emperor when Charles's ally the Duke of Bourbon sacked Rome in 1527. The diplomatic arrangements of the League of Cognac were upset, and the period ended with a desperate attempt to have the imprisoned pontiff agree to Wolsey himself establishing a deputy papacy in exile at Avignon. The situation was also enormously complicated by Henry's desire to divorce Queen Catherine in order to marry his new love, Anne Boleyn. The pope, as the prisoner of Catherine's nephew the emperor, was hardly in a position to acquiesce to the king's demands. Eventually, France and the Empire made their own peace in 1529 with the Treaty of Cambrai, which left England isolated and which was certainly a factor in Wolsey's downfall.

Historians have widely diverged in their interpretations of this diplomacy. Was the foreign policy really Henry's or Wolsey's, and what, if any, were the major principles behind it? In the eighteenth and nineteenth centuries, when the idea was a current preoccupation, Wolsey's foreign policy was interpreted as an attempt to maintain the balance of power in Europe. However, the twentieth-century debate began with A. F. Pollard's *Wolsey* (1929), which argued that 'he consistently followed a papal policy and was led by personal interests in the same direction'.[11] That is to say, Wolsey slavishly followed papal foreign policy mainly because he himself wanted to be pope. Thus with Pollard we have the spectre of England always dancing to the pope's tune, with the king amazingly allowing it to happen.

The Pollardian view was largely demolished in the 1960s by D. S. Chambers who disproved the notion that Wolsey eagerly wished to be pope.[12] It was indeed the king who pushed Wolsey forward in 1521 and 1523, thinking how marvellous it would be for his lord chancellor to be pope. Only on one occasion, at the very end – in 1529 – when it (wrongly) appeared that Clement VII was about to die did Wolsey himself covet the papal throne, because its possession would have given him the power necessary to solve his major problem by this date, the granting of the royal divorce.

J. J. Scarisbrick in 1968 presented a portrait of Wolsey as a notable Renaissance 'peacemaker', but his pacific intentions were spoiled by the belligerent pose of the king. Above all, Henry was truly desirous of conquering France, a policy which was generally popular in England. Scarisbrick emphasised the Treaty of London in his view of Wolsey's sincere peacemaking intentions, and pointed to Wolsey's reopening of negotiations with the French before Pavia.[13] Such a noble view of Wolsey was undermined by the researches of Peter Gwyn, who initially demonstrated that in the diplomacy of 1521 Wolsey was merely posing as a peace-maker, only pretending to reconcile Francis I and Charles V, while secretly plotting France's destruction in concert with the emperor.[14]

Gwyn maintains that Wolsey's prime aim was to give England a leading role in Europe, which was not really deserved, judged by her size or resources, and to that end Wolsey used both war and peace as the occasion demanded. The diplomatic revolution of 1514 was concluded because the *entente* with Louis XII actually enabled England, allied to France, to dominate Europe. Despite being only a second-rate power, England was given a leading role in international affairs until 1527, thanks to Wolsey. Another important argument of Gwyn's is that after 1515 the idea of invading France was less important than in traditional accounts which make it one of Henry's obsessions. Threatening invasion was merely to increase England's bargaining power at the nego-tiating table, and despite all the big talk there were no military preparations commensurate with a genuine planned invasion. Even the 'Great Enterprise' of 1523 was more bluster than reality. If the two great powers of France and the Empire were destined to be at war then England could not just opt out of military activity: Henry's honour would not permit that.

Both Peter Gwyn and George Bernard agree that Henry and Wolsey were in harmony over the main thrust of foreign policy;

both agree that maintenance of the king's 'honour' might demand either a warlike or a peacemaking stance; foreign policy was thus opportunistic. Bernard believes that the negotiations carried on with the French during 1524 were merely an insurance policy, and that Henry and Wolsey genuinely wanted an Imperial victory and an English invasion of France.[15] In Gwyn's interpretation, however, Pavia was seen as a heavy blow to England's position as a decision-maker in Europe; with France completely humiliated and with the emperor all-powerful there really was no way that Henry could play the role of arbiter of Europe that Wolsey had designed for him. Wolsey's aim was, after all, not so much victory for either side, but maintaining a role for England, and for Henry, in a European settlement. Wolsey's calculations were that, no matter who should win in Italy, England's help would be needed by both sides, victor and vanquished. However, the sheer magnitude of the emperor's victory upset all such calculations: France seemed all but destroyed, and the emperor was beholden to nobody.[16] Hence the diplomatic revolution of 1525 designed to prop up France in order to ensure a European role for Henry.

The fall of Wolsey

Wolsey fell from grace at the end of 1529, an event which has provoked much debate in recent years. Was Henry simply tired of Wolsey, or was he tricked by factional intrigue into dismissing the cardinal? There has been a general consensus that Wolsey was brought down by 'an aristocratic *putsch*'.[17] Starkey and Ives have both argued in favour of Anne Boleyn's enmity towards Wolsey and the force of faction politics in explaining his disgrace. In this version of the story the gullible Henry was being led by those around him, especially Norfolk, Suffolk and the Boleyns. There is certainly some contemporary evidence for the factional interpretation of Wolsey's end, notably from ambassadorial reports as well as from his first biographer George Cavendish, who in particular blames Anne for his master's disgrace. Cavendish reports that Anne had hated Wolsey ever since his role in breaking up her earlier liaison with Lord Henry Percy. David Starkey has emphasised the rising political influence of Anne

Boleyn and her ambitions to be queen, obtaining the re-entry of expelled members of the privy chamber and the introduction of new ones to form her own faction there:[18] notably her brother George Lord Rochford, cousin Francis Bryan, together with Francis Weston and William Brereton. Wolsey's grip is seen to be slackening, to the extent that even a conservative supporter of Catherine of Aragon returned in the form of Sir Nicholas Carew. The privy chamber was now supposedly tense with intrigue and divided into Boleyns, Wolseyans and Aragonese. The inability of Wolsey to gain the king his divorce and his failure in international affairs would lead to the ascendancy of Anne Boleyn, who plotted the elimination of the cardinal. Eric Ives has argued that Anne was a Lutheran, an ideological position that made her a natural enemy of Wolsey. By January 1529 she had finally turned against him because he seemed to be dragging his feet on the divorce issue, hoping that the king would tire of her. According to Ives, Wolsey was lukewarm over the divorce because he apparently feared that he would lose his power to the Boleyns. During 1529 the Norfolk–Boleyn faction organised themselves to topple Wolsey, and on 1 July 1529 a detailed plan was formed. Nevertheless, in this interpretation, the king still retained confidence in Wolsey, and the only success of the conspirators consisted in persuading the king, who was open to manipulation now because of foreign-policy differences with Wolsey, to call Parliament.

Even after Wolsey's disgrace the king apparently remained friendly towards him. Cavendish relates that Henry Norris was sent to Wolsey at Putney to comfort him by displaying the king's ring and to tell him that Henry had consented to the cardinal's disgrace 'only to satisfy more the minds of some which he knoweth be not your friends'. Ives regards this as a genuine attempt at consolation. In Parliament a book of articles of accusation against Wolsey was read out, and these charges then tipped the balance of Henry's mind against him; and Ives believes that the articles of complaint derived from the articles of conspiracy of 1 July. But Parliament was not in the event to be used to disgrace Wolsey; that was to be achieved by the old statute of *praemunire* in King's Bench. Ives cites the Milanese ambassador as reporting that Henry was soon regretting Wolsey's loss.[19]

This factional view of Wolsey's fall is plausible but not secure, and has been challenged by Peter Gwyn and George Bernard.[20]

Gwyn paints a portrait of a king disillusioned by Wolsey from early 1529 because of his failure in the divorce, all confidence having evaporated by the end of May, when Suffolk was sent with a 'secret charge' unknown to Wolsey to the French Court. It was therefore the king alone who decided to humble his great cardinal. Gwyn sets little store by the contemporary hearsay reports of intrigue, and finds little concrete evidence of enmity between Wolsey and the alleged faction leaders; even Anne Boleyn had every reason to hope for success from Wolsey in his prosecution of the divorce. The winding up of the legatine commission on 23 July meant that Wolsey was no longer essential and could now be abandoned. Stephen Gardiner became royal secretary on 28 July, taking over most of Wolsey's duties. Wolsey was not immediately dismissed because his services might still be needed regarding the advocation of the divorce question to Rome, but during August and September Wolsey was purposely kept away from the royal presence. Wolsey still maintained hope and was indeed kept on a string by Henry, but only with formal consultations on technical matters. Thus Wolsey's downfall in October came as a complete surprise, the unscrupulous king alone determining his servant's disgrace.

Henry allowed Wolsey to live in honourable retirement in his diocese of York. However, Wolsey never entered his cathedral at York for his official enthronement, set down for 7 November 1530, because he was arrested on 4 November on charges of treason. On his way south for trial Wolsey died at Leicester Abbey on 29 November. Whether or not Henry was seriously contemplating the cardinal's execution is unknown. The episode remains murky, even if some recently discovered evidence sheds extra light on the charges, which were that Wolsey had plotted his own return to power by plotting with the pope, the emperor and the French for them to assist Queen Catherine's cause by waging a ruinous war on England, which would then need Wolsey's services to be delivered from such a catastrophe. This plot, revealed in a letter from the king, seems too far-fetched for belief. Wolsey was certainly corresponding with the French and Imperial ambassadors, and it is therefore possible that Wolsey was regarded by the government as a loose cannon up in the unreliable north. It is also possible that factional enemies invented the story to manipulate gullible Henry. However, against the faction theory and a malleable king, Peter Gwyn has argued most forcibly for the treason charges against Wolsey to be interpreted as part of Henry's machiavellian scheming, the king using the final degradation of Wolsey as part of the pressure being applied to the pope to grant the divorce.[21]

The fall of Wolsey left government in the hands of Norfolk, Suffolk, Wiltshire (Anne's father), Sussex, Stephen Gardiner and others. The traditional leading minister, the lord chancellor Sir Thomas More, was not a member of the political inner ring because of his opposition to the divorce. Thus one has the reversal of the situation under Wolsey, where the council in Star Chamber around the cardinal had been large and all-important, leaving the council attendant on the king very small: now the politically important 'secret' or 'privy' councillors attended on the king, while only the less significant attended More in the Star Chamber and dealt with mainly legal business.

Whether or not Wolsey fell because of factional intrigue, there can be no doubt of the existence of factions in the 1530s simply because of the new element of religious ideology that now intruded into courtly politics. A radical group emerged that wanted evangelical reform as well as the marriage of the king to Anne Boleyn: this Boleyn faction included Anne's brother Rochford, Thomas Cranmer, Edward Foxe and later Thomas Cromwell. The conservative religious position and support for Queen Catherine were upheld by a group which historians today dub the 'Aragonese', and which included More, the Earl of Shrewsbury, Bishop Fisher, Cuthbert Tunstall, John Clerk and Father Peto. This conservative Aragonese party conspired with conservatives in the Commons to block radical government policies. Out of the struggle to gain the divorce the radicals emerged supreme, and continued to dominate the Court until the downfall of Anne Boleyn in 1536. By that date England had thrown off its subjection to the papal supremacy and established the Church of England as an autonomous Church in Christendom. These religious developments will be surveyed separately in Chapter 4. The immediate political result of the break with Rome was Henry's marriage to Anne and the birth of Princess Elizabeth, whose sex was such a great disappointment to her father that he refused to attend her christening. Nevertheless she was heir to the throne on the bastardisation of her half-sister Mary.

Thomas Cromwell and the decade of reform

The 1530s were a decade of profound changes in the history of the English state. Whether these reforms were part of a constitutional blueprint or simply pragmatic responses to crises remains a matter of contention. G. R. Elton believed that the reforms were generated in the mind of Thomas Cromwell, whom he dubbed 'the most remarkable revolutionary in English history',[22] far more important than the descendant of his sister, Oliver Cromwell. In Elton's original analysis Cromwell presided over the modernising 'Tudor revolution in government' in the 1530s, as well as being the sole architect of the break with Rome. Later research by others forced Elton to modify such stark views, but he remained to the end convinced of the very special imprint of this individual on English history. But whether Cromwell was a conscious constitutionalist and theoretical reformer or simply used whatever means he could to bolster the power of the king remains controversial.[23] Like his patron Wolsey, Cromwell rose to the top from humble circumstances through sheer talent and hard work, and by the opportunity they each presented the king for getting his way. Cromwell, again like Wolsey, was a late starter in the world of politics, being at least 45 years old when he entered the royal service in 1530. Cromwell had been in the cardinal's employ since about 1516; he had sat in the Parliament of 1523, where he had certainly prepared, and most probably delivered, a speech attacking the misconceived and expensive war against France, and recommending instead the subjugation of Scotland as top priority. It is possible that Cromwell on that occasion was doing the cardinal's bidding in the ever-complex world of foreign policy and misinformation, but as the speech so contradicted Wolsey's and the king's policy at the time it seems wiser to deduce a degree of independent thought on Cromwell's part and his interest in uniting the British Isles.

The fall of Wolsey shook Cromwell to tears but it also spurred him to make his own way in politics. With Wolsey's blessing, and also with the king's permission, Cromwell sought a late return to the Parliament called for November 1529. As Elton pointed out, a modern aspect of Cromwell was that he was the first English statesman purposefully to use the House of Commons to launch his political career. Cromwell undoubtedly showed great courage in remaining loyal to his old master, but when it became clear that Wolsey would not be restored to office Cromwell joined the royal service, perhaps as early as April 1530, or as late as after Wolsey's death in November. As a result of his activities in the Commons, Cromwell's ability was soon recognised, with his entry into the council by January 1531, and into the 'inner ring' by the end of that year. Whatever his contribution to policy discussion at this time, what brought him dominance in the administration was his ability to achieve the first major breakthrough in the Reformation: the 'Submission of the Clergy'. Henceforward he was the king's right-hand man.

There can be little doubt about the revolutionary nature of the jurisdictional break from Rome, which upheld the idea of the supremacy and omnicompetence of statute law. Although judges in the fifteenth century tended to support the positivist view that statute law was to be obeyed whether it was good or bad, and that it was not invalidated by any higher law such as natural law, this view was not universally accepted before the 1530s, when for the first time statute law impinged on truly religious issues. The creation of a national Church under the king as supreme head (who could determine religious belief) amounted to this very thing. The use of the word 'empire' in the Act of Appeals of March 1533 was meant to indicate in a novel way the modern concept of a national sovereign state. Cromwell's use of statute must certainly be seen against the background of the advance of the positivist notion of lawmaking in the previous century, but true omnicompetence had to wait until the 1530s. Later attempts to invalidate statutes by appeal to a higher law cannot detract from the importance of this extension of the power of lawmaking by Cromwell in this decade. However, Elton's assertion that Cromwell was solely responsible for the intellectual arguments in the break with Rome has been refuted; but the minister still scores high marks for his practical ability in getting parliamentary legislation drafted and passed.

By the term 'revolution in government', Elton meant a transformation from medieval household government (dependent on the personal involvement of the king) to a more impersonal and modern national bureaucratic system. Many of the changes involved are seen clearly only after Cromwell's death; therefore proving that they emanated from his mind presents difficulties.

For example, the reformed privy council was definitively established on 10 August 1540, a fortnight after Cromwell's execution, but it is clear that it had existed earlier under him and that he had been intimately involved in a fundamental reorganisation of the council. This reorganisation had led to the abandonment of the large formal council inherited from the Middle Ages and to its replacement by a small executive corporate board of no more than 20 members, which would meet in whole or in part at any time of the year wherever the king and his Court happened to be, and which would be known consistently thereafter as the 'privy council'. It was a board of politicians, mainly leading officers of state and household, but without the law officers. The term 'privy council' itself was not new, but the earlier use (in the fifteenth century) of the word 'privy' or 'secret' to denote members of an 'inner ring' should not obscure the important changes made in the late 1530s. Because of the dire need for secrecy in dealing with the divorce issue a political 'privy' council had been in attendance on the king in his privy apartments since Wolsey's fall, and this small council had become more important than the council in the Star Chamber with a lord chancellor who was unsympathetic to the divorce. This select council actually governed the realm during Henry's absence in France in 1532, but it still included the judges and others who were to have no seat in the later true privy council. By January 1533 this 'council attending upon our person' had been given its own paid clerk, although this clerk seems to have been active since the resignation of More as lord chancellor the previous May. The true privy council would emerge out of this secret council attendant, and this same clerk would be referred to in 1538 as the clerk of the privy council. In June 1534 Cromwell made a note 'To remember the king for the establishment of the council'. Elton proved that the new privy council of 19 members was in existence at the latest by the autumn of 1536 and can be seen during the crisis to the regime posed by the Pilgrimage of Grace. However, the idea of an intellectual exercise in improved government has been attacked by John Guy, who perceives the privy council being formed as a pragmatic response to that crisis, when a small 'war cabinet' which signed documents collectively against the rebels was deemed necessary to safeguard the regime. After the crisis its collectivity seems to have been undermined by Cromwell's reassertion of his personal control, so that the refoundation of August 1540 was, in Guy's view, a return to the principles of its original creation in 1536 rather than to those of Cromwell.[24]

In finance the royal chamber now began to lose its supremacy with the creation of the first of a number of new 'bureaucratic' revenue courts, each with its own central staff, records and seals, and its agents in the localities. Although only one was fully founded in Cromwell's lifetime, Elton argues that the principles articulated in the creation of the court of augmentations in 1536 were carried on into the others set up after his death. The court of augmentations was founded because of the pressing need to deal with the moneys and legal problems emanating from the first wave of monastic dissolutions, and it was modelled on the late-medieval duchy of Lancaster, with its simplified bookkeeping and its national system of local receivers of revenue. Cromwell's earlier financial moves had shown some indecision. He himself acted as a kind of informal royal treasurer, but tightened up the bureaucratic element within the chamber and reduced its dependence on the household by making the two statutory general surveyors of crown lands permanent, and preventing the chamber from gaining new sources of revenue. And when it came to handling the new clerical taxes of first fruits and tenths, he entrusted these to an informal treasurer, his old colleague John Gostwick. It was clearly the magnitude of the task of handling monastic wealth that led to the bold move of the court of augmentations. Then just before his fall in 1540 Cromwell organised the creation of the court of wards to deal with the Crown's business in feudal land rights, which had been much increased by the traffic in monastic lands. After Cromwell's death, but clearly in the same spirit, the full court of first fruits and tenths was created in 1540 under Gostwick; and in 1542 the general surveyors were also turned into a full court to specialise in those crown lands acquired before 1530. With the medieval Exchequer dealing with the ancient revenues of the shires, parliamentary taxation and customs receipts, and the duchy of Lancaster looking after its own property, there were by 1542 six discrete revenue courts no longer dependent on the close involvement of the king.

Elton saw this as a major step in modernising the finances and the state, but medievalists have attacked his argument, stressing

that the keynote of late-medieval government had been bureaucracy, and pointing to the importance of the Exchequer; what was
now being overturned in the late 1530s was that primitive aber-
ration of chamber finance brought in by Edward IV and Henry
VII. The fact that the inspiration for the new revenue courts was
the medieval duchy of Lancaster, and that later in 1554 the
Exchequer would regain its supremacy by absorbing first fruits
and tenths and the enlarged augmentations are taken by medievalists as proofs of this. Therefore, they argue, the system was
really bureaucratic throughout, and no 'revolution in government' ensued except in the sense of the wheel turning full circle
backwards.

The antithesis perceived by most historians between backward-
looking household government and forward-looking departments of state should not be pushed too far. Medieval
departments of state were not 'modern', and household government had shown its ability to get things done (the major criterion
for institutional success) with improved bookkeeping and faster
audits; indeed both can be seen as 'bureaucratic' in the medieval
sense of having fixed routines and trained personnel. There
were thus no two rival 'systems' in operation with one winning
out over the other, and what is noteworthy is that the same
personnel could operate in both of them. All that mattered was
convenience. Whether done wittingly or not, the major result of
the changes made in the 1530s and 1540s was that royal finance
moved one step away from the personal involvement of the king.
In 1500 Henry VII could be found lovingly counting out his
money in his chamber. But later monarchs showed less interest
in such intimate involvement with their cash, and in the later
sixteenth century royal finance was overwhelmingly in the care of
the Exchequer, which took its orders mainly from the privy
council. The reformed Exchequer of 1554 was neither medieval
nor modern but had adapted itself to change, notably the use of
the new accounting methods, often using arabic rather than
roman numerals, derived from the royal chamber via Cromwell's
revenue courts, as well as a greater use of cash in the lower
Exchequer of receipt.

There can be little doubt of the importance of Cromwell's work
in transferring government from household to departments of
state, but this was not completed overnight because of the

existence of the privy chamber as a spending department (though never a collecting one) through the privy purse and the privy coffers. There was no change to a modern constitutional government as England remained a personal monarchy and it would be anachronistic to think that Cromwell envisaged the future constitutional development of England. His aims were the traditional ones of convenience and efficiency because under Henry VIII the personal involvement of the monarch in the nitty-gritty of government could not be taken for granted.

Although Cromwell was not averse to cooking the books against his enemies, he was not aiming to build up a Tudor despotism, but believed in the rule of the king under the law. He used parliamentary statute whenever he could, rather than creating a French-style system of government through the prerogative. Even royal proclamations were validated by an Act of Parliament in 1539. He brought the monarch clearly within the institution of Parliament by emphasising the trinity of King, Lords and Commons. The Dispensations Act of 1534 was the first to state explicitly that the king was a member of Parliament. That this now became constitutionally clear can be seen in comments by Henry VIII to Parliament in 1543, when he stated that

> We be informed by our judges that we at no time stand so highly in our estate royal as in the time of Parliament, wherein we as head and you as members are conjoined and knit together in one body politic.

Here was due recognition that sovereignty lay in the concept of monarch-in-Parliament, just as it does in Britain today.

Cromwell also oversaw reforms designed to unify the realm and strengthen the enforcement of the Reformation. Both Wales and the north of England posed serious problems of lawlessness. In 1531 the chancellor of the council in the Marches had come up to Court with the suggestion of turning Wales into counties on the English model, but the suggestion was not acted upon by the king. By 1533 Cromwell was pondering the 'necessity of looking to the state of Wales', and in April of that year jotted down a reminder note for the 'establishing of a council in the marches of Wales', by which he meant reforming the ineffectiveness of the current one. Then in December 1533 the central council's draft agenda contained an item 'to reform the administration of Wales so that peace should be preserved and justice done'. When this agenda was redrafted and items grouped together in themes, the Welsh question was linked up with the Irish problem and four topics dealing with the defence of the realm. Ireland and Wales were obvious back doors into England for any potential invader, and no one could forget that the Tudors themselves had gained the throne by invading through Wales. However, in Cromwell's mind probably more than just defensive measures were hatching – issues of uniform administration and justice. Ten years previously, as we have already seen, Cromwell had been advocating the subjection of Scotland into one uniform realm with England so that 'both they and we might live under one obedience, law and policy for ever'. Now he was thinking on the same lines, especially as he did not want the validity of Reformation legislation, despite Parliament's traditional claim to be able to legislate for Wales, queried on the grounds that the region was not represented in Parliament.

A new policy for Wales was presented in the last session of the Reformation Parliament in 1536, when a bold initiative was outlined with the first of the two so-called 'Acts of Union' (the later one of 1543 made some amendments in the light of experience) which completely assimilated Wales and made it unequivocally part of the kingdom of England, with the same laws and rights as the English (and openness to greater taxation than had previously been known in Wales). Now the whole of Wales was converted into shire-ground. The English common law overrode any surviving Welsh law, and English was to be the sole language of government and the legal system. Wales now became part of the kingdom of England, with membership of Parliament. However, the Act was soon suspended by proclamation (provided for in the Act). There were technical reasons for the delay, but it also seems that Henry VIII himself was not convinced: in 1540 there would be a plan to scrap the Act of 1536 in favour of creating a Principality for young Prince Edward with government in the hands of the prince and a Welsh court of chancery rather than by the council in the Marches.[25] However, this retrograde scheme was soon abandoned, and the policy outlined in the Act of 1536 put into effect, with a more elaborate second 'Act of Union' in 1543, which filled in the details as well as making some minor changes in the light of experience. Also by this second Act the council in the Marches acquired statutory validity, rather than resting purely on the royal prerogative, and it was thereafter no longer linked to a royal household there.

Also revamped by Cromwell to combat far-flung lawlessness was the council in the north. This was undertaken in 1537 in the wake of the Pilgrimage of Grace which had shown up the unreliability of most northern magnates. Now its jurisdiction was extended from just Yorkshire to the entire northern region. The council of the north was no longer based on a royal household as previously, nor did it now supervise crown lands in the region; instead it was a purely bureaucratic administrative and judicial body that governed the north, exercising, like the Welsh council, both a common-law and an equity jurisdiction.

Faction politics in the 1530s and 1540s

We now return to the dramatic but murky world of courtly politics, where it is very difficult to see what is going on below the surface of the mosaic of colourful events. We have already noticed the increased importance of the Court as a political centre and the civilianising of politics. In a personal monarchy factions are likely but not inevitable: there were no factions allowed, for example, under the strong and involved Henry VII. Factions sprang up whenever a king was weak or uninterested in government; such factions were then liable to be in a position to influence or manipulate him. Alternatively, a powerful but suspicious king might allow factions to flourish, pitting them against each other in order to ensure his own survival at the centre – a policy of 'divide and rule'. Historians have painted Henry VIII as suspicious and uninterested in government, and some recent historians have also seen him as an often weak and gullible king. One should bear in mind that in a personal monarchy closeness to the king could bring considerable political influence, and recent emphasis on the privy chamber has accorded great political influence to the well-born royal body-servants there. Whether or not factions existed earlier in the reign, there can be no reason to doubt their existence in the 1530s, mainly because there was now a brand new element in politics – namely, religious ideology. True factions, as opposed to rival patronage networks, in Tudor England were the product of the combination of aggressive patronage acquisition with political and religious differences. As to the role of the king and his personality and psychology, there is simply no agreement among modern historians – hence the enormous divergence among recent interpretations of that crucial episode in factional politics – the downfall of Anne Boleyn.

The fall of Anne Boleyn, 1536

The downfall of the king's second wife so soon after the momentous break with Rome remains a very enigmatic affair. After all, a large reason for the Reformation had been Henry's passion for one woman, now about to be discarded. There has been a general consensus among historians that Anne was not guilty of the scandalous charges brought against her – of adultery, incest and plotting to kill the king. Was Henry VIII really as monstrous as to condemn an innocent woman to death just because he was tired of her or in order to marry another? This seems too wicked to be true. In May 1536, in the space of only three weeks, Anne and five men – George Lord Rochford, Henry Norris, William Brereton, Francis Weston and the humble musician Mark Smeaton – were charged, found guilty and executed for treasonable adultery. All were members of the privy chamber. Rather than envisage Henry as a monster it has been claimed that it is easier to understand Anne's death as a consequence of factional politics. The king is to be viewed as not being in complete control; instead he was duped or misled by factional intrigue. In this interpretation the privy chamber assumes a crucial role. Anti-Boleyn factions gained the king's ear and persuaded him of her guilt.

Most of the dates and places of the illicit assignations of Anne and her alleged lovers can today be shown to be wrong (14 out of 20): this may be proof of fabricated evidence, or they may be simply clerical errors.[26] The portrayal of Anne as a religious reformer of an evangelical persuasion, especially by Ives, has tended to support her plea of innocence. Was it all just the trappings of innocent 'courtly love' that became misunderstood?

If the king was being duped who were the factional leaders who wanted to get rid of Anne?

In January 1536 Henry's heart was gladdened by the natural death of Catherine of Aragon, but saddened by the miscarriage of a male foetus by Queen Anne. How significant this latter loss was to Anne Boleyn's fate is still a matter of contention. On 14 April the Reformation Parliament ended and the members returned home. This fact tends to suggest that a crisis at Court had not yet blown up; had Anne's end already been foreseen at this juncture the Parliament would have been continued or prorogued to deal with it. Instead a new Parliament soon had to be called to help Henry get rid of his queen. On 18 April, according to Ives, Anne's position still appeared secure because Henry was anxious for the Imperial ambassador to acknowledge her at Court, and Rochford was still being employed in diplomatic negotiations. But ominously on 24 April *oyer and terminer* investigations were launched into certain unspecified treasons, and these were to start the ball rolling. Nevertheless, on 25 April the king wrote to his ambassador in Rome that he still expected heirs by his 'most dear and entirely beloved wife'. Again this might seem to suggest that all was still well. But on Saturday 29 April accusations against Anne were brought to him, and at a council meeting at Greenwich the next day the issues were discussed. Anne realised that something was wrong, and was glimpsed at a window holding up Princess Elizabeth in her arms while trying to reason with Henry. Events then rapidly escalated. The musician Mark Smeaton was interrogated at Cromwell's house in Putney, and possibly tortured in the Tower. The next day, May Day, Henry and Anne sat together at the jousts, but then Henry, in a bad temper, suddenly left, and they never saw each other again. Henry Norris, one of the jousters, returned to Whitehall with the king, and Henry gave him the chance to confess his adultery with the queen and save his life, but this Norris refused, claiming outright innocence. Norris was dispatched to the Tower, and then Anne was arrested the next day. Norris, Brereton, Weston and Smeaton were all tried in Westminster Hall on 12 May, but Anne and her brother Rochford were tried in the great hall of the Tower on 15 May. The five men were beheaded on Tower Hill on 17 May; Anne was beheaded by the sword on Tower Green on 19 May. That same day Henry held a betrothal party for Jane Seymour, whom he went on to marry quietly at Whitehall on 30 May.

Eric Ives opened up the factional interpretation in 1972.[27] Henry did not always know what was going on, he claimed, rather he was at the mercy of the factions. If Anne had really been guilty of adultery why was it necessary to execute her? Adultery with a fully consenting queen was not treason under existing law; and to make it treasonable additional arguments had to be employed to show that Anne and her lovers had plotted the king's death by magic. Only a later Act of 1542 would make adultery with a queen a treasonable offence in itself. It seems significant that no woman was accused as an accomplice, yet ladies in waiting would have been needed for the queen to have had secret assignations. If, as most historians have concluded, the queen was innocent, so too were the accused men. Ives viewed the removal of the queen and the five men as the consequence of political intrigue. The link between them was that they were all members of the king's privy chamber. In Ives' view, Henry did not fall out of love with Anne; he was led away from her.

It was the conservative 'Aragonese' faction, devoted to Queen Catherine and her daughter Mary, that was behind the king's change of heart. The Aragonese had been grooming Jane Seymour to steal the king's affections, and in this they were soon to be joined by Thomas Cromwell. The king seems to have been interested in Jane from September 1535; and by early March 1536 he had Jane, along with brother Sir Edward Seymour and his wife, secretly housed at Greenwich Palace in a suite that he could reach by a secret passage.[28] Whether Henry wanted a mistress or a new wife remains unclear. Was he involved at this early stage in replacing Anne? Was he the originator of the scheme or only reluctantly persuaded of the charges against Anne? Ives considers the king to have been quite simply duped. Yet one would have expected a man who truly loved his wife to have reacted to such an allegation with extreme anger towards her accusers, but there seems no evidence of this. David Starkey, also following the faction model, believes that the king was eager to get rid of Anne.[29] Retha Warnicke argues that Anne's miscarriage was critical in killing the king's affection for her, especially as the foetus was deformed: Henry could thus persuade himself that he had been bewitched.[30] As for Cromwell's role, if Henry was eager to get rid of the queen then his job was obvious: to do it efficiently and quickly. If, however, Henry was not eager to lose his wife then it must be explained why Cromwell would want to throw in his lot with the conservative Aragonese (whom he hated) against his former allies the Boleyns. After all, an Aragonese victory might spell ruin for him and his plans. This was certainly an enormous challenge, whether he was working with or without the king's approval: that is, to use the Aragonese but not to be crushed by them. Basically the Aragonese wanted Anne's divorce from Henry and the reintroduction of the Lady Mary into the succession. This could be done by arguing that Anne's marriage to the king was nullified by her pre-contract (if there had been such) to Henry Lord Percy, while Mary could be legitimated while not accepting the validity of the Aragon marriage by claiming that Mary had been born in the parents' good faith. It was certainly Cromwell (with or without the king's permission) who changed the charge against Anne from adultery to treason, thus requiring the death penalty. Cromwell could not face the possibility of her revenge if she were to live. Clearly those behind the charges wanted to remove Anne permanently.

It is possible that Cromwell wanted to be rid of Anne for political reasons of his own. We know that Cromwell was negotiating with Chapuys, the Imperial ambassador, for a *rapprochement* with Charles V. This meant a great deal to Cromwell, who was extremely upset by Henry's reluctance in the matter (April 1536). Anne Boleyn was pro-French, and Cromwell may well have thought that Anne was a hindrance in the pursuit of a pro-Imperial foreign policy. Ives says that Anne herself had decided to abandon France if a deal could be made with Charles V; it was now Henry who stood out against this *rapprochement* in opposition to the wishes of the various factions. The crucial point, argues Ives, is the kind of alliance being negotiated. Charles V was insisting that Mary's exclusion from the succession be lifted; and this was something that Anne simply refused to contemplate. Thus the existence of Anne might have represented a limitation on diplomatic negotiation.

The only contributor to the recent debate who genuinely believes Anne to have been guilty of adultery is G. W. Bernard. In his eyes there is no need at all to invoke the faction model to explain her elimination. The queen had committed adultery with Norris and Smeaton. Bernard rejects Warnicke's view that Anne's miscarried foetus was indeed deformed as being based on too flimsy evidence, from 50 years later. Bernard lays much emphasis on the poem *Histoire de Anne Boleyn* by Lancelot de Carles, who was an attendant on the French ambassador, and who in this poem refers to the evidence of Elizabeth Countess of Worcester, sister of the Aragonese supporter Sir Anthony Browne. Sir Anthony scolds his sister for her immoral lifestyle, but the countess replies that the queen's lifestyle is worse, committing adultery with Smeaton and her own brother Lord Rochford. Sir Anthony then informed the king. Bernard regards this poem as an independent contemporary source which clinches the matter. However, it may well simply express the government's official propaganda position as fed to the French embassy. Ives prefers to believe the later boast of Cromwell to the Imperial ambassador that he had organised the whole scheme. This might be true or a complete bluff.

Whether by the king or by the other faction leaders, Cromwell was placed in charge of getting rid of Anne, and in so doing won promotion, becoming Lord Cromwell and lord privy seal. The alliance formed to secure Anne's removal did not last long. The Aragonese failed to get Mary restored to the succession, and, according to Ives and Starkey, Cromwell turned against them and threatened them with worse. To save her supporters Mary had to recognise her father's supreme headship over the Church and her own illegitimate status. Cromwell is thus portrayed as a double-crosser.

According to Elton, the Pilgrimage of Grace can be viewed as the work of a desperate Aragonese group, now rendered impotent at Court and taking their quarrel into the localities. This might partially explain the involvement of lords Darcy and Hussey, but as a general explanation of the rebellion, as simply an extension of factional intrigue, it seems extremely unlikely, especially as most Aragonese leaders stayed aloof. However, the Aragonese were to suffer a severe onslaught during 1538–9 at Court. About 16 conservatives were put to death, including the Marquis of Exeter and Lord Montague, grandsons respectively of Edward IV and George Duke of Clarence, and also the supposed faction leader, Sir Nicholas Carew. Sir Geoffrey Pole,

Montague's brother, had been interrogated in the Tower, and on the basis of what he said the others were hauled in for questioning. Above all, it was support for the traitor Cardinal Reginald Pole which brought them under suspicion. The last of this group to die – in 1541 – would be the aged Margaret Pole, Countess of Salisbury, Clarence's daughter and mother of the three Pole brothers. No wonder the French ambassador could regard Henry as 'the most dangerous and cruel man in the world'.

Obviously Cromwell was pleased to see the end of these factional foes, but the impetus for their removal seems to have come from the ever-suspicious king himself. They were essentially dynastic rather than factional casualties. Exeter's father had been imprisoned by Henry VII simply on the basis of his proximity to the throne, while Exeter and Montague had been under suspicion since about 1530 for recruiting retainers in the southwest. There had been rumours that Exeter had his eyes on the throne, and his support for Mary had got him thrown off the council in 1536. Also his sympathies for Cardinal Pole and his hatred of the radicals about the king ('I trust once to have a fair day upon these knaves which rule about the king') led to his downfall. The king's paranoia about the succession was at its height during these years, and the birth of Prince Edward in October 1537 had in no way reduced them: indeed the king was now determined to protect his son from all other claimants, especially as Queen Jane had died in the process and no other heir could soon be expected. The *rapprochement* of France and Spain in June 1538 meant the real possibility of an invasion of the realm, and the most vulnerable region would have been Cornwall and Devon under the thumb of the white rose. Therefore there is no reason to overemphasise the factional role of a manipulative Cromwell in the removal of these Yorkist elements. However, there was certainly a factional consequence in that Cromwell was now in a position to get more of his supporters into the privy chamber to make up the losses sustained by the conservatives. In came new men, of a reformist bent and not obviously courtier material, such as Ralph Sadler, Anthony Denny and Philip Hoby. Cromwell himself became the nominal head of the privy chamber in 1539, and as lord great chamberlain in 1540 was henceforward in a position to dominate the Court.

The search for a new wife for the king got under way in earnest from early in 1538. Of the many suggested ladies, Henry fancied Mary of Guise (soon to marry James V of Scotland) and especially Duchess Christina of Milan (a 16-year-old widow), with whose portrait by Holbein the king fell in love. Both were tall ladies, but both were worried over Henry's matrimonial record, and Christina is supposed to have quipped that although she had a tall body she had a small neck. Nevertheless, it was not personal but diplomatic problems that prevented any possibility of these marriages. Having married his second and third wives for love (or lust), Henry now had to return to the more usual path for a king – an arranged diplomatic marriage.

The fall of Cromwell

This fourth marriage was to be Cromwell's undoing. Because of the *rapprochement* of France and Empire in 1538 there was at last the possibility of enforcing the papal excommunication against Henry. Early in 1539 in order to gain a European ally, Cromwell got the idea of a marriage for the king into the House of Cleves, which although at the time not a Protestant state was linked to Lutheran Saxony. Holbein's portrait of the lady helped Cromwell persuade the king, and the betrothal of Henry to Anne of Cleves was concluded on 4 October 1539. Unfortunately, as soon as Henry first caught a glimpse of her at Rochester in December, he was not amused: 'I like her not', he reportedly commented. Holbein's portrait had done the lady too much justice, it seems. Nonetheless, the wedding to his 'Flanders mare' (an apocryphal description) took place on 6 January 1540 at Greenwich. Yet straightaway Henry demanded to get out of this latest marriage, which had now been rendered diplomatically unnecessary by the collapse of the Franco-Imperial truce.

The fiasco involving Anne of Cleves finally gave the conservatives sufficient ammunition to undermine Cromwell in the king's eyes just as the minister was about to enjoy further honours. He was elevated on 17 April 1540 to the earldom of Essex and the office of lord great chamberlain. Whether this was again the result of factional machinations or a machiavellian ruse on the part of the king is unclear. The downfall of Cromwell had, it seems, been discussed at the French Court by Francis I and the Duke of Norfolk as early as February 1540. The conservatives were eager to help the king jettison Anne of Cleves, whereas Cromwell was hopeful of the king getting used to her. Cromwell was reluctant to accede to a speedy annulment especially because the king's roving eye had now wandered to a lady from the blood of his hated rivals, the Howards.

The minister had lost the king's confidence, and his enemies drove home the accusation in April 1540 that he was a heretic who supported the Lutheran views of Robert Barnes and whose laxity allowed a nest of heretics to flourish at Calais. Cromwell tried to retaliate by exploiting the existence in Calais of a papist priest named Gregory Botolf in the employ of the governor Arthur Viscount Lisle. This Gregory Botolf seems to have made a visit to Rome and to have been in contact with Cardinal Pole. Cromwell was playing on Henry's unquenchable hatred of Pole to make him suspicious of all conservatives. The upshot was the arrest of a large number in Calais, including Lisle himself, whose papers were seized. However the conservatives were now making all the running, grasping the trump card of a possible new queen in the person of Catherine Howard.

The tension at Court continued for some time, with conservatives berating Cromwell for thwarting Henry's wish to be rid of Anne of Cleves. But the actual event of Cromwell's arrest at a council meeting on 10 June came as a complete surprise after a normal morning's business. In the council chamber Norfolk and Southampton led the wolves in tearing off the badges and symbols of the fallen minister. Cromwell was peremptorily disposed of by an Act of Attainder which specified heresy and treason as the crimes, including his support for the views of Robert Barnes. The inclusion of heresy in an attainder was completely novel. Cromwell was beheaded on 28 July 1540 on Tower Hill. Earlier, on 9 July, Convocation had given Henry his annulment: this decision was based on the notion of a pre-contract undertaken by Anne of Cleves with Duke Francis of Lorraine. Henry was also forced to use the argument of non-consummation of his marriage despite their having shared a bed – an argument which he had regarded as ridiculous when used previously in reference to his brother Arthur's marriage to Catherine of Aragon. The royal physician Dr Butts was summoned to prove that the king was not impotent because he could still obtain wet dreams! On the same day as Cromwell was beheaded, Henry married Catherine Howard at Oatlands (Surrey) to solidify the conservative victory. According to the French ambassador, Henry was later to blame his ministers for their false accusations against Cromwell, whom he had come to regard as his most faithful minister ever.

The conservative reaction

Despite the fall of their master, the Cromwellians remained at their posts, but power reverted back to the religious conservatives led by Norfolk and Stephen Gardiner, Bishop of Winchester, with the support of the ex-Cromwellian Thomas Wriothesley, who now became chief secretary, and later in 1544 lord chancellor, even though he was neither a common lawyer nor a cleric. The conservative euphoria was not long-lived, however, on account of the infidelities of Catherine Howard. She was not a spotless virgin, having previously had a sexual relationship with one Francis Dereham while staying in the Duchess of Norfolk's household at Lambeth; indeed she may well have been pre-contracted to marry him. None of this was known to Henry when he eagerly ventured into marriage with her. In August 1541 Catherine foolishly made Dereham her secretary. Henry's 54-inch waist and ulcerous legs made dalliance with another man understandable, but foolhardy. The continuation of a sexual relationship with Dereham after her marriage to the king seems doubtful, but it is clear that her relationship with a new man, one Thomas Culpepper of the privy chamber, was a sexual one. Culpepper confessed that full sexual intercourse was intended though not obtained; nevertheless sexual behaviour was involved. Catherine wrote Culpepper a love letter: 'It makes my heart die to think I cannot be always in your company.' Catherine's downfall began when evidence relating to her previous attachment to Dereham was supplied to Archbishop Cranmer by the religious radical John Lascelles (whose sister had been a servant to the duchess at Lambeth). Cranmer's revelation of this to Henry made him wild with anger – so very different from his reaction to the revelations concerning Anne

Boleyn – and both Dereham and Culpepper were tortured for evidence of immoral behaviour with the queen after marriage. The investigation of the queen's adultery was conducted by ex-associates of Cromwell: Thomas Audley, Ralph Sadler and Cranmer. The pre-contract with Dereham might have meant that Catherine could have been spared, but Henry was genuinely angry that he had been misled, since any children by Catherine would have been rendered illegitimate by it. And the queen's own behaviour after marriage reduced any chance of clemency; Jane Viscountess Rochford, the widow of Lord Rochford, supplied evidence about the various secret meetings she had helped arrange between Catherine and Culpepper. After a public trial both men were executed on 10 December 1541, Culpepper being beheaded and Dereham (because of his common stock) suffering the worse fate of hanging, drawing and quartering. Most of the Howards, except for Norfolk, were held for a time at the Tower. There was to be no public trial of the queen, however. On 21 January 1542 after a speech by the king, an Act of Attainder against Catherine was passed in Parliament. Whether it was Henry's spiteful decision to make Catherine pay the full price, or whether it was his reformist councillors who pushed for the attainder to prevent the king from forgiving her, is a matter of conjecture. Both Catherine and Lady Rochford were beheaded on Tower Green on 13 February.

Henry's last years

Henry depended on no single minister after Cromwell's death. To G. R. Elton this period signified Henry's 'truly personal rule'.[31] Lacey Baldwin Smith has argued that one sees the real Henry in these last years because he had to take the important decisions himself. This is not quite true because Henry still ruled with the advice of the newly reformed privy council. Nevertheless the fact that Henry appointed no vicegerent-in-spirituals to replace Cromwell indicates that Henry saw himself as shouldering more of the burden of government. Baldwin Smith also floats the theory that in old age 'man casts off a portion of the protective shield hammered out during childhood and adolescence and reveals the raw personality beneath'.[32] If this is true then it is not an attractive personality that we behold in the king, although it must not be forgotten that during this last decade Henry was a sick man and towards the end had to be carried around Whitehall in a sedan chair (or 'tram').

The demise of Catherine Howard led to a gradual decline in the influence of the conservatives at Court. They still dominated the privy council, but reformers were ensconced in the privy chamber. There was a definite struggle between the two factions attempting to influence the king, especially as both sides were looking forward to the next reign. They took every opportunity to undermine each other's position. Cranmer's reforming policies in his own diocese were staunchly resisted by conservatives among his own clergy. In the so-called 'prebendaries plot' of 1543 they tried to tar him with the brush of heresy; also involved in this were the conservative son and son-in-law of Sir Thomas More – John More and William Dauntsey. Gardiner and the conservatives tried to convince Henry that the archbishop should be investigated for heresy, and Henry seemed to play along with them, but in fact warned Cranmer against them and gave him a ring to show his enemies should they try to arrest him. This story suggests that now Henry understood the workings of faction. Perhaps he was at last waking up to factional machinations after the loss of Cromwell.

The king's last marriage would be of enormous benefit to the reforming party, because the new queen, Catherine Parr, whom the king married in July 1543, was a lady of intellectual and reforming tastes. Edward Seymour, Earl of Hertford, was the leader of the reforming party at Court, which also contained the new queen's brother William Parr, Earl of Essex. Both Sir William Herbert and Sir Thomas Seymour were also linked to Queen Catherine. The reformers were younger, well organised, and were fortunate to win over that great administrator Sir William Paget. The younger men, especially Hertford and Viscount Lisle, were brought to the fore by the warfare of the 1540s. The conservatives were older and being thinned out by death, Sussex and Southampton dying in 1542 and Suffolk in 1545 (although in truth neither of the last two had displayed much religiosity). Henry really had little choice but to promote the younger men at Court, and they tended to be reformers. Even Norfolk's son, Henry Earl of Surrey, had converted to

Protestantism, and had got into trouble for eating meat in Lent in 1543. An attempt by Gardiner and Wriothesley to convince the king of his new queen's religious heterodoxy failed when Catherine made a complete submission to Henry and said that it was not a woman's role to meddle with religion. This was enough to satisfy Henry, who was in no mood to lose another wife, especially with no serious chance of marrying again. When Wriothesley came to arrest her, Henry rounded on his lord chancellor calling him a knave and a fool. This gives us a very clear indication that the king was perfectly capable of looking after his own interests as he perceived them, and that he was now extending to Catherine Parr the personal protection that – significantly – had not been forthcoming for Anne Boleyn.

The last years were to be dominated by war – Henry's paramount interest – and economic ills, above all the rise in prices. The warfare of the last decade was against England's two traditional enemies, Scotland and France. The warfare against Scotland was secondary to the main goal of reinforcing Henry's 'honour' by belittling France and was not primarily part of a grand vision to unite the British Isles. France and the Empire were no longer bound by a truce, and both as usual wanted England for an ally. In 1542 Henry and the emperor made an unofficial agreement (written up in 1543) that they would combine to attack France, and indeed capture Paris. But before that could be achieved Henry had to address the side issue of Scotland. War with France could not be entertained while Scotland was free to come to her ally's aid. Henry needed an excuse to provoke war with both his foes. Accordingly he sent an invitation to his nephew James V of Scotland to meet him at York. To this end Henry went north and waited at York for nine days, but James never turned up. Henry publicly confessed anger at being mocked by the Scottish king, although it was clear from earlier English reports that James would not keep the appointment; this was possibly because of the danger involved to the Scottish king, who had no legitimate heir, but more definitely because his ally and father-in-law Francis I refused to allow him to go.[33] The non-meeting gave Henry an excellent excuse to initiate hostilities in Scotland that he hoped would provoke France into war. When Francis declared war on the emperor in July 1542, Henry increased his aggression towards the Scots, culminating in his sending Norfolk into Scotland, where at Solway Moss on 24 November an English force of 3000 beat a Scottish army more than three times its size. The Scottish king survived the day but died within three weeks, leaving Scotland with a new-born sovereign, Mary Queen of Scots. Henry's imperialistic aim was now to incorporate Scotland into England and undo the 'Auld Alliance' of France and Scotland by arranging the marriage of the infant Mary Queen of Scots to his own son Prince Edward. This was resisted by the majority of the Scots, and so Henry embarked on what Sir Walter Scott later dubbed 'the rough wooing' to enforce his wishes; the Earl of Hertford was sent north to try and make the Scots comply. However, despite some limited success, the pro-French party would remain in power during Henry's lifetime.

The main prize for Henry remained France, and in July 1544 he accompanied his army across the Channel to Calais, besieging Boulogne and Montreuil. Boulogne eventually fell, and this was greeted as a great victory by the king, although (as should have been expected) the emperor immediately extricated himself and made peace with France. In July 1545 the French raided Portsmouth and the Isle of Wight, in which action Henry's flagship the *Mary Rose* keeled over in Portsmouth harbour within sight of the king, incurring the loss of some 500 men. This disaster, which involved denting the king's honour, plus the soaring costs of war led the council to urge peace with France. The king's honour was restored by the condition that England should keep Boulogne until 1554 after which date it should then be purchased by France for £600 000 – a sum nowhere near the cost of capturing it, maintaining and fortifying it. Also previous French pensions to Henry were to be renewed. The expense of war led to the largest debasement of the coinage seen heretofore, and the Parliament of 1545 allowed the king to dissolve the chantries, although in the event these church moneys were not to be touched before the new Chantries Act of 1547.

Struggle for the succession and the will

As the reign drew to its weary close the factions were looking to the reign of a boy-king, with all the possible problems that this might involve, as witnessed by the recent past. By the third Act of

Succession (1543) the Crown was to go to Edward as the king's legitimate son or to his issue, but failing this, it should then descend to Henry's two bastardised daughters, Mary and Elizabeth, in that order. The two girls were – surprisingly – not made legitimate by the Act. During Edward's minority there would be a Regency council, but its composition and other details were left to be decided in the king's will, to be 'signed with his most gracious hand'. Thus factional rivalry in the last years of the reign was directed at winning Henry's support for inclusion on the Regency council. The winning faction, conservative or reformist, would be able to mould policy, and indeed the future of the state, during the boy's minority, by inculcating in him the religious ideology of which the winning faction approved.

The main instructions of the final will of 30 December 1546 provided that there should be a Regency council of 16 equal members to govern until Edward reached the age of 18, and majority decisions would be binding. Notably absent from the named councillors was Bishop Gardiner. Also notable was the absence of any mention of a lord protector. The will repeated the arrangements for the succession mentioned in the Act, but if all of the king's children were to die without heirs, by the will the Crown was to go to the descendants of his sister Mary, but the descendants of his other sister Margaret of Scotland – the Stuarts – were ignored.

Henry's last act of kingship has provoked a long academic debate. Historians used to follow Pollard in regarding the will as Henry's refusal to acknowledge his disappearance from the political scene and as an attempt to rule England from the grave. Pollard believed that the will was genuine and manually signed by the king on 30 December.[34] This scenario was attacked in 1962 by Lacey Baldwin Smith, who regarded the will as an absurd document if it had really intended to lay down the rules for the next reign.[35] Smith argued that the will was devised solely to control and manipulate competing factions at Court in Henry's own lifetime. They had to stay good boys or lose their chance to be on the Regency council. The will was not Henry's last word because on 26 December 1546, when he called for his will to be drafted, he did not expect to die; indeed he was planning another attack on Scotland. A month later however, on 28 January 1547, before he could sign the will personally Henry suddenly died. Instead, the dry stamp (a metal impression of the royal signature, to be inked in by a clerk) was applied to the will. Paget later gave evidence in 1553 that the will had indeed been dry-stamped. This was a breach of the Act of 1543 which explicitly demanded a true royal signature. Although officially dated 30 December 1546, the will was dry-stamped only a few hours before Henry passed away. It was mandatory for all stamped documents to be listed every month so that the 'forgers' could receive a pardon. Henry's will was duly included in the list of stamped documents for the month of January; it was the last but one on the list, the will being referred to as made on 30 December. According to Smith, Henry had never intended a council to govern, which is why just before he died he reportedly gave the will into the hands of Edward Seymour, Earl of Hertford. He expected his son's uncle to rule as lord protector.

Smith's interpretation was in turn criticised, but all the theorising was based on the premise that even from his sickbed the king was in charge, manipulating factions for his own benefit on the principle of 'divide and rule'. Scarisbrick doubted Smith's argument because he considered it 'difficult to believe that the king needed any such extra grasp on those around him'.[36] As we have seen, the notion of an all-dominant Henry VIII has been under challenge since the arrival of the faction model in the 1970s. Especially in his sick old age Henry might be misled and duped by those around him.

The faction model has been applied in recent years to the issue of the will. The new 'factional' scenario is that during the second half of 1546 the radical party became dominant at Court. The conservatives still had the upper hand in the summer as witnessed by their successful drive against heresy. But on the return of Hertford and Lisle from the war in August the new reformist faction became dominant at Court. The Imperial ambassador was to write that the 'great persecution of heretics and sacramentalists...has ceased since Hertford and the Lord Admiral have resided at Court'. The reformers already possessed the dry stamp, and the man who controlled its use, Sir Anthony Denny, became groom of the stool in October 1546. Only two other men were allowed to use the dry stamp, the clerk of the privy seal and Denny's brother-in-law, John Gates. Supreme in the privy chamber they also began to challenge the conservative preponderance on the privy council. Gardiner fell out with the king and was absent after November. The Howards fell when the Earl of Surrey was charged on 2 December with treason in quartering the royal arms with his own, and also with plotting to make his sister Henry's mistress in order to ensure their own dominant position. The old Duke of Norfolk followed his son into the Tower. Thus Henry was largely surrounded at the end by one faction, clustered around the Earl of Hertford. Other conservatives like Wriothesley and Sir Richard Rich may have been bought off or agreed to acquiesce rather than suffer the arrogance of the Howards.

A case has been made out for seeing the will's final revisions as emanating more from the supreme faction rather than from the supreme head. The Imperial ambassador reported home in December: 'The Court is closed to all but the privy council and some gentlemen of the chamber.' Even Queen Catherine could not gain access to her husband. David Starkey believes that the will was doctored in the secrecy of the privy chamber, and that the final will did not represent all of Henry's wishes but instead was a gerrymandered document to promote the interests of the winning faction. According to this conspiracy theory, between December and January important changes were made: especially the infamous 'unfulfilled gifts clause', by which unnamed courtiers were to be rewarded with grants and gifts which the king had intended to distribute but which he had found no time to so do. Under this clause the great men of the next reign were scandalously to enrich themselves. Starkey sees this clause as being inserted in the will without the king's permission. A single faction was thus now able to steal rewards and the government of the next king, and there is little reason to suppose that Henry knew much about what was going on.[37] The Starkey conspiracy theory seems most plausible, although it has been attacked recently by Eric Ives, which might seem surprising in view of his own general belief in factional conspiracy at Henry's Court. But now for technical reasons Ives finds it improbable that the will could have been seriously manipulated or changed, and he concludes that Henry agreed with the final contents of the will, which should therefore be seen as conferring power on the reformist group with the king's implicit blessing for further religious change.[38] This last point, however, seems dubious. There will be no agreement on Henry's final aims and policies, just as there has been no agreement by historians on Henry's psychology and role in politics throughout his reign. Was he a machiavellian monster, or just weak, misled and misunderstood?

4 The Henrician Reformation

The king's 'Great Matter'

The immediate cause of the Reformation in England under Henry VIII in the 1530s was political and personal. If Henry VIII had not wanted to divorce his ageing wife Catherine of Aragon in order to marry his new love Anne Boleyn, the Church in England would have stayed obedient to the papacy, at least in the short term. Whatever might have happened later in English history, we can be sure that as far as Henry VIII was concerned the only thing that drove him to break with the pope was his dire need to remarry and beget a male heir to ensure the survival of the dynasty. After all Henry had been a notable champion of the papacy in the quarrel with Martin Luther. Henry VIII was not a Protestant nor ever would be, although some historians have speculated on a possible change of mind right at the end of his life. Because of political circumstances Henry was forced to reject papal supremacy while for the most part maintaining essential Catholic dogma; this is what most differentiates England from the rest of Europe where religious change was undertaken. On the continent repudiation of papal supremacy in the sixteenth century went hand in hand with theological change. Not so in England. Protestantism was to reach England only later, in the reign of Henry's young son Edward VI. Of course, removal of papal authority would eventually lead to theological change, but it is unlikely that Henry himself foresaw this. There would be some tampering with theology in the late 1530s because of the actions of religious radicals at Court and the demands of diplomacy, but from 1539 onwards, with the very strictly orthodox Act of Six Articles, right down to 1546 Henry maintained essentially an idiosyncratic non-papal reformed Catholicism and burned Protestant heretics. The thousands of requiem masses that Henry ordered to be said for his soul as well as the invocation of the Virgin Mary in the royal will seem overwhelmingly to confirm his conservatism to the very end.

What exactly was the political and personal problem which had led to the Reformation? The very survival of the new Tudor dynasty was at stake simply because Henry did not have a legitimate male heir to succeed him, and by this time it looked as though Queen Catherine would not conceive again. But after some 18 years of marriage to Catherine, despite numerous pregnancies and stillbirths, only one child had survived, Princess Mary. Before Catherine had married Henry, she had been the wife of his elder brother Arthur. It now seemed to Henry that because of Catherine's infertility the law of the Church had been proved correct after all, and that the papal dispensation granted by Pope Julius II in 1503 had been invalid. Canon law prevented in the normal course of affairs the marriage of a man to his brother's widow. This prohibition was based on two texts in the Old Testament book of Leviticus:

> Do not have sexual relations with your brother's wife; that would dishonour your brother. (Leviticus 18: 16)

> If a man marries his brother's wife it is an act of impurity; he has dishonoured his brother. They will be childless. (Leviticus 20: 21)

Henry, of course, was not childless, only sonless, although the king tried to show that in the original Hebrew 'sons' were specifically meant. The first of these texts comes from a chapter on unlawful sexual relations, the brother in question clearly still being alive; this seems not to have much bearing on Henry's case. In the second text, also, there is no guarantee that the brother mentioned is dead; the passage seems a condemnation of two brothers sharing the same wife.

Henry's case in canon law was difficult: he had to show that the condemnation of Leviticus was relevant and absolutely binding, a task complicated by an apparently contradictory text in the Book of Deuteronomy:

> If brothers are living together and one of them dies without a son his widow must not marry outside the family. Her

husband's brother shall take her and marry her and fulfil the
duty of a brother-in-law to her. (Deuteronomy 25: 5)

This quotation, which refers to the institution of the *levirate* to
perpetuate a tribe, proves that there is no eternal divine commandment against marrying a brother's widow. The medieval
Catholic Church had taught that in normal circumstances such a
levirate marriage was not permissible to Christians, but this prohibition sprang from the positive law of the Church, not from the
law of God. Hence the papal dispensation of 1503. However, by
1527 Henry had convinced himself that the curse of Leviticus
was absolute and the cause of his dynastic problems. The Tudors
had been given the throne by God; it must be sin that was now
the hindrance to the succession. It has to be understood that
Henry's case was also based on the premise that Catherine's
first marriage to Arthur had been truly consummated, whereas
Catherine always denied this and asserted that when she became
Henry's wife she was still a virgin. Wolsey gave the king good
advice not to pursue this line but to argue instead on the basis of a
technical flaw in the papal dispensation caused by the oversight
of not clearing the 'impediment of public honesty' occasioned by
the public betrothal and marriage of Arthur and Catherine.
However Henry disowned this option and in 1527 he told Wolsey
to arrange a papal annulment of the marriage on the basis of
consanguinity – the 'impediment of affinity'. In normal times
Henry would almost certainly have gained his wish, but since
1527 the pope was a prisoner of the Emperor Charles V, who
would not hear of his aunt being put aside. Unable to get his
divorce, Henry after some six years of debate finally threw out
papal jurisdiction, creating not so much a Reformation as a
schism. The reign of Henry VIII witnessed the establishment of
a schismatic Catholic Church, not a Protestant one.

Can one attribute such momentous changes in the Church
solely to the wishes of a single individual, even such a pivotal
one as the king? The Tudors were not despots and had no
standing army to impose their wishes on a reluctant people.
Many traditionalist historians have seen the changes in the
Church as being generally popular and indeed as a response to
public opinion. A. G. Dickens, for example, painted a picture of a
people profoundly dissatisfied with later-medieval Catholicism,

thirsting for the Bible and seeking fundamental change.[1] Even without a divorce problem, the argument here is that the Reformation would have come about sooner or later because this is what the people wanted. Since the mid-1980s this notion of the inevitability of the English Reformation has been radically challenged by revisionist historians, notably J. J. Scarisbrick, Christopher Haigh, J. A. F. Thomson, Eamon Duffy and Richard Rex, who have all argued for the general popularity of Catholicism on the eve of the schism. One fact is not in doubt, namely the successful implementation of the changes with only small amounts of resistance. Does the lack of resistance point to popular approval of the changes, or does it underline the large degree of obedience and loyalty the Tudors could expect no matter how uncongenial their demands might be?

Religion in England on the eve of the Reformation

One of the main arguments of the traditionalists has been the widespread existence of anticlericalism among the laity. In 1510 Archbishop Warham of Canterbury was voicing the opinion that the laity were hostile to the clergy, while in 1512 Dean Colet of St Paul's blamed the wickedness of the clergy in general for such hatred. Certainly there were many examples of vices, corruption and immorality in the English Church, just as there were in the Church in Europe. In the traditional story of growing anticlericalism in England the story of the London tailor Richard Hunne plays a large role: the celebrated Hunne affair. Between 1511 and December 1514 Richard Hunne was involved in a dispute with the church courts over payment of a mortuary fee for the burial of his infant son. The priest had asked for the burial robe as payment, but Hunne had refused to give this up. In reply to the Church's legal action in the archbishop's court at Lambeth, where the clerical plaintiff won, Hunne brought a counter-suit in King's Bench in 1513, claiming that the Church had breached the statute of *praemunire* (1393) for having exercised a separate spiritual jurisdiction through its church courts.[2] Bishop Fitzjames of London was a conservative defender of the rights of the Church and ordered Hunne's arrest, as well as a search of his house which resulted in the discovery of heretical books. Hunne, while awaiting trial, was imprisoned in the Lollards' Tower of old St Paul's, and there in his cell in December 1514 he was found hanged. The church authorities insisted that Hunne had committed suicide, but a London coroner's jury found that he had been murdered and indicted the bishop's chancellor and two gaolers. Later, one gaoler confessed to the murder and implicated the others. The result was uproar and commotion in the City of London, to such an extent that the affair was picked up by the Parliament of 1515, sparking off a dispute over benefit of clergy (the immunity of the clergy from secular law). The laity supposedly voiced their anticlericalism in no uncertain terms, and later the Hunne case was used as evidence of the depravity of the Church in its wealth, sin and scandal by the arch-anticlerical Simon Fish in his *Supplication for the Beggars* (1528).

However, the original coronial inquest records no longer exist, and the only transcript of the proceedings is an edited version in an anticlerical pamphlet published in 1539. Thus the exact truth is hard to find. Did Hunne commit suicide because he felt that he was losing his heresy case? Did the gaolers kill Hunne through over-energetic interrogation? Whatever the truth, the Hunne affair was not a typical or representative example of profound hatred of the laity for the clergy. Indeed the Hunne case is really the only one of its type.

Colet's criticisms of the clergy were traditional, and unfair. Quarrels over mortuary fees were rare, especially as mortuary fees were frequently waived for the poor. Indeed the whole notion of anticlericalism before the Reformation has been challenged by revisionists. What anticlericalism existed was more common in the capital than in the rest of the country. Also the legal disputes involved in the Hunne affair, namely *praemunire* and benefit of clergy, evaporated fairly quickly and were absent from debates in the Parliament of 1523. Altogether there were not many complaints about absenteeism, pluralism or vice in this period. In the large diocese of Lincoln, for example, it has been shown that between 1514 and 1521 there were only some 25 reported cases of priestly lapses from celibacy in over 1000 parishes, not enough in Haigh's opinion to have caused widespread resentment.[3] The bishops were on balance a worthy and respected group of pastors and administrators. Nor were the priests treated as an alien caste, as in the traditional view, but as fellow-villagers and family members. Indeed, Haigh views anti-clericalism as a consequence of Protestantism rather than as a harbinger of it.

Lollardy

England was not totally Catholic on the eve of the Reformation. The old native heresy of Lollardy still survived. Lollardy was a popular, simplified version of the teachings of the radical Oxford theologian John Wycliffe (*d.* 1384), who had taught many of the same doctrines which later Protestant theologians were to hold: above all, he had rejected the authority of the pope, whom he identified with the Antichrist, transubstantiation, clerical celibacy, pilgrimages, prayers for the dead, and monasticism, and instead he upheld the sole authority of the Bible (which he thought should be read by people in their native tongue) and also the predestination of the saved. He was moreover an Erastian, believing that the Church should have only a moral and spiritual influence with no worldly jurisdiction, wealth or power. However, the great distinction between Wycliffe and the founder of Protestantism, Martin Luther, was that the former did not advance to the latter's mature doctrine of 'justification by faith alone'.

Lollardy was never destined to gain acceptance by the state. The Lancastrian regime supported the bishops in their attempt to extirpate the heresy. After the failure of the Lollard rebellion of 1414, when heresy and treason became entwined, Lollardy lost support in the upper classes, and instead developed into a persecuted underground movement. It never formed a separate denomination, and it did not have a clear set of doctrines or definite creed; but it was always anti-sacramental, with a common-sense rationalism, and anticlerical, with a hatred of tithes to support the despised priesthood.

Lollard groups could be found especially in the Chiltern region of Buckinghamshire, in Kent, Berkshire, Essex and in Coventry, Birmingham and London. Heresy was largely confined to the south of England; the north saw no real Lollardy in the fifteenth century, and the first recorded northern Lollard in the sixteenth century, in 1512, had been converted by an outsider. From 1528 to 1547 there are some 30 noted cases of heresy in the archdiocese of York, and A. G. Dickens has argued that the vast majority of these were new Lollards, a sign that the native heresy was indeed spreading on the eve of the Henrician Reformation.[4] Historians have often argued that Lollards were mainly humble people, especially artisans, craftsmen and small tradesmen, with only a smattering of clergy and professional men thrown in, but recent work has shown that many Lollards were quite well off. Some London Lollards were leading members of liveried companies, and one was the widow of a lord mayor. Lollards could be found in both urban and rural areas, and they probably also had some gentry support because their manuscript Bibles and sermon cycles were preserved by people who had the means and space to store the group's literature. Thus it has been argued by Dickens and J. F. Davis that the old native heresy was still very much alive in England on the eve of the Henrician Reformation and influenced public opinion into going along with the king's actions against the pope.[5]

There can be no doubt that England had an irritating minority of heretics on the eve of the Reformation. The clergy themselves, although they tended to exaggerate the problem, are witnesses to this danger. Dean Colet, despite the fact that Lollards came to hear his Bible-based preaching at St Paul's, warned against their prevalence in 1512: 'We are also nowadays grieved of heretics, men mad with marvellous foolishness.' What the Lollards liked about Colet was his attack on the veneration of images and his emphasis on an inner faith, attitudes which led the extreme conservative Bishop Fitzjames of London to regard Colet himself as a heretic and to bring charges against him. However, revisionists claim that Lollardy was not numerically significant or expanding,[6] and those northern cases referred to by Dickens were essentially linked to new Protestant strands of heresy that were infiltrating the country.[7] Lollard survivalism was thus not a major contributory factor to the Henrician Reformation.

Early Protestants in England

How influential were truly Protestant ideas in creating an atmosphere for change? Certainly Lutheran ideas had penetrated England before 1529. How much did Lutheranism and Lollardy have in common, and were there any connections between the old heresy and the new? The answer seems to be that both groups felt drawn to each other and there were many links between them. The Lollards provided one of the main markets for imported Lutheran books.

Lutheranism proper first appeared in England among London merchants and lawyers, and within university circles, especially at Cambridge. Lutheran works had been imported into England from late 1518, about a year after the initial upheaval in Wittenberg that had started on 31 October 1517 with the nailing up of the 'Ninety Five Theses' by an obscure professor of biblical theology named Martin Luther, inviting discussion on the question of papal indulgences and their efficacy in gaining salvation for purchasers. Other people took up Luther's cause straightaway and the new ideas spread like wildfire in the German lands. It was probably German merchants in London who first imported Lutheran works into England. Certainly the intellectual challenge which they presented found an interested audience. By 1520 Lutheran doctrines had found a home for discussion among students at Cambridge University, at the White Horse tavern in the town, where meetings (known as 'Little Germany') were presided over by Robert Barnes, prior of the Augustinian house there (he belonged to the same order as did Luther). Other Protestants known to have been in Cambridge during the 1520s include Miles Coverdale, Hugh Latimer, Thomas Cranmer, John Frith, John Lambert and Matthew Parker. These university intellectuals often took their message to London and made contact with the reformist 'scripture men' there. The greatest of the early English Lutherans was undoubtedly William Tyndale, an Oxford graduate. Tyndale was the most single-minded of the early radicals, wanting above all to make the Scriptures available in English in printed form; he came as a priest to London in 1523 determined to undertake a translation of the Bible into English and offered his services in this regard to Bishop Tunstall of London, but employment was refused. Tyndale consequently entered the service of the 'scripture man' Humphrey Monmouth, a wealthy cloth merchant, who had heard Tyndale preach in a London church. It was in his London home that Tyndale began his great translation of the New Testament into English. Tyndale did not stay long there but soon went abroad and met Luther in Wittenberg during 1524, with Monmouth sending him an allowance; the great work of translation would be completed in Antwerp, printed in Germany and smuggled into England, to the indignation of the bishops and official church censors. Tyndale also received financial support from members of the Merchant Adventurers in Antwerp, in whose house he was to live for many years. Tyndale's version became basic to all later English translations of the New Testament before the 1960s, including the Authorised Version of James I (1611), mainly because of its avoidance of Latinisms and its essential simplicity. Thus many familiar biblical phrases today derive from Tyndale, including 'fight the good fight,' 'the salt of the earth' and 'prepare ye the way of the Lord'. The Tyndale New Testament became the leading smuggled book of the late 1520s.

A clampdown by the English authorities on the new heresy of Lutheranism had begun as early as 1520, especially in London and the two universities; and in 1521 Wolsey led a ceremonial public burning of Lutheran works outside St Paul's Cathedral. In this charged atmosphere of counter-attack against Luther's prolific output, Henry VIII himself joined the fray and had himself named as the official author of a work in defence of the traditional Catholic sacraments, although in reality Sir Thomas More and others had ghosted it. The pope showed his gratitude by making Henry 'Defender of the Faith'.

The 'traditional' view that the Reformation was both a good thing in itself and thus inevitable has been described as 'Whiggish'. Protestantism has thus been seen as a progressive, individualistic, even capitalistic, movement and an essential rung in the ladder of modernity, in contrast to the decadence of feudal and corporative Catholicism. Whatever one's private thoughts on Protestantism, modern-day revisionist historians of the Reformation argue that Protestantism in the early sixteenth century was neither inevitable nor even likely if one judges by the surviving evidence of popular religious sentiment, rather than by narrowly listening only to the (admittedly clever) enemies of late-medieval Catholicism. In this revisionist account there was no groundswell of opposition that put religious change on the agenda in the first half of the Tudor period; instead the changes are seen purely as the result of high politics – of the king's need to gain his 'divorce' and of the generally unprincipled ambitions and factional rivalry of Tudor politicians. True and deep theological sentiment plays only a small role in this revisionist account. J. J. Scarisbrick's judgement has been echoed by most recent writers: 'on the whole, English men and women did not want the Reformation and most of them were slow to accept it when it came'.[8] No longer is the old Church seen as a hated and extortionate intruder but as a popular institution where the laity had much more of an active role than previously thought. The popularity of the Church can be gauged by the amount of money and gifts people were leaving to it in their wills, which overwhelmingly demonstrate the conservative religiosity of the vast majority of ordinary people, high and low, in early Tudor England. Susan Brigden has revealed that some three-quarters of London wills in the early sixteenth century were thoroughly Catholic in tone and invoke the 'glorious company of heaven' for spiritual assistance; and some half of will-makers asked their parish priest to attend as a witness, demonstrating the close affinity between priest and parishioner in the pre-Reformation period.[9] In northern England nearly 40 per cent of will-makers requested prayers after death, and while figures from elsewhere are lower than this, though always substantial, there are grounds for believing that actual provision of prayers for the dead was much greater than the formal request in wills might suggest.[10] Scarisbrick stresses his conviction that no one had any inkling of what the future held for the Church; there was no intuition of major changes to come – such knowledge was the privilege of only a tiny number of people right at the heart of Henry's government. Indeed even such a nobleman as the Earl of Shrewsbury had not detected how the religious wind was blowing, because when he made his will in August 1537 he left money for thousands of requiem masses to be said to help his soul, as well as bequests to a number of religious houses. However, by the time that his will had undergone probate in 1539 these houses which were to receive the earl's gifts had been dissolved by an Act of Parliament.[11] The fact that Shrewsbury did not suspect that this might happen shows clearly that there was no great popular clamour or campaign for the complete abolition of monasticism, which was to come like a bolt out of the blue. There was no general feeling that old-style Catholicism was on the way out. No one was certain, not even the courtier-politicians locked in factional intrigue with each other.

Such a vision of the immense popularity of the traditional religious system has been confirmed in most recent works, notably Eamon Duffy's *The Stripping of the Altars* (1993). The judgement here is that 'the Reformation was a violent disruption, not the natural fulfilment, of most of what was vigorous in late-medieval piety and religious practice'.[12] Duffy denies that most people felt a sense of alienation from the Church and affirms the essential unity of the Catholic population of England. The Church had taught its flock well, using printing and the plastic arts to get its message across. Printing had not proved an inherent enemy of traditional religion because Catholic books had poured out of the earliest printing presses during the fifteenth century. The notion of 'liturgical alienation' is also attacked by Duffy – the belief that the very barrier of the rood-screen in the parish church divided the clergy and laity in more than one sense, that the laity were only passive spectators of a mystery known only to the priesthood. In fact the laity were more involved than the liturgical separation might at first suggest: the drama of the mass was indeed highlighted by the separation, and those desiring a more intimate mass could always find it on weekdays, especially in small side-chapels. The separating rood-screens might themselves be ordered and made by parishioners. Duffy's denial that liturgical separation in itself led to a sense of alienation seems borne out by the success of the Orthodox churches among the peoples of eastern Europe.

Whether or not one approves of late-medieval Catholicism, it does not look as though there had been enough of a change in public opinion to have made the Reformation inevitable at this date. The evidence points towards there needing to be a major move at the top to make the English change their religious habits – and this was indeed to come through the king's 'Great Matter'.

The break with Rome

The Reformation of the 1530s, with the creation of a schismatical, independent Church of England controlled by the king as supreme head, must be seen as a revolution rather than as the inevitable product of a simple evolutionary process. As a revolution it had to be defended intellectually. The government of Henry VIII could not just say that these changes were necessary or good without trying to prove that they constituted a return to a much purer past. History was seen at the time as being cyclical: it was believed that there had been a golden age in the past from which modern times had deviated with the consequent loss of perfection. No one could brazenly argue that a schism was required just so that Henry could obtain a 'divorce'. Thus the government's problem was to prove that an independent Church of England was part of the divine plan and based on past precedent.

The debate on the intellectual origins of the Reformation has until fairly recently focused on two personalities: Henry VIII himself and his leading minister of the 1530s, Thomas Cromwell. A. F. Pollard thought that the king changed from being a lazy playboy to a serious-minded reformer. Henry VIII 'sought the greatness of England, and he spared no toil in the quest'.[13] The Reformation was part and parcel of Henry's great design for England, a reform that would be popular with the people at large. That notion was challenged in the 1950s by G. R. Elton, who regarded Henry as only a mediocre man without vision. Instead the great revolution in Church and state was the achievement of Thomas Cromwell. Elton attacked Pollard's notion of the unity of the reforming years from 1529 to 1547, and instead argued that the decade of the 1530s was so full of achievement in contrast to the disastrous and barren 1540s which were filled only with war and economic dislocation. Elton's simple explanation for this was that during the 1530s Thomas Cromwell was at the helm and the government pursued a consistent and successful policy in practically every sphere of activity. The only point in common between Pollard and Elton was that they agreed that the year 1529 marked a watershed in the king's reign in that Henry was now forced to think hard. Some recent historiography, however, has challenged this seemingly impregnable view of a watershed. Peter Gwyn, George Bernard and Glyn Redworth have emphasised Henry's eagerness for substantive change right from the start of the reign, with a policy of subjecting the Church to the state. Redworth and Bernard believe that Henry may have amended the coronation oath in 1509 to reduce the independence of the Church.[14] The surviving undated document, however, is more likely to derive from the 1530s. Nevertheless, Gwyn, Bernard and Redworth deny that the year 1529 marks a significant break from the earlier years. Gwyn sees Henry throughout as a powerful, unscrupulous king determined to keep the Church obedient, using Wolsey as his tool.[15] Yet even if one accepts much of this account, it remains true that Henry had acted like a convinced supporter of the papacy. It still required a revolution in thought for Henry to proceed to abandon the pope and the international Catholic Church to which England had been joined since the days of St Augustine of Canterbury in the sixth century.

The making of the Reformation is in many ways the central issue of the reign since upon it so much of our conception of the larger-than-life Henry depends. Elton's theory that Cromwell's was the great brain behind the break with Rome was a brilliant one, provoking historians to reassess the personality and kingship of Henry VIII. But while dominant for a time in the 1960s this interpretation never won universal acceptance, and it was two of Elton's students who provided the empirical basis for its overthrow – namely J. J. Scarisbrick and Graham Nicholson. Scarisbrick, in his mammoth biography of the king, attempted to reinstate Henry VIII as the architect of religious change, though without employing the same reasoning as Pollard's. Scarisbrick was no admirer of Henry VIII; he did nevertheless see the king's scheming mind as being crucial, with Cromwell acting only as a royal instrument. Scarisbrick's concentration on the king is nowadays less important than his evidence, gleaned from the Vatican archives, of new ideas before Cromwell's arrival on the scene. The work of Graham Nicholson revealed that these new ideas emanated not from the king but from an advisory panel of intellectuals. Thus neither Henry nor Cromwell was the single crucial agent of change.

The Reformation Parliament, 1529–36

The legatine court under Cardinal Campeggio opened in June 1529 to hear the king's suit for an annulment of his marriage, but it broke up on 31 July, with the case being revoked to Rome.

Wolsey had failed to gain his master a quick divorce on English soil. Then at the beginning of August Henry made plans to call a Parliament to meet in November. Now a parliamentary meeting so close to the festive season of Christmas must be seen as proof that a crisis had developed. This Parliament was to last on and off down to April 1536: meeting in eight sessions, it would go down in the annals of parliamentary history as the 'Reformation Parliament'.

Traditionally the calling of the Reformation Parliament has been viewed as the opening act in the drama of overthrowing papal power in England. However, nowadays it is rather more difficult to be so certain as to what Henry's real intentions were in calling it. It may have had something to do with plans to disgrace Wolsey, but in the event it was not used for that purpose. Possibly it was summoned in order to cancel Henry's foreign-policy debts incurred by the fallen chancellor. The government certainly had no other legislation to put before the assembly. This first session has become famous for the so-called anticlerical debates. Long regarded as a sign of widespread general hatred of the clergy, these anticlerical outbursts now appear to be the campaign of only specific interest groups against the fallen Wolsey, notably London merchants and common lawyers. Enacted reforms reduced the amount of mortuary and probate fees, and regulated pluralism and non-residence in the Church. Another, more comprehensively anticlerical, petition has recently been noticed, emanating probably from court nobles, but it was not acted upon by the Commons.[16] There was no full-scale attack on the Church at this stage, and it is difficult to see in the desultory reforms a clear royal policy of trying to bully the pope. Thus Parliament met without any real work to do: perhaps Henry was hoping for suggestions! The ministers overseeing policy in the years 1529–31 were hardly politicians of any stature – namely the triumvirate of Suffolk, Norfolk and Wiltshire – but they were certainly hostile to the church hierarchy. Only Lord Chancellor More was a man of intellectual substance, yet he disagreed with the king's wish for a divorce and thus did not play a directing role in affairs.

England was always in a weak position attempting to intimidate foreigners: bullying was easier to achieve at home. In 1530 and 1531 Henry decided to use the statute of *praemunire* as a weapon against the clergy. In 1530 some leading bishops and clerics, most of whom were public supporters of Queen Catherine, were indicted in King's Bench with having breached *praemunire* by acknowledging Wolsey's legatine powers. This prosecution of a select few was then abandoned in favour of indicting the entire clergy of breach of the statute for having exercised a separate spiritual jurisdiction through the ecclesiastical courts. The penalty for *praemunire* was loss of property; and rather than lose their property the Church surrendered early in 1531. The Convocation of Canterbury agreed to pay a fine of £100 000, while York paid up £18 000. Henry also wanted the Church to grant him the clear title of 'supreme head of the Church,' but this was something the clergy refused to do at this stage. Instead, Archbishop Warham suggested a more acceptably vague title of 'only and supreme lord, and as far as the law of Christ allows even supreme head'.

When the Reformation Parliament reassembled in 1531 it embodied the so-called 'Pardon of the Clergy' in a statute. What is one to make of the events of 1530–1? Henry had come to the brink of schism, but then had gone back and merely compromised with the clergy. According to Elton's original theory, by the end of 1531 Henry had devised all of the expedients that he could think of – and these amounted to little more than the old, tired use of *praemunire* – and they had failed miserably. Elton saw the turning-point in the royal fortunes, and a real change in policy, coming in 1532 with Cromwell's acquisition of power. A new policy was then perceived, that of abandoning the pope and asserting the doctrine of the national sovereignty of England. This notion of Cromwell's importance was challenged by Scarisbrick based on his researches in the Vatican archives. This new evidence suggested that Henry's policy changed, not in 1532, but much earlier – in late summer 1530. In 1530, because of Catherine's appeal, the case was revoked to the Church's matrimonial court in Rome, the Rota. This was the last thing that Henry wanted as it effectively guaranteed his defeat. Before late summer 1530 the king had never denied the right of the pope to decide the issue; but now Henry began to question the right of the pope to adjudicate the matter with the statement that no Englishman could be summoned before a foreign court. Thus papal jurisdiction was challenged for the very first time. In September 1530 Henry declared that he had 'no superior on earth' and had 'a pinnacle of dignity'. Also this month, it was claimed that Henry 'was absolute both as Emperor and Pope in his own kingdom'. At about the same time Henry told his agents in Rome to locate evidence in the papal archives to confirm what he termed his 'authority imperial' – that is, evidence to prove that the King of England was not subject to the pope for anything except heresy. Here essentially is the idea of 'empire' as later embodied in the Act of Appeals. However, the agents had to report no luck in their search for such evidence: earlier popes had recognised no such imperial authority vested in English kings. Yet Henry's claim to an imperial authority was not to be so easily abandoned. The Duke of Norfolk insisted on the claim in a conversation with the emperor's ambassador in 1531.

Scarisbrick showed that from the late summer of 1530 onwards Henry began to claim the three essential ingredients of the later full royal supremacy over the Church of 1533: first, no obedience to the pope (from 1530); second, a God-given cure of souls (from 1531); and 'erastianism' (from 1531).[17] The last two ingredients were seen in the *praemunire* indictment of the clergy in 1531. Although the Church in that incident was able to modify the king's title of supreme head with the phrase 'as far as the law of Christ allows', Henry himself was not so content with the clerical interpretation of the new title's meaninglessness. In a letter Henry claimed to be head of the clergy in more than purely temporal things: for, says the king, 'all spiritual things, by reason whereof may arise bodily trouble and inquietation, be necessarily included in a prince's power'.[18] Henry was claiming jurisdictional power over the Church, but not the spiritual power of holy orders.

The work of Graham Nicholson supports Scarisbrick's argument for a major change of policy from midsummer 1530, rather than in 1532, but this recent work gets away from the alternatives of the 'King or Minister' debate.[19] Nicholson discovered a manuscript book of intellectual arguments to be used by the king in prosecuting his campaign for a divorce: this *Collectanea Satis Copiosa* ('Sufficiently Full Collections') was compiled in 1530. It is not clear who was primarily responsible for collating this collection, but the best opinion rests on Edward Foxe and Thomas Cranmer. There is no doubt that there was a 'think-tank' of clergy at Court from 1529 onwards looking for new concepts that Henry could use. Between 1529 and 1530 the royal team dealt with arguments for the divorce, but in 1530 they shifted their interest to the wider ground of Church–state relations. The *Collectanea* (finished by September 1530) was the fruit of this new initiative; and all of the ideas of the royal supremacy and concept of 'empire' are contained within this volume of arguments. It is most probable that Cranmer and Foxe, not Cromwell, were responsible for the new ideas that led straight to 1533.[20]

Whatever his exact role, Thomas Cromwell certainly had made a name for himself in the second session of the Reformation Parliament in 1531, and as a reward was invited into the inner circle of the Council in December. According to Elton, the first clear evidence of new thinking came in the third session of the Parliament which began in January 1532, when for the first time a clear government legislative programme can be detected. Among the various official measures was the first major attack on the papacy – in the first bill of Annates (fees payable to Rome each time a new bishop or abbot was appointed). The aim of this bill was to stop these payments; furthermore, if the pope were to react by prohibiting the appointment of bishops and abbots, then they would be consecrated in England without reference to Rome. The Annates bill provoked a great deal of opposition in both the Lords and the Commons. Henry had to attend Parliament in person to secure the bill's passing, but only after the first ever recorded division in the House of Commons. The spiritual peers in the Lords voted as a bloc against the bill, but many temporal peers were also unhappy with it. Against this display of opposition the government had to work out a compromise under which a clause was inserted in the bill suspending its provisions until later confirmation by royal letters patent. In this modified form the measure was passed. What was behind this show of opposition? There was evidently a large group who wanted to maintain the independence of the Church. We now know that Lord Chancellor More, while not opposing the government publicly, was secretly fomenting opposition within the Commons, especially employing Sir George Throckmorton as his spokesman there.

The second important event in the third parliamentary session of 1532 was a renewed attack on clerical abuses, culminating in the so-called 'Submission of the Clergy' in May. Although it is not absolutely clear, it looks as though Cromwell had retained a draft of those various Commons complaints, especially in regard to ecclesiastical jurisdiction, voiced in the first session back at the end of 1529. Cromwell now took up this list of grievances and piloted through the Commons what became known as 'The Supplication against the Ordinaries' (i.e. bishops), and presented the document to the king. Henry then passed it on to Archbishop Warham for the clergy's reply. Convocation completely rejected these charges, but Henry announced that he found the clergy's reply 'very slender' or unconvincing, which was an open invitation for the Commons to attack the Church. Henry threatened to have canon law put under examination by a commission of equal numbers of clergy and laymen. Fearing a lay attack on canon law, the Church agreed to submit personally to the king and place itself on his mercy: this was the non-parliamentary 'Submission of the Clergy'. By this document the Church surrendered ecclesiastical law into the hands of the king, as a result of which from May 1532 onwards Henry VIII became supreme legislator for the Church in England: it was he, not the pope, who would decide what laws the Church would maintain.

The Reformation began in earnest in 1533. Some historians suggest that the final decision to throw out papal power was the result quite simply of Anne Boleyn's pregnancy. She had conceived during December 1532, and she married Henry the following month. Now one must bear in mind that since 1527 at least when Henry had begun courting her Anne had refused to go to bed with him; she did not want to end up as a discarded mistress, like her elder sister Mary, who had already been the king's lover. Anne wanted to be queen. So her decision to go to bed with Henry towards the end of 1532 certainly denotes a change of policy on her part. Did she surrender because of Henry's badgering (unlikely), or was it because she now knew she would be queen? Certainly once the pregnancy had been confirmed it was vital for the couple to be legally married so that the child's position would be totally clear; there would be a possibility of civil war if the first son were born illegitimate and a later one legitimate. Elton argued that Anne's pregnancy was the result, the first fruit, of the new policy and the assurances of Cromwell that all would be well. The death of Archbishop

Warham in August 1532 certainly allowed the next stage to proceed more easily, but it seems most unlikely that Henry was simply waiting for him to expire.[21]

The new policy was evident in the Act in restraint of Appeals of March 1533, a bill which Cromwell had been working on since the previous September. This Act, which Elton described as Cromwell's 'masterpiece in statute making,' prevented appeals in legal cases, with the notable exception of heresy issues, from going outside the realm. Queen Catherine's appeal to the Rota was now invalid. The famous preamble to the Act sums up the new political philosophy:

> Where by divers sundry old authentic histories and chronicles it is manifestly declared and expressed that this realm of England is an empire, governed by one supreme head and king having the dignity and royal estate of the imperial crown of the same. . . .

These were, of course, blatant untruths. No 'old authentic histories and chronicles' had been found supporting Henry's imperial pretensions – but no matter. The king's position as supreme head of the Church was thrown in without any attempt to defend its inclusion or its revolutionary import. In an age that found it hard to justify change or novelty, recourse had to be made to the past, in this case a fictitious past. The Act is significant for its assertion of England's independence and sovereignty as an 'empire'. Previously kings had referred to themselves as emperors, but now the term 'empire' was used for a piece of territory without reference to foreign conquests to denote national autonomy or sovereignty. Elton regarded this usage as very novel, the use of 'empire' rather than of emperor. There certainly seems to be a new element introduced into political discussion by it, even though the word had been used shortly before. Bishop Tunstall in 1517, in a letter to the king regarding the next election for the Holy Roman Empire, had stated that 'the crown of England is an empire of itself'. But Tunstall was here referring to England's freedom from the Holy Roman Empire, not from the papacy. The fact that appeals to Rome on heresy questions remained open suggests that the king himself had not decided irrevocably on a split with the pope.

Between 1534 and 1536 Cromwell drafted a series of statutes which completed the policy outlined in the Act against Appeals. Most important were the second (confirmatory) Act of Annates; the First Act of Succession, which bastardised the Princess Mary (now demoted to Lady Mary), vested the succession in the heirs of Henry and Anne, and included an oath to be taken by all adult males; the Act of Supremacy, which worked out in greater detail the king's claim to the headship first mentioned in the Act against Appeals. The Act did not grant or create the supremacy; the theory was that this was personal to the monarch and a trust from God. All that Parliament could do was to advertise and enforce this ancient royal right of which English kings had been kept in ignorance by successive popes. The Act of Supremacy cut all links to Rome by prohibiting even appeals in heresy cases. The Treasons Act made it a treasonable offence to call the king a heretic or a usurper. The Convocations of Canterbury and York were forced to declare that the pope had no more jurisdiction in England than any other foreign bishop.

The Church of England, 1536–40

St Augustine of Hippo described heresy as 'schism grown old'. The Henrician Church of England was schismatic, but did it leave the path of Catholic orthodoxy and become heretical? Henry, most historians agree, was conservative doctrinally, and he certainly did not break with the pope in order to embrace Protestantism. Henry's own religious attitudes and his theological grasp have been debated by historians, but still no clear picture emerges. Did Henry know what he wanted or was he led in different directions by factional intrigue? Of course, Henry had got his 'divorce' solely by giving power and influence to the radical group, and these men wanted religious change in a Protestant direction. They could not, of course, own up to this because Henry remained a staunch anti-Protestant and continued to burn those who adhered to heresy. Yet theological modifications were made, resulting both from the pressure of radicals, such as Cromwell and Cranmer, and from diplomatic moves in an attempt to get the support of German Protestants against the Habsburg emperor, who was threatening invasion.

The Church was administered on behalf of the king by Cromwell in his capacity as vice-gerent in spirituals, which like Wolsey's old legatine powers allowed him to govern the two English provinces of York and Canterbury. Cromwell used his powers to appoint reforming bishops, and there were nine such in the years before 1536, including Nicholas Shaxton, Hugh Latimer and Edward Foxe. The earliest modifications in a Protestant direction that the radicals were able to secure came in the Ten Articles of mid-1536, the very first Anglican confession of faith. While it taught a largely traditional Catholicism, only three sacraments were emphasised, namely baptism, penance and the eucharist (or holy communion), while ignoring the four other traditional sacraments of marriage, holy orders, confirmation and the last rites. There was also much vagueness on eucharistic theology, which could be read in a Catholic or Lutheran way (the term transubstantiation being avoided); either way the Real Presence of Christ in the sacrament was reaffirmed. There was also studied ambiguity in the statement on justification (or salvation). Purgatory was defended although specific papal teachings on it were criticised (indulgences had already been banned by proclamation). Also the superstitious use of images was attacked, though not images in themselves. Then in Cromwell's first Ecclesiastical Injunctions of August 1536 the clergy were urged to teach the Lord's Prayer, the Ten Commandments and the Creed to their parishioners in English. These Injunctions denied the need for pilgrimages and attacked the whole cult of relics.

More substantially, there appeared the *Bishops' Book* (or *Institution of a Christian Man*) in September 1537, the work of the bishops led by Foxe and Cranmer, and corrected by the king only after publication. The king's attention had been focused on Jane Seymour's pregnancy and he had given no thought to the compilation of the work. The political background was the need to gain German Lutheran diplomatic support. The *Bishops' Book* included an explanation of the Nicene Creed, the Ten Commandments, the Lord's Prayer, the Hail Mary and all the seven sacraments. However, three of the sacraments (baptism, penance and the eucharist) were deemed more important than the others. The book moved away from papal Catholicism in two ways: transubstantiation was not defined as being obligatory (a telling omission) and the notion of the sacrifice of the mass was ignored.

Furthermore, the main work of the priest was now seen to be preaching rather than administering the sacraments. These changes were small but very significant, and show the Protestant thrust behind the radicals at Court. The king himself did not read the work until December 1537, after the death of Queen Jane, when he had spare time. Henry's annotations to the *Bishops' Book* suggest that Henry was a rather poor theologian without even a firm grasp on traditional Catholicism. However, he certainly fancied himself in the role and made over 100 corrections – 'a monument to his theological enthusiasm'.[22] Henry was against Lutheran justification (or salvation) by faith alone and preferred almost Pelagian ideas of meriting salvation, long condemned by the Church as heretical. Where the book emphasised three superior sacraments, Henry wanted the sacrament of marriage added to that more essential group! He also wanted the Tenth Commandment ('Thou shalt not covet thy neighbour's wife') to be extended, to include the phrase 'without due recompense'! Even more radically, Henry seems not to have regarded holy orders as something special: he wanted the word 'holy' dropped as it made the clergy into a separate caste. Henry's religious views are hard to reconcile, and seem to have been rather shifting and incoherent.

Cromwell's Second Injunctions (September 1538) condemned the cult of relics and began the campaign to destroy superstitious relics and shrines, and stated that the Bible was the only source of religious truth, a copy of which in English had to be placed in every parish church by next Easter. Furthermore, parish priests were to start keeping registers of baptisms, marriages and deaths. Yet any trend towards true Protestantism was soon to be curbed. Henry's innate conservatism was revealed in his personal involvement in the condemnation of John Lambert's eucharistic heresy in November 1538, with a proclamation reaffirming the Real Presence and the necessity of clerical celibacy; another proclamation in February 1539 vindicated many traditional customs and ceremonies, including creeping to the cross on Good Friday. The international situation was also looking menacing with the *rapprochement* between France and the Empire; thus Henry was more eager to appear orthodox to his brother rulers and not as the protector of heretics. The Parliament of 1539 was induced to pass the Act of Six Articles, which included the reaffirmation of transubstantiation, the denial of which now led to death without the customary opportunity to recant; one of those who suffered was the 15-year-old Richard Mekins despite his recantation. Also confirmed in the Act were communion in only one kind, auricular confession, private masses, clerical vows and a celibate clergy. But this was not a complete return to the past because many reformist attitudes were to remain, such as the dislike of the cult of relics and pilgrimages.

The dissolution of the monasteries, 1536–40

Henry VIII did not agree to the dissolution of the monastic system for fundamental religious reasons, except in so far as the monastic orders belonged to an international system. Apart from a small number of monks who had opposed the break with Rome, notably the Carthusians of the London Charterhouse, the Observant Franciscans and the Bridgettines, the heads of religious houses fell into line with the government's plans. The monks proved not to be great defenders of the papacy when the need arose.

Although the idea of a partial monastic dissolution was possibly first aired by conservative nobles in 1529, the push for the change in the mid-1530s came from the radicals led by Cromwell, who had religious – Protestant – reasons for wanting the end of a system that was intrinsically Catholic and wedded to the notion of prayers for the dead: one of the major tasks of monks was to pray for the souls of the founders and supporters of the individual monastic houses. Such objections meant nothing to the king, who continued to believe in the mediation of the saints and prayers for the dead. Henry was won over solely by the financial rewards accruing from the confiscation of monastic estates and buildings. From the government's point of view there was an urgent need to make the English state financially viable to defend itself from all possible enemies. Having briefly considered stealing episcopal lands, Cromwell decided that the easier alternative would be to target the monasteries, even though Parliament had shown its opposition in 1534 to disendowing them. Cromwell had learned something of monastic dissolution from his time serving Wolsey, and he got under way

in 1535 that comprehensive valuation of all church properties
and offices known as the *Valor Ecclesiasticus* (Ecclesiastical Valuation). This was undoubtedly an amazing administrative achievement. Armed with this information Cromwell then proceeded
against the monasteries with a formal visitation, ostensibly to
discover the objective facts but in reality to scrape together
enough damning evidence to justify dissolution.

Any sense of a revolutionary wrenching away from the past was
to be blunted or smoothed over by the decision initially to dissolve only the smaller religious houses with incomes of less than
£200 p.a. Some 400 or so of the 800 or so houses were affected by
this line of demarcation, but 70–80 secured exemption by offering money, while the government made soothing and reassuring
noises to surviving houses, where 'thanks be to God, religion is
right well kept and observed'. Those monks ejected in 1536 were
given the choice of becoming secular priests or joining a larger
house of the same order. Cromwell's faction seems to have been
determined on the utter destruction of monasticism, and the
erection of the court of augmentations to receive the proceeds
from the closed houses indicates a long-term strategy. However,
the king probably did not realise this: hence his refoundation of a
dissolved house in December 1537. The radicals' strategy seems
to have been one of stealth – 'little by little, not suddenly,' as
Cromwell himself put it.

The final phase began in November 1537 with the first of the
voluntary surrenders that would lead to to the closure of all
houses by 1540. In the process some 9000 monks plus their
servants and some 2000 nuns were turfed out to make a new
life for themselves. Although the great age of monasticism had
long gone and the religious life was not attracting the large
numbers it once had, monasticism was still a lively force and
there were more men in religious vocations than employed as
secular beneficed clergy (about 8000). The government's method
of proceeding was very clever: abbots were bought off with large
pensions of £100 p.a. plus as an inducement to lead their respective houses into quiet surrender. Only three abbots resisted (those
of Glastonbury, Reading and Colchester), and were murdered at
their houses; all the others acquiesced quietly. Ordinary monks
fared less well financially, however, with only a small pension of
£5–10 p.a.; but they could find other better paid work in the

Church (and forgo their pension). Of the male religious only the friars received no pensions (but a small cash handout). Nuns also did very badly, receiving only £2 p.a. but with no prospects at all of paid work within the Church. Moreover, they were not allowed to forget their vow of celibacy (always a tender point with the king) and marry. The new life of the former nuns would thus be a desperate fight with poverty, relieved only by being welcomed back into the old family home. Much of medieval life disappeared with the destruction of the monasteries. While many art treasures were rescued and given new homes, so much was lost or irreparably vandalised. The king pocketed the revenues from the forfeited monasteries; this could be viewed as an act of theft since most houses had had private founders or benefactors.

The acquisition of so much monastic land (about three times the value of the royal estates) meant that potentially the monarchy was so rich the king might become a tyrant, never needing to call Parliament again for supply. Cromwell had no wish to create a despotism, but he probably wanted a financially strong monarchy. However, the long-term beneficiaries of the dissolution would not be the Crown but the gentry, because the lands were soon transferred by lease or sale to those gentry who had the ready cash. Because so much land flooded the market it became a buyer's paradise with low prices. The resale of ex-monastic land to the gentry would within a short time represent the largest transfer of land since the Norman Conquest. There was thus a revolution in landholding but it was not accompanied by social revolution since the well-entrenched gentry were the group who bought up the new offerings, thus consolidating their own social supremacy. By 1547 half of the monastic estates had gone to the gentry; by Elizabeth's reign only a quarter remained in royal hands. From the Crown's long-term point of view the whole business was very poorly managed.

Opposition and the Pilgrimage of Grace

The massive changes in religion provoked little overt opposition from leading churchmen after 1532. A group around the supposed visionary Elizabeth Barton had tried to warn the king against changes. Only Fisher among the bishops refused the king's new title of supreme head, and in the religious orders only some Carthusians, Observant Franciscans and Bridgettines were prepared to sacrifice their lives. Among the governing secular elite only Sir Thomas More stood out as a fervent champion of the old model of the Church international; he was the most famous lay victim, a humanist scholar of international renown, but sacrificed by Henry VIII because he was an impediment to his goal. More had resigned in May 1532, the day after the 'Submission'. He was later imprisoned for refusing the oath of succession: he had conceded that Parliament could change the succession, but the oath also assumed agreement with all other legislation of the Reformation Parliament. He was condemned on the perjured evidence of Richard Rich that he had spoken out against the royal supremacy, although he had tried to retain his life by a studied silence on the subject. After condemnation More made clear his view that no single country could make a law 'disagreeable with the general law of Christ's universal Catholic Church'. More was thus a Catholic universalist, not the upholder of the autonomy of the modern state – in stark contrast to Cromwell and his group. More was condemned for supporting papal supremacy, although what this exactly involved, beyond the need for the pope as the guarantor of the universality of the Church, is unclear.

The amount of opposition to the Henrician Reformation before the monastic dissolution was in general small. However, not all was smooth sailing and the government had to face in Lincolnshire, Yorkshire and six other northern counties the largest peasant uprising since 1381 – the rebellion known as the Pilgrimage of Grace. This complex rebellion has sparked much debate as to its real leaders and their ambitions. Were the major aims truly as religious as they seem, or more secular? Was it a spontaneous peasant rebellion or a neo-feudal revolt controlled by the aristocracy? The traditional interpretation of a spontaneous religious uprising of the commons against the government's religious innovations has been restated by Scarisbrick.[23] But A. G. Dickens argued against the primacy of religion in favour of more secular, economic ones.[24] G. R. Elton questioned the widespread nature of the rebellion, and detected the key to the problem in factional politics, arguing that it was a crisis manufactured by the Aragonese group after their defeat at Court by Cromwell.[25] Most recently, Michael Bush has viewed it as a general uprising by all groups against religious changes and government innovations.[26]

Among the common people trouble began in Lincolnshire in early October 1536 at a time when three different commissions had been roaming the shire: one dissolving the smaller monasteries, a second assessing taxpayers for the parliamentary subsidy (unusual in time of peace) and a third to investigate the quality of the clergy. Many rumours were circulating: that all valuable church plate would be confiscated from parish churches, indeed that parish churches might be dissolved, and that new taxes were proposed on christenings and burials, as well as on horned cattle. All these fears propelled a small insurrection that began at Louth on 2 October which soon swelled to about 3000 insurgents. What seems to have started as a genuinely spontaneous reaction to the infiltration of government commissioners was soon taken over by members of the local gentry, and with their support rebel numbers increased to around 10 000. A banner was designed showing the Five Wounds of Christ; other symbols were a chalice (probably representing their fears over church plate), a plough (symbolising fears over enclosing of arable land for sheep farming), and a horn (denoting the rumour of a proposed tax on horned cattle). The rebels took an oath to be true to God, Christ's Catholic Church, the king and the commons. Whether the gentry were a part of a conspiracy from the first, or whether they jumped on a convenient bandwagon, or were forced in against their wills, has been a matter of much debate; but this first stage ended when the Lincolnshire gentry withdrew their support on hearing that the Duke of Suffolk was drawing near at the head of an army to crush them.

Although tempers were cooling in Lincolnshire they were flaring up in neighbouring Yorkshire, where the lawyer Robert Aske put himself at the head of a movement designed to defend the Holy Church. Now he raised men in Yorkshire, and the gentry soon joined in. Some 10 000 men marched into the city of York on 16 October. The rebellion was viewed by Aske specifically as a 'Pilgrimage'. He drew up an oath (in imitation of the oath of supremacy) for the rebels, pledging to fight for the Church and for the removal of evil royal officials. The overwhelming strength of the Pilgrims forced the government to negotiate with them. On 3 December the king announced a general pardon for those who had taken up arms, promised a Parliament that would discuss their grievances, and in particular an overturning on the policy of monastic dissolution. It looked as though the rebels had got their way. Aske declared his loyalty to the king and told his men to return to their homes.

It is impossible to say what might have ensued had this been the end of the affair: Henry might have decided on a rethinking of his policies towards a general pacification, but it would have been more in character for him to have bided his time waiting for an opportune moment for revenge. The latter is certainly what (the Protestant) Sir Francis Bigod believed: he thought that the promises of the king and Norfolk were false, and in January 1537 in the East Riding of Yorkshire Bigod led an unsuccessful attempt to capture Scarborough and Hull. This time, despite peasant support, the gentry remained aloof, and the government's reaction was the clear one of ending the rebels' threat once and for all. The Duke of Norfolk declared martial law, and rebels were summarily hanged in Carlisle and the villages of Cumberland. Among the 179 people executed were Lord Darcy, Lord Hussey, Bigod, Aske and Sir Thomas Percy. The aftermath of the rebellion was a reorganisation of the government in the north: the power of the Percy family was broken, and the council of the north was reformed. Michael Bush has suggested that the Pilgrimage was not a total failure but indeed successful in preventing further theological change in Henry's reign.[27]

The English Bible

The most important, and long-lasting, of the positive achievements of the radical group at Court in the 1530s was undoubtedly the publication of the Bible in English. This was the work of English Lutherans patronised by Cromwell. As early as 1534 the Convocation of Canterbury had been influenced to petition the king for the Scriptures in English. The first complete English Bible was the work of Miles Coverdale, the former Augustinian friar and follower of Barnes at Cambridge. Coverdale had fled abroad and in exile had produced his translation which he dedicated to the king. Coverdale did not read Hebrew so that he had to rely on a Catholic Latin translation of the Old Testament for his English version, but he knew German and was influenced by Luther's German Bible. Henry VIII was persuaded to allow publication of this Bible, which was reprinted at Southwark. This Coverdale Bible was to have been placed in every parish church by the Ecclesiastical Injunctions of 1536, but this arrangement was abandoned with the overthrow of Anne Boleyn and her reformist faction in May. Another English Bible was produced in Europe shortly afterwards, the 'Matthew Bible', the work of John Rogers, who used the pseudonym of Thomas Matthew to avoid Tyndale's fate. This too was licensed by Cromwell for publication within the kingdom. Both of these Bibles were inspired and heavily influenced by Tyndale's New Testament. Then finally, in 1539, appeared the *Great Bible* of Henry VIII, an official translation that had been called for by the Articles of 1538 which ordered that a copy should be placed in every parish church. This new version was based on the previous two. The title page showed Henry receiving holy writ directly from God and passing it down to the bishops and through them to the jubilant common people. The publication of the *Great Bible* was the high-water mark of radical success at the Henrician Court. The radicals would soon fall from power and their leader removed; but despite Cromwell's execution and the subsequent ascendancy of religious conservatives the English Bible would remain as his greatest legacy to the English people.

The Church of England, 1540–7

The return to conservatism in the Act of Six Articles, underlined by the victory of the conservative faction at Court, was further clarified by the *King's Book* of 1543 (a revision of the earlier *Bishops' Book*), which now taught transubstantiation and held the teachings of the Early Church commensurate with those of Scripture as authority for belief. Prayers for the dead were defended, although papal teachings on the expiatory nature of purgatory were criticised, in views reminiscent of those of the Orthodox Church. There was no leap to Protestantism, and Henry's later years have been seen as a period of reformed Catholicism. The

English Bible was to remain, although the conservatives secured an Act to limit its sale to gentlemen in 1543. No new vice-gerent in spirituals was appointed after Cromwell's fall, which suggests that the king contemplated no further reforms. The king himself was adamant for orthodoxy and spurred on a vicious campaign against heretics as late as 1546. Doctor Edward Crome, who had denied the sacrifice of the mass and prayers for the dead, was forced to recant, while two London heretics were burned, the young Anne Askew and John Lascelles, for denying transubstantiation.

Some historians have claimed that, despite this drive against heresy, Henry VIII at the very end of his life was contemplating further reformation. For example, during the making of the peace treaty with France in 1546 Henry urged Francis I to throw out the pope and to convert the mass into a non-Catholic communion service. Second, there is the fact that Henry chose to entrust the tutorship of his son Prince Edward to three Protestants: John Cheke, Dr Richard Coxe and Anthony Cooke. Third, there was the alleged commission to Cranmer to peruse certain liturgical books and to change the sacrificial character of the mass, replacing it with a more Protestant kind of communion service. Fourth, there was an Act which in 1545 aimed to dissolve the chantries (endowments to support prayers for the dead). Add to all this fact that leading conservatives like Gardiner and Norfolk were absent from the Regency council to govern for his young successor, and that possibly the king handed the will personally to the reformist Edward Seymour (Hertford), and a good case can be made out for a major change of religious direction at the very end of Henry's reign. However, such a case disintegrates when each argument is individually scrutinised. The stories of the French treaty and the commission to reform the liturgy come from Cranmer himself in the reign of Edward VI, when he was certainly claiming respectable ancestry for his later reforms. Prince Edward's tutors were not known as Protestants while the old king lived: indeed Coxe had been assigned the task of ensuring Dr Crome's recantation. The attack on chantries had, like the dissolution of the monasteries, only a financial motive not a religious one in the king's mind. The absence of Gardiner and Norfolk from the Regency council owed little to their religious views, while the domination of

Seymour and the reformers at most can be seen as a guarantee in Henry's mind of the continuation of the royal supremacy. If the final document of the reign is anything to go by, namely the king's last will and testament, that remains a solid pointer to Henry's innate conservatism: it opens with the call for the help 'of God and of the glorious and blessed virgin Our Lady Saint Mary and of the holy company of heaven'. This Catholic preamble is followed with arrangements for thousands of requiem masses to be said for the dead king's soul, which suggest he had not lost his fear of purgation after death. Henry was never a visionary and it is very doubtful if he foresaw any major changes in the religious complexion of his country.

5 Mid-Tudor Turbulence, 1547–58: Edward VI and Mary I

The Duke of Somerset and the protectorate

When Henry VIII died during the night of 28 January 1547 in the arms of Archbishop Cranmer, he was succeeded by his nine-year-old son Edward VI, whose reign of six years would be one filled with crisis and drama because he would remain a puppet-king with real power being wielded by ambitious nobles, whose designs threatened the stability of the state. Such a minority would be an interruption to over half a century of strong Tudor rule and an invitation to reopen the wounds of civil war. Yet despite a great deal of tension at the top, England would not descend into domestic strife, owing to the effectiveness of Tudor propaganda warning of the evils of chaos, to the demilitarising process within the nobility, and to the material self-interest of the ruling class.

After Henry VIII's death, the changeover in power was effected smoothly and effectively, thanks to the length of time taken by the factional plotters to plan their moves under the expert management of William Paget. The conspirators kept news of Henry's death a secret for three days before being announced in Parliament. In the meantime Edward Seymour, Earl of Hertford had taken possession of young Edward and brought him to the Tower, where at a council meeting on 31 January, Seymour was made protector of the realm and governor of the king's person by a majority of the council. Only a small number opposed it, grouped around Wriothesley. But the general consensus seems to have been voiced by the conservative Sir Anthony Browne that a protectorate was 'the surest kind of government and most fit for this commonwealth'. This majority decision could be seen as being in conformity with Henry's will. However, the will would be overthrown on 12 March 1547 when, with new letters patent from Edward VI, Seymour as lord protector was given full powers to appoint his own council. This was claimed to be in accord with Henry's final wishes, and was later endorsed by Parliament.

Thus after 12 March Edward Seymour could rule like a king, and the council's power diminished to such an extent that it became nothing more than a rubber stamp for Seymour's decisions. Before the establishment of the protectorate in March, there had been a scramble for rewards by the conspirators. The will had included a gifts clause, allowing the council to confer those honours and rewards which Henry himself supposedly had not had time to deal with. This clause was probably completely phoney, but it justified the distribution of titles and rewards. In February 1547, Seymour became Duke of Somerset, William Parr Marquis of Northampton, Thomas Wriothesley became Earl of Southampton, Sir Richard Rich Baron Rich and John Dudley became Earl of Warwick. Wriothesley did not survive long at the top and was dropped from the council on 6 March, essentially because of his dislike of the protectorate. Thereafter the privy council went into a decline with the lord protector governing through his own household council. Somerset's brother-in-law Sir Michael Stanhope was made chief gentleman of Edward's privy chamber and the custodian of the king's dry stamp; Edward's signature was not a sufficent warrant without also the application of the dry stamp, which rendered Somerset all-powerful. This was resented by his brother Thomas Seymour, who over the next 18 months conspired against him, trying to build up an affinity in the country and followers in Parliament, and seemingly prepared to kidnap Edward VI and Princess Elizabeth, thus fomenting civil war.

Somerset ruled the kingdom as lord protector until October 1549, and in that time he acquired a reputation as 'the good duke', trusted, if not revered, by the common people. On the basis of Somerset's fame in his own day, A. F. Pollard painted a portrait of him as a liberal reformer, a champion of the people, an enlightened idealist well in advance of his own day and surrounded by a far-seeing 'party' of social reformers, 'the commonwealth men' – a man who was brought down by greedy, selfish colleagues.[1] Pollard's view of the enlightened Somerset survived for some 70 years, and was last repeated in the major two-volume

study of the reign by W. K. Jordan (1968–70).[2] But the ortho-
doxy was completely demolished by M L. Bush's *The Government
Policy of Protector Somerset* (1975), and Dale Hoak's *The King's
Council in the Reign of Edward VI* (1976).

It is now clear that Somerset was more in the mould of a
normal sixteenth-century politician – tough and grasping –
rather than being a modern idealist born ahead of his time in
the way that Pollard depicted him. Somerset's supposed idealism
was to a large extent based on the great Act of Repeal in his first
Parliament (which met in November 1547). This involved the
wholesale repeal of Henry VIII's treason legislation (with only
the denial of the royal supremacy itself and opposition to the
third Act of Succession remaining as treason) as well as other
legislation including the Act of Six Articles and the 'despotic' Act
of Proclamations. Pollard concluded erroneously from this that
'the Protector was a believer in constitutional freedom'. Yet even
if true, it was unwise to pull down all the barriers against anarchy
at this critical stage as it could stimulate demand for further
change and cause greater instability – a point actually made by
Paget to Somerset: 'Then [under Henry VIII] all things were too
straight and now they are too loose.' However, it was not really an
experiment in liberty at all. It was partly an attempt to gain
popularity for the new regime while making concessions to the
minority of radicals who were already campaigning for change;
but more importantly the Act of Repeal was viewed as necessary if
new policies were to be undertaken, especially in religion. Bishop
Gardiner had already told Somerset that there could be no religious innovations as long as the Henrician legislation was still in
force. The Act of Proclamations of 1539 was repealed not because
that measure had attempted to bring in despotism (which it had
not) but because Somerset aimed to use proclamations autocratically himself, and the 1539 Act had laid down that proclamations
needed majority council support. Gone therefore is the great Act
of Repeal as the evidential basis for Somerset's 'idealism'.

The beginnings of the Protestant Reformation, 1547–9

Somerset's regime is notable for the introduction of Protestantism, albeit in a moderate form. Somerset was a genuine

Protestant who corresponded with the Swiss reformer John Calvin, and who surrounded himself with Protestant converts, but his exact religious views are difficult to pinpoint. Somerset clearly wished to move away from Henricianism. On Henry VIII's death the services of the English Church were still in Latin. However, the new government was determined on change, and above all on the use of English in worship, while Protestant agitators were demanding reforms and ridiculing the mass. By the 1547 Church Injunctions the Gospel and Epistle were to be read in English during the Latin Mass. Also in 1547 the *Book of Homilies* (or sermons) was issued which included an exposition of the Lutheran doctrine of justification (or salvation) by faith alone:

> And this justification or righteousness, which we so receive by God's mercy, and Christ's merits, embraced by faith, is taken, accepted, and allowed of God, for our perfect and full justification.

When Parliament met, an Act against Revilers of the Sacrament was passed which tried to prevent public disputation over the mass but allowed also for communion in both bread and wine during mass (rather than just bread for the laity as previously). The Act for the dissolution of the chantries meant theologically the end of prayers for the dead, a measure which encountered some stiff opposition in the Commons. Then in 1548 some distinctive Catholic practices were abolished: candles at Candlemas, palms on Palm Sunday, ashes on Ash Wednesday, the veneration of the cross on Good Friday; holy water stoups and images in churches were all to be removed. In the same year *The Order of the Communion* was issued – a booklet which supplied the English words for use in the Latin mass at the distribution of bread and wine to the laity in realisation of the Act of 1547 for double communion.

Finally in 1549 the first Prayer Book was published – the great achievement of Thomas Cranmer whose beautiful language made it a milestone in the history of the English language. It rested on an Act of Parliament and not simply on the authority of the Supreme Head, and never seems to have been formally examined in Convocation. The book's very title was important: 'The book of Common Prayer and administration of the

Sacraments and other rites and ceremonies of the church: after the use of the Church of England.' 'The Book' signified for the first time that there was a comprehensive collection of church services in one volume, replacing five different medieval books. Only the ordination of priests was reserved for a separate volume, to be published a year later (the Ordinal of 1550). The phrase 'after the use of the Church of England' meant that there was to be liturgical uniformity rather than the medieval diversity of service books (or uses); previously different parts of England had their own liturgies – such as the uses of Salisbury and Lincoln. Now every priest in every church throughout the realm was to use the same liturgy, which represented a very important development for the growth of a national state Church, as well as helping to break down dialect barriers and creating a national English language.

Theologically it is difficult to interpret the first Prayer Book. The communion service, 'commonly called the mass', was unique in Reformation Europe to follow the general structure of the old Latin mass – although now of course in English. Nevertheless, the elevation of the host (bread and wine) was forbidden, thus denying the Catholic concept of the sacrifice of the mass: instead there was now only 'a sacrifice of praise and thanksgiving'. It was also ambiguous on the heavily debated nature of Christ's presence in the bread and wine. There was a move away from transubstantiation when the words of the consecration of the elements were changed: where the Latin missal had (the equivalent of) '*may be made* unto us the body and blood of thy dearly beloved son', this was now changed to '*may be* unto us'. But the words at the distribution of communion might lead the unsuspecting to believe that a corporeal doctrine of the Real Presence was still being supported: 'The body of our Lord Jesus Christ which was given for thee preserve thy body and soul unto everlasting life.' Furthermore, traditional vestments were to be worn by the priest, and the word 'altar' (implying sacrifice) was used. There was even a prayer for the dead in the central section of the service.

The new Prayer Book was made mandatory on the clergy by the first Act of Uniformity 1549; but the people's attendance at church was to be enforced by the church courts as previously. The aim in having such a conservative liturgy as well as the reforms coming in piecemeal fashion was to prevent discord and rebellion, because it was obvious that the majority of the people were still wedded to the old ways; and Cranmer and Somerset hoped to wean people off their traditions by reform through the back door, with substantial changes hidden beneath a familiar veneer. Somerset also seems to have supported such a slow rate of religious change because he did not want to alienate Charles V now that England was at war with Scotland. Paget stressed to Somerset the absolute necessity that changes should both 'as God be pleased and the world little offended'. Another measure of 1549 was to allow the marriage of priests, and many were to seize the opportunity.

Somerset's foreign policy

Somerset was first and foremost a soldier and his main concern before any social or religious reforms was to continue the war against Scotland in which he himself had played such a notable role, and which had fuelled his rise to power. But whereas for Henry VIII Scotland had always been seen as secondary to a primary French adventure, for Somerset Scotland took pride of place – at least in the short term; he probably saw the acquisition of Scotland as greatly strengthening English claims against France at a later date. He thus refused to declare war on the French, waiting for them to do so in August 1549. Somerset was obsessively determined to tie Scotland dynastically to England by the betrothal of Edward VI to the infant Mary Queen of Scots, and led an army across the border in September 1547. For the next two years he spent more money on aggression against the Scots than Henry had since 1542. Somerset immediately won a great victory over the Scots in September 1547 at Pinkie, which probably made him even more arrogant thereafter, but which militarily and politically solved nothing. He set up a network of some 24 garrisons along the border and east coast of Scotland, but this was to cost him a fortune. Yet he failed because of the determination of the Scottish magnates to resist him and because of the help (and generous pensions) which they were given by the new French king Henry II, who thus became Somerset's great obstacle in his policy of conquest through garrisons. The Scottish

Parliament agreed in July 1548 to the betrothal of Mary Queen of Scots to the Dauphin and the eventual absorption of Scotland into France. In August 1548 the young Queen of Scots was taken to France, so that Somerset was deprived of the essential prize of his adventure. The 'rough wooing' was over. He would finally have to confess failure. But there can be no doubt that Somerset's first ambition was in the field of foreign affairs and not in social reform.

Somerset's social policy

Somerset has been regarded as possessing an altruistic sympathy for the poor, as a man with a 'stubborn and highminded devotion to a programme of revolutionary reform'[3] which was not shared by his selfish colleagues who consequently brought him down. Jordan's view seems wide of the mark because Somerset had no wish to reorder society or redistribute wealth but instead was eager only to curb the abuses that undermined the traditional hierarchical order. Happy peasants grew food and were loyal, supplying healthy men for war.

What was the basic social problem at the time? What we today call inflation was then known as 'dearth', or dearness. Prices had been rising since the 1520s and shot up alarmingly in the late 1540s – something new and horrible in the sixteenth century coming after late-medieval price stability. People did not know how to deal with inflation and did not understand its causes, but the rise in prices was causing widespread unrest. There was a tendency to blame the vogue for sheep-farming instead of tillage as the cause of the mischief. Historians today blame inflation especially on the growth in population which put a strain on agriculture; but inflation was also exacerbated by the profitable practice of debasing the coinage to pay for war in the 1540s. Somerset took seriously the call of the moralists who claimed that greedy men wanted to make money from sheep and to depopulate villages. There was no clear appreciation at the time that the population was rising, only that more people were poor and homeless. Putting the blame on enclosures for sheep-walks, especially if it involved enclosing former common land, was a traditional government attitude from Henry VII's time onwards.

However, it was the wrong answer, and thus Somerset was following the same wrong path. Somerset could thus continue happily debasing the coinage to pay for his Scottish adventure.

The campaign against depopulating enclosures began in earnest in June 1548 with a proclamation that the existing laws would be enforced and commissions of investigation set up. The reformer John Hales tried to get three agrarian reform bills passed by Parliament in 1549. However they failed against the various interest groups, and all that was passed was legislation imposing extra taxes on sheep-farming. Rejection in Parliament led to a new commission to curb enclosures by proclamation in May 1549 on Somerset's sole authority. The main consequence was that ordinary people believed that enclosures were the root of all evil; that if they agitated they could depend on the government for help against the selfish gentry. As for the other privy councillors, they expressed no opposition to the general drive against enclosures and the decay of tillage, although many regarded Somerset's enclosure commissions to be badly timed, likely to foment discontent rather than to calm the situation.

The rebellions of 1549

Somerset's proposed agrarian reforms and the commissions were aimed at preventing peasant unrest: in this they failed dismally. Between May and September 1549 some 15 counties in southern England and the Midlands witnessed largely uncoordinated peasant uprisings owing to the harsh economic climate. In most places conciliation and the traditional measures of control by the aristocracy and gentry soon restored order. But in two major areas full-scale rebellions blew up which necessitated government intervention: in the south-west (Cornwall and Devon) and in East Anglia (Norfolk and Suffolk). The major reason for this was that in both areas a political vacuum existed at the very top, because neither region had a dominant aristocrat who could nip the rebellion in the bud. In East Anglia the absence of the Howards counted greatly, with the Duke of Norfolk imprisoned in the Tower, while in the south-west the execution of the Marquis of Exeter back in 1538 meant that there was no great local figure there who could quickly rally troops on the basis of loyalty and good lordship. Exeter's replacement in the region, Lord Russell, may have been wealthier but he lacked sufficient local prestige to be immediately effective.

In the south-western rebellion grievances were mainly religious. Anticipation over the introduction of the new Prayer Book at Whitsun 1549 sparked off the commotion in Cornwall and Devon. These rebels wanted at least a return to Henrician Catholicism, calling for the return of the Act of Six Articles and transubstantiation. To the Cornishmen the new English Prayer Book was no advance because most of them did not speak English but Cornish, a Celtic tongue similar to Welsh. The new system they described as 'a Christmas game'. The Cornish people were also generally resentful of the English and of their own gentry who had embraced Protestantism: they wanted to 'kill the gentlemen and we will have the Six Articles up again'. There were thus religious, racial and class aspects to the rising. The rebels opposed government policy on both religion and enclosures. They disliked Hales's new tax on sheep because enclosure was not a problem in the area. There may have been a political angle also: it is possible that some obscure remnants of the Courtenay (Exeter) family were involved. This idea is strengthened by the rebels' demand for the exiled Cardinal Pole to be pardoned and made a member of the privy council. This was a very serious uprising because of the rebels' aim to march on London, and also because of the large numbers involved: the united forces constituted about 8000 men, and of the 3000 Cornishmen about 2000 were fully equipped for battle. Eventually the rebels were crushed in August by Russell and Sir William Herbert. All together, about 2500 Cornish and Devon rebels died, not to mention the hangings that followed.

Another major rebellion broke out in Norfolk on 7–8 July 1549, which although very different in its aims from the one in the west shared the same common denominators of peasant unrest and hatred of the gentry. The rebellion in Norfolk began over anger against enclosure hedges and against the avaricious behaviour of the gentry. The leading malcontents comprised mainly yeomen and tenant-farmers and were led by a minor gentleman, Robert Kett, who had been involved in a personal quarrel with a local lawyer over enclosure hedges. This was an apparently loyalist rebellion in sympathy with the protector's religious and economic policies: pro-Protestant and anti-sheep. Indeed they did not look upon themselves as rebels at all. In Norfolk although enclosures were not everywhere a huge grievance, nevertheless sheep rearing was a big business that was disliked because of the Norfolk fold-course custom which allowed individual lessees the right to pasture their sheep wherever they wished on anyone's land in the manor. Some pro-rebel small farmers might even have used enclosures to try to impede the pasturing of other men's sheep on their lands. What really bound the rebels together was a hatred of the antisocial effects of sheep-farming, but unlike the western rebels the Norfolk insurgents had no wish to march on London but instead established camps near some of the leading administrative centres in Norfolk and Suffolk. This static 'camping time' was remembered for years afterwards in the region and certainly alarmed the government because the encamped rebels aimed to govern the local area independently of the central government: this was setting a hor-rifying precedent, with those rebels (like Kett) who were just outside the circle of the ruling class taking over local government and indeed making a rather good show of it. The gentry proper were either away from home or made themselves scarce, waiting for the central government to deliver them from the danger. Many gentlemen were immobilised by the fact that their relatives were hostages of the rebels.

Kett assembled some 16 000 men encamped at Mousehold Heath outside Norwich, but made no attempt to take the city, although he forced the authorities there to accept his rule. Kett established a camp council with delegates elected from the vari-ous districts of Norfolk, and he issued orders in the king's name. Kett did not see himself as a rebel, but as an agent of the govern-ment against the rapacious local gentry. The rebels even used Cranmer's new Prayer Book and demanded a proper preaching clergy.

It is true that Somerset was sympathetic to the complaints of the Norfolk men against enclosures, and he certainly did not want to own up to the failure of his social policies; but a rebel was still a rebel, and there is no evidence that Somerset's attitude towards rebellion was any softer than that of the other members of the council. Delays in crushing the rebellions of 1549 were due more to inadequate local information and to the lack of available troops than to any genuine sympathy for the rebels. Eventually Somerset realised that only stern measures would count, and he had to call on Warwick to finish off the task. This was accomplished with about 10 000 troops at Dussindale, near Norwich, when on 27 August some 3000 rebels died.

Somerset could not be criticised for his handling of the rebellions because he had the agreement of his colleagues on the council. 'In the military treatment of peasant rebellions Somerset and Warwick saw eye to eye': both believed in conciliation before the use of force. But Somerset certainly lost prestige once his rival Warwick took the field against Kett. What brought Somerset down was the very fact of rebellion; and after the dust had settled he was blamed for having caused unrest by his radical social reforms. He was made a scapegoat, as there was no great opposition to the general lines of traditional social policy, only the timing of his particular measures which had provoked some plain speaking from colleagues. In July 1549 Paget had upbraided him: 'What is the cause [of the tumults]? Your own levity, your softness, your opinion to be good to the poor.' Somerset was getting the quite undeserved reputation of being a radical. Peasant support for his continuation in office virtually guaranteed his overthrow by his colleagues.

Somerset's social schemes had blown up in his face at the same time as his foreign policy lay in tatters: he had been forced to evacuate Scotland at the end of July because of the cost, and soon afterwards France declared war on England, which left the realm fearing a French invasion while its coffers were empty. This all amounted to massive incompetence, now to be added to Somerset's earlier arrogance in ignoring the privy council. No wonder, therefore, that his colleagues resented him as they had been excluded from power. Thus when in 1549 with mounting problems surrounding him he was forced to recall the privy council he found only a group of malcontents. Somerset's fall was probably not the result of a spontaneous revolt against him in September after order had been restored. A conspiracy to oust him can be traced back to mid-August 1549, at the latest, in which Princess Mary was invited to join Warwick, Arundel, Southampton and William Paulet.

Somerset, confronted by opposition, was prepared to embark on civil war, and on 1 October ordered loyal people to repair to

Hampton Court in his and the king's defence. Both Somerset and the council wrote to the City of London requesting its aid, and the two letters were read out to the City fathers, who decided in favour of the council. There emerged for a brief moment the spectre of civil war, especially as some 4000 peasants had come to Hampton Court to the duke's aid. However, the council did not resort to the army in retaliation against Somerset. Instead Warwick sent the yeomen of the guard to Windsor, to which Somerset had fled with the king. On 14 October Somerset, having surrendered, joined Kett in the Tower.

The conspiracy that was hatched against Somerset was essentially a conservative one initially, to install Princess Mary as regent for her half-brother and perhaps even to restore Catholicism. But Warwick reneged on such promises, and in December had a showdown with the conservatives who now wanted to oust him along with Somerset. These were the conservatives who had been bought off in January 1547 or had disliked the assumption of the full protectorate: especially Southampton and Arundel. They wanted to tar Warwick along with Somerset as a traitor. Warwick was fighting for his life in an extremely vicious and sordid game, and was rescued only by the intervention of Archbishop Cranmer, who was in a position to persuade King Edward to appoint a number of radical supporters to the privy chamber. One of these was Warwick's brother, Sir Andrew Dudley; another was Sir John Gates. These moves placed Warwick in a better position to get the king to make four new appointments to the privy council. With a majority support among councillors Warwick was able to foil the conspiracy against him, and indeed in February 1550 to oust the conservatives entirely from the council and achieve his own true domination.

The regime of John Dudley, Earl of Warwick and Duke of Northumberland

Whereas Somerset has traditionally been seen in a modern altruistic light, his successor John Dudley, who remained Earl of Warwick until his elevation to the dukedom of Northumberland in October 1551, has been painted as a villain – 'the subtlest intriguer in English history', according to A. F. Pollard. There has indeed been an amazing degree of consensus among historians down the ages that he was unprincipled and grasping. Was this just the result of his having failed, and his history being written by the victors? Part of Pollard's condemnatory judgement of Dudley was to contrast the visionary nature of Somerset. But recent research has downplayed and softened this contrast: Somerset was not whiter than white, but neither was Dudley black and evil. Indeed both emerge a similar hue as typical Tudor politicians. Like Somerset, Dudley was essentially a soldier with little experience of government; he also had the misfortune of Edward VI's early death to contend with. But it was his attempt to exclude Mary from the throne that sealed his reputation as the embodiment of evil.

Somerset was imprisoned in October 1549, but he was not eliminated at this stage, not even after the defeat of the conservatives in December which had made Warwick the leading politician by February 1550. Indeed Somerset was able to return to membership of the privy council in April 1550. An era of cooperation between the two men was signalled by the marriage in June 1550 of Warwick's eldest son John to Anne Seymour. Yet Warwick was still suspicious of Somerset – with good reason because he continued to intrigue to regain his old supremacy. Finally in October 1551 Somerset was charged with high treason in a trial before a hand-picked jury, and executed on slender charges in January 1552.

Warwick did not repeat Somerset's damning error of arrogantly dispensing with the council, nor did he wish to succeed to the position of lord protector. The privy council was no longer merely a rubber stamp but now regained its proper role in government. It increased in size, although never to more than 33 members. Warwick was able to dominate the council through his position as lord president of the council, allowing him to create and eject members. This presidency was his automatically by virtue of his being master of the household during a royal minority. Using these powers, he expelled Southampton (2 February 1550) from the council, and also filled the household with reliable men, notably Sir John Gates. Warwick then rewarded himself with the dukedom of Northumberland in October 1551. There followed a purge of conservatives from the council in May

1552, with the removal of Rich and Tunstall. Although less obviously authoritarian than Somerset, Northumberland still often behaved autocratically, but hid behind the claim that Edward was beginning to take decisions and that he was merely acting on the king's behalf.

Financial reform

Northumberland's most important achievement was in combating inflation by reforming the currency and with the help of Thomas Gresham restoring the government's credit-worthiness. Between 1551 and 1552 the face value of coins was reduced to correspond more closely to their real content in precious metals. By a policy of peace with France (including the return of Boulogne) and by selling more crown lands Northumberland was also successful in greatly reducing the country's foreign debt.

The financial agencies were also rationalised. Cromwell's attack on household methods had left too many expensive bureaucratic departments. In 1547 the court of augmentations had absorbed the court of general surveyors. Now in 1552 a royal commission was set up to survey the whole financial apparatus. The commission reported in December 1552 and recommended the absorption of all the financial courts into a reorganised Exchequer. This suggestion (although modified by leaving the courts of the duchy of Lancaster and wards and liveries separate) was to be acted on in Mary's reign, but one must give credit to Northumberland's team of advisers (Winchester, William Cecil and Sir Walter Mildmay) for creating the reform scheme which enabled the Exchequer once more to gain supremacy over the national finances.

Further religious reformation, 1550–3

John Dudley presided over a vigorous campaign of protestant-isation in England, but whether this was driven by conviction or by self-interest it is impossible to say. Those who were eager to believe in him might, like John Knox, regard him as an 'intrepid soldier of Jesus Christ', yet Northumberland's preparedness to go back to Catholicism at the very end of his life suggests either opportunism or (at best) loyalty to the monarch but certainly not 'intrepid' faith. Dudley allowed reforming divines to formulate a programme of religious change that began with the new Ordinal of 1550. A service for the ordination of priests had been the only omission from the otherwise comprehensive first Prayer Book of 1549 so one was urgently needed. The Ordinal is important for omitting any notion of a sacrificial priesthood (i.e. one able to offer the sacrifice of the mass), although the historic ceremony of the laying-on of hands was still adhered to. This was followed up by the removal of stone altars (as signifying sacrifice) from their traditional place at the east end of churches and their replacement by wooden communion tables positioned in the chancel or in the nave.

The ambiguous nature of the theology of the first Prayer Book meant that more radical minds would demand a clarification. This was partly achieved by the second Prayer Book of 1552. It was a work that departed radically from medieval liturgical tradition. The thrust of the new English service was to emphasise the communion as only a memorial of the Last Supper. The words at the distribution of the bread and wine at the end reflected this: 'Take and eat this in remembrance that Christ died for thee, and feed on him in thy heart by faith with thanksgiving. Drink this in remembrance that Christ's blood was shed for thee and be thankful.' However, Anglicanism (as a creed to comprehend all English people) could never afford to be crystal clear, and for those who wished to cling on to a notion of the Real Presence there was a prayer in the text that communicants 'may be partakers of his most blessed body and blood'. Other contradictions include the word 'priest' (rather than minister) and the necessity to kneel while receiving communion. This second Prayer Book has remained the basis of the Anglican communion service. The new Prayer Book was enforced by a second Act of Uniformity, which for the first time also enforced by state law people's attendance at Sunday worship. The last period of Northumberland's rule saw a concerted iconoclastic campaign to remove objects of value from the parish churches, especially serving objects made of gold and silver, which the government appropriated and melted down.

The problem of the succession

The most acute problem for Northumberland during 1553 was that of the succession, because his own power depended solely on the life of a sickly boy. If Northumberland's policies and his powers were to survive then Princess Mary had to be ousted from the succession. The issue of the succession was complicated at this time for two reasons: because all those in line were females, which was a completely novel situation; and second, because three changes had already been made to the succession by Henry VIII, and thus pure legality had been superseded by the notion of concern for the best interests of the realm. It could now be argued that the best interests of the realm could be served by the removal of Mary from the line of succession. Henry VIII's will had left the throne to his three children, and then to Frances, Duchess of Suffolk (daughter of Henry's sister Mary by Charles Brandon) and to her daughters by Henry Grey, Duke of Suffolk – namely Jane Grey, Catherine Grey and Mary Grey. Finally in Henry's will came Margaret Clifford, a grand-niece of Henry VIII and daughter of the Earl of Cumberland.

Edward VI's last illness came upon him in February 1553. In May, although still a minor, Edward VI drew up in his own hand his 'Device for the succession', which was a draft form of a will and which excluded both of his sisters from the throne. The legality of this document could be challenged on two fronts: Edward as a minor could not make a binding will, and it could not withstand the parliamentary Act of Succession of 1543. What was needed to overturn Henry VIII's arrangements was an adult king's will supported by a new Act of Parliament. In the original draft of his 'Device' Edward aimed to leave the throne to a male – to the sons of Lady Frances, Lady Jane, etc. At the time of writing the 'Device' none of these ladies had any sons, and to remedy this a marriage was arranged that same month between Lady Jane and Lord Guildford Dudley, Northumberland's son (21 May). With luck, in nine months there would be a male heir to the throne, who would be the duke's grandson.

Such a scheme depended on Edward clinging on to life until the new birth. However, at the very end of May the king took a turn for the worse: something desperate now had to be done to prevent Mary succeeding. Therefore the 'Device' was changed with numerous insertions and deletions, with the most crucial being the change of the phrase 'Lady Jane's heirs males' to 'Lady Jane and her heirs males'. These changes were almost certainly forged by someone other than the king, because he was too ill to write, although it was possibly done with his approval. The Crown could now go directly to Lady Jane Grey. Northumberland's hand has always been seen behind this treasonable conspiracy to exclude Mary, but W. K. Jordan believed that the attempt to exclude Mary was Edward's own doing, with Northumberland 'being entrapped in a great conspiracy not of his own contriving'.[4] The real truth will probably never be known, but it seems wisest to regard the amendments as the fruit of active cooperation between the king and the duke. To exclude the Catholic Mary made sense from their point of view, but why also exclude the Protestant Elizabeth if the main aim had been to preserve Protestantism? One can argue that Elizabeth's illegitimacy worked against her, but primarily Northumberland's personal ambition must be seen in the wish to exclude Elizabeth, which meant effectively bringing the Tudor dynasty to an end. It is noteworthy that in the same month of May a marriage was projected between Northumberland's brother Sir Andrew Dudley and the claimant Margaret Clifford, while Northumberland's daughter Catherine actually married another possible contender, Henry Hastings, the future Earl of Huntingdon.

Nevertheless, Northumberland failed in what should have been an easy undertaking: he was too late to capture the person of Princess Mary. Northumberland had invited Mary to Court to stay with the sickly king, but Edward's death from tuberculosis on 6 July came when Mary was at Hunsdon in Hertfordshire. Being forewarned by an unknown friend, she made her escape into East Anglia, first to her manor-house at Kenninghall in Norfolk, from where she sent a letter on 9 July to the privy council claiming the throne. Mary then moved on to Framlingham Castle in Suffolk, where more of her supporters flocked to her side. Edward's death was kept a secret by the privy council until 8 July; then on 10 July Lady Jane Grey was proclaimed queen at the Tower of London. The official proclamation pointed to the illegitimacy of both Mary and Elizabeth. Letters sent by the council to the counties stressed that Mary would bring back 'the Antichrist of Rome'. The arrival in London of Mary's letter on 11 July threw the privy councillors into total confusion. On 14 July Northumberland ventured from the capital with his leading supporters, especially Northampton and Gates, and an army of 600 men to crush Mary's uprising, leaving the rest of the privy council locked up in the Tower. But by 19 July the remaining privy councillors, led by Arundel, Pembroke, Bedford (Russell) and Shrewsbury, had repented of their earlier behaviour and managed to escape and proclaim Queen Mary in London. The following day Northumberland realised that all was lost and surrendered at Cambridge to the Earl of Arundel.

Why did Mary win the day? The traditional answer is that the nation put the principle of legitimacy before Northumberland's selfish scheming; people wanted the stability of the rightful monarch – and this is certainly a part of the explanation. However, those who sprang to her call immediately and so made her bid for the throne possible were loyal Catholic-minded gentry of East Anglia – men like Sir William Waldegrave and his brother-in-law Clement Heigham. It was the gentry who first rallied to Mary, not the nobles – only the earls of Bath and Sussex were prominent in her support at the start. Protestants were divided between those who put zeal for their religion first and those whose minds eventually came down on the side of legitimacy. Two ardent Protestants who nevertheless sided with Mary in the crisis were Sir Peter Carew and Bishop Hooper. Clearly motivation was mixed and no dogmatic judgement can be made, but support for Catholicism was a more potent reason than traditionally assumed.

Mary I and the Catholic restoration (1553–8)

Mary became queen at the ripe age of 37, a lonely and embittered woman, with little experience of government. Completely alienated from the Protestant Court of her brother, who had tried to forbid her private mass, she had unsuccessfully devised plans to flee to Spain. Mary was the first queen regnant in English history;[5] there was certainly general apprehension over a female ruler, which to many seemed contrary to both nature and God's law. Mary was not a typical Tudor: she was the odd person out in the dynasty, putting religion before political convenience –

something no other Tudor would have done. Yet she was not as weak or foolish as often supposed, but a shrewd negotiator.[5]

Mary's unhappy, short reign was dominated by two major policies: the restoration of papal Catholicism and marriage into the Spanish royal house from which her mother had come. Unfortunately, as a result of her policies which tied Catholicism to the Spanish alliance she made both the papacy and Spain the objects of English hatred for generations to come. It was a great blow to Mary that Pope Paul IV was an enemy of Habsburg power, which he wanted ejected from Italy, and that ironically towards the end of her reign England was actually at war with the papacy.

The reign of Mary Tudor was to end miserably in November 1558, with war and pestilence raging, and with the persecution of heretics fully ablaze, and consequently most historians tradition- ally have condemned her reign as one doomed to failure. The attitude of the English Protestant establishment has been to view her reign as a stagnant interlude between the dynamic age of Henry VIII and Edward VI, on the one hand, and the glories of the Elizabethan England, on the other. Pollard's famous negative judgement that sterility was the conclusive note of Mary's reign was repeated by most historians until the recent advent of revi- sionism. Revisionists, however, emphasise Mary's achievements and point to the shortness of her life and her sheer bad luck rather than the impossibility of her goals. Had she lived a little longer, perhaps till 1568, which would have given her policies more time to work and made them harder to dislodge, or had Elizabeth died before her – perhaps in 1562 when indeed Elizabeth did nearly die of smallpox – then England's history might have been alto- gether different. A permanent Catholic restoration was not an impossibility; a policy of force had succeeded elsewhere in Europe in eradicating heresy, so why not in England? Protestants were not complacently waiting for the end of this 'interlude' but were struck with fear and uncertainty over the future.

Mary's new government

Although important changes were made, it is necessary to bear in mind the high degree of continuity in government. There could be no clean sweep of the council board, because faithful Catholics (such as those in her household) had no experience of government. Only Bishop Gardiner was a man who fulfilled both criteria of orthodoxy and experience, and he was made lord chancellor. Yet even he had been a Henrician Catholic, who had reverted to papalism because he realised that only the papal supremacy could prevent a drift towards heresy. The other experienced councillors were untrustworthy in religion, but they were needed, and so 17 members of Edward's privy council were forgiven for having signed the 'Device' and remained on. This partly accounts for the real amount of governmental stability underneath the dramatic flow of events. But there was an undeniable cleavage between the Court and the privy council. Mary's old household officers formed the nucleus of the new (and much larger) royal household. The privy chamber, now staffed by women, lost most of the political influence it had possibly enjoyed under Henry VIII and Edward VI. Because Mary had to reward the faithful who had flocked to Kenninghall and Framlingham, the privy council was greatly inflated to around 50 nominal members, and this huge unwieldy council used to be seen as a hallmark of unstable Marian government. Now, however, we know this not to be true. The normal working council consisted of 10–20 men, a small council of the late-Henrician sort. Cromwell's disciple Paget seems to have been responsible for this as well as for the creation of some 12 standing council committees in February 1554 to deal with different aspects of government. The purpose of these was to exclude the nominal and non-experienced councillors and to prevent Gardiner from exercising too great an influence. Within the council one can discern factional rivalry: Gardiner was the leader of the clericalists – bishops Tunstall, Bonner and Heath – who wanted to revive the powers of the Church, while Paget was the leader of the lay group on the council which was determined to maintain the 'Cromwellian' lay revolution. But the council was not Mary's sole source of advice: more important was the Imperial ambassador, Simon Renard, to whom she regularly turned first. Indeed councillors who wanted to approach the queen usually needed to go through Renard – an amazing and alienating situation. Once again Mary proved herself not to be a genuine, nationalistic Tudor.

Mary's great aim was to erase all memory of the changes in religion made by her father and brother and to return England to Rome. However, because the Reformation had been constructed constitutionally by Parliament it could now be demolished only by Parliament. The frequency of Parliament in this short reign is not a sign of the queen's love for the institution but of her constitutional need of it. Mary hated being the supreme head of a schismatic Church but until this could be changed by Act of Parliament she was forced to remain so. The best that she could do was to hide the fact behind the use of *etcetera* in her title: she was Queen of England, France and Ireland *etc*.

Although most people wanted traditionalism in religion, there seems little doubt that had a referendum been possible they would have voted for a nationalistic Henrician Catholicism, and many of Mary's initial supporters may have hoped that this is what she would bring in. There was no great love for a foreign and distant pope: thus when the taxes of first fruits and tenths were returned by the Crown to the Church in 1555, the bill had to be amended in Parliament to ensure that the money would not go to the pope but instead remain with the Church in England and be used to increase poor priests' stipends. It was the conservative bishops who were now the pope's greatest supporters in England, having repented of their earlier acquiescence in the royal supremacy. The country in general would loyally obey the restoration of Roman Catholicism, apart from one major point of resistance: the gentry (even the most Catholic) refused to give up their monastic and chantry lands. The pope had to guarantee the safety of these lands before any formal reconciliation was allowed to take place. The restoration of the old religion was undertaken in stages and through parliamentary statute.

Mary's first Parliament (October–December 1553)

The first Parliament abolished Northumberland's treason legislation, which brought the return of the medieval treason law of 1352: thus there were no longer any penalties for impugning the supreme head. Also the queen's previous illegitimate status was overturned by an Act declaring the validity of her mother's marriage. Theologically there was a return to Henrician

Catholicism by the abolition of the two Edwardian Acts of Uniformity: the Prayer Book was now illegal. The Act of 1549 allowing the marriage of priests was also rescinded. Although the legislation got through, it was not all plain sailing: in the Commons opposition was clearly voiced to the religious reaction. According to the French ambassador, a third of the Commons were hostile, while Gardiner told Renard that 80 MPs out of 350 had opposed the changes. Furthermore, a list of Members survives for this Parliament on which 60 names are asterisked as having 'stood for the true religion' (i.e. Protestantism).[6] Protestant hostility can also be glimpsed in the episode when on the day of this Parliament's dissolution a dog with a shaven head (as a symbol of a tonsured priest) was thrown into the queen's presence chamber at Court. Clearly the Protestants in the governing class, though a minority, were prepared to use Parliament to voice their grievances. This makes Mary's success in getting her legislation through both Houses all the more notable.

The second major event of this first Parliament was Mary's announcement of her decision to marry Philip of Spain, which surprised almost all of her councillors and shocked the realm. Of course, everyone expected her to marry and, unlike her half-sister Elizabeth later, Mary agreed with conventional wisdom and even secretly gave over the choice of her husband to a man – the emperor – who in September came up with the name of his son Philip. Most people wished her to marry an Englishman, and a party around Gardiner had canvassed for the Plantagenet descendant Edward Courtenay, Earl of Devon. However, Mary made a secret pledge on 29 October to marry Philip of Spain, and when this news leaked out much criticism was voiced in Parliament; and on 16 November a Commons delegation in an audience with the queen tried to persuade her to marry an Englishman instead. However, Mary's mind was made up, and her betrothal was officially announced the day after Parliament was dissolved.

Wyatt's rebellion (January 1554)

The decision of the queen to marry Philip and the reluctant acceptance of that decision by the council drove some hotheads to bolder action. Although they claimed that they wished only to force the queen to change her mind, their real ambition was probably to force her off the throne and to install Princess Elizabeth in her place, married to Courtenay. The four principal conspirators, who inveigled the handsome and ambitious, but also unstable and dissolute, Courtenay into their enterprise, were Sir Thomas Wyatt in Kent, Sir Peter Carew in Devon, Sir James Croft in Herefordshire and Henry Grey, Duke of Suffolk in Leicestershire. Although they had toyed with the notion of assassinating Mary, their agreed scheme was for four simultaneous local uprisings that would then move on to the capital; the day set was Palm Sunday (18 March) 1554. However, the government got wind of the affair in January, and when Carew refused to answer a summons to appear before the council, suspicions were aroused. Then on 21 January Gardiner squeezed information out of Courtenay. Carew fled to France, Suffolk made an abortive attempt at rebellion in Leicestershire, while Croft failed to make any move at all. Only Wyatt in Kent was able to get an uprising started, which began at Maidstone on 25 January. This was potentially very dangerous because of its proximity to the capital and the recruitment of some 3000 rebels. Indeed the royalist force sent against them disobeyed their commander and went over to the rebel side. Wyatt was successfully capitalising on the widespread dislike of the Spanish marriage among Kentishmen, but Mary rose to the occasion and in a burst of typical Tudor oratory was able to keep the loyalty of Londoners. The rebels could not cross London Bridge from Southwark, where they had pillaged Gardiner's palace, but succeeded in moving west, crossing the Thames at Kingston and trying to invade the City through the western entrance at Ludgate. By this time, however, Wyatt's force was much depleted and was forced to surrender. Whether or not this rebellion was driven primarily by political opposition to the Spanish marriage or by Protestant hostility to Mary has been debated with no firm conclusion being reached. The rebellion certainly got no clear backing from Protestant leaders. Both Carew and Croft had earlier supported Mary in the crisis over the succession, so that what sent them into disloyalty was principally the Spanish connection. Yet no matter what the original motives, if the rebels had won the result would have been to oust Mary and her catholicising policies.

About 100 people were executed in the aftermath, including Lady Jane Grey and her husband Lord Guildford Dudley. Elizabeth was sent to the Tower for two months and was lucky to survive. Renard and Gardiner wanted her eliminated, but Paget protected Elizabeth and her right to remain in the succession, while Courtenay could thank Gardiner for his extra lease on life. The main result was that the rebellion strengthened Mary's resolve and weakened the opposition within the government to the match. Affluent Protestants, some 750 of them, fled into exile in Europe, largely unmolested by the authorities.

Second Parliament (2 April–5 May 1554)

This was summoned to ratify the marriage treaty which both Gardiner and Paget had cooperated in drawing up and which secured essential English interests; it would also be necessary to extend the treason laws to Philip because the 1352 Act had not envisaged a female ruler with a male consort. This was indeed a quieter Parliament than the first mainly because of Wyatt's rebellion, but there were ripples of discontent in the Lords, where the personal quarrel between Gardiner and Paget dominated the proceedings; this represented an unprecedented spillover from the council chamber to the floor of the House of Lords, a fact which again underlines the queen's poor control of her councillors. This rivalry can be seen in the problem of getting the medieval heresy laws revived. Although there was surprisingly no recorded opposition in the Commons to Gardiner's attempt to revive them, the measure was actually defeated in the Lords. The reason for this setback lay with Paget, who agreed with the Imperialists on the need not to inflame the religious situation and thus spoil plans for Mary's marriage; Paget was additionally not eager to augment the power of the clericalists. His ploy in the Lords was to persuade his colleagues that Gardiner's heresy bill would somehow jeopardise their monastic property. The defeat meant that the government was left with no means of prosecuting heretics already in gaol, like Cranmer, who had initially been held mainly on political charges. Also defeated by Paget for factional reasons in the Lords was a bill to extend to Philip the protection of the English treason laws. This was truly amazing

since it was Paget who among the councillors most favoured the
Spanish match. The only explanation for this is that Paget, furious with Gardiner for the heresy bill, wanted to show the queen
how powerful he was. Mary was extremely displeased with these
developments, and Paget was forced to lurk in disgrace for some
time. Nevertheless it must be remembered that the House of
Commons had shown itself loyal enough to pass the heresy
laws, without any Protestant outburst. On the other hand, it was
perfectly clear that Parliament would never accept Mary's desire
to disinherit Elizabeth.

Despite the taciturnity of the Commons in this Parliament, it
was decided before each of the next three Parliaments (November 1554, 1555, 1558) to send out circular letters to the sheriffs
(as the returning officers) requesting the election of reliable
Catholic Members, which indicates that the government could
not take consensus or loyalty for granted. In the meantime Philip
arrived at Southampton on 20 July, and five days later he and
Mary were married at Winchester Cathedral by Bishop Gardiner.
The arrival of Philip meant a scramble by councillors to obtain his
favour (if not a pension). Paget re-entered political life after his
disgrace by ingratiating himself with Philip, whose cause he had
indeed supported from the start.

Third Parliament (12 November 1554–16 January 1555)

This third Parliament reunited England with Rome, and a prayer
for the pope was offered during the opening ceremonies. A bill
was passed reversing the attainder of Cardinal Pole so that he
could re-enter the country after his long exile and act as papal
legate, and eventually after Cranmer's deposition in 1555 as the
new Archbishop of Canterbury. While the pope and Pole had
agreed that the monastic lands could remain with their new lay
owners, Pole insisted that this should be seen as a gift from the
Church rather than as a legal right of the laity to appropriate
church property. This attitude of the cardinal bred continuing
uncertainty among the laity that at a future date the Church
would revoke its 'gift'. Apart from the temporary refusal of Sir
Ralph Bagnall to take the oath to the pope, there seems to have
been no overt opposition to the reunion with Rome, nor to the

reviving of the medieval heresy laws. A Regency Act was passed which, in the event of Mary's death, would give Philip the governorship of a daughter to the age of 15 and of a son and heir to the age of 18; Philip was thus to rule England during the period of minority, and the treason laws were duly extended to him.

While this appeared a peaceful enough assembly there is evidence of some possible opposition. In January 1555 106 MPs were absent when a roll-call of Members was made on 12 January; some of these absentees were later fined in King's Bench for their truancy, but others were not. It is difficult to say precisely why some were punished but not others. The 'seceders' were not linked by Protestantism, and if they had opposed the Regency bill they would have stayed on to fight rather than leave defeated before the final passing of the bill in the Commons on 14 January. Despite this the beginning of 1555 seemed to augur well for Mary's hopes, but as the year wore on disillusionment and opposition were to grow.

Fourth Parliament (21 October–9 December 1555)

This Parliament, which was called for taxation, witnessed the largest amount of opposition to the queen. For three reasons the political climate had changed by the time this assembly met: first, the burning of heretics had already started – in February, with the martyrdom of John Rogers; second, the queen's eagerness to return former church lands in the Crown's possession was worrying the landowners, especially with the return of the Franciscans to Greenwich and Richmond; and third, Mary's phantom pregnancy. The belief in her pregnancy had been published before the last Parliament and a *Te Deum* had been prematurely sung at St Paul's in November 1554. The child had been expected in April 1555, but as time elapsed it became obvious that nothing would eventuate. Mary's misery was compounded by the departure of Philip from England at the end of August in order to take over the Netherlands and Spain on the abdication of his father the emperor.

This new Parliament saw opposition to two government bills: the bill to restore first fruits and tenths to the Church, and the exiles bill. As for first fruits and tenths, the government's original intention was to restore these moneys to the pope, but this aim was defeated in the Commons, and the amended bill insisted that the tax should remain within the English Church. Many MPs feared that the loss of this income would impoverish the Crown and lead to greater demands for taxation. The House had already whittled down the queen's tax demands in order to persuade her to hang on to her church lands. The amended bill was passed on 3 December by 193 votes to 126, with the government resorting to the ruse of keeping the House sitting until 3 p.m., with the consequent departure of MPs hungry for their midday meal, who might otherwise have voted against it; the government then had the doors of the Parliament chamber locked to prevent the return of opponents to cast their votes.

The exiles bill was a measure to confiscate the lands of those Englishmen who had gone abroad and who now refused to return home at the queen's command. Only a temporary confiscation was intended until the owners returned, but substantial sums in land revenue were involved, and this was a clear intrusion into the property rights of people who had not broken any law by leaving the country, especially as many had actually obtained official permits to so do. Opponents of the bill, led by Sir Anthony Kingston, seeing after the third reading of the bill that there was a majority in the chamber opposed to it, locked the chamber door with a key seized from the sergeant-at-arms and forced the Speaker to take the vote. This unpopular bill was defeated.

There was thus clearly a more organised opposition in this Parliament than in any other. Both the government and the 'opposition' had a good idea of who their supporters and opponents were – proved by the two incidents of locking the chamber door when on the visual evidence a favourable outcome could be predicted. The Venetian ambassador's report that the Commons were 'for the most part suspected in the matter of religion' was undoubtedly an exaggeration but not a complete figment of his imagination. A number of these 'opposition' MPs (or 'right Protestants') were wont to meet at Arundel's tavern in Poulteney Lane, where parliamentary matters were discussed and opposition plans laid. The council must have thought that some MPs were nuisances because, according to the Venetian ambassador, it tried to bring in a bill to exclude gentry from borough seats by reimposing the old residence qualifications for burgesses. Also Gardiner's death in November 1555 probably encouraged opposition within the House by weakening council management there.

Conspiracy and war

Following the dissolution of this Parliament, opposition was forced outside into the conspiracy of February 1556 named after its leader Sir Henry Dudley, which included some dozen MPs from the last House. This conspiracy was centred on the west of England and aimed to bring in a force of Marian exiles with French support to put Elizabeth on the throne. After the French showed little enthusiasm, the conspirators planned to finance their venture by robbing the treasury, at which point they were discovered, and ten were executed. Had the French been deeply involved in the Dudley conspiracy this could have provoked war right then, but the actual trigger for war against France was Thomas Stafford's capture of Scarborough Castle in April 1557, when he proclaimed himself king.

Philip had returned to England in March in an attempt to gain England's entry into his war against France, essential because of Spain's bankruptcy, and the Stafford event was now used as an excuse by the queen to overcome opposition within the council for England to declare war on France in June. The ironic thing was that the papacy was allied to France in reaction to the Spanish invasion of the Papal States in September 1556, so that England was at war with the Holy See. The fiercely anti-Habsburg Pope Paul IV revoked Cardinal Pole's legatine commission in April 1557, which deprived him of much authority. The Catholic cause thus became hopelessly divided.

The Anglo-Spanish war against France was to prove a catastrophe for the reputation of Queen Mary, but this was not inevitable. The war itself was not the problem: although there had been patriotic resistance to the idea of England's being dragged into a Habsburg quarrel, there were good reasons for English participation now, especially given the ambitious designs of Henry II of France and the need to safeguard the Netherlands for English trade. French support for Stafford tipped the scales and gained the council's support for war. But, apart from Paget, the bureaucrat-councillors remained half-hearted, although many of Mary's nobles, notably Pembroke, were pleased at the chance to resume their military careers. The war also offered the opportunity for reconciliation to former opponents of the Marian regime. Sir James Croft and Sir Peter Carew, together with Sir Ambrose Dudley and Sir Robert Dudley, Northumberland's sons, were all allowed to serve Mary in the war. Thus a good war had every prospect of reuniting the ruling class. At first all went well with the notable, if exaggerated, English success at the storming of St Quentin (10 August 1557), but then English morale collapsed after the fall of Calais in January 1558. England's last vestige of European empire vanished, and while in the long run that loss would certainly be beneficial to England's development, directing attention away from Europe, at the time it seemed to many as further confirmation of God's disapproval of Mary's regime.

Such loss of confidence might be expected to have had the same immediate destabilising effects at home, as in 1450 after the loss of Normandy. But the Parliament of 1558 (January–March, and 5–17 November) was the easiest the queen ever experienced. This may have been due to the return of good Catholics (unlikely) or (more probably) the natural unity experienced in the midst of war; perhaps the eagerness to escape a disease-ravaged capital reduced any attraction to drawn-out opposition. The Parliament was called for taxation to pay for the war, but because of an economic slump the queen had to accept a smaller amount than she had sought; even so she obtained £168 000 to be paid by the end of the year. Measures were also passed to improve the unclear system of army recruitment: the Arms Act and Militia Act tried to guarantee that recruits, according to their income, brought with them usable, modern weapons (e.g. pikes and arquebuses), and that there were no absences or corruption in the mustering of the shire levies – reforms which despite their faults were to bring rewards in the Elizabethan period. The first session of the Parliament passed without trouble, apart from some murmurings over the few restored religious houses and some fears voiced by the Protestant Thomas Copley over the possible exclusion of Elizabeth from the throne. Nevertheless, had Mary lived she would doubtless have had a difficult task of maintaining unity in the face of military defeat and consequent recriminations.

Mary and religion

The old idea of Mary's reign as a 'sterile interlude' in religion seems harder to maintain nowadays. Protestants of the time had no idea that the Catholic restoration would only be temporary but instead had been very fearful for the future, with only a very short period of Protestant experimentation behind them in the reign of Edward. Although the exiled Protestants printed many pamphlets against the Marian regime, it does not appear that this Protestant propaganda was very effective. The calls by John Knox and John Ponet for the forceful removal of the queen were not imitated by other pamphleteers, who preferred to stress patient suffering rather than conspiracy and were more passive than revolutionary. What revisionists emphasise is just how much was achieved in religion by Mary in such a short time: in general people accepted loyally, indeed enthusiastically, the return of Roman Catholicism. There had been much popular rejoicing at Mary's accession, with the colourful accoutrements of traditional worship being brought back without the need of any official commands. Huge numbers turned up at St Paul's cross in London to receive official absolution in November 1553. The speed with which parishes voluntarily restored the mass and repurchased vestments, fabric and plate for their churches out of their own pockets seems proof of this enthusiasm. There was also a significant increase in bequests to the Church compared to the days of King Edward. And there was a huge increase in the number of ordinations to the priesthood. At Oxford, for example, there had been no new ministers at all ordained between 1551 and 1553, whereas in the years 1554–7 some 97 new priests were consecrated – clear evidence that no one thought in terms of a short interlude.[7] Nevertheless it has been argued that the queen's policies chosen to achieve her goal were not always the best. Mary and Cardinal Pole believed that the heretics who had caused all the trouble were small in number, and just eliminating them and removing married priests would suffice. Was there perhaps not enough understanding of the power of

Protestantism or the appeal of Tyndale's New Testament? Was there too little idea that a major missionary campaign was necessary to make Catholicism secure? Certainly Pole put his mind against any aggressive missionary enterprise that might create deeper divisions. Ignatius Loyola, the founder of the greatest Catholic missionary order of the time, offered his Jesuit priests for the task in England, but this offer was rejected by Pole. It has been said that returning to the past was his main ambition rather than looking to a bright new future for Catholicism in tune with some of the new thinking from Counter-Reformation Europe. However, this is unfair. Pole had only a short time at his disposal and he was up against the physical despoliation of the churches and the problem of irregular priests. More positively, the cardinal called the synod of Westminster in 1555–6, where a series of reforming decrees was passed dealing with the clergy; these included ensuring priestly residence in parishes, and sermons on Sundays and feast days, as well as the far-sighted creation of seminaries for the training of priests. Given time for implementation these would surely have made a large impact. Pole and Mary certainly chose bishops noted for their theological and pastoral gifts rather than their legal training, and plans were also mooted for a Catholic English New Testament. Among other concrete achievements one can mention a spate of Catholic books, such as *A Profitable and Necessarye Doctryne* of Bishop Bonner of London, the *Holsome and Catholyke Doctryne* (1558) of Bishop Watson of Lincoln and a collection of official sermons. The aim of such works was to ensure an educated priesthood that in its turn could teach the laity. It is impossible to say what might have been achieved if Mary and Pole had been granted more time on earth: whatever criticisms one might make of their policies it is clear is that their work was not doomed to failure.

Yet no matter how dynamic Mary had been or how successful and popular in general her policies, everything came to nought with her early death on 17 November, followed within hours by the passing of Cardinal Pole. Mary died too soon without an heir of her body, and her crucial policies were all overturned, and so her story was to be written and distorted by the enemies who succeeded her. All her mistakes were therefore magnified, but her good points, such as her frequent generosity and kindness, were ignored, and she became the 'Bloody Mary' of legend. The reign ended ingloriously in a welter of military disgrace, economic misery from bad harvests, and devastating plague and influenza epidemics. The nearly 300 burnings of committed Protestants would scar her regime indelibly in the national memory. Protestants believed that God had spoken on the day of her death, closing a chapter of English history. The future lay with the Protestant half-sister who, when news of Mary's death was brought to her at Hatfield, was found seated under a tree reading the New Testament in Greek.

6 The Reign of Elizabeth I, 1558–1603

'And great Eliza's glorious name may ring':[1] **the monarchy of Elizabeth I**

The woman who became the last Tudor sovereign was only 25 years of age at her accession and unmarried. No one in November 1558 had any idea that she would rule for such a long period – nearly 45 years – down to 1603, or that she would preside over one of the truly great epochs in English history. Indeed the keynote of 1558–9 was one of tension and uncertainty. England seemed beset by crises: a religious crisis occasioned by continual changes in belief and devotion; a dynastic crisis created by the claim of Mary Queen of Scots to the English throne; an international crisis engendered by the inherited war against France and the French presence in Scotland; and an economic and demographic crisis owing to a vicious bout of influenza that seems to have reduced the population quite substantially in the years after 1556. Sir Thomas Smith might well bemoan that 'I never saw England...weaker in strength, money and riches.'

Yet despite this inauspicious start Elizabeth stamped her personality on the second half of the century, and there can be little doubt of the great reputation that Elizabeth I has enjoyed over the centuries as the saviour of her country and as the epitome of Englishness. The vast majority of historians have praised her highly, beginning with William Camden in the early seventeenth century. David Hume in the eighteenth century, although disliking the Tudors as unenlightened despots, praised the queen's abilities which 'appear not to have been surpassed by any person who ever filled the throne'. Hume concluded that '[f]ew sovereigns of England succeeded to the throne in more difficult circumstances; and none ever conducted the government with such uniform success and felicity'. In the nineteenth century even the Whig Lord Macaulay regarded Elizabeth's age as a golden one, whose 'memory is still dear to the hearts of a free people'. Bishop

Mandell Creighton enthused that '[s]he represented England as no other ruler ever did'. Among the throng of admirers only J. A. Froude in the mid-nineteenth stands out as a major exception for his carping criticisms, attacking her indecisiveness and judging that the successes of her reign were due principally to her ministers and not to her. However, the vast majority of historians have given the queen a good report card, even if they could not endorse all her policies. The Catholic writer John Lingard in the nineteenth century disliked her religious policy naturally, but he could still assert that she was 'among the greatest and most fortunate of princes'. Thus Elizabeth has generally been seen as a politician of genius, a woman whose self-mastery after years of uncertainty was the essential prelude to her mastery of government. The orthodox view has been that the queen's success was largely due to the fact that she followed a middle path (*via media*) avoiding the extremism and fanaticism so prevalent elsewhere at the time – a view which went back originally to Camden, and which was reinforced by the influential work of J. R. Green (1874). Green's view of a middle path of peace and stability has influenced all modern discussion of the queen. Sir John Neale, writing in 1958, perceived 'the recognition of her greatness by the consensus of the centuries'.[2]

In recent years, however, the chilly winds of revision have begun to blow, with the aim of toppling the queen off her pedestal. Foremost among the revisionists is Christopher Haigh, who writes that '[t]he monarchy of Elizabeth I was founded upon illusion...images which have misled historians for four centuries'.[3] One of these illusions, he claims, is that there was chaos on either side of her reign: the destabilising reigns of Edward VI and Mary, on the one hand, and the unpopular rule of her Stuart successor James I, the first step on the 'highway to civil war', on the other. Drawing on revisionist work rehabilitating those surrounding periods, Haigh can thus argue that the reign of Elizabeth was nothing special, not 'a golden age of national harmony'. Revisionists maintain that whatever successes were achieved by the Elizabethan regime came more through luck than by design; and that Elizabeth was an irresponsible housekeeper who merely swept the dust under the carpet rather than thoroughly cleansing and reforming her home. She was fortunate enough to have survived, but only at the cost of leaving unresolved problems to her successors. Injecting a note of sceptical realism is always a healthy corrective to high-flown mythology, but such revisionism seems prone to miss the big picture, namely Elizabeth's successful presiding over a major transition in the symbolism and direction of the English state. Elizabeth's achievement lay in her exerting a moderating influence at the critical passage from a Catholic to a permanently self-conscious Protestant state. It was not just a matter of time. Long reigns in themselves tend to prove troublesome rather than praiseworthy, so the key must lie elsewhere, probably in her fine judgement of character, especially regarding the men she chose to serve her.

Elizabeth's success was linked to the new Protestant establishment which took over the country and which needed her as its symbol; accordingly she became the embodiment of English Protestant nationalism. Initially she had to overcome the prejudice against female rule. She was only the second queen regnant, and immediately found herself attacked by John Knox's book (directed in fact at two Catholics, Queen Mary and the Scottish regent Mary of Guise), *The First Blast of the Trumpet against the Monstrous Regiment of Women* (1558), which had lambasted female rule as 'repugnant to nature, contumely to God, a thing most contrarious to his revealed will and approved ordinance'. To counteract such a widespread view the government first had to present Elizabeth as an Old Testament heroine, such as Deborah the judge and saviour of Israel – someone chosen by God despite her gender.

In her later years, from 1578 onwards, she would become a Protestant icon, the subject of a cult which aimed to put her almost on a par with the Virgin Mary in Catholicism. Although Elizabeth played along, the Elizabethan cult was the creation of others – those who needed her as a symbol of a staunch Protestant England surrounded by hostile Catholic states. A hatred of foreigners, which had militated against her sister Mary, could be fully employed in Elizabeth's favour. The new queen boasted that she was 'mere English' with no foreign blood in her veins (which was not quite true). As a symbol she was physically and temperamentally ideal, with a tall handsome figure (about 5 ft 10 in.) which good painters could exploit. She was also a fine actress who could change her mood quickly for any diplomatic reason. She made full use of the pomp and splendour of the Court, and was also a brilliant orator, with a scintillating use of words. Her scolding of MPs and their impertinent speeches on her marriage as 'lip-laboured orations out of such jangling subjects' mouths' is a good example of the new flexibilty of the English language, and there can be little doubt that her own eloquence was a spur to the literary genius of her age. She also possessed the common touch and communicated easily with her ordinary subjects.

One of the revisionist charges is that Elizabeth was irresponsible over her refusal to marry, that she 'risked instability after her death for the sake of stability in her own lifetime'.[4] The lack of a successor could have plunged England into civil war in 1562, when she nearly died of smallpox, and in 1578, when she narrowly missed death in a hunting accident. Elizabeth was naturally expected to marry in order to beget a male heir to continue the dynasty under strong rule. So why did she not marry? There has been a tendency to assume that she never intended to, perhaps because of negative psychological considerations stemming from childhood and adolescent experiences, or else because, more egotistically, she did not wish to diminish her own new-found authority and thus lose her role as the sole centre of attraction at Court. More altruistically, she has also been viewed as a modern career woman, a 'radical celibate' sacrificing domestic joys for the good of England. She made many comments that suggested her wish to remain single. In April 1558 she had said that 'I so well like this estate [of being single] as to persuade myself that there is not any kind of life comparable to it.' She told her first Parliament, when she was petitioned to marry:

> And in the end this shall be for me sufficient, that a marble stone shall declare that a queen, having reigned such a time, lived and died a virgin.

Again in 1563 she opined that it was better to be 'beggar woman and single, far rather than queen and married'. One of her suitors, Sir William Pickering, said 'he knew she meant to die a maid'. However, Elizabeth's attitude to Pickering might have been just designed to put him off. Indeed the evidence suggests that she was seriously considering marriage for emotional reasons to Robert Dudley in 1560–2, but desisted because of opposition from the council, especially from William Cecil, who spread rumours that Dudley had killed his wife Amy. Later, in 1579, Elizabeth appears to have been eager for political reasons, and also because she may have thought that this was her last chance, to wed Francis Duke of Anjou. Recently Susan Doran has suggested that Elizabeth remained a spinster only because of divisions within the council over a choice of husband, and not because of any personal wish to remain single.[5] The cult of the Virgin Queen was developed only from 1578 onwards by Protestants eager to sabotage the match with the Catholic Anjou, and as a kind of compensation for her not marrying. The plain fact is that Elizabeth's marriage problem was insoluble. If she married a foreigner – and among her European suitors were King Eric of Sweden, the Archduke Charles of Austria and King Philip of Spain – England risked being sucked into European entanglements and an inflexible foreign policy. If she married an Englishman, such as Pickering, Dudley or Arundel, she risked factionalism at home. Whatever the legal restrictions on the male consort there was always the danger that the Court would look for guidance from the consort first, rather than from the queen herself: hence Elizabeth's outburst against Dudley in 1564 that 'I shall have but one mistress and no master.' If she married at all she risked dying in childbirth, with all its attendant political miseries and uncertainties. Marriage and a sex life did not guarantee political stability. Her increasing preparedness to remain single did not induce her to name an heir, simply because she feared that people would look for favours from the successor rather than the queen – as no one knew she would last till 1603. She recalled how she was herself the focus of plots against her half-sister. On balance it can be said that Elizabeth made the best of her situation, and that celibacy was a sacrifice: this seems proved by her jealousy of other people's sexuality. Indeed she may have desired marriage to Anjou in 1579 because of her recent painful discovery of Dudley's new (third) marriage.

Also complicating marriage prospects was Elizabeth's exalted view of her own abilities: she knew that she was the equal of any man. Of course, she could not say this in a patriarchal world. She had no concept of modern feminism, and boxed the ears of her ladies-in-waiting when she discovered them discussing politics. Politics was for men, and for the queen who saw herself as an honorary man – a special instrument of God. She played to the popular conception of womanhood and her own unique position in politics: 'Although I have the body of a weak and feeble woman, I have the heart and stomach of a King, and a King of England too.' Sexism and chauvinism could be exploited to make her own position seem even more clearly divinely ordained. From the late 1570s she revelled in the cult being created for her and the adulation surrounding her. She was exalted as the pagan goddesses Cynthia and Diana; she was the virginal Astræa. She was Gloriana of Spenser's *Faerie Queene*. In the various later portraits of the queen Renaissance symbolism is used to depict her as a spotless virgin, a paragon of virtue and as the very embodiment of England, her reign possessing a cosmic dimension. Moreover, the antiquated and unrealistic painting technique, especially of the 'Ditchley portrait', was used to emphasise Elizabeth's role as an icon – on a par with medieval icons of the Virgin Mary. Altogether the propaganda campaign on the queen's behalf was the most systematic and developed ever used for any English, or indeed contemporary European, monarch. By the 1630s Elizabeth's life was commemorated in many London churches with the verse:

> Chaste Patroness of true Religion,
> In Court a Saint, in Field an Amazon,
> Glorious in life, deplored in death,
> Such was unparallel'd ELIZABETH.

She would prove to be a very hard act to follow.

Elizabethan courtly politics

The queen was a conservative, authoritarian monarch, while the vast majority of the ruling class wanted peace and harmony. All this made for an age that was in essence politically stable. Only a minority of religious zealots of both Catholic and Protestant hue posed a threat to the Elizabethan regime. Elizabeth herself was probably the most conservative ruler of the Tudor line. The reigns of her Tudor predecessors had been filled with change. Now with Elizabeth it became time to take stock of the situation and to establish harmony and a sense of permanency out of the discordant flux of the first half of the sixteenth century.

Her motto was *Semper Eadem* ('Always the Same'), emphasising her resistance to change and novelty, and her policies were drafted mainly in response to other people's actions. It certainly seems that the Elizabethan governments had 'lost the initiative' and were on the defensive.[6] Unlike her father, Elizabeth had no military ambitions in Europe – she would actually refuse the sovereignty of the Netherlands – and so her reign promised less sanguineous excitement. The queen aimed to put a cap on disruptive change. At the top there was stability but under the surface there were bubbling tensions created by the disruptive forces of the growth of capitalism and the novel surge in the population: between 1558 and 1603, it rose from under three million to over four – a massive increase in the context of the age, putting enormous burdens on agriculture, and leading to unemployment, underemployment and vagabondage in an economy which could not expand enough to find work for all its members. Despite contemporary emphasis on order and degree, the reality underneath was one of social mobility and economic change.

As with previous monarchs, the Court was the permanent but peripatetic centre of politics; and Elizabeth exploited a magnificent Court for its full propaganda effect. At its apex the leading courtiers had to make ritualised love to the queen, flattering her outrageously, which she always saw through but enjoyed and demanded. In the lower strata the Court was a place for doing deals and soliciting patronage. At its political heart was the queen's privy council. The Elizabethan council was small, with no more than 20 members, and with the real work being done by an inner ring of between 4 and 11 councillors. As Elizabeth stated in 1558: 'a multitude doth make rather discord and confusion than good counsel'; and thus she was adamant not to repeat Mary's mistake of a large council vulnerable to factionalism. The queen did not normally attend its meetings unless the matter under discussion was very serious. Although it acted as a corporate board in administering the realm, the queen viewed it as a collection of individuals whom she had appointed and could dismiss at will. Policy suggestions were generated by the council, which tried to persuade the queen on the course of action to be adopted. However, the queen had the last word, so that policy always remained personal to her. She was not bound by even the unanimous advice of her councillors, and like her sister Mary she could go outside the council for advice, as when she called upon Robert Dudley before he was officially admitted late in 1562, or upon the Earl of Sussex before he joined at the end of 1570. On some issues the councillors were united against the queen – especially on her need to marry or to name a successor – but in these matters the queen relied on her own judgement much as the councillors might try to persuade her through agitation in Parliament. If the queen did not wish to be moved nothing could budge her. Increasingly, Elizabeth chose professional bureaucrats from the household and departments of state as her councillors – men like Sir William Cecil – rather than noblemen whose claim to appointment was their standing and blood.

Most earlier historians emphasised the importance of factions at Elizabeth's Court, seeing the period as constituting a classic example of them. Such a notion largely derived from the contemporary courtier Sir Robert Naunton in his *Fragmenta Regalia* (Royal Fragments, *c*.1630), which stated:

> The principal note of her reign will be that she ruled much by faction and parties which [she] herself both made, upheld and weakened as her own great judgement advised.

Naunton thought that this was more correct than the general view of his time that Robert Dudley, Earl of Leicester had been 'absolute and alone in her grace'. Naunton's verdict has misled most historians in the past. However, the situation was not as clear as Naunton's judgement implies. After all, he wrote from the unsavoury perspective of the Stuart Court where power had become monopolised by a favourite, and saw the old Elizabethan Court by contrast in glowing terms. It now appears that Naunton's description of the queen's role is unreliable, and the very existence of Elizabethan factions has been the subject of controversy. Simon Adams is sceptical of the use of the term 'factions' to describe the rival patronage networks of the great courtiers prior to the 1590s and the advent of the very factious Earl of Essex.[7] This judgement seems to be correct if by 'faction' one means something on the lines of the bloodthirsty political factions of the 1530s and 1540s. Henrician factions had an aggressive aspect to them as well as an ideological or religious axe to grind. Later under the early Stuarts there would be major policy differences between the factions involving religion and foreign alliances. However, the Elizabethan Court was noted for its high degree of what might be termed 'consensus politics'. After 1570 religious conservatives were largely absent from the Court, and the differences within Protestantism were not sufficient to threaten the consensus. Protestants realised only too well that they lived in a hostile world beset by Catholics so that they could not indulge in too much internal bickering. The Court became a homogeneous Protestant one after 1570, and just as there had been a conscious desire by the political elite to avoid civil war in 1549 and 1553, so too under Elizabeth the courtly elite did not wish to return to the gruesome politics of her father. Nor was the Court such a threat to the virtual monopoly of power exercised by the privy council; there was no rivalry between privy chamber and privy council as there had been in the 1540s. This was partly due to the fact that the privy chamber was a female one, and its ladies less important politically than the gentlemen had been in the later years of Henry VIII or under Edward VI. However, it would be false to say that the ladies of the chamber had no political influence at all, but it was indirect – through the gossip and rumours so prevalent at Court and through the husbands and relatives of the queen's ladies. The stability of the Elizabethan Court was also partly based on its monopolisation by the same families who made up a charmed circle from which outsiders were largely excluded. Offices at Court were often passed from father to son and even mother to daughter. Only two outsiders from minor gentry families broke into this charmed circle – Sir Christopher Hatton and Sir Walter Ralegh – because of their charismatic good looks.

No one, of course, has ever doubted the existence of personal rivalry in Elizabeth's Court, especially between William Cecil and Leicester, between Sussex and Leicester, between Norfolk and Leicester, and later between Ralegh and Robert Cecil and also between Ralegh and Essex. At times these tensions could superficially appear close to Henrician factionalism, as when Norfolk and Sussex tried to prove that Leicester had murdered his wife Amy Robsart; and when in 1569 a number of nobles ganged up against William Cecil and tried to bring him down. Besides personal animosities there were also the policy differences over how best to defend Protestant England. Leicester and Sir Francis Walsingham tended to demand intervention in Europe with a forward foreign policy, while Cecil agreed with the queen on the need to be cautious of European entanglements. However, there were no hard lines of demarcation, and to contrast Leicester as a hawk with Cecil a dove is misleading, because Cecil could play the hawk too when circumstances were right. Certainly personal prestige was involved, and leading patrons were anxious to gain as many clients as possible beholden to them in order to emphasise their own elevated position. Thus William Cecil, Lord Burghley was annoyed when William Camden was given a heraldic office through someone else's patronage and was mollified only when told that Camden had done nothing to seek out the honour. But these personal or policy differences were not great enough to create true factions before the 1590s.

In opposition to the picture of a non-factional, stable Court, ruptured only by petty jealousies, Christopher Haigh has recently recreated the older picture of 'dangerous factional conflicts which destabilised English politics'. He speaks of 'the struggle between the Dudley and Howard alliances', and judges that because of the rivalry of Leicester and Sussex 'for a time civil war had seemed the likely outcome'. Haigh argues that the Court was increasingly aggressive because of the fiercer competition for patronage among the courtiers occasioned by the queen's meanness and also because Elizabeth brought sexuality into politics and so 'raised the emotional temperature of the Court to a dangerous level'.[8] This all appears a gross exaggeration of the dangers involved before the 1590s.

The Essex rebellion, 1601

The spectre of true factionalism can be discerned only in the 1590s. The queen had never allowed true political 'favourites' to emerge, certainly not the kind who obtained power simply because she liked them. She was often infatuated with handsome men, but she never gave them power unless they had earned it. Only in the 1590s can one say that the queen's firm grip began to relax, but even then she remained in overall control. A new situation developed mainly through the appearance at Court of Robert Devereux, Earl of Essex. The ageing Elizabeth was besotted with this handsome and cultivated young man – perhaps seeing him as the son she never had. So many of the stalwarts of the regime had recently died: her beloved Leicester ('Sweet Robin') in 1588, Mildmay in 1589, Walsingham in 1590, Hatton in 1591. Old Lord Burghley was ailing but would soldier on till 1598. All this meant that a political vacuum was opening up, and Essex was determined to fill it with himself and his supporters. On the other hand, Burghley was grooming his younger hunchbacked son Robert Cecil to take over the Cecil interest. Robert Cecil and Essex would become the great rival leaders of opposing factions in the 1590s, but the evidence suggests that only Essex was seriously interested in monopolising power for himself and his faction. Robert Cecil was pushed by Essex into heading a rival group, so that this became a decade of factional intrigue of the type not seen earlier in the reign.

Essex was Leicester's stepson and had first come to Court with him in 1584 at the age of 18. After Leicester's death many of his affinity rallied to find a new master in Essex, who thereupon began building up a party in the country, at Court and even in Parliament; indeed 'Essex was the one man in this period, not excepting his great political rival Sir Robert Cecil, with whom parliamentary patronage became an obsession'.[9] Factional disputes now even extended to local appointments. Essex regarded himself as the heir not only to Leicester but also to Sir Philip Sidney and his literary circle. Among Essex's supporters were Sir Robert Sidney and the brothers Anthony and Francis Bacon. Essex made his London home of Essex House the meeting place for a large group of restless men with grudges, unfulfilled ambitions and literary interests and imagination. William Shakespeare, through his patron the Earl of Southampton, belonged to the Essex affinity, and may well have been inspired to write *Romeo and Juliet* by the family feuding in Wiltshire involving two of Essex's adherents.[10] It has also been suggested that Shakespeare could have written his *Richard III* in the early 1590s about an evil hunchbacked king as a sly way of attacking the deformed Cecil.[11] Another Essex admirer was the poet Edmund Spenser, who in his *Prothalamion*, alluding to the famous Cadiz raid of 1596, praised Essex as

a noble peer,
Great England's glory and the world's wide wonder,
Whose dreadful name late through all Spain did thunder.

Essex tried to get his clients appointed throughout the Court and clashed accordingly with the Cecilians. Politically, Essex, like Leicester before him, supported bold and brash military intervention in Europe, but found the queen and the Cecils reluctant to follow. The problem for Essex was that as a soldier who was eager for glory on military adventures he had to be away from Court, where during his absence his enemies could undermine his power. It was during his absence in France during 1591–2, he believed, that he had been stabbed in the back by his enemies at Court when Robert Cecil was made a privy councillor. This grudge drove Essex to try and monopolise court office and favour for his faction. He had an initial victory over Cecil in 1593 when he successfully unravelled a conspiracy to murder the queen by her Portuguese doctor, a conspiracy that had earlier been denied by Cecil. During his absence on the Cadiz raid of 1596, when Essex became a national hero, Robert Cecil was appointed secretary of state (after acting in this capacity for six years) and master of the court of wards, thus perpetuating Cecil influence in government. The rivalry was created by Essex, not by Cecil. Francis Bacon's wish for appointment as solicitor-general was vetoed by the queen, whereas Robert Cecil had actually put in a good word for him. Essex took the rejection personally and developed a persecution complex. He was also absent from Court when he was appointed lord lieutenant of Ireland. He then went to Ireland hoping against the odds to have a great victory over the rebellious Earl of Tyrone. But in this he failed – indeed he had not engaged the enemy at all – and returned home unannounced in 1599 without the queen's permission in order to surprise and indeed overthrow the Cecil group at Court. There then occurred the famous scene at Nonsuch Palace when in the morning he burst in on the queen before she had had time to put on her make-up or arrange her hair. She hid her displeasure at being seen in such an unkempt state and received him graciously, but a little later she had the Court closed to him. Essex had bargained on the queen's forgiveness, but he had fooled himself and a period of disgrace ensued. By August

1600 he was free again, but had lost all his crown offices. Essex was not a great landowner or wealthy man in his own right; his riches had come from his court connections. He was heavily in debt, and the queen now witheld his lucrative monopoly on the import of sweet wines. Being powerless and poor drove Essex to extreme measures. The members of his party had pinned all their hopes on him, and they were ready to rise in rebellion. This is just what Essex's feverish brain now plotted. The planned uprising broke out in February 1601 with the aim of capturing London, the Tower and the Court. However, rumours of the impending event began to spread, and Essex was summoned to Court to answer them. He refused and instead was forced into trying to rally the City to his cause. But owing to Cecil's intelligent handling of the matter and the disinclination of Londoners to rebel the enterprise failed. It is significant that on the day before the rising Essex had paid the actors at the *Globe Theatre* in Southwark to stage Shakespeare's *Richard II*, a play about a monarch who was forced off the throne for bad governance (and then killed); such a fate was now intended for Elizabeth. Shakespeare's patron the Earl of Southampton was involved in the coup and imprisoned in the Tower. But Southampton would be forgiven, thanks to Robert Cecil's intervention: not so Essex, whom not even the queen's love could save. He went to the block at the age of 34 as a warning to all that Elizabeth would never surrender her control.

Christopher Haigh's conclusion that 'Elizabeth had brought the Essex rising upon herself'[12] because of her parsimony in patronage seems wide of the mark; Essex's vaunting and unbridled ambition alone caused his ruin. Essex had sought to monopolise the Court in a way quite uncharacteristic of the Elizabethan age. Elizabeth had rewarded Essex but she had realised his shallowness and irresponsibility, and had refused him any high office at Court. It was the queen rather than Robert Cecil who had stood in his political path. Not even in her dotage did Elizabeth lose all sense of political reality. Yet the result was that Robert Cecil was now able to dominate the Court in the way his father had not. The balance was now tilted, and as the queen's death approached the Cecilians scooped all the prizes. The balance of 'factions' was gone, and this was a foretaste of what was in store under the Stuarts – disequilibrium.

Elizabethan Parliaments

Parliaments in the sixteenth century were intermittent and not the regular heart of government. Elizabeth called only ten Parliaments, in 13 sessions, in all her long reign.[13] The average length of a session was three months, so that the total time of parliamentary sittings was just over three years out of a reign of nearly 45 years. Sir Thomas Smith saw 'few Parliaments' as a blessing, not as a deprivation. They were not eagerly desired by anyone, mainly because of the expense involved in the Members having to lodge in London, as most of them had by this time waived their right to payment of wages for the local prestige of being elected. Yet Parliaments had to be called when the queen needed new taxes or legislation. Indeed the almost certain knowledge that a new Parliament meant a new vote of taxation (which otherwise was not regular) was another reason why people might welcome an absence of Parliament. So what exactly was the role of Parliament in the Elizabethan period?

Until the 1970s the history of the Elizabethan Parliament was normally viewed in the light and knowledge of the Great Civil War of the mid-seventeenth century, which ended with Parliament gaining supremacy in 1649. Historians tended to look for the seeds of that later victory back in the reign of Elizabeth, and they interpreted the Elizabethan Parliament as a self-conscious political assembly that was flexing its muscles to challenge the power of the Crown. They perceived the origins of the 'rise of Parliament' in the Elizabethan age which was supposed to have witnessed a struggle between Puritan radicals in the House of Commons and the conservative queen, thus preparing the groundwork for the more obvious struggle under the early Stuarts.

Sir John Neale believed that the growing importance of Parliament as an institution in the Elizabethan period could be gauged by its growing size – from 296 Members in 1500 to 462 in 1600 – and by the greater definition it had achieved under the Tudors. The Commons were certainly developing a real self-consciousness and were eager to defend the liberties of the House. But did this mean that they envisaged more power for themselves? Neale thought that they did. Neale emphasised the growth of conflict between the Commons and the queen. He linked their rebelliousness to the growth of Puritanism. In the session of 1566, for example, the House was 'singularly independent, not to say rebellious'. To start with, the government's nominee for Speaker, Richard Onslow, was accepted by a margin of only 12 votes.[14] Neale believed that an opposition 'puritan choir' existed in this session on the evidence of a 'lewd pasquil' written by a Member in which were characterised some 43 of his fellow-Members. Ten years later in 1576 Peter Wentworth made a famous speech on the theme of liberty when he eloquently declaimed that '[s]weet indeed is the name of liberty, and the thing itself a value beyond all inestimable treasure'. Thus the origins of the modern Parliament were to be sought in the Elizabethan age, propelled by religious imperatives.

This attractive theory which dovetailed so well with that of the Civil War being caused by a revolutionary Puritan Parliament has suffered a severe battering since the 1970s. To begin with, in 1963 the medievalist J. S. Roskell revived the older idea that the power of the Commons had been greater in the later fourteenth century than it was to be in the late sixteenth and that the Tudor Parliament was therefore in no sense modern. Both the Yorkist and Tudor periods, he argued, witnessed a decline in the power of Parliament. Before 1460 there is evidence that the Commons were able to withhold their assent to taxation and punish royal councillors by process of impeachment even against the wishes of the king, neither of which was possible in the sixteenth century. Roskell denied that the evidence cited for the growth and greater definition of the Tudor Commons in any way meant that Parliament gained more power in the state. The guarantee of freedom of speech (officially granted in 1523) was 'largely illusory in practice', he maintained, if one looks at the frequent imprisonment of Elizabethan Members who spoke their minds. Certainly Elizabeth did not believe in true freedom of speech for MPs but made the novel distinction between 'matters of commonwealth' (such as economic and social issues) which could be discussed spontaneously by the House, and 'matters of state' (such as religion, foreign policy, her marriage and the succession) which were part of her prerogative and which could be discussed only with her express approval. Roskell saw Parliament remaining an essentially medieval body until 1689, when annual sessions of Parliament became the norm after the Glorious Revolution.[15]

Roskell's challenge to the importance of the Tudor period was taken up by G. R. Elton, who tried to validate the modernity of the Tudor Commons by reference to its constitutional development and the modernising work of Thomas Cromwell. Elton attacked both Neale and Roskell for using the criterion of the growth of conflict as the yardstick to measure the modernity of Parliament. Instead Elton posited the clearer constitutional position of Parliament as 'the body of the whole realm' to indicate its maturity. Whereas before Cromwell's time the king could be viewed as being outside or above Parliament, from 1534 onwards it became the convention to regard the monarch as one part of the trinity of king, Lords and Commons – three separate institutions which made up the single institution of Parliament. In many European states, even those which had experienced assemblies that had been very successful in conflict, those assemblies or estates tended to vanish with the growth of royal absolutism: not so in England, where the medieval convention of political sharing was now buttressed by the inclusion of the monarch in the Parliament, making sovereignty reside in the concept of monarch-in-Parliament.[16] Thus Sir Thomas Smith could write in 1565 that '[t]he most high and absolute power of the realm of England consisteth in the Parliament'. Here clearly Parliament included the queen or the statement would have been gibberish. William Cecil could say that '[o]f these three estates [queen, Lords and Commons] doth consist the whole body of the realm, able to make laws'. Bishop Aylmer could write that 'the regiment [government] of England is not a mere monarchy... nor a mere oligarchy, nor democracy, but a rule mixed of all these, the image whereof... is to be seen in the Parliament House, wherein you shall find these three estates'.

Elton attacked Neale's criterion of conflict to gauge the growing modernity of Parliament. Neale, he thought, had misread the history of the Commons by using the diaries of Puritan MPs which distorted the reality of parliamentary proceedings by recording religious debates to the exclusion of more mundane issues which in fact took up most of Parliament's time. Elton viewed Parliament as a place for getting business done, not as a place for political conflict. Indeed Elton's view, after the

'Cromwellian revolution' of the 1530s, was of an essentially stable society, not one filled with tension. Elton probably underestimated the amount of political conflict in Parliament, which truly desired to be consulted on major issues. Yet he was right to deny Parliament's wish to usurp power.

As for some of the highlights of Neale's conflict story, the problem of Richard Onslow was a technical rather than a political one because he believed that his oath as solicitor-general (an office which gave him a seat in the Lords by a writ of assistance) was incompatible with that of the Speaker of the Commons, and it was over this technical point that the House divided. As for the 'Puritan choir', Neale was wrong to regard these men as forming a Puritan party. If William Strickland – 'Strickland the stinger' – was certainly a Puritan, another mentioned in the pasquil, Francis Alford, was a conservative in religion and supporter of the Elizabethan Church Settlement, while 'Browne the blasphemer' hardly seemed to qualify as a religious zealot. The pasquil pokes fun at the small number of regular speakers in contrast to the dozing majority rather than supplying evidence of an 'opposition' group.[17] There certainly were attempts to put pressure on the queen to name her successor, but these seem to have been the joint effort of Parliament and many members of the privy council.

The making of the Elizabethan religious settlement, 1559

Tudor England was a religiously based state; its monarchy claimed divine sanction. Therefore the most important question for Elizabeth and her advisers to settle immediately on her succession was the religious complexion of the state. The various changes already made since the 1530s had undermined people's faith in both religion itself and the authority of the government. Whatever kind of church system now had to be agreed upon, it would be a comprehensive church to include all English people. Pluralism in religion was not to be countenanced. As William Cecil put it later: 'They that differ in the service of God can never agree in the service of their country.' Elizabeth's problem was to find a formula of faith that would be acceptable to the majority of the nation. Had she conducted a referendum to discover people's wishes there would almost certainly have been an overwhelming majority vote for the return of Henrician Catholicism. Neale thought that this is what Elizabeth initially desired but was frustrated by ardent Puritans from gaining it. She reportedly remarked to the Spanish ambassador that she 'resolved to restore religion as her father left it'. However, this idea has now been generally rejected. From the start Elizabeth was committed to a Protestant settlement, if only because her friends and advisers during her years of adversity were staunch Protestants and she herself had been the focal point of anti-Catholic conspiracies in Mary's time. She made known her opposition to both papal and Henrician Catholicism when on Christmas Day 1558 she walked out of her chapel during the Christmas mass in protest against the elevation of the host. Her main problem now was to decide which brand of Protestantism to enforce.

What guided Elizabeth in formulating her religious policy? There has been a tradition of saying that Elizabeth was 'secular' and that her religious policy was guided solely by political requirements. However, Elizabeth was not secular in the modern sense of the word, but had a deep knowledge of the Bible. Nevertheless, she was not as doctrinaire as her sister had been, but instead believed that she should 'not make windows into men's hearts and minds'. Elizabeth was a Protestant, yet only in the negative sense that she was not a Catholic. What she needed now was a religious formula that would satisfy the largest number of people in her realm. Her Church had to be a comprehensive one, not one so narrow as to exclude or alienate large numbers from it.

In the 1950s Sir John Neale believed that the uproar generated in the Commons over the religious settlement set the tone for the rest of the reign by allowing religious radicals, or Puritans as they would soon be called, to score a victory over the queen's more moderate proposals. This gave them confidence to oppose Elizabeth in later Parliaments so that the reign of Elizabeth became notable for friction and conflict based on religious ideology. Neale's thesis became the orthodoxy until it was challenged in the 1980s by Norman Jones, who denied that the final settlement represented a victory for an 'opposition' and argued that the settlement was what the government desired from the start. If there was an obstacle to it, this was to be found in the conservatives in the Lords, not among any radicals in the Commons.[18]

Over Easter 1559 a disputation was held in Westminster Abbey between Catholic and Protestant divines – not so much to seek truth as to discredit the conservative side. Afterwards two Catholic bishops were imprisoned – White of Winchester and Watson of Lincoln – which further reduced the conservative party in the Lords. When Parliament reconvened after Easter, a new Supremacy bill was introduced, which (as a sop to both sides) made Elizabeth supreme governor (rather than supreme head) of the Church of England. This bill had an easy passage in the Commons but met some resistance in the Lords. The Catholic bishops there put up the biggest fight, with all of them, plus the temporal peer Viscount Montague, voting against the Supremacy bill, which nevertheless got through.

The bill for Uniformity (and a Prayer Book) sailed through the Commons but just squeezed through the Lords, with nine lay peers supporting the consolidated resistance of the Marian bishops. Catholic arguments about novelty in religion struck a chord in the minds of many and almost led to the government's loss of this bill. It was touch-and-go, with the bill passing by 21 votes to 18. There were five other Catholic votes possible, but two of the voters (Lincoln and Winchester) were still in the Tower, Bishop Goldwell and Bishop Tunstall had not been summoned to Parliament, while Abbot Feckenham was mysteriously unavailable on the day. Had these five been allowed to vote the bill would have foundered.

So the government just won, and the thorn in their flesh was not the radical exiles, as Neale had supposed, but the conservative bishops and their lay allies in the Lords. Indeed there were not many returned Marian exiles in the Commons in 1559 – only 19 in fact. There certainly were former exiles around in 1559, but they had greater influence in the Court and council than specifically in the House of Commons. For example, all but one of the Protestant disputants at Easter had been exiles under Mary.

In the final Settlement the queen's position as supreme governor was to be obeyed in oaths from all clergy, public officials and university graduates. Everybody was to attend church on Sundays and holydays or risk being fined 12d. a time. Norman

Jones argues that this final settlement was really what the government wanted throughout: Supremacy, Uniformity and a Prayer Book. This is almost certainly the case. When Lord Keeper Nicholas Bacon opened the Parliament, he stated that it was urgently required to have 'a uniform order of religion' – which clearly implied a Prayer Book. But which one? The conservative Book of 1549 or the more extreme one of 1552? Jones argues that the second Prayer Book was always the one in mind, but there are solid reasons for doubting this. Although Elizabeth was a Protestant she was a very moderate one who liked both candles and a crucifix in her private chapel. Moreover, one clause of the Settlement was that the vestments allowed to priests included those in existence in 1548: that is those before the first Prayer Book, including ornate copes – in fact all the vestments of the Middle Ages (which is the reason they can all be employed in the Church today). This clause specifying the year 1548 could have come only from the queen. Furthermore, the fact that the Latin version of the Prayer Book released in 1560 for college chapels and for private prayer allowed requiems and reservation of the sacrament for the sick tends to suggest that Elizabeth may well have preferred the 1549 Prayer Book. Neale was probably on the right track to argue that there was some kind of struggle between the queen and the radicals over the exact form of service. The radicals won out with the 1552 version, but the queen insisted that it should be subject to conservative modifications: in particular the two sets of words for the distribution of communion[19] were included from both the 1549 and 1552 Prayer Books to allow greater latitude in interpreting the nature of Christ's presence in the bread and wine. Thus the resulting Settlement was not a parliamentary victory over the queen. However, it might be argued that on liturgical details the queen was indeed defeated – by her councillors and her radical divines, on whom she depended at first.

Tension was built into the Settlement of 1559, with a Protestant Church housed in a medieval framework which made the Church of England unique in sixteenth-century Europe. It was the creation of Parliament and had to be obeyed by all English people. But there were two groups in society in particular who were extremely reluctant to concede that the final word on religious matters lay with the queen and Parliament: the Puritans and the Papists, both of whom sought a higher authority to govern their beliefs. However, the vast majority of parish clergy conformed to the Settlement. Of the 8000 or so clergy of England it is difficult to number exactly those who refused to take the oath of Supremacy, but it is clear that the vast majority of ordinary parish priests conformed. This means that it was mainly Marian clergy who were still in charge of the parishes in the early years of Elizabeth. But at the top there was a clean sweep (or almost) when all but one of the Marian bishops refused to subscribe to the oath of Supremacy and were sacked, being replaced by convinced Protestants – the sole exception was the aged Anthony Kitchen of Llandaff, who had agreed to every change since 1545. Most of the other higher Catholic clergy also resigned. The new bishops appointed on the sacking of Mary's bishops were radicals to start with: all but three were from Cambridge and most (17 out of 25) had been in exile during Mary's reign, imbibing advanced religious thought. Most were dissatisfied with the Settlement, to be sure, but decided to conform to the queen's wishes: men like John Jewel of Salisbury, Edmund Grindal of London and Edwin Sandys of Worcester. Although forced to employ Marian exiles, Elizabeth chose as her first archbishop a moderate who had remained at home under Mary, Matthew Parker.

Elizabeth and the foreign danger: France and Scotland, 1559–60

Elizabeth's own aims in foreign affairs appear to have been confined to national defence. She had no desire to win land in Europe or colonies outside; and she was usually very conscious of the cost involved in foreign adventures. Elizabeth's main initial worry was over who controlled the other side of the English Channel. Her first problem was to deal with the inherited war with France. Negotiations, which had indeed begun shortly before Mary's death, to end the war were restarted in February 1559 and would lead to the Treaty of Cateau-Cambrésis (April 1559). There was a face-saving clause for Calais to be returned to England after eight years or else France would pay 500 000 crowns for it. The treaty was due to the bankruptcy of all three participants – not because anyone had learnt any lessons. What the future held for Anglo-French relations was still anyone's guess. No one could have foreseen the accidental death of Henry II of France after a jousting accident in July, and his removal greatly lessened the threat to Elizabeth's monarchy. Henry's strong and ambitious rule was replaced by a long period of weak monarchy in France, and from 1562 by over 30 years of civil war. Indeed both England's 'greatness' under Elizabeth and the Spanish 'preponderance' in Europe under Philip II owed much to the absence of France as a great power during its period of chaos. Henry II had devised plans not only to continue the 'Auld Alliance' between France and Scotland but also to absorb Scotland entirely into France. He married off his heir Francis II to Mary Queen of Scots, and Francis was given the crown matrimonial of Scotland, which meant that he would succeed there should Mary predecease him, or else a son would succeed them in both kingdoms: either way France would get Scotland. Henry also pressed the claims of his daughter-in-law Mary Queen of Scots to the English throne, and had England's arms quartered with those of Scotland on her coat of arms.

Had he lived, Henry would have posed a formidable threat to Elizabeth. England's two traditional enemies of France and Scotland would have made a potent union of opposition, but in both countries the situation turned in Elizabeth's favour. In Scotland Elizabeth's burden was eased by the rise of a Protestant party, the Lords of the Congregation, originally formed in 1557 to undermine both Catholic and French power in Scotland. However, French policy of trying to dominate Scotland did not cease immediately on Henry's death. The Scottish regent, Mary of Guise, was the mother of Mary Queen of Scots and a member of the mighty Guise family that now held sway at the French Court under Francis II. French troops arrived in Scotland in August 1559, and Cecil advised Elizabeth to intervene in Scotland on the side of the Protestant Lords; indeed he threatened to resign if she refused to consent. So much for the notion of Cecil the dove! The queen gave in and an English squadron was sent to the Firth of Forth (January 1560), and in March a military force crossed the border. The main beneficial effect of this was to encourage the Scots to resist the French and the regent. In the midst of this crisis Mary of Guise died in Edinburgh Castle (June 1560), and by the Treaty of Edinburgh (July 1560) France and England agreed to evacuate their troops from Scotland. This amounted to a French defeat, as did the success of the Protestant Lords of the Congregation putting through the Scottish Parliament in August measures to ban the Catholic mass and papal power in Scotland. Finally, the death of Francis II in December 1560 broke the dynastic link between France and Scotland. The danger to Elizabeth was now receding; Scotland was on the road to Protestantism and the military aspect of the 'Auld Alliance' was now dead – although, of course, this was not clear at the time. Scotland was still a separate country from England, and nobody could accurately predict the future state of Anglo-Scottish or Franco-Scottish relations. A Catholic resurgence was possible, as was a new bid by the French to resurrect their old alliance, but for the moment all looked very satisfactory from the window of the English Court.

The religious problem: the Puritans

The term 'Puritan' made its first appearance in the language in 1565–6 as a term of abuse levelled against certain opponents of the Settlement in the so-called 'vestiarian controversy' – over the wearing of the prescribed clerical vestments. As a term of abuse it had no clearly defined meaning, but much has since been made of it, both theologically and sociologically.[20] The abstract term 'puritanism' was first coined around 1571, but any attempt to see 'puritanism' as a coherent body of ideas or as a necessarily dynamic and revolutionary force in society should be resisted. Too easily a historian can slide into unfounded generalisations about 'puritanism', especially sociological assumptions about Puritans as capitalists or revolutionary politicians. And we should certainly not think in terms of simple continuity between Elizabethan Puritans and those later Puritans who engaged in the Great Civil War and the Puritan Republic. The whole notion of revolutionary 'puritanism' in the period before the Civil War has been the subject of a great deal of revisionism in the last 20 years, and much scepticism now hangs over the modern developed concept of 'puritanism'.

The term 'Puritan' was first used against those clergy who in objecting to have to wear any clerical garb at all were accused of wishing to purify the Church of popish remnants from the Settlement. They were also called 'precisians' or 'precisionists' because they wanted to make the Church more 'precise' and less ambiguous. Puritans condemned the Settlement as 'a crooked halting betwixt two religions' and a 'mingle-mangle'. At one time it was believed that Puritans and Anglicans were two separate groups and that the Puritans were trying to overthrow the Anglican Church, but today that view has been discarded. Puritans were really Anglicans who wanted further godly reform to make the Anglican Church more like the Church of the apostles. They wanted to purify the existing state Church, not get rid of it. The Puritan debate was an internal quarrel for control of the Church of England. The big stumbling-block was the queen because she refused to change one iota of the Settlement.

What sort of people were the Puritans? One must immediately rid oneself of the common stereotype of a plain, middling-sort kind of person who wore peculiar clothes or a broad-brimmed hat. That usually applies to the seventeenth century rather than the sixteenth – to the Quakers rather than to Elizabethan Puritans. Puritans spanned many status groups in the Elizabethan age – from courtiers and government officials through the landed gentry to the yeomanry and town merchants. No one group was exclusively Puritan, and every group of importance contained Puritans. They were certainly represented in both Parliament and the Court. Two leading courtly Puritans, who certainly did not look like the popular stereotype, were the earls of Leicester and Warwick – the brothers Robert and Ambrose Dudley. Other noble Puritans were the dowager Duchess of Suffolk, Henry Hastings, Earl of Huntingdon and Francis Russell, Earl of Bedford. The patronage that could be exercised by notables like these was very wide indeed; they could place Puritan clergy directly into church livings in their possession, and into parish lectureships and university positions. Puritan academics were especially important as they could educate a whole new generation of Puritan clergy. The two universities produced Puritan graduates because both chancellors had Puritan sympathies: Cecil at Cambridge, and Robert Dudley at Oxford. London too was a hub of Puritan activity, where at a very early date in the reign the Genevan Brotherhood was formed by activists inspired by Calvin's Geneva.

Above all, Puritans were rabidly anti-Catholic and eager for a 'reformation of manners' among their neighbours by enforcing godliness and curbing immorality. Most Puritans can be classed as moderates who were prepared to accept episcopacy and the role of the queen as supreme governor but who also wanted greater accountability by the bishops to the ordinary congregations. A smaller but more dangerous group were the Presbyterians who wished to abolish episcopacy and bring in a form of ecclesiastical government more reminiscent of Calvin's Geneva. A third group were not really Puritans at all in the original usage of the term, namely the Separatists, who desired not to reform the state Church but to leave it altogether because it was beyond redemption in their opinion. The Separatist Puritans were to be more important under the Stuarts, some fleeing England for the greater freedom of America aboard the *Mayflower*.

In the Elizabethan period there were few genuine theological differences between the Anglican establishment and its Puritan critics. The Puritan tract *The Admonition to the Parliament* (1572) conceded that 'it must be confessed that the substance of doctrine delivered by many is sound and good'. This was because for most of Elizabeth's reign the leading bishops shared with Puritans a basic Calvinist theology. There was a Calvinist theological predominance among church leaders down to the 1590s, with the acceptance of Calvin's teaching on double predestination and the denial of free will in gaining salvation; the world was divided into a minority of the elect and a majority of the reprobate, whose fate had been decided by God from the beginning of the world – 'the truly terrifying decree'. Calvin's own criteria for knowing whether or not one belonged to the elect were clarified by the Cambridge Calvinist theologian William Perkins, who argued that one could be certain of one's own election.[21] The quarrels between the Puritans and Elizabeth's government were over the need for a campaign of Protestant evangelisation to wake up the people (or more correctly its elect members) and over the reform of the government of the Church. All Puritans would have agreed with the *Admonition to the Parliament*, a Presbyterian tract by John Field and Thomas Wilcox, when it claimed that the Word of God was not being purely preached in the parishes and that the sacraments were not being 'sincerely' administered. This was an attack on the fact that most parish clergy were poor preachers, or 'bare readers' who at best could merely read out from the official book of Homilies, rather than deliver an erudite and impassioned sermon that would touch the hearts and minds of the hearers. Puritans were renowned for their 'gadding to sermons' – and long sermons at that – which they mostly regarded as necessary to salvation. Puritans wanted a preaching ministry to evangelise the elect, not in the hope of converting the apathetic reprobate majority; they approved of 'painful' (that is, painstaking) preachers. The queen was reluctant to allow theological preaching because it created discord and disputation and because she did not want ordinary parishioners dejected by the thought of their own ineluctable damnation. The Thirty-nine Articles of 1563 referred only to the elect, and not to the damned. As for the sacraments, the *Admonition* claimed that the Prayer Book was impure, with such popish forms as the Nicene Creed, the use of the ring in marriage or the need for godparents in baptismal services. None of these things could find a warrant in Scripture and were therefore damnable.

On these two general areas Puritans agreed on a common indictment of the Anglican Church; but when it came to the third point raised by the *Admonition*, namely that there should be true discipline (or organisation) in the Church – and the Scottish Presbyterian model was praised – then the various strands of Puritan opinion fell apart. Moderate Puritans could accept the rule of bishops if those bishops were humble men and elected by the local congregations; even Calvin had accepted the validity of such bishops. Presbyterian Puritans, however, strove to abolish episcopacy and the whole hierarchical system that went with it and replace it with a 'parity' of clergy. Instead of power starting at the top with the queen and her archbishops and filtering downwards to the humblest curate, the Presbyterians wanted the four equal officers of pastor, doctor, lay deacon and lay elder, which was what Calvin claimed was the system in the Early Church. Pastors were preachers, doctors were theologians, while deacons handled charity and elders supervised discipline and morals. Furthermore, power was to start at the bottom with the local presbytery (or parish). Presbyteries of a region were to be joined up into *classes*, which were to send delegates to provincial and then national synods – the notion of an ascending polity, or power starting at the bottom. In reality it was not quite as democratic as this, but it stood in marked contrast to the descending polity of Elizabeth's Church. No wonder she hated Puritanism because of its threat to monarchical control of religion. Theoretically Puritanism might be suspected of being revolutionary: the equality of the saints, or the elect, might make them devalue worldly authority, and much has been made of the notion of revolutionary Puritanism. However, Puritans were more conservative in practice than in theory, and they could never forget that only the queen really stood between them and the great likelihood of a Catholic restoration under Mary Stuart. Perhaps the Puritans needed Elizabeth more than she needed them.

The first major quarrel arose in 1565 over the wearing of the surplice (the white gown), when a number of clergy refused to wear any official clerical dress on the grounds that it was not sanctioned in Scripture but was indeed a popish remnant 'consecrated to idolatry'; even the surplice was surplus to requirements. Essentially the Puritans wanted no distinction between the laity and a clerical caste, which they identified as a Roman corruption. But Elizabeth was adamant that order be maintained and that the clergy should wear at least the surplice as a distinguishing garment, and drilled the bishops into persecuting dissidents on the issue. The bishops, many of whom had earlier been radicals, were now seen as increasingly conservative and compliant supporters of the queen and thus the main enemy.

The Presbyterian wing mounted the greatest attempt at change, being well organised by the brilliant John Field and inspired by Professor Thomas Cartwright of Cambridge University. The Presbyterians resorted to Parliament to try and amend the Settlement. There were two waves in the parliamentary campaign: an early one between 1570 and 1574, and a later attempt between 1584 and 1588. In the Parliament of 1571 William Strickland spoke to a bill to reform the Prayer Book and to abolish all ecclesiastical vestments. The council intervened to stop him and forbade him from attending the House for a day, but he was not arrested. There was another campaign during the next Parliament of 1572, in which the Settlement was described as having been made by those 'blinded by superstition', a remark to which the queen naturally took great exception. A demand was voiced that godly ministers should be given exemptions from the law.

Between the end of the first Presbyterian campaign and the second in the 1580s, hopes for change were emerging right at the centre of the church establishment in the figure of Archbishop Edmund Grindal. He endorsed a programme of clerical and lay improvement through those prayer and Bible-study meetings known as 'prophesyings', which had wide support from the godly, including many local bishops and JPs. But 'prophesyings' offended the queen, whose zeal for conformity and obedience was greater than that for a well-educated clergy and laity. It might be argued that the queen lost a golden opportunity to reform the Church in this moderate way which would have taken the fire out of the more radical Presbyterians. The queen feared the threat to her own power in the Church, and she told Grindal to suppress prophesyings. The archbishop refused, telling her that he preferred 'rather to offend your earthly majesty than to offend the heavenly majesty of God'. Grindal was forced to retire and placed under under house arrest on account of his recalcitrance in the matter.

Such conservatism on the part of the queen drove the Presbyterians into a further wave of reform in the 1580s, especially in regard to improving their organisation. The most important development was the formation of the 'classical movement', so-named after the *classes* referred to earlier. A *classis* was a conference or group of presbyteries (or parishes), and was a link in a true Calvinist alternative order of church government stretching up to national synods at the top. But because the 'classical' movement was a forbidden, underground development it was never as coordinated or unified as it might theoretically have been. *Classes* came into existence in many parts of the realm quite often spontaneously and were not the fruits of central planning; and the job of welding them into an organisation was a later development. The main group that took up the job of imposing some kind of order and unity on them was the London Presbyterian group led by John Field. One should not exaggerate the degree of unity, as it fell considerably short of the Calvinist ideal: there were few lay elders involved, the system being almost entirely clerical. The rudimentary classical system was in existence by 1582, and the most famous *classis* was that at Dedham (Essex), which lasted from 1582 to 1589, with its minute books surviving. Not all those who attended the Dedham *classis* or any other were necessarily devoted Presbyterians or adamantly opposed to episcopacy. But the movement allowed the influence of the Presbyterians to flourish.

Indeed Presbyterianism seemed to flourish precisely because of the wave of persecution unleashed against them in the 1580s by Grindal's successor, Archbishop Whitgift, who would stand no nonsense from them. Although a Calvinist in theology he was determined to enforce conformity to the Settlement. He issued articles of conformity to be presented to all members of the clergy for their subscription. Between 300 and 400 ministers refused to accept them and were initially suspended by Whitgift until over-ruled by other privy councillors led by Burghley; finally only a small number were suspended. The Puritans regarded Whitgift as an old-style pre-Reformation lordly bishop, and his ferocity may have been counter-productive in driving moderate Puritans into the arms of the Presbyterians.

The Presbyterian threat was more theoretical than real, and the numbers of true Presbyterians were very small. Moreover, with the death of John Field in 1588 the movement suffered a tremendous blow. It had been his organisation rather than the numbers of converts that had made Presbyterianism seem a great danger. The movement was further undermined by the desper-ate ploy of using the anonymous and scurrilous *Martin Marprelate* tracts of 1588–9 to attack the bishops, who were described therein as a 'swinish rabble'. Many Puritans, and even some leading Presbyterians such as Walter Travers and Cartwright, wanted nothing to do with these vulgar pamphlets (the first of which – the *Deanepitome* – deliberately misspelled 'vicars' as 'fyck-ers'). Privy councillors who were sympathetic to Puritan reform were thoroughly alienated from these propagandist tracts in favour of Presbyterian church government. The author is now believed to have been Job Throckmorton, a cousin of the queen's maid of honour, Bess Throckmorton.

The 1590s saw the triumph of the Anglican establishment over the Puritans. Under Whitgift, supported by his chaplain Richard Bancroft, they were mercilessly persecuted. Thomas Cartwright and eight others were prosecuted in the conciliar courts of High Commission and Star Chamber; and although they were finally acquitted the process showed that the government meant business. After 1592 Presbyterianism seemed thoroughly vanquished, and the privy council could now turn to a new source of danger, that presented by the Separatists.

The Separatists did not wish to purify the established Church but to abandon it completely as thoroughly evil, and instead to found their own independent or 'gathered' churches – as holy communities set apart. But in a looser sense they can be viewed as Puritans, especially in their detestation of all Catholic remnants. Indeed the very existence of an authorised, all-embracing church they regarded as papistical. The Separatist movement did not emerge until the 1580s. However, in 1593 the government decided on an all-out effort against extremists with the passing of the Act against Seditious Sectaries, which led to the executions of Henry Barrow, John Greenwood and the Welshman John Penry.

The decline of Puritanism in the last years of Elizabeth's reign must also be attributed to that great outburst of intellectual energy in defence of the conformist Anglican standpoint. A number of well-organised defences of the Church appeared to combat the Puritans' criticisms, above all by Richard Hooker in his monumental eight-volumed work *Of the Laws of Ecclesiastical Polity*, the first four parts of which appeared in 1593 as part of the official drive against the Puritans. Hooker's was a reasoned defence of the official Church, pointing out against the Puritans that Scripture was not the only guide to valid practice in the Church. While the Bible was self-sufficient and the final arbiter in all matters affecting salvation, it could not be appealed to for many minor matters. In church government, for example, man had to use his own reason and look to Christian history, the teachings of the Fathers and the acts of ecumenical councils.

Puritanism was defeated for the moment and retired to lick its wounds in quietism and the religion of the home. But it was not dead, and found enough strength to organise the massive Millenary Petition on the accession of King James. But if England was not specifically Puritan it was overwhelmingly Protestant by 1600, and much of the old Catholic popular culture of church ales and miracle plays had vanished along the way.

The religious problem: the Catholics

Clearly, most people in Elizabeth's early years were religious traditionalists, but the numbers of papal Catholics who explicitly refused to accept the royal supremacy are harder to determine. Those who refused to attend the Anglican parish church (and were duly fined) were known as recusants (from the Latin *recusare*, to refuse). The major problem for genuine Catholics was that they would be deprived of the services of validly ordained clergy who could say mass and perform the sacraments. This used to be seen as a grave handicap, but recent research has emphasised that as the majority of serving ministers within Elizabeth's Church were validly ordained Catholic clergy there indeed existed a large pool of men who could bend the law and thus maintain the continuity of the Catholic faith. Many clergy said both the Prayer Book communion service and the Latin mass in areas where the gentry were conservative and could protect them. Sir Ralph Sadler described the survival of Catholicism well when he stated that the 'ancient faith still lay like lees on the bottom of men's hearts and if the vessel was ever so stirred came to the top'. Christopher Haigh has emphasised the importance of the surviving Catholic clergy in the long-term story of the evolution of a separate Catholic community.[22] However, this situation could not last indefinitely; as validly ordained priests died off the existence of any kind of Catholicism would be threatened.

When the Settlement was made in 1559 most people probably thought that it would last no longer than previous Tudor religious formulae. The queen could die young, therefore resignation was the more hopeful option for Catholics than overt resistance. The queen for her part hoped that in time loyalty to the pope and the old faith would die out, and preferred to turn a blind eye to recusancy than to persecute it. The less committed Catholics attended the Anglican parish church to avoid any fines and were later known (from the 1580s) as 'church papists'. The pope had certainly forbidden the faithful to attend the heretical church but most Catholics did not know of his pronouncement. Both sides therefore played a waiting game. Only the Puritans, who wanted popery extinguished at once, refused to tarry. Concern over the inevitable loss of Catholic priests through ageing and death led to a new departure being made in 1568 when William Allen established a seminary at Douai in the Spanish Netherlands precisely to train young Englishmen as seminary priests to return home to keep the faith alive. The other major problem for Catholicism was its increasing link to political treason.

Mary Queen of Scots and plots, 1568–72

The new seminary, and also the flight to England of Mary Queen of Scots, changed the scenario. Mary, with her burning ambition to gain the English throne, would pose a continuing problem to Elizabeth for nearly two decades. Mary would become in England the focal point for a Catholic resurgence that she had never been in Scotland. Indeed because of her seeming apathy towards maintaining the faith in Scotland and her immoral lifestyle she had been disowned by the pope in 1567. But during her English captivity she would play the role of a suffering servant for the international Catholic cause. Mary and Elizabeth would become juxtaposed as religious icons for their respective faiths. As Protestantism had not so far put down deep roots, and with Elizabeth still unmarried, there was much fear for the religious and dynastic future of England. The political danger presented by Catholicism came sharply to the government's attention with the rebellion of the northern earls in 1569. This was not a planned Catholic uprising but the uncoordinated offshoot of an attempt among some members of the nobility, including the Protestant earls of Leicester and Pembroke, to marry Mary Queen of Scots to the outwardly Protestant Duke of Norfolk. The ambitious duke, who felt that despite being the premier nobleman he was not being appreciated by the queen, now hoped to improve his chances by marrying Mary and returning with her to rule in Scotland, while awaiting Mary's succession in England. In this scheme Norfolk had the support of his former enemy Leicester, who was hoping for an excuse to get at his rival Cecil, as well as trying to insure his own future on the assumption that Elizabeth would probably not last too many more years and that the younger Mary would then succeed her. Both Norfolk and Leicester attacked the whole of Cecil's policy at a council meeting in February 1569 at a time when the secretary was vulnerable owing to his order to seize the Spanish treasure in December 1568. This had led to a harmful trade embargo from both Spain and the Spanish Netherlands, and the real possibility of war – an outcome which Elizabeth did not relish after many years of keeping Spain friendly. Also in the marriage plot were the earls of Arundel and Pembroke, two conservatives who disliked Cecil's antagonistic policy towards Spain. The scheme was all based on Mary's agreement to convert to Protestantism and on her returning to Scotland with the support of the Scots themselves as well as of Elizabeth. Other conspirators, however, were hopeful that a Catholic restoration would ensue upon this marriage. The Florentine banker Roberto Ridolfi tried to interest Spain and France in the marriage, while the Catholic Earl of Northumberland followed Mary's orders even though he would have preferred her to have married a Spaniard. The queen picked up the rumours through her ladies-in-waiting, and Leicester blurted out the whole story, with the consequent arrest of all the schemers (bar Leicester himself). Norfolk fled to Kenninghall, and the government was fearful of a rebellion centred on East Anglia. However, Elizabeth behaved coolly and defused a potentially dangerous situation. She treated the plotters as a schoolma'm would treat naughty schoolboys, putting them into detention for a time, and hoping they had learned their lesson.

On his way to the Tower, Norfolk warned his fellow plotters, the Catholic earls of Northumberland and Westmorland, not to rise in rebellion. The aims of these Catholic earls had differed from Norfolk's as they seemingly gave a higher priority to their Catholicism. They had reluctantly gone along with the Norfolk match simply because that is what Mary wished. Initially rumours abounded in the north that Norfolk was about to stir the realm against the queen, and plans were made for a northern rebellion, but when Norfolk capitulated confusion reigned supreme. The two earls panicked when the queen summoned them to Court, suspecting that her aim was to imprison them. They refused and were persuaded by others to lead a force of 5000–6000 tenants and dependants into rebellion (November 1569). Lady Westmorland was Norfolk's sister and egged her husband on into treason, and the Countess of Northumberland also goaded her husband into action. Reverence for the old faith was the most significant ingredient in the uprising, with the mass being restored in Durham Cathedral; other factors in the rebellion included the hatred of southerners by northerners. However, Catholics elsewhere refused to rise in support or to help release Mary. Lacking support from Lancashire or Cheshire, or from Spain, the earls fled to Scotland; and, apart from the siege of Barnard Castle, the only actual fighting was between the rebel Leonard Dacre and Lord Hunsdon in February 1570, when some 500 rebels were taken or killed. The downfall of the Nevilles and the Percys meant the end of a feudalised rebellious north. One hundred years previously the Percys and others had tried to undo the Yorkist hold on the throne and the supremacy of the Nevilles; now both families together were unable to withstand the growth of Tudor centralisation. The queen sent in the Puritan Earl of Huntingdon to bring the north to heel.

If the political dangers of Catholicism could be discerned in the rebellion, they were even more underlined by the papal bull of excommunication issued against Elizabeth by Pope Pius V in 1570, which declared her a deposed heretic and ordered all Catholics to abandon their allegiance to her. Up to this point the papacy had not taken a hard line against Elizabeth, mainly because of Spanish pressure, but now there was a rather unworldy pontiff in Pius V who threw diplomatic caution to the wind. He had received an over-optimistic report on the preparedness of English Catholics to rebel and had viewed the northern rebellion as proof of this. Indeed the pope sent money to aid the rebels. The bull was untimely as it was issued just as the rebellion fell apart. Philip II of Spain was extremely annoyed as he knew nothing about it, and it was canonically a flawed document as it did not give Elizabeth a chance to defend herself nor did it allow one year's grace before being implemented. It merely made matters worse for English Catholics by tarring them with suspicion of treason.

The House of Commons in 1571 reacted harshly by trying to stamp out recusancy with heavier penalties and with the obligation on everyone to receive Anglican communion annually. But Elizabeth wanted only outward conformity not inward obedience, and vetoed such attempts. Nevertheless she agreed to a new Treasons Act which punished anyone who denied the queen's title to the throne or who called her a heretic. By another statute it was also deemed treason to be caught in possession of any papal bull whatsoever, and it was a *praemunire* felony to be apprehended with any papal object of devotion, such as rosary beads or pictures. Another measure in this Parliament deprived Catholic exiles of their moveable goods and the profits of their lands if they indulged in hostile action abroad.

The need for such stern measures seemed to be vindicated by the discovery of the plot organised by the intriguer Ridolfi and supported by Spain and the papacy. Having initially failed with Norfolk and the northern earls, Mary was now forced to play the Spanish Catholic card. She made common cause with Ridolfi, who enticed Norfolk back into conspiracy to marry Mary, but this time with the clear intention of restoring Catholicism, aided by Spanish troops from the Netherlands. Details reached the government and Norfolk's secretary revealed all. Norfolk was rearrested in September 1571, found guilty of treason and condemned to death, but Elizabeth was reluctant to sign his death warrant until she realised that it was easier to save Mary from the execution that Parliament was demanding if she made a sacrifice of Norfolk, who was duly axed. Parliament wanted Mary attainted and barred from the throne, but Elizabeth vetoed this bill: she had allowed Parliament to discredit Mary, but Mary was still a Queen and to have dealt with her in this way would have discredited the very idea of monarchy. Elizabeth had to perform a tight balancing act between the demands of her office and the interests of the state. The Ridolfi plot indicated the lengths to which Elizabeth's enemies would go to overthrow her. Its unravelling by Cecil brought stricter incarceration for Mary.

The Catholic seminary priests

It was the slow erosion of Catholic life that made the work of the seminary priests so critical. The surviving Catholic recusant priests had done much to maintain the old faith among their flocks, but the new blood of the missionary priests trained in Europe would be vital for the long-term health of English Catholicism. The kind of priest produced by Allen's seminary at Douai was something new in England with a devotion, courage and ability to preach of the highest order. The first ordinations at

Douai took place in 1573, four in all, and they arrived in England the following year. By 1580 there were some 100 priests at work, a small but influential group of men who undermined the queen's attempt at a comprehensive Church of England. In 1579 another college for the training of English priests opened in Rome, which would soon be taken over by the Jesuit order.

The influx of seminary priests from the mid-1570s increased the numbers of recusants and greatly alarmed the Elizabethan authorities, who became more keenly vigilant in hunting down people who secretly heard mass in private homes. The first Douai seminarian to be martyred was Cuthbert Mayne, having been found in possession of a papal bull (but not that of 1570) in Cornwall. The success of the seminarians was, however, being jeopardised by, of all people, the pope. The missionaries themselves believed, and were at pains to make clear to others, that they presented no political danger to the queen and were engaged only in pastoral work. But papal policy, which was encouraged by William Allen, tended to go in a different direction, with the pope and Philip II of Spain being politically committed to the overthrow of the heretical government. In 1579, with papal and Spanish support, a fleet under James Fitzmaurice Fitzgerald landed in Ireland. Rebellion broke out in Munster in support of it, and fighting went on, with the landing of Spanish reinforcements in September 1580, right until the end of 1581. This two-year rebellion was used as proof by the government that Catholicism was synonymous with treason.

In 1580 the first Jesuit mission arrived in England, consisting of Robert Parsons and Edmund Campion. It had been William Allen who had called upon the Jesuits to help in reconverting England. Officially, the work of the Jesuits was to be entirely spiritual and non-political, and most historians have followed this line, but there are grounds for doubting it, at least in regard to Parsons.[23] Certainly in 1580 the pope had interpreted the bull of excommunication of 1570 in a way that seemed to render it a dead letter, and the Jesuit missionaries were instructed not to advocate rebellion in any way but to offer only spiritual comfort. This may have been whitewash to conceal the real goal of a long-term plan of forcible reconversion. However, on their way to England the news of the papal–Spanish invasion of Ireland must have caused them some embarrassment. Unperturbed, Campion published the aims of the mission in a manuscript document known as 'Campion's brag', which boldly asserted that they should have the right to dispute in public before the queen's council and the universities, and that the Catholic faith would eventually be restored no matter how great the persecution. Campion was arrested in 1581, and on his appearance before Elizabeth he did indeed acknowledge her as queen and maintained that his mission was purely spiritual; so cogently did he argue his case that the queen offered him a living in the Church of England if he took the oath of Supremacy. As a result of refusing he was one of many indicted in a large propaganda show trial for having aimed at the assassination of the queen and for having helped the cause of foreign invasion of the realm – charges that were plainly false and contrived. Campion in his defence claimed to be a good subject of the queen but was found guilty and hanged, drawn and quartered in December 1581. With Campion dead, Parsons decided that the best part of valour lay in returning to Europe.

As a reaction to the papist threat, the Parliament in 1581 wanted to introduce a severe measure to crush recusancy completely. But the bill which the Lords and Commons wanted was toned down by the queen's intervention, and the bill that was finally passed made it treason for someone to convert another person to Catholicism if that conversion meant that the other person gave up his or her obedience to the queen: a nice line was thus drawn between the spiritual act of conversion, which was not a crime, and the possible political consequence of the convert becoming disloyal, which was deemed treason. Also under this Act a priest apprehended while saying mass would be fined 200 marks (£133) and spend a year in gaol; members of the congregation could expect a fine of 100 marks and a year in gaol. Non-attendance at Anglican services would be punished at the stinging rate of £20 a month. This Act had a modern angle in that it claimed to be punishing only disloyalty, not the rights of conscience: no other government in Europe bothered making such a point. However, it was a distinction easily blurred, and the reality would be that as interpreted in the courts the Act made conversion to Catholicism as such a treasonable crime. No longer would the government need to fabricate evidence of involvement in plots as they had done in Campion's case. However, the government took the high moral ground, and Burghley's *The Execution of Justice in England* (1583) maintained that the Catholic priests at work in England had as their avowed intent to inform English Catholics of the papal excommunication and deposition of Elizabeth and to foster sedition. Although Burghley's fear that if an invasion force should come then priests might well fan up support for it had some justification, his attempt to prove that the missionary priests were actually plotting such an invasion was unjust.

William Allen replied to Burghley's tract in his *True, Sincere and Modest Defence of English Catholics* (1584), where he tried to show that English Catholics were not disloyal at all, and did not contravene any ancient treason statutes, only the invented ones of Elizabeth's reign. Allen accepted that the pope did indeed have the power of deposing monarchs but added that Catholic rulers did not find this much of a problem. Allen was here emphasising the purely spiritual work of the missionary priests, but he was glossing over the political dangers involved. Both Burghley and Allen were guilty of dishonesty in their arguments. The government's argument that it was not explicitly persecuting Catholicism itself was dubious. The reality was that one could be a Catholic in Elizabethan England only as long as one went to a Protestant church and led a Protestant life. Cardinal Allen also set out to deceive, because while there is no need to doubt the sincerity of the individual Catholic priests who protested that they had not come to meddle in politics, the fact was that the papacy had already asserted its right of deposition of Elizabeth, and Allen himself would be a leading organiser of the Spanish Armada in 1588. The missionary priests were guilty of political myopia in thinking that their work could be confined to purely spiritual matters. The pope had said that the bull of 1570 was not operative, but only in fact until sufficient means could be found to execute it. The more Catholic conversions, the better the chance of a Spanish invasion. In the event, of course, the vast majority of English Catholics did not support the Spanish Armada but remained loyal to the queen. However, a small number of hotheads were eager for her removal. In 1583 Francis Throckmorton, Dr William Parry in 1584–5, and then in 1586 Anthony Babington were all admirers of Mary Queen of Scots and organised abortive attempts to assassinate Elizabeth. So fearful of the queen's safety were the Protestant leaders that they banded together to sign the Bond of Association to prevent the accession of Mary on Elizabeth's death. Indeed Burghley had plans for a Protestant interregnum should Elizabeth be murdered. Mary was at last caught in the noose of the Babington plot, and Elizabeth was forced to assent to her execution in February 1587. The execution warrant contained the signatures of both Queens.

After the failure of the Armada and the loyalty shown by native Catholics, the government could afford to relax its grip and not worry too much about Catholicism, which survived as a minority grouped around the houses of Catholic gentry – what is called 'seigneurial Catholicism' – rather than as an active force among the people at large. Whether more could have been achieved by the seminarians has been the subject of a debate.[24] As a political threat English Catholicism was also weakened by divisions within its own ranks: the 'archpriest controversy' involving George Blackwell saw a split between the majority of priests who were seculars and the minority of regulars (Jesuits). The majority preferred an accommodation with the state and took the oath of allegiance, whereas the Jesuits wanted to carry on conspiracies to change the religion of England by force.

France, Scotland, the Netherlands and Spain

When the French civil wars broke out in 1562 between the Catholics and the Calvinist Huguenots, England had to decide whether or not to aid the Protestants. Elizabeth received overwhelming advice from her councillors to intervene to support the Huguenots and she agreed to it on condition that Newhaven (Le Havre) should be captured and kept as a pledge for the return of Calais. An agreement was made with the Huguenots in August 1562, and a force under Ambrose Dudley, Earl of Warwick took Newhaven and Dieppe. However, the situation deteriorated, and the Huguenots concluded their own peace with the Catholics (March 1563), leaving the English high and dry in Newhaven in the midst of the plague. Elizabeth's demand for Calais seems to have united French opinion from both sides against her. This dismal failure induced the queen and Cecil to much greater caution in the future.

Relations with Spain, England's traditional ally, remained superficially friendly. Philip II, despite Elizabeth's heresy, was more concerned to prevent Mary Queen of Scots gaining the English throne and the inevitable French influence which would accompany that event. It was Philip who twice prevailed on the pope not to excommunicate Elizabeth. For her part the queen wanted to avoid an open rupture with Spain. Yet the old diplomatic friendship between England and Spain was not destined to last but to give way to a life-or-death struggle, with Spain becoming viewed as England's (and God's) greatest enemy.

Religion played a large part in the estrangement, of course, but the actual breakdown in their relationship emerged out of the revolt of the Netherlands against Spanish overlordship. When the Netherlanders resisted, they were crushed by the Duke of Alva and his Spanish army between 1566 and 1568. The imposition of Spanish-style, dogmatic Catholicism so close to Protestant England was naturally worrying to the English Protestant establishment. But what could England do? England did not have the necessary political might to take on Alva. In any case the queen disliked the idea of helping rebels against their sovereign lord. Spain had every right to be in the Netherlands, and all that Elizabeth could do was to reduce the danger presented by Spain on the other side of the Channel by making life difficult for Philip. The first real break with Spain came in November 1568 when, on Cecil's advice, the queen ordered the seizure of bullion from on board those Spanish ships which had sought shelter in English ports from storms and pirates. The official excuse was that this bullion did not belong to Philip but was a loan to him from Genoese bankers; therefore stealing was not involved! After this date Philip began helping the opponents of the Elizabethan regime, beginning with the northern rebels of 1569 and the Ridolfi plot of 1571. Even so, he was dismayed to learn of the papal excommunication of Elizabeth in 1570, for he was still eager for a working relationship; hence the ending of the trade embargo between the two countries in 1573. For the next few years Elizabeth refused to give approval to any English sailors venturing into Spanish colonial waters: such voyages were to be purely private.

The trouble with Spain over the seizure of the Spanish bullion in 1568 led to peace-feelers with France, and the suggestion by Cecil that the queen might marry Henry Duke of Anjou, the heir to the French throne. A defensive alliance with France was concluded in April 1572 as a protection against Spain, but with the slaughter of some 2000–3000 Huguenots at the St Bartholemew's Day massacre in August great revulsion was felt at the English Court – admittedly not enough to rescind the treaty but enough to call off any marriage negotiations.

Elizabeth had no wish to annex Scotland or interfere in its politics except out of sheer necessity prompted by fear of French influence returning there, mainly through the machinations of the House of Guise. To keep French influence out of Scotland Elizabeth acceded to the council's request (including Burghley's) that to guarantee the Protestant ascendancy an English force should be sent in November 1572 to Edinburgh to help Regent Morton consolidate the Protestant hold on Edinburgh by squeezing out the remaining Marians from the castle. When this was successfully accomplished in 1573, the queen refused any further aid so as not to antagonise the French.

It was the renewal of war in the Netherlands from 1572 that was to begin the escalation of enmity between England and Spain. However, before 1576 there was little real hope that the Dutch could actually win against the Spaniards, and Elizabeth's policy aimed at reconciling the parties from a neutral position and without any official English aid for the rebels. English policy changed during 1575 after Spanish successes suggested that the rebels might turn to France for help, and Elizabeth now demanded from Spain the removal of its troops and the guarantee of the Netherlands' liberties.

Walsingham wanted support for the Dutch Protestants (who were increasingly Calvinistic), but the queen disliked the idea of giving succour to rebels against their anointed king, while Burghley feared the growth of French influence in the Netherlands when the Dutch rebels called on Francis of Anjou[25] to head their resistance movement. Burghley was even prepared to help the Spaniards provided that they guaranteed the traditional religious toleration and liberties of the Netherlands. The one thing no English politician could stomach was the entrenchment of Spanish 'absolutism' just across the Channel. The massacre of the citizens of Antwerp by mutinous Spanish soldiers in November 1576 – the 'Spanish fury' – sparked off a truly national resistance movement in the Netherlands against the Spaniards. This was a golden opportunity to eject the Spaniards once and for all, and Elizabeth seriously considered aiding the Dutch, promising that if the Spaniards did not leave and guarantee local liberties she would lend the Netherlanders £100 000 to fight on, a policy which led to a short-term Spanish withdrawal. Later, when war resumed, she could not bring herself actually to deliver the men and money that she had promised; she could not convince herself that her allies in the Netherlands were reliable enough. In 1578 Elizabeth offered the Dutch £40 000 to hire mercenaries, but the Dutch also invited Anjou to join them. Increased French influence in the Netherlands was not what England wanted, and Elizabeth offered the Dutch more money if they abandoned Anjou. Walsingham, Leicester and Burghley all agreed that Anjou had to be removed from the Netherlands, and the best way to do this was to give more money to the rebels. Elizabeth vacillated, of course, listening to the warnings of the Earl of Sussex, but by the time she decided to loosen her purse strings, the Dutch had abandoned all hope of her help and had signed an agreement with Anjou, which elevated him to the title of Defender of Belgic Liberties. Elizabeth had agreed with the advice of most of her councillors but had delayed too long in coming to a decision.

Anjou's renewed prominence led to the reopening in 1579 of marriage negotiations between Elizabeth and Anjou, and the first serious courtship between them. Burghley and Sussex were all in favour of the marriage, but Walsingham was entirely against it, as were all other councillors. In August 1579 Anjou, Elizabeth's 'frog' as she called him, made his first appearance at the English Court. Staunch Protestants were aghast at the thought of her marriage to a Catholic, and John Stubbs, who had written a tract denouncing the marriage, had his right hand chopped off as a punishment for intruding into the queen's prerogative. It was Elizabeth herself who seemed most eager for marriage, and a number of historians have regarded her ardour as genuine – for diplomatic reasons or even personally, perhaps as her last chance. If she were play-acting she was most convincing. But she stipulated that the marriage could take place only if her people were in agreement with it. Elizabeth enjoyed the wooing period with its opportunities for theatricality, but it was partly to keep some control on Anjou, to whom in January 1580 the Dutch offered the sovereignty of the Netherlands in place of Philip II. Elizabeth tried through both Anjou and Henry III to keep France antagonistic towards Spain, especially after Philip's support for the papal invasions of Ireland in 1579–80 and Spain's annexation of Portugal. In September 1581 Henry III insisted on his brother's marriage to Elizabeth as the price of an alliance with England. Indeed Anjou paid a second, and longer, visit to England between October 1581 and February 1582, but Elizabeth was no longer serious about marriage. Elizabeth gave Anjou the loan of some money, but no formal alliance ensued. Anjou's military defeats in the Netherlands led to his quitting the enterprise in 1583, and he was to die the following year. Spanish hopes revived also in 1584 with the assassination of the Dutch rebel leader William of Orange, which the English took as a great blow, while in France the pro-Spanish Guises were in the ascendant and made a treaty between the Catholic League and Spain. Henry III was forced to join the Guise-dominated Catholic League in 1585, and he was no longer in a position to help the Dutch.

In their hour of desperation the Dutch offered the sovereignty of their country to Elizabeth in 1585 to gain England's protection, but she refused, both because she did not want to be everlastingly committed to them and because she still believed that Philip was their true sovereign. However, as Philip's victory over them would be ruinous to England's safety, some kind of help had to be given to the Dutch. Leicester and Walsingham wanted to give direct aid, but Burghley stuck to his wonted caution and distrust of the Dutch, to the extent of inflaming Walsingham's anger. Eventually Elizabeth decided to take the Dutch under her protection, but what this meant exactly was not clear. Finally, she was pushed into the arms of the Dutch by the action of Philip II in seizing English ships in Spanish ports; by the Treaty of Nonsuch Palace (August 1585) she promised £126 000 p.a. for the duration of the war to maintain an English military presence in the Netherlands. This treaty now committed England to war with Spain, although no formal declaration of war was made, and indeed Elizabeth remained ever hopeful that conflict might be avoided.

The Spanish Armada and the later years

In order to reconquer the Netherlands Philip realised that England would have to be dealt with. Ideas for some kind of direct attack on England dated back to 1583, but more definite plans for the 'Enterprise of England' began to be aired in Spain from December 1585 onwards as the English problem grew more acute. Apart from the Treaty of Nonsuch, the existence of Ralegh's Roanoke colony in North America, which threatened Spanish communications there, was another major Spanish grievance, to be followed by Drake's West Indian raid (1585) and his attack on Cadiz (1587). England was growing more troublesome, certainly, but there were also encouraging signs for Spain: Brussels and Antwerp were recaptured in 1585, and after the execution of Mary Queen of Scots in 1587 Philip could regard himself as her Catholic heir in England. English aggression in no way induced Philip to negotiate: these insults to his honour had to be avenged.

The Spanish Armada of 1588 was not principally aimed at invading and subduing England, but instead ending English help for the Dutch and making the Channel safe for the transportation of Spanish troops to the Netherlands. There was also the optimistic possibility that English Catholics would avail themselves of the opportunity to overthrow their heretic queen. If not, the Spanish forces could hardly conquer the entire country unaided; but possibly the south-east and London could be taken and Elizabeth's government forced to conclude a treaty by which they abandoned the Dutch rebels. The Armada of 130 ships and some 22 000 men left Lisbon on 18 May 1588 under the Duke of Medina Sidonia, but got scattered and delayed for a month by winds off Corunna. Drake and Lord Howard of Effingham led a fleet to try to defeat the Armada off Portugal, but they were forced back by the same wind that allowed the Spaniards now to sail northwards; the Armada made its entrance into the English Channel on 19 July, tightly formed in a crescent shape. The plan was for Medina Sidonia to rendezvous with the Duke of Parma at Calais, with strict instructions not to engage the enemy in battle before the rendezvous. Although English ships shadowed them the Spaniards' discipline was tight enough to keep to the plan. On 27 July the Armada anchored off Calais, rather than in Calais harbour as Parma had expected, and Medina Sidonia became apprehensive at being informed that Parma would not be ready for another six days. Medina Sidonia's problem now was to keep his fleet together, and this was to be thwarted by the English use of fireships, which were directed at Spanish vessels off Gravelines (29 July). Although little direct damage was done to the enemy ships, the device scared them into breaking formation and caused general chaos. Spanish ships now became easier targets for English firepower. Three Spanish vessels were sunk, many others were damaged, whereas English vessels emerged intact, and seemingly only one man lost his life. No longer was any rendezvous between Medina Sidonia and Parma possible, especially as the wind now pushed the Spaniards northwards. By 3 August Medina Sidonia had to give the order to return home to Spain by going into the North Sea, around Scotland and the west coast of Ireland, a perilous journey in gale-force winds that caused Spanish vessels to lose their anchors and run aground. Only between one-third and one-half of the fleet made it back to Spain.

England's victory over Spain was immediately hailed as the judgement of God in favour of Protestant England. George Gower was commissioned to paint the Armada portrait, which depicts a glamourised queen in front of two window-views of the events at sea. On the left the glorious English fleet is shown with the flag of St George; on the right the window-view is of the Spanish ships foundering in the North Sea. The queen has her hand on the globe, with the clear, but premature, message that Spanish world dominion must now give way to English world dominion. This English boast was, of course, nonsense in the context of 1588: not only was there no English empire apart from the Roanoke colony, which was about to disappear from sight, but also the failure of the Armada was not seen at the time as definitive. It had been a major achievement for Philip II to have done as much as this, for certainly no other European monarch could have put on such a great enterprise, which failed mainly because of inclement weather. Nor was this the only Armada planned; two later Armadas would be prepared and would also fail; but nobody could know this in 1588. Nevertheless the defeat of the Spaniards put enormous heart into the English, who convinced themselves that they were truly God's elect.

In the period after the Armada both the Earl of Essex and his rival Sir Walter Ralegh were champions of an aggressive policy against Spain: so too was the treasurer of the navy Sir John Hawkins. The two Cecils were supporters of cautious aid to the Huguenots and to the Dutch rebels. Parliament was called in 1589 for money for military operations, and a double subsidy was willingly conceded. In France Elizabeth, on the assassination in July 1589 of Henry III, came out in support of the Protestant claimant Henry of Navarre against the Catholic aspirant the Cardinal of Bourbon, who was supported by the League and by Spain. The first English troops were sent to France in September 1589 – a force of some 4000 men. Then the arrival of Spanish forces in Brittany in 1590 set off all the alarm bells in England. Just as France could not be allowed to extend its influence over the Channel coastline neither could Spain. In the civil war in France the Earl of Essex was sent to Henry of Navarre to help him capture Rouen from the Catholics, but after a long siege (October 1591 to April 1592) the arrival of the Duke of Parma's troops saved the city for the Catholic side. More English troops were sent to northern France in 1593, and the government secured a triple subsidy from Parliament.

One of the last great successes of the reign was the attack made in 1596 on the Spanish fleet being assembled in Cadiz. The English fleet led by Lord Howard of Effingham, Essex and Ralegh destroyed Spanish ships and captured the city of Cadiz. In retaliation Philip sent another Armada in 1596, but it was wrecked by storms on the way. The Spanish siege of Calais in March 1596 led to the Treaty of Greenwich in April, when Elizabeth undertook to send another 4000 men to help France regain Calais. In 1597 England, France and the Dutch Republic signed the Triple Alliance against Spain. But thereafter Elizabeth rapidly reduced her land commitments, and only action at sea against Spain would continue on to her death. France and Spain made peace in 1598, and the undisputed rule of the nominally Catholic (but pro-Protestant) Henry IV in France meant a check on Spanish aggrandisement. Elizabeth had succeeded in defending English national interests and the Protestant religion. The Dutch Protestant rebels would fight on to win their independence from Spain, but the Spanish southern Netherlands, which remained Catholic, were allowed to keep much traditional autonomy. The nightmare of Spanish absolutism opposite England's shores had been averted.

Colonisation under Elizabeth

The English state in our period took its first steps towards its colonial future, although this aspect of the Elizabethan age is prone to exaggeration because little was achieved. Nevertheless, the first initiatives and justifications were taken then, and some acknowledgement needs to be given to this aspect of the growth of the English state. Paintings of the queen from the end of the 1570s containing symbols representing imperial or world dominion[26] emanated from a group of ardent colonisers at Court, led by Hatton and John Dee.

In Elizabeth's reign Plymouth replaced Bristol, which had been prominent in early Tudor exploration, as the focus of maritime activity. Earlier English interest had been in trying to get around America and reach the spices of China directly by a north-west passage or a north-east passage: but now under Elizabeth there was a serious interest in the American landmass itself. In 1558 there was still no European presence north of Mexico, leaving a huge area for exploitation. Most of the great Elizabethan seafarers were West Country men, the major exception being the Yorkshireman Sir Martin Frobisher. They included adventurers like Sir Humphrey Gilbert, Sir Walter Ralegh and Sir Richard Grenville as well as intellectuals such as Dee, Richard Hakluyt senior, his cousin Richard Hakluyt the younger, and Adrian Gilbert. It was Humphrey Gilbert, Adrian's brother, who was the first to argue in favour of colonising America in the Elizabethan age. He wanted state help for a project that would aid England's poor and needy by sending them out to a colony, and also be a place of refuge for Catholic recusants. This last suggestion was opposed by the seminary priests who wanted to convert England back to the old faith. Gilbert's ideas were taken up by Richard Hakluyt the younger, whose manuscript 'Discourse of Western Planting', written for the queen in 1584, gave various reasons why the state should support overseas colonisation. He firstly cited historical reasons for England's interest, going back to the Cabot voyages of Henry VII's time.

Then secondly he saw colonisation as a means of preventing the spread of Catholicism. There were thirdly strategic reasons that colonies would be of use against Spain and Spanish supply-lines. Fourthly, there were economic advantages to be enjoyed, such as gaining Mediterranean-type produce and having new markets in which to sell English cloth (to the Indians!). Lastly colonies could relieve England's population pressure and be places to deposit undesirables from England.

Also in 1584 Ralegh was granted a charter for another expedition, which reached what would soon be called Virginia. Ralegh himself was not allowed to go on the voyage because the queen wanted her favourite at Court, but his men brought back two young Indians to England as well as skins and pearls and stories of a paradise over there. Ralegh was knighted on Twelfth Night 1585, and the queen allowed him to call the new colony Virginia after her. There then followed an expedition organised by Ralegh and Grenville, which established in 1585 the first English colony at Roanoke island, with over 108 men. Unfortunately no real effort was made to establish a firm social or economic basis for this first colony: there were no skilled farmers, for example, among those first settlers.

Shortly after the abandonment of the colony, Sir Richard Grenville's ship called in (June 1586) and left 15 men there as a holding party and supplies for two years, thereby establishing the second colony at Roanoke. A third colony was sent out in 1587 with 117 men, women and children and John White as governor. When they arrived, they found the fort at Roanoke destroyed and the skeleton of one of the 15 men; the earlier settlers' homes remained standing but were overgrown, and so the new colonists moved to a different site near by. Mysteriously this whole third colony was soon to disappear during White's return to England for supplies; and because of the Spanish Armada the provisions and White's return to America were delayed. When he finally reached Roanoke again in 1590, he found no trace of his fellow-colonists.

These early attempts at colonisation at Roanoke in Virginia were thus a failure. They had been small-scale affairs with no more than 250 people involved. The financing was the work of private gentlemen and had been inadequate. The queen herself had been too poor to contribute anything except incidentally, through granting favours and monopolies to such as Ralegh. It has been suggested that the failure of the early colonising attempts in North America were advantageous in the long run because established colonies would soon have impelled the Spanish to move north into their Florida, as they called the whole of North America, and take it over. But despite this special pleading, the plain fact was that at Elizabeth's death England had no colonies anywhere – except for Ireland. Yet 100 years later England would be a leading colonial power. Permanent settlement and a commitment to stay in America would come only in the reign of James I, when government backing and commercial sponsorship would take over from the amateur-gentleman attitude of Elizabethan times.

The end of the reign

The last Elizabethan decade was filled with factionalism at Court, problems with Parliament and increasing economic misery for at least half of the queen's subjects. Her reign had seen economic growth, with a diversified trade through Russia, Persia, Venice, Turkey and the East Indies,[27] and even the beginnings of a 'consumer society'.[28] But the new wealth was not evenly distributed. There had been a rapid growth in the population, which led inexorably to an increase in unemployment, underemployment and vagabondage. Economic growth was not swift enough to enable it to keep up with the increasing population, and the inability of agriculture to meet the increased demand for food meant that food prices soared. Attempts to bring back full employment, as in the Act of Apprentices of 1563, had failed before the tide of impersonal economic change. The growth in vagabondage – the 'terror of the tramp' – had alarmed authorities throughout the Elizabethan period, and whipping had been introduced in the 1560s as a new punishment to prevent people moving about the countryside – which was officially not allowed unless one had a domestic passport. Those on the move were mainly people genuinely in search of work, but the authorities often perceived them as criminals. It seems that wage-earners (the lucky ones in work) suffered a real decline in their living standards: the value of wages fell by 25 per cent under

Elizabeth, which might indicate a fall in living standards for ordinary people by that amount. But it was not as simple as that because not everyone was a wage-earner at this period, and fortunately not all wage-earners were totally dependent on wages for subsistence. By the 1570s it had become clear that not all those out of work were lazy but instead victims of the economic system; the able-bodied poor were now to be helped with work, not punished, while the impotent poor were to be given charity. The four bad harvests in succession from 1594 to 1597 meant widespread hardship, even some instances of death from malnutrition in the far north, and provoked the government into further legislative action. After much experimentation, and by emulating the pioneering work of various local authorities, such as in London and Norwich, Parliament passed the great Elizabethan Poor Laws of 1597, which remained the basis of government assistance to the poor until 1834. The unit for relief was the parish; a compulsory poor-rate was established to pay for the upkeep of the poor, and this was to be levied by four overseers of the poor in each parish, these overseers being appointed by the JPs. The overseers were to set poor children to be apprenticed, and hospitals were to be built for the sick. Work was to be found for the unemployed, and stocks of raw materials were to be kept in each parish for them to work on. Wealthier parishes were to help any poorer ones. By a separate measure the JPs were to send the wilfully idle to houses of correction. The surviving evidence suggests that the system of relief was put into effect only at periods of crisis and it never completely replaced private charity. Yet in having such a national system, at least on paper, England led the rest of Europe.

Relief of the poor had to be balanced by relief to the employers, who were chafing under the queen's increasing use of monopolies – the sole right to trade in a commodity – to reward her servants. Monopolies cost the queen nothing but were a great burden on those merchants who were thus excluded from fair competition. Monopolies were an anti-capitalist device and became the great bogey in the Parliaments of 1597 and 1601, so much so in fact that the queen saw sense in bowing to the swelling opposition against them, and she cancelled most monopolies to the delight of the Members, who were eager to thank her. The queen turned a potentially ugly situation to her own advantage. Elizabeth never lost her theatrical touch, and in her dazzling 'golden speech' (as it was later called) of November 1601 to the entire Commons assembled in the council chamber at Whitehall she assured them that:

> there is no prince that loves his subjects better, or whose love can countervail our love. There is no jewel; be it never so rich a price, which I set before this jewel: I mean your love. . . . And though you have had and may have many princes more mighty and wise sitting in this seat, yet you never had nor shall have any that will be more careful and loving.

Elizabeth died at Richmond, after a fortnight of melancholic inactivity, on 24 March 1603 at the age of 69. Francis Bacon, writing two years later, looked back in amazement at the previous half-century of Tudor rule:

> The strangest variety that in a like number of successions of any hereditary monarchy hath ever been known: the reign of a child, the offer of a usurpation, the reign of a lady married to a foreign prince, and the reign of a lady solitary and unmarried.

Like most others, Bacon looked to the future and welcomed the advent of the more fertile Stuarts in place of 'these barren princes'.

The Stuarts and the Republic

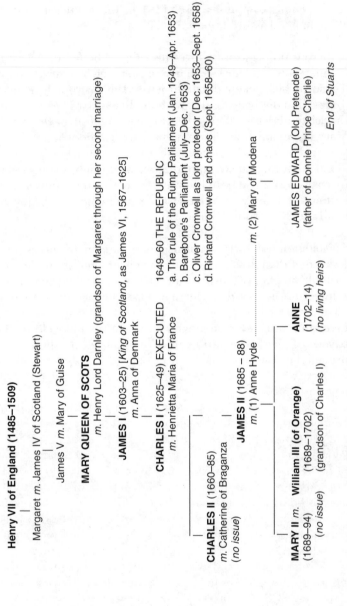

Henry VII of England (1485–1509)

Margaret *m.* James IV of Scotland (Stewart)

James V *m.* Mary of Guise

MARY QUEEN OF SCOTS
m. Henry Lord Darnley (grandson of Margaret through her second marriage)

JAMES I (1603–25) [*King of Scotland*, as James VI, 1567–1625]
m. Anna of Denmark

CHARLES I (1625–49) EXECUTED
m. Henrietta Maria of France

1649–60 THE REPUBLIC
a. The rule of the Rump Parliament (Jan. 1649–Apr. 1653)
b. Barebone's Parliament (July–Dec. 1653)
c. Oliver Cromwell as lord protector (Dec. 1653–Sept. 1658)
d. Richard Cromwell and chaos (Sept. 1658–60)

CHARLES II (1660–85)
m. Catherine of Braganza
(*no issue*)

JAMES II (1685 – 88)
m. (1) Anne Hyde .... *m.* (2) Mary of Modena

MARY II *m.* **William III (of Orange)**
(1689–94)   (1689–1702)
(*no issue*)   (grandson of Charles I)

ANNE
(1702–14)
(*no living heirs*)

JAMES EDWARD (Old Pretender)
(father of Bonnie Prince Charlie)

End of Stuarts

7 The Coming of the Stuarts: James I, 1603–25

The death of Queen Elizabeth led to the end of the House of Tudor[1] and to the peaceful transfer of the kingdom of England to the related House of Stewart.[2] Thus James VI of Scotland, son of Mary Queen of Scots, now also became James I of England in a personal union of the two neighbouring realms. This was indeed a major event, being the first ever peaceful accession of a new dynasty in English history; and with the final subjugation of Ireland in 1603, James was the first monarch to be in full control of all three British kingdoms. Moreover, with the founding of Jamestown in 1607, he became the first king of permanent British colonies in North America.

The House of Stewart in Scotland had been a weak dynasty, owing to the prosaic origins of the family and the large number of royal minorities. The name Stewart originated from the fact that the family had been stewards of the lands of earlier Scottish kings. Coming from such undistinguished beginnings the Stewarts found it hard to assert their authority among the feuding Scottish nobles, who in particular relished royal minorities as a chaotic avenue to their own self-aggrandisement.

Certainly Scotland was a much more primitive society than contemporary England; chaotic conditions reigned supreme there right up to the end of the sixteenth century, in marked contrast to the growing stability of Elizabethan England. James's father, Henry Lord Darnley, had been murdered in 1567, and not long afterwards James lost the company of his mother for ever as the result of her abdication and flight to England. At the age of 13 months James was crowned King of Scotland at Stirling parish church in a Protestant ceremony which ignored the act of anointing (29 July 1567). As a child James was surrounded by a world of thuggery and was certainly starved of affection. His upbringing was extremely strict, with an inadequate diet that gave him rickets. Unlike both parents who were extremely tall and handsome, James was a mediocre physical specimen with a permanently out-turned foot.

At the age of 17, in June 1583, James was declared to have come of age, although the true personal rule was not to begin until 1585. James had no special lingering affection for his mother and ignored her appeals to him to support her return to Scotland as joint sovereign. In fact by 1586 James had completely deserted his mother by accepting an annual pension from Elizabeth with the unspoken assumption that he could look forward to succeeding to the English throne in the distant future. More immediately James needed to guarantee his family's hold on the Scottish throne by marrying and begetting a nursery full of heirs. In 1589 he married the 14-year-old Anna of Denmark. Although James was homosexual he was not an 'inverted' one, unable to relate to women; far from it, the couple would produce seven children over some 17 years, beginning with the rapturously received birth of Prince Henry in February 1594, and end up as good companions. Undoubtedly James took his dynastic duties seriously, and his rule in Scotland in the 1590s as an adult married king must be judged a success, especially in reducing the chaos that the feuding nobles could engender. Now he was called to a larger theatre of politics. How well might he do there?

On learning of Elizabeth's death, James wasted no time in crossing the border and claiming his new throne. Although Elizabeth herself had never formally bequeathed the throne to him the path had been prepared by the secret correspondence between James and Robert Cecil, and the take-over was smooth. The only ripple on the water was an alleged plot to put the English-born Arabella Stuart[3] on the throne with Spanish help, for which Lord Cobham and Sir Walter Ralegh were arrested and imprisoned. There can be no doubt of the general rejoicing and relief at the accession of James I, both because he was a man, after half a century of female rule, and because the transfer had been effected so peacefully. The last years of Elizabeth had been years of tension and strife, and while the old queen could ride out any storm nevertheless many people looked forward to strong masculine rule. James himself immediately wanted a formal union of the two countries under the name of Great Britain, one with a new flag, but his proposals for this met continual resistance. James could not understand the reluctance of

Englishmen to put enmity behind them and embrace a common future. The reasons were partly nationalistic. There was the ancient inbred English hatred of the Scots, made greater by failure to conquer them; there were worries over Scotsmen flooding south and taking over England, whereas few Englishmen contemplated venturing north or wanted to see the proud name of England disappear. There were also legal problems, including the perceived threat to the English common law from the greater use of Roman law in Scotland. This failure immediately to unite two ancient foes was a bitter disappointment for James who was by nature a pacific reconciler. James did not help the situation by surrounding himself with Scotsmen in the most private part of the Court, the bedchamber – replacing the privy chamber which remained merely as an outer service department. Only one English gentleman of the bedchamber was appointed before 1615.

Interpretation of the reign

Traditionally, historians have interpreted the reign of James in the light of their knowledge that a civil war would break out less than 20 years after his death. They have therefore traced the origins of that seemingly inescapable conflict back to his reign, which was seen to be filled with problems which could not be resolved and which were to lead inevitably to that great clash between king and Parliament in the English Civil War. What was prominent in traditional historiography was the stark contrast between Elizabeth, the pure, chaste Virgin Queen, and James, the lazy, dirty, slobbering old man from Scotland who simply did not understand English ways and who wanted to impose an absolutist system on the country, setting the stage for later calamities. Undoubtedly James did not have the personal charisma of Elizabeth. He did not have her regal build, nor her superb gifts in dealing with ordinary subjects; he completely lacked her common touch. Elizabeth had loved the theatricality of monarchy, whereas James hated formal occasions and ceremony. The Venetian ambassador commented that James 'did not caress the people nor make them that good cheer that the late Queen did...but this King manifests no taste for them but rather contempt and dislike. The result is that he is despised and almost hated.' This was undoubtedly an exaggeration, but James was certainly not a public-relations success. He also suffered hostile comments on his personal handicaps such as his over-large tongue that dribbled incessantly and his bent gait, his dislike of washing and his habit of 'his fingers... fiddling about his codpiece'.

Traditionally, James was viewed as a king doomed to failure, and this was because until fairly recently the dominant schools of thought on this period were the Whig–Liberal and the Marxist schools. The Whig historians of the nineteenth century emphasised the importance and the inevitability of constitutional conflict in the Stuart period. As the great Whig Lord Macaulay wrote: 'the time was fast approaching when either the King must become absolute, or the Parliament must control the whole executive administration'. This Whig (and later Liberal) approach emphasised the self-conscious struggle for sovereignty and freedom between an increasingly powerful Parliament and the Crown, a struggle that was to break out in the English Civil War and find its fulfilment in the 'Glorious Revolution' of 1688–9 with the establishment of a truly constitutional monarchy and annual Parliaments.

The Whig–Liberal attitude was built up further by Marxist and sociological historians of the late nineteenth and early twentieth century, who accepted the major Whig components of the story – the inevitability of conflict and the growth of two 'sides' – but regarded the Whig–Liberal view as being an inadequate explanation. It was all true as far as it went, they reasoned, but the underlying reasons for the conflict were economic and social changes: the growth of a capitalist economy and the rise of a bourgeois (or capitalist) gentry who exploited their lands in a businesslike way to give the largest return. The 'rise of the gentry' in both wealth and numbers made conflict inevitable because they would demand political power commensurate with their economic domination, the monarchy and aristocracy being viewed as in financial decline. Thus by the mid-twentieth century the dominant view was a mixture of Whig–Liberal and Marxist ingredients, and historians could publish books with titles such as *The Rise of the Revolutionary Party in the English House of Commons, 1603–1629* (1957). Lawrence Stone as late as 1972 could assume 'the rise of opposition as a self-conscious political force'.[4] The modern Liberal as well as Marxist and sociological historians have emphasised the seventeenth century as marking the great turning-point in the history of England, and indeed of the world. The Marxists emphasised especially the years of Civil War as constituting England's 'revolution', which became in their interpretation the great bourgeois or capitalist breakthrough of worldwide significance.

Such constructs were orthodoxy down to the mid-1970s and the onslaught of revisionism. Through the work of Conrad Russell, John Morrill, Kevin Sharpe and others, the whole period was opened up to keen controversy, which still reverberates. Revisionists are sceptical of the old notion of a deep rift in early Stuart society, either socially or ideologically. They claim that there were no deep divisions in society which made conflict, let alone the Civil War, inevitable. Parliament was not growing more powerful; there was no 'rise of Parliament'. Indeed Parliament was becoming weaker and anxious over its continuing existence. Revisionists certainly do not paint the parliamentarians as revolutionaries. Revisionism claims that England was 'unrevolutionary' before the Civil War, an event which should be viewed as the result of only short-term causes, not of the inevitable breakdown of the system caused by ideological or constitutional struggles. The revisionist John Morrill has claimed that it was 'pilot error rather than mechanical failure' which brought about the Civil Wars. Revisionists also downplay any intellectual motivation in the quarrels of the period: they claim that there was no fight over ideology or the constitution, only disputes over materialistic issues, with 'outs' wanting to become 'ins'. Faction and localism were much more predominant than national, constitutional or ideological considerations. The urge for consensus was far greater than that for conflict. The main strength of the revisionists lies in their vast empirical knowledge of the detail of political and parliamentary affairs which has rendered so many of the old generalisations either meaningless or misleading.

Revisionists regard the reign of James I as a successful one, not the overture to an inevitable Civil War. Conrad Russell's exhortation is to study the reign of James while pretending not to know that the Civil War ever happened;[5] and in this dispassionate way without hindsight, without looking for the seeds of conflict, one must conclude that James solved most of his problems, especially those problems bequeathed to him by Elizabeth I. Accordingly, revisionists deny the customary stark contrast between the two rulers. Elizabeth had been idealised by both pen and paint, whereas poor James not only lacked a lobby group eager to promote him into a cult object but also was later vilified by courtiers who had a grudge against him – notably Anthony Weldon, Francis Osborne and Arthur Wilson, who wrote in the period of the Republic, when the way to advancement was to denigrate the fallen monarchy. It is from such writers that we get the stock portrait of James as lazy, dribbling and overly familiar with handsome young men in public. Thus the reality of both monarchs was distorted, and if one peels back the paint of flattery concealing Elizabeth and discounts the viciously exaggerated insults to James, then the two monarchs, argue revisionists, get similar report cards. James is now portrayed as a successful monarch, as much a seeker of the middle way as Elizabeth is supposed to have been, and one indeed who solved more problems than did the old queen.

Revisionism appears to be the orthodoxy today, especially in Britain, but it has not won a universal following. In opposition a school of 'post-revisionists' has emerged which agrees that the old generalisations will no longer stand up but remains unconvinced by the rather negative conclusions of revisionism. Post-revisionists include both older historians like J. H. Hexter, Theodore Rabb and Perez Zagorin and younger scholars such as Ann Hughes, Johann Sommerville and Richard Cust. Post-revisionists want to reinstate ideological differences and tensions as a main feature of the reigns of both James I and Charles I. They certainly accept the argument of the revisionists that the parliamentarians were not flexing their muscles and conspiring to wrest power away from the monarch: ideas of 'the rise of Parliament' and of revolutionary parliamentarians are decidedly outmoded. However, according to the post-revisionists, the parliamentarians did disagree with the king on fundamental issues of principle, although what is noteworthy is their patience and nervousness rather than any aggressive intent of trying to wrest power for themselves. Parliamentarians were conservative men who wanted a quiet life; they had no model of revolution to inspire them. Nevertheless the issues dividing them from the king were real ones.

James's political philosophy

Undoubtedly James had a high opinion of his own abilities because he had survived so many vicissitudes. Initially, James may well not have understood the nature of English monarchy. He had espoused while King of Scotland what can only be called absolutist notions. He had written in *The Trew Law of Free Monarchies* (first published anonymously in 1598) that kings were answerable to God alone and that they were not bound by Parliaments. 'The King makes daily statutes and ordinances, enjoining such pains thereto as he thinks meet, without any advice of Parliament or estates.' Such ideas would clearly not go down well in England, but did James really mean them and intend to apply them in England? Revisionists are sceptical about this and argue that such absolutist tenets were initially employed as a counter-attack to the clerical Presbyterians who wanted to turn Scotland into an elective monarchy. In England such high-flown words could also be useful against those Catholics who believed in the pope's power to depose kings. However, the post-revisionist Johann Sommerville has written in favour of the traditional view that James pursued a secret absolutist agenda in England, whereas the revisionist Glenn Burgess has taken up the cudgels against that stand and in favour of a widespread consensus about the constitution.[6]

The traditionalists' assumption was that James meant what he said and tried to carry it out in England, but that the wary Commons were ready for him, and a clash between the royal prerogative and the English common law was joined from the very beginning. The very first Parliament of James's British reign drew up the 'Form of Apology and Satisfaction', a 4000-word document that attacked the rise of absolutism in Europe and tried to prevent it getting a foothold in England. 'The prerogatives of princes may easily and do daily grow', it warned in 1604. S. R. Gardiner, the great nineteenth-century traditionalist, saw this as a key document: 'To understand the Apology is to understand the causes of the success of the English Revolution.' The very earliest revisionist critique came from G. R. Elton in 1965 in an essay on the drafting of the 'Apology', where he argued that this document was not really the first call to arms of the constitutionalist opposition, but instead a minority document which the vast majority of the Commons repudiated. Being an unrepresentative document it was never even presented to the king. It in no way should be seen, argued Elton, as the start of the march on the 'high road' to Civil War. Clearly, the traditionalist view of the centrality of the document has to be modified, but whether it is as peripheral as Elton claimed is still open to debate. Post-revisionists agree that there was no confrontational spirit in 1604, but nevertheless find impressive a document that would be continually requoted in later Parliaments. Neither forgotten nor insignificant, the 'Apology' can still be regarded as a carefully thought-out defence of the privileges of Parliament, which would be steadfastly maintained for the next 25 years.

Factional politics

The new king's Scottish origins showed up at once in the new style of politics, especially with the re-emergence of the nobility. Queen Elizabeth had kept her nobility small and had tended to draw her advisers from the gentry. But James in Scotland was used to dealing only with the great nobles because no equivalent group to the rich English gentry existed there. Thus James soon ennobled his leading English servants, which made him feel more at home and also made good sense to give out rewards after Elizabeth's stinginess; on the negative side, however, this meant the loss of their skills to the House of Commons.

Whatever the role that should be assigned to Parliament in this period, we must be very clear that the centre of the political world was still the royal Court, which was always in session, and not Parliament, which was very infrequently called. Unfortunately, the major feature of the Stuart Court was that it became less and less 'a point of contact', less a place to involve a wide spectrum of the governing class and less a centre for reconciliation, being instead increasingly a source of alienation for large numbers of the gentry class. The Court was widely seen as a centre of immorality and corruption. Whether the reality was as bad as much of the literature of the time suggests is a moot point, yet the overwhelming impression remains that James's Court was generally regarded as a centre of wickedness, debauchery and intoxication, where women rolled about drunk, and where the notion of a court virgin was entertained as a contradiction in terms. Corruption was hardly new, and had increased during Elizabeth's last decade, but what seems changed was the level of sexual immorality, which had always been heavily punished by the old queen. The young diarist Lady Anne Clifford noted in 1603 that 'all the ladies about the Court had gotten such ill names that it was grown a scandalous place'.

The first period in the factional history of the reign was dominated by that group which had scooped the pool of prizes in Elizabeth's declining years – the Cecilians led by Robert Cecil (who became ennobled as Lord Cecil, then finally in 1605 as Lord Salisbury), allied to Henry Howard, Earl of Northampton and Thomas Howard, Earl of Arundel. As partners, Salisbury and Northampton tried to prevent the emergence of a new hostile Essex affinity centred on the new third earl – a young boy whom they together arranged to be married off to Northampton's niece, Lady Frances Howard, daughter of the Earl of Suffolk. That lady's sister was also betrothed to Salisbury's son, suggesting partnership rather than political rivalry between the two families.

On Salisbury's death in 1612 a rather fluid factional situation initially emerged. There was a group of Scottish nobles, led by the Duke of Lennox and Lord Hay, who were pro-Protestant and pro-French, but they had no great political ambitions. More important was the Howard faction, which was pro-Catholic and pro-Spanish, led by Northampton. Finally, a mixed anti-Howard group surfaced, led by William third Earl of Pembroke, Archbishop George Abbot and Lord Chancellor Ellesmere, which was above all pro-Protestant and very anti-Spanish. No one succeeded Salisbury as lord treasurer, the treasury being placed under a commission comprising both Howards and anti-Howards. Out of this balance, the Howards were for a while to emerge as the predominant force, thanks partly to James's infatuation with the handsome flaxen-haired Scotsman, Robert Carr, Viscount Rochester. Despite being a favourite, he was not to receive any real political power until his alliance with the Howard family, towards which he was directed by the king. Rochester formed an attachment to Frances Howard, now Countess of Essex. On the grounds that her husband was impotent an annulment was granted to Frances in 1613, thanks mainly to a commission of judges and bishops which James had packed to produce the right verdict for her to marry Carr, now elevated to Earl of Somerset. Only Archbishop Abbot refused to vote in favour of the divorce, so great was his hatred for the pro-Catholic Howards. This travesty of a commission shocked public opinion and brought further odium on the Court. But worse was to follow. The great scandal which ensued was the revelation in 1615 that Frances Countess of Somerset had poisoned a former servant of her new husband's, Sir Thomas Overbury, during his incarceration in the Tower of London in 1613. Overbury had been sent there by James for refusing a foreign posting – just to get him out of the way. Overbury had been a close friend and adviser to Carr – his 'governor' according to Queen Anna – and possibly also his lover. Overbury had abetted Carr's flirtation with Lady Frances by writing his love-letters to her, but he was entirely against the marriage, either out of jealousy or more probably because he did not want his friend to join the Howard faction. Certainly Northampton had influenced the king to imprison Overbury in order to facilitate the annulment. Overbury died in the Tower in suspicious circumstances, his putrid body suggesting poisoning. In 1616 the Earl and Countess of Somerset were put on trial before the House of Lords and were found guilty of poisoning Overbury; Lady Frances pleaded guilty but Somerset maintained his innocence. Sentenced to death by the court, they were pardoned by the king who merely lodged them in the Tower for six years. This scandal and the exaggerations involved in its retelling seemed to confirm the worst rumours about the Court of James I.

The fall of Robert Carr led to the demise of the Howard faction at Court. Northampton had already died, and the Earl of Suffolk, father to Lady Frances, was dismissed in 1618 for gross corruption in mismanaging the finances and was punished by a huge fine in Star Chamber. The decline of the Howards, however, was not entirely brought about by scandals: it was as much the result of a newcomer in James's bed, George Villiers. He was initially a pawn used by the anti-Howard faction, led by Pembroke and the archbishop, with the support of Queen Anna (despite her unofficial conversion to Catholicism), to wield power over the king. But in the end Villiers proved able to checkmate his patrons and become master of the situation, exerting great influence over

James. He was able to do this solely because he became the king's sexual partner in August 1615. Writing many years later, Buckingham reminded James of their first night together at Farnham, Surrey:[7]

> whether you loved me now... better than at the time which I shall never forget at Farnham, where the bed's head could not be found between the master and his dog.

Queen Anna, who had not shared the king's bed since about 1606, proved herself to be an extremely understanding wife. She had a pet-name of 'dog' for Villiers. Queen Anna, writing to 'My kind dog', praised him for doing 'very well in lugging the sow's ear, and I thank you for it, and would have you do so still upon condition that you continue a watchful dog to him and be always true to him, so wishing you all happiness'. The king referred to him as 'sweet Steenie' after the angel-faced St Stephen, and called Villiers 'my sweet child and wife'. James verged on blasphemy in 1617 in equating his relationship to Villiers to Christ's with the beloved disciple John: 'Christ had his John and I have my George.' Accordingly, Villiers soon became truly top dog at Court, and finally Duke of Buckingham (1623) – the first English duke since 1572. This last phase in the factional history of the reign of James I, from 1618 onwards, saw the almost complete domination of the Court by one man. The Elizabethan model of a sharing of patronage so that the Court could attract and reconcile different political groups and interests had been shattered. Buckingham now succeeded where Elizabeth's Essex had failed. The Court had become a centre for alienation rather than for reconciliation: opposition to him was no longer being neutralised at Court but taken out into the provinces.

James and finance

The longer James reigned the worse the financial position of the government became despite genuine attempts at reform. Undeniably the king was personally extravagant. He believed that he had come from impoverished Scotland to a land flowing with milk and honey, and he was determined to reap the rewards. He spent £64 000 on jewellery during his first year as king. He gave large gifts to his Scottish favourites; Lord Hay got some £400 000 (about £6 million in today's money) out of the king. No wonder that Hay's motto was 'Spend and God will send'! James was a very poor businessman with no understanding of credit, although he was tight-fisted enough with cash which he could feel in his own hands; a contemporary said that James 'was liberal with what he had not in his own grip, and would rather part with £100 he never had in his own keeping than one 21/- piece within his own custody'. This extravagance was in marked contrast to the parsimony and frugality of Queen Elizabeth, who despite all the costs of a long war against Spain had left an essentially balanced account at her death. However, when James died, he left the government in debt to the tune of a staggering £1 million. The reasons for this were essentially structural rather than personal to James, although his spendthrift ways obviously exacerbated the problem.

The underlying fault lay in the continuing medieval way of financing the state. James was still expected to 'live of his own', that is to pay his way without going to Parliament for grants of taxation, except in emergencies, such as wartime. But 'to live of his own' was getting harder in an age of inflation. The recent subjugation of Ireland was also terribly expensive, costing some £30 000 p.a. by 1612. Queen Elizabeth had undertaken drastic economies, but she had only her own household to upkeep. King James needed a household for himself and separate ones for Queen Anna and his heir Prince Henry. That was all normal and customary, but of course it cost much more money. James maintained a magnificent and costly Court even though he himself did not enjoy public ceremonies. By 1606 the royal debt stood at £735 000. By careful management both the Earl of Dorset and Lord Salisbury brought down the debt to £280 000. But all this good work was sabotaged by James who went on happily spending, as did the pleasure-loving Queen Anna. Nevertheless, despite the sums that he spent on himself and the Court, James never managed to look regal or inspiring. In that sense such spending was money wasted, merely evoking criticism from the more staid and Puritan-minded members of the gentry.

The major sources of income that James could depend on regularly were the crown estates, fiscal feudalism, purveyance and customs duties. The problem with the royal estates was that they were a continually diminishing asset. Elizabeth had sold large tracts of the royal estates to pay for the war with Spain. James sold a similar amount, but in his case the sale was to finance his peacetime government, and by his death they stood at only half their value. As the king lost lands so he tried to squeeze more money out of those landowners who held their lands from the Crown by a feudal tenure. The feudal rights of wardship and marriage were especially exploited. There was nothing new in this exploitation, but it was becoming even more resented now than in the past by the landowning class, mainly because of the growing capitalist nature of land management. The king's intrusion into a family's estates and his right to sell wardship and marriage sorely impeded the building up of secure estates. It was the major grievance in the parliamentary session of 1604. Purveyance was another medieval custom that now seemed out of step with changing times. This involved the ancient right of the monarch to buy commodities for the royal household considerably below the market price at amounts determined by the king's purveyors. Those items not for consumption by the Court could be resold for a profit on the open market. In the parliamentary session of 1604 the Commons refused to accept the legality of purveyance, but as it meant an annual profit to the Crown of £40 000–50 000 the king was loath to abandon it; his only retort was that purveyance was an ancient custom.

The king's major source of income was customs duties. This financial source tripled in value during James's reign partly because trade was flourishing for most of the time and partly because of the increased tariffs levied by the Jacobean government. In 1604 James sold the right to collect customs duties to a syndicate of London businessmen for £112 000 p.a., rising later to £140 000. This privatising of customs collection certainly led to greater efficiency and receipts. However, the big quarrel in James's reign was over the extension of customs tariffs to new commodities not previously taxed – tariffs known as impositions. Queen Elizabeth had led the way here with some new tariffs. In 1606 the merchant John Bate was brought before the Exchequer for having refused to pay an Elizabethan imposition on currants. The Exchequer ruled against Bate and in favour of James on the grounds of regulation of trade, which was judged to be part of the royal prerogative. But the Exchequer's verdict implied more than simple regulation of trade; it suggested that the king had the right to impose taxes at will. This seems to have given the government the go-ahead to enlarge greatly the scope of these novel impositions in the new Book of Customs Rates of 1608 (the first since 1555), as well as to increase the traditional tariffs. The increase in customs rates was moderate and easily justifiable, but nothing could prevent the storm of criticism that ensued, especially over the new impositions, which were now levied on some 1400 items. There seem to have been two major anxieties in the minds of opponents of the government's policy: first, there was an understandable fear that the king could use his prerogative of trade regulation simply to tax at will and make himself entirely independent of the landowning class in Parliament; and second, it certainly looks as though the landowners wanted more of a say than previously in the running of the economy, objecting to the medieval convention of the king's sole authority in such matters. Impositions were the main focus of contention in the parliamentary session of 1610 and in the 'Addled Parliament' of 1614. However, as impositions brought in £70 000 p.a. the king was not too worried over the complaints. Revisionist Conrad Russell regards impositions as sparking 'the only profound constitutional conflict of the reign of James I'[8] because of the perceived threat to the very existence of Parliament if the king could raise money in this way.

Another source of income was the sale of honours: ordinary knighthoods and then from 1611 the brand-new honour of hereditary knights baronet, as well as peerages (48 of them). As more honours were sold the prices fell, and those who had paid highly at the start, expecting an exclusive company, were resentful at the bargains that came later for others. The sale and dilution of honours thus brought in quick money, yet it was a short-sighted policy, creating jealousy and resentment among a large segment of the ruling elite.

As for parliamentary taxation, this was among the least important source of royal funding. Parliaments were infrequent and objected to paying taxes for peacetime government now that the war against Spain was over. Although Parliaments granted subsidies, sometimes triple subsidies, the amounts were small, because of the system of assessment which was entrusted to the gentry themselves, who undertaxed each other and their friends. The Members, of course, believed they were being very generous, but they were living in a fools' paradise.

Thus James sold off his capital, raised money by other means but still ended up in debt. What was needed was a radical overhaul of the whole financial system to move away from the antiquated medieval, feudal basis to one based on cooperation with the ruling gentry class represented in Parliament. Such a scheme was indeed devised by Lord Salisbury and presented to both king and Parliament in 1610. Salisbury's plan, known as 'The Great Contract', was for the king to surrender his hated feudal incomes from wardship and marriage as well as purveyance and impositions. James was reluctant at first, but he was eventually persuaded by Salisbury to accept the scheme. Under the deal the king would get £200 000 p.a. from Parliament in return for what he had abandoned, as well as a one-off payment of £600 000 to extinguish the king's existing debts. The understanding was that James thereafter would live within his means. This proposal was both reasonable and viable, and there was much initial enthusiasm for it from the Commons. However, when MPs reported to their constituencies during the recess, doubts arose over who exactly should pay what. How exactly was the money to be raised? The abolition of wardship suggested to many that it should be replaced with a permanent land tax, while to others the abolition of purveyance, which suited the merchants, should be made up by an excise tax. Those who had not been subject to wardship or purveyance could see no good reason why they should shoulder a new general tax burden. And Parliament as a whole began to worry that the king might not need to call it again if his income were assured. Eventually both Parliament and the king myopically vetoed the scheme, and its failure was a major blow personally to Salisbury.

The years following Salisbury's death in 1612 saw corruption on a large scale in the unreformed finances. The king's need for money saw him turn to yet another fiscal device, the revival of the practice of granting patents of monopoly – that is, the sole right to import or trade in a particular commodity. The granting of monopolies to courtiers and privileged merchants, who could then ask whatever price they wished without the discipline of competition, was a major source of royal patronage. But monopolies were a major obstacle to the growth of business and capitalism, and had been enormously resented in the last years of Elizabeth, who had had the good sense to abandon the most hated of them. James had followed suit initially, but now in dire straits after 1612 he revived them on a scale far larger than Elizabeth's. Monopolies became the great bogey in the Parliament of 1621, when a huge attack was made on them, and the leading monopolist Sir Giles Mompesson was impeached. As a result of this uproar James had to back down and surrender all major patents of monopoly. In the next Parliament of 1624 the king accepted a new Monopolies Act which allowed them only on new inventions.

After the failure of the 'Great Contract' the only other serious attempt to bring order to the finances was that undertaken by Lionel Cranfield, the London businessman brought in initially by Northampton and taken up by Buckingham. Cranfield began by pruning the expenditure of the royal household, the navy and ordnance, and by reforming the treasury itself. By 1619 he had just about balanced the ordinary account, although past debts of £900 000 remained unfunded. Queen Anna's death in this year meant a future annual saving of £60 000, although at the time there was no money to bury her and her funeral had to be delayed. In 1622 Cranfield became lord treasurer and Earl of Middlesex, and began cutting back on the fees, pensions and sinecures of courtiers. This naturally enraged the courtier element, who wanted reforms as long as they themselves were exempted, and Buckingham soon turned against his client. Once more, vested interests prevented reforms to the royal finances. And as the reign was coming to a close the costs of military intelligence and planning increased, now that Europe was in the initial stages of the Thirty Years War. Middlesex opposed all expensive warlike demands, and indeed desired a Spanish alliance and accompanying dowry, which led to his impeachment and disgrace in 1624 through Buckingham's machinations. As England entered a new period of war at the end of James's reign the royal finances were atrocious, and it soon became obvious in the new reign that England could not afford warfare on an antiquated financial base.

James and Parliament

James called only four Parliaments in his reign of 22 years, but the first Parliament of 1604 consisted of five sessions stretching down to 1610. The 'Addled Parliament' of 5 April–6 June 1614 was the shortest and most barren, with a long gap then until the next in 1621 (January–June, November–December), and the last in 1624 (February–May). As with most previous monarchs since 1460 it was not usual to invoke Parliament for the regular day-to-day running of the state, so that the infrequent use of Parliament should evoke no amazement. Nevertheless, the central place of Parliament has been accepted as axiomatic in traditional accounts of the period. The familiar story was that of 'the rise of Parliament', wherein the growingly assertive House of Commons campaigned in an organised and systematic way to reduce the power of the Crown.

The old interpretation was first questioned by G. R. Elton, but the full onslaught of revisionism began in 1976 with Conrad Russell's challenge to the very foundations of the 'rise of Parliament' thesis. In his view there was no struggle for sovereignty in early Stuart England, no continuous 'opposition' because Parliaments were infrequent, and in any case the Members had no wish to form an opposition, which was seen as disloyal. If one judged the supposedly growing strength of Parliament by its ability to win victories over the king, then Parliament could be said to be losing out, rather than going from strength to strength. Parliament made no real attempt to use the granting of taxation as blackmail to secure concessions or the redress of grievances, which one might have expected if their intentions had been aggressive. Subsidies were voted easily when asked for in 1606, 1610, 1621 and 1624. Only in the 'Addled Parliament' of 1614 was supply used as a weapon against the hated impositions, and much of the chaos in that Parliament could be attributed to court factionalism. Although Parliament continually called for the end of impositions no notice was taken of their demand. When there were conflicts, the king normally won; and if anything, parliamentarians, far from feeling confident of ultimate victory, actually feared for the end of all Parliaments in England with the growth of royal power. 'Before 1640, Parliament was not powerful and it did not contain an "opposition".' Moreover, argues

Russell, this weak Parliament was saved only by the intervention of the Scots in 1640 and by the Dutch later in 1688–9.[9]

Revisionists are essentially empiricists who examine the minute details of events rather than concern themselves with long-term theories. Accordingly, they argue, if one studies the events in Parliament closely they undermine the old Whig–Liberal–Marxist generalisations about 'the rise of Parliament'. Revisionists have striven to explode the significance of various traditionalist 'milestones' on the road to parliamentary supremacy. According to the traditionalist Wallace Notestein, the House of Commons 'won the initiative' against the Crown by developing a procedure of opposition. Notestein thought that the creation of the Committee of the Whole House in 1606 (it was actually first employed earlier under Elizabeth) was a method of reducing government authority in the Commons.[10] A normal session of the House was guided by the Speaker, a government nominee, but when the entire House became a committee the normal rules of debate were abandoned and the authority of the Speaker evaporated, while Members could speak as many times as they wished rather than just once as normally. Notestein interpreted committees in themselves as being a device of opposition. This idea was attacked by Sheila Lambert (Lady Elton), who maintained that committees were first devised for the sake of business efficiency rather than to foment opposition, and they were chaired by government men.[11] Whereas in ordinary debate government spokesmen could speak only once, in a committee of the Whole House they could air their views as often as possible and thus impress their audience with the government line. This was above all designed to gain consensus, and was not an example of a special procedure of opposition. However, despite such innocent origins, post-revisionists retort that the Committee of the Whole House was undoubtedly used as an instrument of opposition, especially in 1614 and 1628.

Perhaps the most celebrated of parliamentary confrontations occurred in 1621 when, according to the old story, the Commons invaded the royal prerogative by discussing foreign policy without the approval of the king. The convention developed by Elizabeth was that 'matters of state' (such as foreign policy and religion) could be debated in Parliament only at the request of the sovereign; on the other hand, 'matters of commonwealth' (such as the poor laws or economic issues) could be debated spontaneously at any time. James followed this recent distinction, and was thus furious when the Commons invaded his prerogative with advice on foreign affairs. In a very dramatic episode James had the *Commons Journal* brought to him at Whitehall, where he tore out the offending page containing 'The Protestation' in defence of the right of free speech in the House. What could be a more clear case of constitutional conflict? Once again the revisionists have shown by a wealth of detail that the real story is rather different, more confused and less pregnant with future civil war. Conrad Russell pointed out that the first formal motion that the Commons should support a policy of general war with Spain – which was the advice that James did not want to hear – came from somebody close to the government. Russell showed that members of the government – Lord Keeper Williams and Lord Treasurer Cranfield – actually invited the House of Commons to discuss foreign policy; there was no conspiracy by the Commons to invade the prerogative. The House was eager to know the king's mind, but James showed himself a poor parliamentary manager and left the House confused and in the dark. Certainly James was hostile to the call for an all-out war against Spain, and this idea may have been aired in the Commons precisely to drive the king into dissolving Parliament. It was an event engineered by a Court faction, the Members of the Commons appearing docile rather than aggressive. What angered the king was the Commons' petition for Prince Charles to marry a Protestant instead of the Catholic Infanta of Spain.[12] Once again, whatever the true intentions of the participants, the event now cannot so easily be read as a clear threat to the king's power: it is no longer the milestone of traditionalism. Nevertheless, post-revisionists, while accepting that a misunderstanding was involved, still see a 'profound gulf' developing between the two sides.

Revisionists concede that there were areas of conflict, but these were conflicts not between a united Parliament on the one hand and a united government on the other, but between different factions at Court linked to their clients in Parliament. As Russell says: 'On none of the great questions of the day did Parliamentary leaders hold any opinions not shared by members of the Council.'[13] Factionalism and self-interest were the main motives for political behaviour, according to the revisionists, not ideology and principle. Certainly some of James's statements might seem inflammatory, such as his claim that 'the privileges [of Parliament] were derived from the grace and permission of our ancestors'. He also threatened to punish Members when Parliament had been dissolved for what they had said in the House – on the basis of his stated principle that 'the Parliament not sitting the liberties not sitting'. Accordingly James detained nine MPs after the Addled Parliament for speeches in the House, four of whom were sent to the Tower. Revisionists ask whether this was really any different from Elizabeth's imprisoning difficult parliamentarians, and conclude that there was no new, imported policy of royal absolutism.

On the other hand, James was so angry in 1614 that he tore up the Addled Parliament's bills and papers. Post-revisionists point out that these arrests of 1614 were never forgotten, but were brought up in the next Parliament of 1621 despite the many years intervening, thus highlighting a real continuity of concern.[14] To post-revisionists, the Addled Parliament cannot be so easily dismissed as the victim of faction politics. While it is true that the Howards were against calling it because they did not want their pro-Spanish policies criticised, and they undoubtedly fanned up hostility within the House when it met, there is little real substance to the view that John Hoskins, who made a speech attacking the Scots and intimating a possible massacre of Scots in England, was a dupe of the Howards. The speech certainly frightened James, who thereupon dissolved Parliament, but he had clearly been aiming at its dissolution earlier because of the Commons' refusal to give supply until grievances over impositions had been redressed.[15] There were perhaps more genuine differences in 1614 than revisionists concede. However, one must not view the Addled Parliament in too revolutionary a light either despite some of the speeches delivered. True, Thomas Wentworth of Oxford seemed threateningly to suggest that James might be assassinated as Henry IV of France had recently been, but he later apologised and said that no allusion to King James had been intended. And while Sir Edwin Sandys had implied that all monarchy was elective and that impositions signified tyranny, he too became eager to conciliate the king. Although Sandys is regarded as a leading activist in this Parliament it must not be forgotten that he owed his seat to Court patronage. What truly alarmed the Commons was the freedom that impositions seemed to give to the king never to call Parliaments again, as well as the perceived attacks on their privileges. The Addled Parliament seems to reveal genuine tensions. Furthermore, after the next Parliament in 1621 a number of Members were imprisoned, notably Sir Edward Coke, Sir Robert Phelipps and John Pym. Were these men eccentric and untypical, like the Puritan malcontents of Elizabethan Parliaments? A case can be made out for seeing these Jacobean victims as being more typical parliamentarians of their age than their Elizabethan predecessors had been. They seem to have been standing up for a concept of liberty at variance with that espoused by the king.

Revisionist scepticism of the king's wish to be an absolutist takes comfort from the fact that James himself banned by royal proclamation a book advocating absolutism, namely *The Interpreter* (1607) by Dr John Cowell, a leading civil lawyer. This was a top-selling law dictionary, which claimed that the king 'is above the law by his absolute power'. Common lawyers obviously disliked the work, but it was the king who took action against it, proving in the minds of revisionists that James did not agree with its ideas and was thus no aspiring absolutist. Post-revisionists are not convinced by this argument. J. Sommerville's view is that James banned the book because he did not want the royal prerogative discussed by anyone at all, since this was beyond all debate, and because he did not want Parliament wasting its time on this matter when it should be voting him money.[16] Revisionists point to the king's speech to Parliament in 1610 wherein James espoused the view that he had a duty to rule according to the constitution and the law, since anything else made the king into a tyrant. This sounds constitutionally immaculate, but it may not be the convincing evidence that revisionists claim, because absolutists could easily voice the same sentiments: that is, that in normal times they ruled in accordance with known laws rather than just by arbitrary whim. The important question was: could the king ever disregard the known laws, and if so for how long? Absolutists answered yes to the first question because they were above the laws; and as for the length of an emergency situation the king alone had the discretionary right to decide that.

James and religious problems

The Puritans

The religious problems of the reign have traditionally been viewed by historians from the vantage point of the Civil War, with this war usually being seen as the 'Puritan Revolution'. Such a view stressed the alienation of the Puritans, whose demands for reform had been ignored so that the Church was left unpurified and 'papistical'; consequently mounting Puritan anger exploded in the 'Puritan Revolution'. Calvinist Puritans were viewed as religious revolutionaries, indeed the first political revolutionaries of the modern world. Hierarchy, it has been claimed, meant little to the Puritans, who felt a bond only with their fellow 'saints', and whose prime ambition was to sweep away the abomination of Catholicism. There is much still of worth in this interpretation of the Puritan world view, but modern revisionist work suggests that Puritans were neither as radical nor as aggressive as this. Their boldness was blunted by their need of the Protestant monarch who alone could defend them from the furies of international Catholicism.

The Puritans were hoping for a greater degree of toleration at James's accession in 1603. James's education had been Calvinist, but he had come to regard Presbyterianism as the greatest threat to his position as King of Scotland. Nevertheless, English Puritans had their hopes up, and on the king's journey south presented him with the 'Millenary Petition', supposedly signed by 1000 Anglican clergy of a Puritan persuasion calling for the removal of 'abuses', such as the wearing of the surplice, bowing at the name of Jesus, the use of the sign of the cross in baptisms, as well as demanding a better educated, preaching clergy. The result of this and other petitions was the three-day Hampton Court conference of January 1604 where a delegation of bishops debated with a group of four specially appointed Puritans, with the king acting as chairman – and with a larger group of Puritans waiting outside. The old idea about the conference was that James and the bishops stood firm against the Puritans and completely alienated them, thus missing a wonderful opportunity for consensus and instead storing up trouble for the future. But the truth is not as simple as this. There is no doubt that James sympathised with many of their demands, especially with their call for a preaching ministry, yet James hated Presbyterian-type Puritanism.[17] His two famous sayings from the conference bear this out: Presbyterianism, James maintained, 'agreeth as well with a monarchy as God and the devil'. And even more famous was his outburst in reaction to the Puritan dislike of episcopacy: 'No bishop. No King.' Such sayings reveal his hostility to the democratic tendencies inherent in the Puritan outlook and his amazing perceptivity, putting his finger on one of the main themes of seventeenth-century English history, namely the importance of hierarchy in both Church and state, a threat to the one being seen as a threat to the other also. James had already tried to revive episcopacy in Scotland and would continue later to do so successfully. James lost patience at the conference and warned: 'I shall make them conform themselves or I will harry them out of the land.' As a result 90 hard-core Presbyterian ministers were ejected from their livings – about 1 per cent of the clergy. According to Patrick Collinson, the conference and James's decision against the Puritans did not mean the end of them, 'but it proved to be the end of the puritan movement in the form of a concerted effort mounted from within the Church to alter the fundamental terms of the Elizabethan settlement by political means'. The Puritans were no longer the danger to monarchy that they had seemed to be earlier. By the new church canons passed by Convocation in 1604 a test was devised to weed out extreme Puritans: candidates for the ministry had to subscribe to the royal supremacy, the Prayer Book and the Thirty-nine Articles. But it seems that despite this test Puritan ministers were generally left alone and not forced to subscribe. Most Puritans were moderate in their outlook, were willing to conform, and were therefore not a major problem. However, even though James was as suspicious of Puritanism as Elizabeth had been, his mind was less resistant to reform in the Church than hers had been, and he made improvements that to some extent blunted Puritan criticism. He went quite a way to meeting their demand for a learned, preaching ministry – something which Elizabeth had always resisted – and enforced high standards. Revisionists regard the Jacobean period as a stable, quiet time in the Protestant Church of England, not an era of alienation – a peaceful interlude between the tensions of the Elizabethan and Caroline periods. The king himself maintained a close interest in what was to be the greatest religious legacy of his reign, the publication of the Authorized Version of the Bible (1611), a reform stemming directly from the Hampton Court conference.

The Catholics

Catholics, like the Puritans, were hoping for a lightening of their burden at the accession of the new monarch, especially because James had already had dealings with the papacy and had intimated that he would tolerate those lay Catholics who obeyed the law. Such early hopes of the abolition of recusancy fines were to prove unfounded when James became king, and led to a sense of disillusionment on the part of some. One former advocate of peaceful coexistence and an opponent of Jesuit machinations, the secular priest William Watson, was incensed enough to plot a hare-brained scheme to capture the Tower and James himself, forcing him to allow toleration or else threatening his removal. The 'By Plot' (or priests' plot) was denounced to the authorities by the Jesuits, and Watson and another secular priest were executed.

James had no wish to persecute over religion; he had a scheme to reunify Europe religiously and he had called for an ecumenical council to decide the main issues. But he was firmly against the political pretensions of the papacy, and accordingly Jesuits and seminary priests were banished by a proclamation of 1604. Even so, despite all the official prohibitions against their religion, lay Catholics now suffered lighter recusancy fines and indeed became emboldened to stay away from the parish church. It was to be Parliament's disapproval of this leniency on James's part which forced him abruptly to change course in 1605 and order a stricter enforcement of the recusancy laws. Accordingly, a small number of extremists now plotted to be rid of the new monarch, just as they had plotted Elizabeth's death. The conspiracy known as the 'Gunpowder Plot', which aimed to blow up the assembled Parliament along with James and Prince Henry at the official opening of the second session on 5 November 1605, was hatched among some remnants of the old Essex affinity, led by Robert Catesby and his cousins, Francis Tresham and Thomas

Winter. The most famous of the plotters, Guy Fawkes, was a convert to Catholicism and had served as a captain in the Spanish army in the Netherlands. Besides blowing up the king and the government, the plotters aimed to synchronise their activities with a rising in the Midlands to capture Princess Elizabeth, who was at Coventry, and place her or Prince Charles (whose capture was less clearly envisaged) on the throne. Fortunately, the government got wind of the affair when the Catholic Lord Monteagle received an anonymous note tipping him off about the explosion, and decided to inform the council. This note was almost certainly from his brother-in-law, Francis Tresham. Guy Fawkes and the gunpowder were thereupon discovered in the cellars of the Palace of Westminster. The revelation of this audacious plot led immediately to a rigorous persecution of Catholics, but its lasting results were less than might have been predicted. The harsh enforcement of the recusancy laws softened with time, and the number of executions of Catholic priests declined. There were only 17 such executions beween 1607 and 1618, and none at all in the last years of the reign. This was a far cry from the large numbers of priests (129) condemned to death under Elizabeth. What was to be left behind indelibly was the notion of an ongoing 'popish plot' that could be used to inflame any situation at a critical time in the future by extreme Protestants.

The revisionist claim is that, as regards both dissident religious minorities, the reign of James can be viewed as a healing period rather than one of continued strife, and can thus be reckoned as a great success; in no way can the religious tensions of the Civil Wars be traced back to James's reign. However, this view ignores the fact that from 1621 onwards James fell out with Archbishop Abbot, an evangelical Calvinist, in a situation reminiscent of Elizabeth's quarrel with Archbishop Grindal. Although Abbot was not forced to retire, he lost all influence with the king thereafter. There were two reasons for this estrangement: first, Abbot opposed the king's foreign policy of peace and a dynastic tie with Spain, which was seen as being a betrayal of Protestantism; and second, James issued a proclamation in 1622 forbidding the preaching of Calvinist double predestination. In a letter to the king, widely known but never delivered, Abbot condemned the king's policy as 'a liberty to throw down the laws of the land at your pleasure'. The revisionists Russell and Nicholas Tyacke argue that the Puritan problem would be reopened not by James but by Charles I through his embracing Arminianism, and they regard the year 1625 as a crucial watershed in the religious history of England. However, the 'success' of James's religious policy remains controversial, especially as it was he who encouraged the 'Arminian' Richard Montagu to publish his *New Gag for an Old Goose*, a book which in its refusal to endorse Calvinist predestinarianism made it hateful to Puritans and which was published only after James's death. Therefore the first major religious dispute of Charles I's reign stemmed from that of his predecessor.

James, foreign affairs and the drift to war

James was a peace-loving king, 'pacific' rather than 'pacifist'. He had a genuine desire for peace, and he realised that war simply could not be afforded; accordingly peace with Spain was concluded in 1604. Spain had been the great enemy in Elizabeth's reign; that attitude was now to change radically under her successor. James is usually portrayed as being pro-Spanish, and in traditional accounts his friendship with Spain is usually linked to his perceived absolutist ambitions in England. But this is doubtful: James was not so much pro-Spanish as simply not as vehemently anti-Spanish as were so many of his subjects. James, as a foreigner, undoubtedly underestimated the smouldering embers of Hispanophobia in England, only too easily rekindled. Moreover, his close friendship with Count Gondomar, the Spanish ambassador between 1613 and 1617, seemed to confirm to his subjects his veering towards Spain. However, James knew that in the last resort his only duty was to support the Protestant anti-Habsburg alliance in Europe: thus in 1610 he became allied to Henry IV of France (although James had no inkling at the time of Henry's desire to go to war), and in 1612 he allied with the Protestant Dutch and the Evangelical Union in Germany. James's heartfelt desire in all this was to maintain the peace rather than to open up a new round of fighting. He aimed to use dynastic links to bring peace. In 1613 James married his daughter Elizabeth to Frederick, the Calvinist Elector Palatine. Having married off his daughter into the Protestant camp, James thought he could balance the account by marrying his heir Prince Charles to the Catholic Infanta of Spain. But this plan initially foundered on Spanish conditions that there should be freedom of worship for English Catholics and that children of the marriage should be raised as Catholics. No way would the English Parliament allow this, and the king's policy of reconciliation made little sense to most Englishmen.

The last years of James's reign were bedevilled by the opening phase of the so-called Thirty Years War (1618–48) in Europe. James's son-in-law, the Calvinist Elector Palatine, had ventured his fortune on accepting the offer of the Bohemian rebels to become King of Bohemia, thus ousting the Catholic Habsburg occupant, the Archduke Ferdinand (who had since become the Emperor Ferdinand II). The Bohemian rebels and the forces of the Elector Palatine were crushed at the Battle of the White Mountain, near Prague, in November 1620. Frederick lost not only Bohemia but also his home, the Palatinate, which fell to Spanish forces, and he and his wife Elizabeth had to flee to the Dutch Netherlands. James had disapproved of Frederick's gamble in putting himself at the head of the Bohemian rebels, especially as this jeopardised James's role as mediator and involved rebellion, something which he loathed. But the milk was now spilt and James felt obligated to help his son-in-law, who was widely regarded as an international Protestant hero. The question was how best to help – by war or by negotiation? If by war, what sort of war – a general war at sea against Spain in the great Elizabethan manner, or a limited land campaign to recover the Palatinate? James wanted to remain friendly with Spain, and accordingly had sacrificed Ralegh to execution in 1618 for infringing the Spanish monopoly in South America. This seemed an evident reversal of the great days of Elizabeth.

Despite not wanting a war, James called Parliament in 1621 to get money to finance one, on the assumption that the very threat of hostilities would bring peace and Frederick back to Heidelberg. James had to appear to be doing something to help. War was very expensive, and although the House of Commons in 1621 was very free and generous with words, promising to help Frederick 'with their lives and fortunes', they did not back this proud boast with hard cash to mount a viable land campaign. Such reluctance was understandable in view of the dire economic depression at the time. Nevertheless, two subsidies (£140 000) were granted to organise for war. James wanted to do nothing which would cause the war to spread further in Europe. If he were forced into playing some role, then he preferred to start up a limited land campaign to put pressure on the Emperor, while maintaining good relations with Spain in the continued hope of the Spanish marriage, which he still saw as his best opportunity for resolving the conflict. This was a difficult balancing act which most MPs could not appreciate. In the view of most Members 'a war of diversion' (an all-out war at sea with chances of plunder) was 'more profitable'. Being given no decipherable lead by the government, the House began calling for Prince Charles to marry a Protestant, and this greatly angered the king. This was the occasion of that quarrel discussed earlier between James and the Commons which resulted in the king's tearing out their 'Protestation' on parliamentary privileges from the *Commons Journal*. Although not the great constitutional clash of legend, it nevertheless revealed genuine differences over the prosecution of a war against the Habsburgs, and James felt that his prerogative of deciding foreign policy was being challenged, while the Commons believed that their freedom of speech was being trampled upon.

The proposal for the marriage of Prince Charles to the Spanish Infanta was revived in 1622. Again it was hoped that this initiative would influence the Habsburgs to reinstate the Elector Palatine at Heidelberg. Prince Charles and Buckingham decided impetuously to go to Madrid incognito (as Jack and Tom Smith) to woo the Infanta. This was a rash move, and James heartily disapproved of it but could do little to stop them. Charles and Buckingham spent six months in Spain (February to October 1623) without bringing up the question of the Palatinate until after Charles had agreed to become a Catholic and to have any children brought up as Catholics. Philip IV went further and demanded the abolition of all anti-Catholic laws in England. Charles, it seems, had fallen in love and was prepared to give away too much. The Spaniards in return had agreed to nothing.

Charles had botched the deal, and Buckingham soon realised the extent of Spanish designs and the danger which they posed to England; on their return they reversed their position and now demanded war against Spain. Buckingham's absence from Court had threatened his continued predominance there, and Cranfield had taken advantage of it to groom a homosexual favourite to succeeed Buckingham in James's favours. However, by the time Buckingham returned, he had secured the full confidence of the heir to the throne, so that such scheming came to naught. Buckingham and Charles began making deals with some key Members of Parliament to gain a new compliant House for a war against Spain. They agreed not to raise disputes over parliamentary privilege, while Buckingham undertook to persuade James to call a new Parliament to abrogate the marriage negotiations and to pursue a policy of war with Spain. Buckingham created a team of key players who could convince the House into an aggressive policy against Spain, and in this he was supported by Pembroke's faction. The Lords (including the bishops) were also eager for war, the Earl of Southampton claiming that they were ready 'with our persons and estates'. The House of Commons seems to have been less belligerent than the Lords and more concerned with the problems of paying for a war at a difficult economic time, but the Members were being talked into it by Buckingham's and Pembroke's men. James said he needed six subsidies and 12 fifteenths to pay for a war, and agreed that parliamentary treasurers could oversee it – proposals designed to reduce Parliament's clamour for war. James was, of course, very hesitant about any such risky and expensive enterprise. The Spanish marriage treaty could be abandoned only if Parliament voted enough money. Parliament offered merely three subsidies and three fifteenths, but James accepted this because he wanted only the threat of war rather than the real thing. However, the prince and Buckingham gave promises to Parliament for an all-out war at sea against Spain. Buckingham was more successful in his personal vendetta against treasurer Cranfield, who was one of the few to oppose any war, and who was now charged with bribery as master of wards. Despite the hysteria generated in this last Parliament of the reign for a great war against idolatrous Spain, all that the old king sanctioned was a limited land campaign to recover the Palatinate, employing an expeditionary force under the German mercenary, Count Ernst Mansfeld. The death of the pacific James in March 1625 at the age of 58 would lead to a new period of war and internal tensions in the reign of his successor Charles I.

8 The Reign of Charles I to 1640

The accession of Charles I on 27 March 1625 was marked by broken promises, the first of many that would characterise his reign and leave the political nation alienated and disillusioned. He had vowed in the Parliament of 1624 to make no concessions to Catholics and to wage a war at sea against Spain. Despite these pledges, in the negotiations for his marriage to Henrietta Maria of France he agreed to relax the recusancy laws, while the war with Spain was being conducted on land – in Germany – in the shape of Count Ernst Mansfeld's expeditionary force to regain the Palatinate.

Although revisionists have given us a probably exaggerated picture of harmony in James's reign, one must nevertheless concede that England at his death was not hurtling towards crisis, let alone revolution. Yet a great and dramatic change in atmosphere suddenly occurred in the first years of the new reign, so that already by 1628 John Hampden could fear for the 'subversion of the whole state'. What had caused this early crisis? Was rebellion or revolution an imminent possibility? The answer must be no, but some fundamental issues were to be raised. Revisionists have argued that it was not absolutism which caused the early crisis of Charles's reign, but the sheer impact of war with the two great powers of Spain and France and the unwillingness of the House of Commons to shoulder the burden of a war that they had seemingly been clamouring for.

A major reason for the gathering storm must be sought in the personality of the new monarch. It was an undoubted blow to the Stuart dynasty that James's elder son Prince Henry had died so young, as he had embodied the Protestant swashbuckling qualities of the Elizabethan age which had made him so popular. Not so the brother who replaced him. It would indeed be difficult to find someone temperamentally less suited to lead the nation at this, or any other, time. There can be no doubt that Charles I must be regarded as one of the most incompetent of all English kings, completely failing in the major task of kingship, namely the sowing of concord between himself and his leading subjects, the 'political nation'. Charles I was aloof and out of touch, preferring to retreat into an artistic fantasy land; and the history of the new reign is that of the worsening isolation of the Court. Charles was not only more provocative and energetic than James but also less prone to theorise. He stood on his prerogative even more than his father had, refused to compromise and failed to communicate with his subjects. His pronounced stutter was probably a major reason for this. James might have said much (especially on the subject of divine right), but in fact did little that was unequivocally contrary to constitutional convention – whether through laziness or wily circumspection. His son Charles was neither lazy nor circumspect. Hardly anyone had a good word to say about Charles I, despite his upright morality and despite the fact that he developed into a model family man. He was always regarded as untrustworthy and vindictive; he was loyal to no minister except Buckingham, and that was to cost him dearly. It is very doubtful if Charles had any notion of his favourite's sexual relationship with King James, and there was certainly no sexual relationship between himself and Buckingham. However, Buckingham's influence undermined the relationship between Charles and his queen; the marriage blossomed only after the favourite's death.

The reign opened on a sour note with the news that Count Mansfeld's expedition to the Rhine, which had set out in January 1625, had been a farcical failure on account of dysentery among the troops. This blow to the Protestant cause in Europe was exacerbated by the young king's decision to marry a Catholic, which caused widespread unease. Now that Charles had turned against the idea of a Spanish match, negotiations had been under way since 1623 for a marriage to Henrietta Maria of France. However, the final arrangements had not yet been agreed upon when Charles became king. Because of this the first Parliament, initially called for 17 May, was delayed until 18 June. Charles realised that his treaty with the French would provoke opposition in Parliament. This delay heightened MPs' fears when they were already faced with a vicious attack of the plague in London, killing one person in every five. Indeed the outbreak of the plague in 1625 was attributed by many ardent Protestants to

God's wrath for England's failure to rally to the Protestant standard; they sought to appease God by attacking idolatry, namely Roman Catholicism.

When Parliament finally met, the king wanted it to vote money for a war with Spain. In addition to the renewed popish scare, the Parliament of 1625 was to be notable for its attack on the growth of 'Arminianism' within the Church of England. By 'Arminianism' one means essentially the refusal of a number of divines to adhere to the strict Calvinist belief in 'double predestination' and the denial of free will which many people believed had characterised Anglicanism under Elizabeth and James I. Whether or not the Church since 1559 had in truth accepted such an austere Calvinist position is open to doubt, but the point is that many staunch Puritans believed this to have been the case and also that dangerous changes within the Church were now under way owing to a conspiracy of 'Arminians', with their Catholic notions of free will, to monopolise the Church. John Pym and Sir Edward Coke led the attack on the cleric Richard Montagu for being an 'Arminian'. The rise of 'Arminianism' undermined a crucial peg in their theology and rendered up to confusion what the Protestant Anglican Church stood for, lessening what they had regarded as the incontrovertible dividing line between truth and falsehood.

There was also an attack mounted in the first Parliament on Buckingham in his capacity as lord high admiral for having (unwittingly) lent English ships to Catholic France in 1625 in order to suppress the Protestant rebellion at La Rochelle. However, the first Parliament was especially notorious for the famous conflict over the levying of customs dues – the issue of tunnage and poundage. Only once (in 1614) had supply been withheld from James I. Now the Commons refused to grant tunnage and poundage to the king for life, as had been customary for every new king in his first Parliament since 1484. The old interpretation of this event was that it showed the growing self-assertiveness of the Commons and their wish to weaken the monarchy by attacking its financial base, but Conrad Russell's analysis has reduced the constitutional significance of the event.[1] The reason for the dispute was that the government's levying of the hated impositions under James I had been based on the tunnage and poundage Act of 1604. The Commons now wanted a tunnage and poundage statute which would deal with impositions. It is not clear what was being envisaged: either impositions would be excluded altogether or they would be regulated by parliamentary authority. At all events they could not be left purely to the royal prerogative. Parliament wanted to keep its authority over customs revenue, but not necessarily to diminish such revenue, perhaps even to augment it because there was a real appreciation of the king's need to widen his customs base. Because the drafting of such an Act would take time and because of the outbreak of the plague, an interim measure was devised on the suggestion of Sir Robert Phelipps, granting tunnage and poundage for only a certain period, not for life. This measure the Lords refused, so that this Parliament produced no act at all to allow the king to collect customs duties. The king, of course, would continue to collect customs revenue even without parliamentary approval, and this would prove unpalatable to parliamentarians, but it is now clear that this was no great constitutional struggle as in the old 'conflict model' of parliamentary history. There was no solid aim of preventing supply: two subsidies had already been passed, although admittedly small in amount (£120 000) – mainly because the Members had not seen much for the moneys they had given in 1624, as well as on account of plague and economic depression. After an unpopular and inconvenient adjournment to Oxford (1–12 August) the Commons' refusal of a third subsidy led to the dismissal of the Parliament.

Following the dissolution of this first Parliament, Charles and Buckingham attempted to win popularity by an attack on Cadiz as part of a general war against Spain, emulating the feat of the second Earl of Essex back in 1596. Unfortunately, this expedition of October 1625 was not commanded by Buckingham himself, but by the incompetent Lord Wimbledon. It turned into a complete fiasco because when they landed near Cadiz the soldiers discovered stores of wine and drank themselves silly. Little more than half the fleet managed to limp back home.

Charles's second Parliament (6 February to 15 June 1626) was specifically called for money to undertake war. Most Members in both Houses had now grown more hostile to Buckingham. Just before the writs for the new Parliament went out, some six noted opponents of the duke were deliberately excluded from membership by the device of appointing them as sheriffs (and thus returning officers) of their respective counties. Why was this? The government's mismanagement of the war with Spain had certainly provoked criticism, while the merchants disliked the disruption of trade in the Mediterranean. Furthermore, despite the marriage alliance with France, relations were becoming strained there too. French ships had been seized in the English Channel, and trade with France, especially in wine, had become dislocated.

Fear was now growing that through Buckingham's foolishness England would soon be at war with France as well as with Spain – a calamitous situation which all previous governments had sought to avoid. As the Parliament progressed, Buckingham was soundly condemned for his monopoly of counsel and patronage, and for incompetence and corruption. Thus what had begun solely as an attempt to get Buckingham to soften his line towards France built up into a major campaign to get him ousted from office by process of impeachment. Parliament now refused to grant taxation unless the king agreed to impeach Buckingham. The mood turned ugly when the duke was actually accused of having poisoned James I. Furthermore, this Parliament had also revealed the growing hostility between Buckingham and the queen. Buckingham was jealous of Henrietta, especially as her household was a separate centre of patronage. Charles made a threatening remark to this Parliament: 'Remember that Parliaments are altogether in my power for their calling, sitting and dissolution: therefore as I find the fruits of them good or evil, they are to continue, or not to be.' Parliament's refusal to punish the Earl of Bristol for his impertinent remarks about Buckingham's responsibility for the loss of the Palatinate provoked the king to dissolve the assembly.

Failure to get any money from Parliament in 1626 meant that Charles himself had to finance the war against Spain, using his prerogative powers. The king turned to the idea of a forced loan (a privy seal loan); but whereas in the past forced loans were demanded only of chosen individuals and had to be repaid, this time all taxpayers were to contribute, and the promise to repay was made very limply indeed. The forced loan was thus to be taxation without parliamentary authority. It was constitutionally dubious and provoked much discontent, with peers, gentry and even the judges protesting. A large minority of peers and gentry refused to pay up and were subjected to coercion and heavy-handed tactics, with the king making it a personal test of loyalty; and clerics like Roger Manwaring used the pulpit to claim divine-right validity for the loan. Some 76 gentlemen were arrested for refusal to pay. The government ploughed on regardless, with the result that about £184 000 was collected, which meant that financially the forced loan was a huge success – but extracted at a great political cost.[2] Out of this came the celebrated Five Knights' case of November 1627, when five members of the gentry, who had been gaoled for refusing to pay the forced loan, tried to test the legality both of the loan and of the reason for their incarceration. They thereupon applied for writs of *habeas corpus* from the court of King's Bench for cause to be shown why they had been imprisoned; but this request was turned down. While the judges in King's Bench would not deal with the propriety of the loan, they agreed that in an emergency situation the king had a right to imprison people without showing cause. The judges in 1627, as previously, appear to have meant little more by this than refusing bail, and they did not intend to condone indefinite imprisonment on royal warrant.[3] Nevertheless, it appeared that Charles I was acting in an arbitrary way; the tender issue of liberty was highlighted, and this was to be the central topic in the next Parliament in 1628. Also worrying to the gentry was the king's imposition of martial law in the west and south-west of England during this crisis, as it replaced their normal control of local government there. Soldiers were billeted in civilian homes, especially in homes of those who had refused to pay the forced loan. The civilianised ruling gentry class looked askance at the military build-up. The war was not going well: Buckingham in person had led a force of 6000 across the Channel to try and liberate the besieged Huguenot town of La Rochelle, but had failed dismally, losing half his men. There was no good news at all.

The Petition of Right, 1628

The king summoned his third Parliament of 1628–9 because of his desperate need for money both for his troops and for an assault on La Rochelle to help the Protestants there. When Parliament assembled on 17 March 1628, England was at war with both France and Spain – a perilous situation. There now existed a large conscript army under the command of the king with the biggest military preparations seen since the Armada crisis. The very idea of a standing army sent shivers down the backs of the gentry. The work of conscripting men was given over to the local squires, which made them very unpopular with their neighbours. The squires were incensed by the king's emergency measures and what these would mean to the notion of 'English liberties'. The Five Knights' case had shown that there was no legal remedy available to them, so they looked to the new Parliament for answers from the king. For the first time one can speak of a real 'opposition' in Parliament. The Members regarded themselves as speaking for the 'people' (their electors) against what they represented as the tyrannical behaviour of the king. The main complaints were over forced loans – some 5 per cent of MPs in 1628 had been gaoled for refusal to pay the forced loan – and over billeting, the martial law commissions and, of course, the king's power of imprisonment without cause being shown. The major worry of MPs in 1628 was what exactly did the law allow? Sir Robert Phelipps asked: 'If this be law, what do we talk of our liberties?' Was the king ruling under the law, or as an absolutist answerable to God alone? The king's ministers agreed with the Members that the king wanted to act according to the traditional methods. The problem was what to do in an emergency. The common lawyers agreed that the common law gave the king special emergency prerogative powers, but the emergency had to be such that there was no time to call a Parliament to deal with it. The king's opponents denied that the current emergency was of such an acute kind that the normal methods could be overridden. The parliamentarians had no objection to prerogative imprisonment of traitors, but now the machinery of the prerogative was being directed against themselves, the loyal gentry, the backbone of the Protestant realm. If this could be done to them and their precious liberties, what certainty resided in the English common law? Charles did not want to illuminate the grey area of the prerogative but he was forced in opposition to Sir Edward Coke's defences of the common law to say that he had a prerogative from God by which he could imprison at will. This did not mean necessarily that Charles was aiming at absolutism, but he was aiming at a freedom from the law which Coke and the common lawyers were now unwilling to concede. The imposition of martial law had raised fears about the undermining of the common law by Roman law.[4]

The king had called this Parliament for money, but as there was no longer any enthusiasm whatsoever for war the main concern of the Members was to defend and vindicate English 'liberties' against a divine-right monarchy. Both Houses wanted the position made clear by asking Charles, who had refused an Act, to agree to a petition – the Petition of Right – which outlawed forced loans and non-parliamentary taxes, condemned imprisonment without cause being shown, made illegal the billeting of troops on civilians and prohibited the imposition of martial law. Both traditionalists and revisionists agree that in 1628 Parliament put the notion of liberty before everything else. All other issues were set aside for the time being.

Defeat in Germany, and the failure of the second expedition to help the Huguenots at La Rochelle (May 1628) forced the king to assent to the Petition, because he needed the five subsidies conditional on it. Charles had first negated the Petition by a cold reply, but then seemingly accepted it when he used the formula for assent to a private bill. Accordingly, the subsidy bills were passed. However, Charles had no desire to abide by the Petition because when he had it printed he attached his initial (chilly) response to it, denying the MPs' complaints as legitimate and emphasising his prerogative. Charles accordingly seemed determined to ignore the Petition of Right. Parliament appeared powerless to enforce its provisions; the word, even now the signature, of the king was deemed valueless. Once again the king proved he could not be trusted.

On 23 August 1628 Buckingham was murdered at Portsmouth by an aggrieved soldier. At his funeral in Westminster Abbey, Buckingham's body had to have military protection from the crowds who exulted at his death. Charles, however, was so upset that he locked himself away for two days.

The king had not dissolved the Parliament of 1628 but had promised to call another session, initially scheduled for October, but then delayed until January 1629. Despite Buckingham's death and the ending of war with Spain and France (who were back at war with each other) there was still much hostility to the government. This was partly owing to the failure of the third expedition in September to La Rochelle. A month later the Huguenots abandoned their last resistance to the Catholic siege. This exacerbated the sense of disillusionment and power-lessness among Members after the Petition of Right had been so disregarded by the king, who had also thrown fuel on the reli-gious fire by his promotion of those very 'Arminians' condemned by the House in 1628. When the House reconvened, religion and the liberties of the House emerged as the burning issues. The privileges of the House were raised by the treatment meted out just before the House assembled to one of its Members, John Rolle, who had suffered the seizure of his goods for non-payment of customs. The House now demanded the punishment of the customs officers concerned. When the king asked for a tunnage and poundage bill, Sir John Eliot raised the issue of impositions, the original objection to the bill back in 1625, and no compro-mise was possible. The House attacked the continuation of tun-nage and poundage without parliamentary approval. Sir Robert Phelipps was adamant to have the king recognise the liberties of the House, and quoted from the 'Apology' of 1604, while Eliot and the lawyer John Selden set afoot an investigation into breaches of the Petition of Right.

Yet the biggest and most heated issue in 1629 was the religious one. Francis Rous raised the bogey of 'Arminianism', claiming that it was a 'Trojan horse' concealing traitors 'ready to open the gates to Romish tyranny and Spanish monarchy'. Pym went as far as to claim that there was a veritable conspiracy to change the religion of the Church of England. This refrain of a supposed 'alteration' in religion and the state would be Pym's signature tune through the years ahead down to the Long Parliament. These religious zealots whipped up a frenzy in the House, win-ning over those whose concerns had been more political. Pym also voiced his apprehensions over the Irish recusant army – foreshadowing his concerns in 1640. Two sides were emerging in the House, with an astonishing degree of hostility being shown to government Members. Sir John Eliot and others planned a major demonstration against the king to appeal to the people in the country at large. In a dramatic and famous scene the Speaker was held down in his chair just before he had time to dissolve the Parliament so that Eliot could pass three resolutions: the first condemned 'Popery or Arminianism', the second the illegal collection of tunnage and poundage, and the third denounced anyone who paid the tax as 'a betrayer of the liberties of England, and an enemy of the same'. These were undoubtedly revolutionary events, but rather than foretelling immediate civil war they should be seen, argues Russell, as untypical and eccentric deeds, not at all representative of the mood of the country or even of the House, because most Members were absent. Russell's judgement of their behaviour is that they were suffering from delusions of grandeur. The place for an opposition leader was at the head of a rebel army or in the Tower. And to the Tower went the leaders of the parliamentary riot: Sir John Eliot, Benjamin Valentine, Denzil Holles and William Strode. Parliament was dissolved, and the so-called 'Eleven Years Tyranny' began.

Although there had been a genuine 'opposition' in the Parliament of 1628–9, revisionists wish to abandon the old idea of two 'sides' in the wider political nation: the two sides of Court and country. Some leading opponents of the Court in 1628 took up office under the Crown in the 1630s: for example, Edward Littleton, who had chaired the debates over the Petition of Right, became solicitor-general and would be a prominent royalist in the Civil War; Sir Edward Herbert, who had organised the attempted impeachment of Buckingham in 1626, would enter Henrietta Maria's service while William Noy, who had defended one of the Five Knights in 1627, would become attorney-general. Most famous of all those who supposedly abandoned the patriot cause for the Court was Sir Thomas Wentworth. However, argues Russell, there was no real question of these people 'changing sides' because there were no 'sides' at all. The only side was that of the king.

The Personal Rule of Charles I, 1629–40

The description of the years when Charles ruled without calling a Parliament as the 'Eleven Years Tyranny' is owed to the Whig interpretation of the period: the very fact of no Parliaments seemed to signify tyranny to the Whigs, but this was more of a nineteenth-century view rather than one appropriate to the seventeenth century itself. Opposed to the Whig–Liberal view, the revisionists see Parliament as 'an event not an institution', to quote Russell. This statement is technically not true and can be misleading, but certainly one must agree that Parliament was not a frequent assembly and when it did meet it was a great event. Nevertheless, Parliament was a recognised institution, essential for legislation and taxation. A king ruling without it for a long space of time would inevitably be seen to breach English constitutional convention, although such rule might not necessarily amount to tyranny. No one seemed to mind that James I had ruled without Parliament for 11 years between 1610 and 1621 if one ignores the Addled Parliament of 1614. The phrase 'the Personal Rule of Charles I' is more truly descriptive, because the king had no favourite or chief minister, and often took scant regard of the privy council. It was the king himself who dominated government business in the 1630s.

Whether Charles ever intended to call a Parliament again after 1629 is a moot point. It is difficult to decide how long Charles could have governed without Parliament, but it could hardly have been indefinitely. The king said he would call Parliament again when the Members had learned to be more cooperative, but some historians have detected an absolutist streak in him. There is no evidence that Charles attempted to import European absolutist forms of government, such as a centralised bureaucracy, but instead he continued to rely on the traditional forms of local government. However, we know that he studied Richelieu's absolutist work in France, and Charles's actions were certainly leading in an arbitrary direction ever since he embarked on war in 1626 without parliamentary support. Despite this it is difficult to discern any long-term plan of absolutism. The only evidence of genuine attempts at a kind of autocracy comes from Wentworth's rule in Ireland. For most of the 1630s Charles I was to receive the traditional cooperation and consent of the local landowning families. Even his most vocal opponents in the Parliaments of the late 1620s can be found faithfully obeying his commands as commissioners in the 1630s. The Personal Rule was not doomed to failure, but for most of the time can be accounted a great success from the king's perspective. Revisionists take seriously Clarendon's reminiscence that the 1630s witnessed the 'fullest calm and greatest measure of felicity'. Post-revisionists emphasise the sheer patience and loyalty of the discontented gentry until they were goaded into action by the king's cataclysmic policies in Scotland from 1639 onwards, and point to the fact that Clarendon was initially an opponent of the Court in 1640.

Factions in the 1630s

From Buckingham's death in 1628 down to the death of Lord Portland in 1635 the situation at Court was fluid but stable. Not long before Buckingham's death it had been realised that the Court had to be made more accessible: hence the reconciliation effected by the duke with two of his leading opponents, the Earl of Arundel and Sir Thomas Wentworth. Then, after his death the Court was more completely opened up to include men of different persuasions. One hopeful courtier wrote that 'The eyes of all men are upon the King to see how he will dispose of those places that are fallen into his hands' after the disappearance of Buckingham and the patronage he had controlled. In the consequent shake-up a number of former critics (mentioned above) were introduced into the government seemingly with the aim of strengthening the regime, but not of changing the direction of policy.

With no favourite at large and with the king in overall control, the period of the Personal Rule saw a number of factions jostling for position. First, there was the leading faction built loosely around Lord Portland, the lord treasurer, a crypto-Catholic whose policy encouraged peace with Spain and reductions in government spending. Second, and opposed to Portland, came a faction around the young Queen Henrietta Maria, opposing Portland's pro-Spanish stance and economical reform policies, the latter especially because they touched her household. Henrietta's faction of rich nobles and witty courtiers was originally created for her, it seems, by the French ambassador in 1630 to work against the peace with Spain. Among her supporters were two men who later converted to Catholicism, namely Henry Jermyn and Walter (Wat) Montagu, but she also gained some staunch Protestants such as the earls of Holland, Warwick, Northumberland, Pembroke and Leicester. 'The Queen allies herself to the Puritans', the queen's confessor told the papal envoy in 1635.[5] The reason for this seemingly bizarre situation was that the Puritans hoped through her to revive the war with their great enemy Spain, which could be done only in alliance with France, and thus Henrietta Maria was the best figure to rally around at Court in their factional opposition to Portland. For her part, Henrietta believed that there was more chance of gaining concessions for English Catholics from Protestant adherents than by surrounding herself with ineffectual co-religionists. A third faction centred on Archbishop William Laud; he hated Portland, and did not get on with the queen because she criticised his persecution of recusants. Laud is normally linked to Sir Thomas Wentworth in the 1630s in enforcing a policy which they themselves called 'Thorough'. For most of the decade Wentworth was absent from Court, but as lord deputy in Ireland he may be viewed as Laud's agent there. Although Laud was not significant in secular government in the early 1630s, nevertheless throughout the decade he enforced the religious policy of Charles's government, and this certainly caused a stench in the nostrils of traditional Protestants. Whether this ecclesiastical policy was Laud's or the king's primarily is still unresolved.[6]

The death of Portland in 1635 led to another factional scramble. Portland was succeeded as lord treasurer by Laud's friend Bishop Juxon, an appointment that is normally viewed as underlining the archbishop's greater prominence in secular affairs from now on. However, this appointment may not have been due to Laud's influence. Portland's disappearance also led to the collapse of his policy of an understanding with Spain and to a shift towards a pro-French policy which in turn gave greater political influence to Henrietta Maria, who was clamouring for a treaty with France. Her factional success was manifested when her leading supporter, the Earl of Holland, became groom of the stool and chief gentleman of the king's bedchamber. All now seemed ready for Charles to agree to hostilities with Spain as the best means to induce the Habsburgs to return the Palatinate to his nephew Charles Louis. The king even seemed prepared to give some support to those Puritans who wanted to strike at the economic foundations of Spanish power – in Central and South America. Unfortunately for them, Henrietta Maria's faction did not long remain united in its antipathy to Spain. The faction's religious pluralism began to melt away through the promptings of the papal envoys who encouraged Watt Montagu to make the queen's faction an increasingly Catholic one centred on her chapel in Somerset House and eager for conversions. The queen's pro-French policy also evaporated. Henrietta had long opposed Cardinal Richelieu, chief minister to her brother Louis XIII, and had tried to unseat him, but now she abandoned France altogether and instead looked to Spain. This amazing turn-about was mainly the result of the visit to England in 1638 of both her childhood friend the Duchess of Chevreuse and her mother Marie de Medici, two escapees from the cardinal's wrath, who urged the queen to transfer her sympathies to Spain. This change happened in the midst of the king's attempt to impose Anglicanism on the Presbyterian Scots, a move which engendered fears at Court that the French were stiffening the Scots' resistance and trying to renew the 'Auld Alliance' between the two countries. The switch to a pro-Spanish policy alarmed the queen's former Puritan supporters, who were also increasingly alienated from the Court because of the king's Scottish policy. It fuelled the fears of those who suspected that the whole Court was really Catholic and that the attempt to impose Anglicanism on the Scots was but the prelude to the reimposition of Catholicism in England. Henrietta Maria thus played her part at a critical time in another episode of the 'popish plot', a myth that was to be a leitmotiv throughout English history in the seventeenth century.

Financing the Personal Rule

The Personal Rule could survive only in a period of peace, given the normally high expenses of the Court – expenses now exacerbated by the birth of Prince Charles in 1630 with his allocation of a separate household of 300 servants. The war with Spain was brought to an end because it was ruinously expensive – not because Charles desired peace. Financially, the peacetime Personal Rule was a success, despite the Crown's inability fully to exploit its resources. There was no refusal to pay tunnage and poundage on the part of the merchants; indeed the campaign of objection to non-parliamentary customs, which had characterised the years 1628–9, was not to be repeated in the 1630s until towards the very end. Although there was an improvement in trade, the government could not fully maximise the yield from customs because these had already been farmed out, and found it hard to get any increase in the rent from the customs farmers. What could, however, be extracted from the customs farmers were loans and advances on the rent, and these were undoubtedly a significant source of revenue. Later, in 1637, when Lord Treasurer Juxon had successfully concluded a new bargain with different customs farmers, they agreed to pay a higher rent but were less forthcoming with loans and advances, so that what was gained in one way was lost in another. Luckily, impositions, which were outside the customs farm, could be directly exploited, and they were increased in the new Book of Rates of 1635. Other means of tapping commercial wealth included the return of monopolies and licences for the sale of tobacco. Revisionists point to the fact that monopolies and impositions were no longer vehemently attacked as proof of royal success and the absence of a continuing opposition. Landed wealth, in the absence of Parliament, had to be tapped in other ways. The king therefore devised various means to get money out of the landed gentry. These included the Commission for Defective Titles, which attempted to regain former crown land taken over by the gentry illegally. The landed class in Parliament in 1624 had secured a measure to curb the monarch's power to enquire into titles of land held in continuous possession for 60 years. But then in 1628 a new commission was set up to enquire into titles to land held for a shorter period; this same commission was also to attempt to reclaim for the Crown land taken over against specific statutes. Also, an important aspect of the commission's work was the reclamation of areas of the royal forest; leading magnates, including the Earl of Warwick, were made to compound for encroaching on them. Charles also fined landowners worth more than £40 p.a. who had not taken out a knighthood at his accession, as medieval convention required. There was, moreover, a Commission on Depopulation which fined landlords who had wrongfully enclosed common lands. The government's major interest, of course, was in getting the fines rather than in punishing the crimes.

The most notorious of all Charles's financial devices to get money out of all sections of society was that of ship money. This was originally a tax on coastal towns and counties to pay for naval defence and to fight against piracy. Thus when Charles asked for ship money from the coastal areas in 1634 there was no basis for complaint. Problems began in 1635 when the tax was extended to the inland counties as well. A naval tax thus became transformed into a land tax, and the gentry disliked it. However, they paid up at first. Between 1634 and 1638 well over 90 per cent of the full assessed value of ship money was actually collected – a remarkable achievement for the period. But in 1638 and 1639 the yield decreased dramatically. In 1639 the assessed value of the tax was £214 000, but only £43 000 was actually collected. What had caused this sudden decline? Historians have traditionally pointed to John Hampden's celebrated test case of December 1637 over the legality of ship money. The king won the case in the Exchequer in February 1638, but only just – by seven votes to five of the judges. This was a moral victory for Hampden and certainly highlighted this non-parliamentary tax. Hampden did not deny the royal prerogative to raise taxes in an emergency, but challenged the claim that an emergency existed at the time, preventing the calling of a Parliament to legitimate the tax. It seemed once again that Charles had found a financial way to avoid ever calling Parliament. However, there are reasons for supposing that Hampden's case was not the great watershed, and that receipts indeed picked up immediately afterwards. The later refusal to pay was more to do with the king's policy towards Scotland and with the administrative difficulties that the JPs in the counties were encountering in collecting ship money. The justices were becoming very unpopular, and fewer gentlemen were prepared to serve as unpaid royal servants executing such policies. The revisionist John Morrill argues that the great decrease in ship money in 1639 was due not to constitutional objections but to the government's simultaneous demand for payment (in coat and conduct money) to supply troops for Scotland.[7]

Another probable reason for disenchantment was the growing realisation of the pro-Spanish nature of the king's foreign policy and of the uses to which the ship money was being put. At first ship money seemed a good idea – to build up the fleet and defend the sovereignty of English waters, indeed to finance a fleet to fight Spain. But by 1639 it became apparent that Charles was pursuing a pro-Spanish foreign policy at a time when the very survival of Protestantism in Europe was under threat during the Thirty Years War. In 1635 ship money had been used to pay for a fleet which in the guise of clearing pirates and Dutch from English waters put an end to the Franco-Dutch siege of Dunkirk in the Spanish Netherlands. In 1637 when Charles planned to use force in Scotland, he opened up discussions with Spain and the papacy for military help. In 1639 Charles helped transport Spanish soldiers to Flanders in English ships. Thus Charles was helping Spain at the same time as he was attacking the Scots in the two 'Bishops Wars' of 1639–40. The question being asked by worried Protestant observers in 1639–40 was this: would victory over Presbyterian Scotland be but a prelude to a large-scale entanglement in Europe on the side of Catholic Spain?

Policy of 'Thorough' of Laud and Wentworth

The 1630s are always associated with the policies of the two ministers, Archbishop William Laud and Sir Thomas Wentworth, later Earl of Strafford. These were the two men whose blood the Long Parliament was to cry out for; Strafford was to die on Tower Hill in May 1641, and Laud after a long period in the Tower was to suffer in January 1645. Archbishop Laud was the son of a draper, sharing similar low origins with Wolsey a century before, and like Wolsey provoking much hostile comment – 'a little, low red-faced man of mean parentage' observed one Puritan diarist. Laud was intellectually very sharp and made an academic career at Oxford, becoming a client of the Duke of Buckingham. James I did not like Laud much, but through Buckingham he was appointed in 1621 to his first bishopric. Charles I promoted him to the bishopric of London, and then in 1633 to Canterbury in succession to Abbot.

Sir Thomas Wentworth was a rich Yorkshire squire who had sat as knight for Yorkshire in all the Parliaments between 1614 and 1628, except for 1626 when he was kept out of the House by being appointed sheriff. He had shown himself to be an opponent of Buckingham and hostile to the war against Spain; moreover, he had refused to pay the forced loan and had been gaoled. He had been involved right from the start in organising opposition in the Parliament of 1628, including the agitation for the Petition of Right. Then suddenly he changed! In the second part of his career, just before Buckingham's death and at the height of political tension, he went over to the Court, became Baron Wentworth (July 1628), and was appointed lord president of the council of the north; in 1633 he would become lord deputy of Ireland, and finally in January 1640 Earl of Strafford. Did he really 'change sides' and become a traitor to the parliamentary cause, or was there some over-arching principle that could honourably explain the shift? Historians have varied in their interpretations of his motives – conscientious or base? – but most have seen them leading to a 'change of sides'. Revisionists deny this because, they argue, there were no two 'sides'. The post-revisionist response came from Perez Zagorin, who argued for a continuity in the ranks of the gentry who wanted to preserve freedoms against a government which threatened to encroach on them; and he cited contemporary evidence that Wentworth was truly seen as an 'apostate' by his former colleagues, for having been bought off by Buckingham. In 1640 John Pym would denounce Wentworth as one who had been transformed from 'an earnest vindicator of the laws, and a most zealous assertor and champion for the liberties of the people' to become during the 1630s 'the greatest enemy to the liberties of his country, and the greatest promoter of tyranny that any age had produced'.[8] At the least Wentworth appears to be a great opportunist.

What did Laud and Wentworth do in the 1630s to provoke such hatred? Throughout the 1630s Laud was certainly in charge of ecclesiastical affairs for the king, and in many people's minds he was regarded as a crypto-papist, which was really most unfair as he opposed the king's decision to permit two papal agents to appear at Court, and was disliked by Henrietta Maria very much because he was not a Catholic. It was in fact the queen, not the archbishop, who was truly responsible for the Catholic image of the Court in the late 1630s. Laud and Wentworth were certainly allies after 1633, their letters to each other revealing a close cooperation in the policy of efficiency and intrusion which they themselves dubbed 'Thorough'.

In traditional interpretations of the 1630s Archbishop Laud has always appeared at or near the top of the cast of villains of the drama. In 1982 Patrick Collinson judged Laud to have been 'the greatest calamity ever visited upon the Church of England'.[9] In

1984 Robert Ashton criticised as 'one of Charles I's worst mistakes, his espousal of Laudian Arminianism'.[10] This customary emphasis on the malign and leading role played by Laud seemed confirmed by the researches of Nicholas Tyacke, who argued that Laudianism represented a revolutionary assault on the entrenched Calvinism of the Elizabethan and Jacobean Anglican Church.[11] According to Tyacke, the theology of the Elizabethan and Jacobean Church included Calvinist double predestination, which stressed that man had no free will to gain salvation, which was the gift of God to some and withdrawn from others who went to hell. However, in European Calvinism there had recently been a movement away from predestinarian theology towards a greater emphasis on free will and the universality of grace, a movement linked to the renegade Dutch theologian Jacob Arminius (*d.* 1609), whose views were belatedly condemned at the synod of Dort (1618). Hence those English Protestants who adopted free will in this period in preference to double predestination became known as 'Arminians', not always fairly because such free-will views were ancient, and many in the Church of England had espoused such notions before Arminius was ever heard of. The split in the Dutch Calvinist Church between classical predestinarian Calvinists and the minority Remonstrants (as the followers of Arminius were called) had inflammatory repercussions in England with predestinarians feeling a sense of outrage and betrayal, at the same time that Protestantism itself seemed imperilled with the opening of the Thirty Years War. Such predestinarians began looking for traitors within the English Church; Laud became branded in his own time as an Arminian who had betrayed the Calvinist, and thus true Protestant, cause to espouse a doctrine that stank of popery. Laud's 'Arminianism', Tyacke has argued, turned previously loyal Puritans (or staunch Protestants) into opponents of the regime.

Tyacke's interpretation, which Conrad Russell endorsed, had the effect of overturning the old notion of revolutionary Puritans against a reactionary government by claiming that the true innovators or revolutionaries were the Laudians, and that the Calvinist Puritans were upholders of traditionalism. It also underscored the view of the Civil Wars as essentially wars of religion. Tyacke's interpretation has been attacked in recent years, notably by Peter

White, and now seems insecure. To begin with, the notion of a 'Calvinist consensus' under Elizabeth and James I is controversial.[12] While it is true that there were many predestinarians in the Elizabethan and Jacobean Church – the Lambeth Articles of 1595 specified the notion of double predestination, as did the Irish Church Articles of 1615 – the clause dealing with this issue in the official Thirty-nine Articles of 1563 was vague, referring only to the elect, not to the damned. Predestinarians never won a complete victory, partly because Elizabeth would not have the doctrine aired (indeed she banned publication of the Lambeth Articles) and partly because in the practical life of the Church on a parish level such high Calvinist theology was irrelevant. Moreover because the Church of England was a state Church which comprehended all subjects of the Crown, any theological claim that a majority of English people were ineluctably damned would hardly have been conducive to the tranquillity of the realm. Secular considerations of public order and national morale had always been important for the monarch in the running of the Church. Both Elizabeth and James I issued directives against discussing predestination, the latest in 1622. Thus, it is argued, Charles I's proclamations of 1626 and 1628 against the public airing of controversial doctrines hardly represented a new and sinister development.[13] There was, therefore, no sudden revolution in theology.

Was Laud really an 'Arminian'? He was certainly sceptical of the Calvinist position, but rather than being a dogmatic 'Arminian' Laud appears to have been more concerned with avoiding all theological definitions and disputation on such grand matters. Laud wrote nothing formally about the theology of salvation; he regarded the exact nature of salvation as 'unmasterable', and something best left to God. Peter White has argued that there was no campaign in the 1630s to suppress Calvinist thought.[14] Laud seems to have been impeccably in the tradition of the Elizabethan and Jacobean Church. Yet there was a growth in opposition to Laudian policies, which needs to be explained. Laudianism stressed ceremonies and the exalted role of the Church in society, and included the belief that episcopacy (the rule of the Church by bishops) was specifically ordained by God – whereas the Elizabethan and Jacobean Church had largely maintained the view that bishops were an ancient and useful office but without a divine mandate. Laud shared his high view of episcopacy with Roman Catholics and the Orthodox. Laud was not a Roman Catholic and made this clear in his debate with a Catholic theologian, which was published as *Conference with Fisher the Jesuit*, but many of his reforms in the Church could lead the ordinary blunt Protestant Englishman to imagine that he was one because some of the lines of demarcation were too faintly drawn. Although Laud wanted an able preaching ministry he did not put the sermon at the heart of worship as did the Puritans. Laud was a sacramentalist, desiring the sacraments to be administered in beautiful buildings. He was appalled at the dilapidated state of so many parish churches and cathedrals and decided on sweeping changes to refurbish them and make them holy places of beauty. Laud's policy was based on words from Psalms 29 and 96: 'Worship the Lord in the beauty of holiness.' The 'beauty of holiness' to Laud meant orderly worship, including such things as bowing at the name of Jesus and the return of altars (which had been removed under Elizabeth) to the east wing of churches and those altars railed off, rather than the general Elizabethan and Jacobean custom of having wooden communion tables set up in the middle of the nave. The problem with this latter custom was that people often left their hats and coats on it, and Laud believed in complete reverence for the Lord's table. He also wanted reverence for the clergy as a holy caste, again something completely opposite to the Puritan tradition that stressed the lack of difference between ministers and laity. Puritans disliked any clerical garb, and believed one could be as holy in one's kitchen as in a church. Therefore, whereas Puritans demoted the parish church as a religious centre Laud wanted it to be restored to that position in all its magnificence. Laud's emphasis on externals seemed too close for comfort to popery in the minds of Puritans. Laudian clergy were seen as false Protestants, having more affinity with sacramental Roman Catholicism than with biblical Protestantism. Laudianism was seen as opening the door to the nightmare of popery.

The major question remains the extent of Laud's innovation. If he did head some kind of conspiracy to change the Church of England this could be seen as a major religious cause of the Civil Wars. If there was little that was new, if Laud was merely reimposing what were essential elements of Anglicanism comprehended within the 1559 Settlement, then it is harder to see why he was so abused. The key to Puritan anger seems to reside in the growing Catholic menace in Europe during the Thirty Years War. Puritans had suffered Elizabeth because they needed her defences against the common Catholic enemy, but from late in the reign of James the monarch was regarded as being too friendly to Catholicism. James had wanted friendship with Spain, while Charles had married a French Catholic. This had increased Protestant fears, and what had been tolerated earlier was now found to be unbearable. It was probably fear of popery rather than of Arminianism that caused the trouble, and Julian Davies has recently emphasised the king's role, rather than Laud's, in alienating evangelical Protestant opinion.[15] Many of those who were to lead the fight against Charles in the 1640s were in such despair in the 1630s that they were planning to emigrate to America. Furthermore, the religious situation was complicated by the Presbyterianism of Scotland. What the Scots enjoyed the English Puritans also desired in large part. When Charles and Laud tried to extinguish Scottish Presbyterianism from 1637, the Puritan nightmare seemed to be fulfilled. Puritan desperation seems to be the key to the crisis.

Besides theological problems, the Laudian domination also affected the world of politics, because with bishops Juxon and Neile on the privy council there had not been such a clerical presence in government since Wolsey's time. The government's use of the court of Star Chamber and the court of High Commission to attack its opponents made those prerogative courts hated. Star Chamber had been a very popular court for over 100 years, but now it earned an evil reputation that guaranteed its dissolution in the Long Parliament. Laud allowed no dissent and put down the system of Puritan lectureships. Although he spent most time attacking radicals and sectaries, intellectuals were also hounded and punished like common people, with mutilation – notably William Prynne, Henry Burton, John Bastwick and Alexander Leighton. With the growth of individualism, it appears that old-style religious authoritarianism was less tolerable than in the past. Thousands of dissidents emigrated to North America.

Laud also wished to revive the financial position of the Anglican Church, which had lost much land and income during the sixteenth century. The despoliation had left the Church much poorer in worldly terms than it had been before the Reformation, even though now it had to support ministers and their families. Too many livings were in the hands of lay rectors who had purchased them like any other piece of property and paid their vicars only a small stipend. These lay impropriations, where parishioners paid their tithes to a layman, were something that Laud hated and wanted if possible to undo. Nothing much could really be done about it, but Laud prevailed on the king to set up a fund to buy back two lay impropriations a year, using fines collected in the court of High Commission. Laud could do more to pressure clerical rectors to increase stipends to their vicars. Laud wanted a triumphalist, well-endowed Church, and he was supported in this by the king. In 1633 bishops and deans and chapters were forbidden to grant 'leases for lives' on church lands. Instead only shorter leases of fixed periods were to be negotiated so as to raise fines and rents. Laud's major impact was in the style of worship and in appointing supporters in the Church. Otherwise he represented mainly a threat of what might come rather than any concrete gains. However, his ally Viscount Wentworth could point to some far-reaching achievements in Ireland.

Wentworth was successful in Ireland, to which he had gone as lord deputy in 1633, in implementing the policy of 'Thorough' against the various political and social groups in that country. The policy of conquest and plantation under Elizabeth and James I had brought New English and New Scots settlers to rival the former rulers, the so-called Old English, who were of Norman extraction and who had taken over Ireland in the Middle Ages. The Old English were Catholic in religion (like the native Irish) and bilingual in English and Gaelic, whereas the new settlers were monolingual Protestants. Wentworth enforced Laudianism on the ultra-Protestant Church of Ireland (with its predestinarian Church Articles of 1615), which was the Church of the Puritan settlers from England and Scotland, while allowing the majority Catholics, the Old English and the native Irish, *de facto* toleration. His ecclesiastical policies therefore impinged most on the newcomers who were fervent Puritans; they reacted in an even more hostile fashion (if such was possible) than had English Protestants to the consequences of the policy of 'the beauty of holiness'. As Wentworth was not a very religious man himself, it is not clear why he embarked on a religious policy which would inevitably make enemies out of the New English and New Scots. Was Wentworth just myopic or was there an ambitious absolutist design to crush all deviation? Hugh Kearney suggests that Laudianism was the price Wentworth was prepared to pay to have a supporter at Court, namely Laud.[16] The court of High Commission was brought to Ireland to enforce Laudianism. Calvinist bishops either were removed or lost power, so that in Ireland one had the same quarrel as in England but in a more heightened form. Wentworth was successful in reversing the appalling economic plight of the Irish Church. In Ireland lay impropriations were the main cause of clerical poverty. Wentworth dealt arbitrarily with them, and Charles supported him in his attempt to regain impropriations, especially by giving up royal impropriations, keeping only the annual rent. Wentworth retrieved many lay impropriations through the prerogative court of Castle Chamber in Dublin (similar to the English Star Chamber) with no appeal to the common law or to the English privy council. In Castle Chamber Wentworth acted as initiator of the action, prosecutor and judge in all actions for recovery. This was taken as a major threat to the New English and New Scots, whose economic supremacy had been based on despoiling the Church of Ireland. The Old English were alienated by having feudal incidents squeezed out of them, by the Commission for Defective Titles, and by his refusal to confirm their privileges known as 'the Graces', as well as by his determination to colonise Connacht. Wentworth alienated all sections of society by his use of 'a little violence and extraordinary means', as he himself described his methods to Laud. All this meant that the king's cause was even more hated than it was in England. Terence Ranger suggested that Wentworth was systematically building up an absolutism in Ireland that would serve as a blueprint or dress rehearsal for its imposition in England.[17] The Irish opposition had more to lose, and royal authority there was more extensive than in England. The Irish common law was losing out fast. Would this soon be the position with the English common law? Furthermore, Wentworth built up a standing army in Ireland, admittedly officered by Protestants but overwhelmingly composed of Catholic rank and file. This fact could lend credence to the notion that Charles I was secretly a Roman Catholic waiting only for a suitable moment to impose Catholicism on England by force. Hugh Kearney's most recent view is that Wentworth saw himself in a traditional Tudor light, bringing English civility to Ireland, rather than experimenting with absolutism. Whatever the truth of Wentworth's motives, the crucial point is: how were they interpreted by English Protestants? And it seems definite that the likes of John Pym believed that a new policy was being embarked upon, with inevitable future repercussions on England. The most important article of accusation levelled at Wentworth's trial in 1641 was that which accused him of intending to bring over the Irish army 'here to reduce this kingdom'. Pym's long-held convictions concerning the danger from Ireland and the 'popish plot' seemed to be vindicated.

9 The Coming of War, 1640–2

The Collapse of Personal Rule, 1640

In the previous chapter we saw that the traditional interpretation of the Civil War as an inevitable conflict has been seriously challenged by the revisionist argument that, far from being on the verge of revolution, England was 'unrevolutionary' in the 1630s. It has been claimed that England under the early Stuarts was more stable, and thus less prone to internal conflict, than under Elizabeth.[1] The possibility of civil war because of dynastic problems or the military pretensions of the nobility was a thing of the past; there was no longer any fear of foreign invasion; population growth and inflation that had caused misery under Elizabeth were slowing down; violence towards state servants had largely disappeared; centralised state power was on the increase; and until the accession of Charles I the Puritans and Papists were no longer a menace and had settled down into an accommodation with the state. Thus the England that Charles inherited was moving further away from civil conflict rather than towards it. It follows in the revisionist account that the reasons for civil war must be sought mainly within the reign of Charles and not further back. Conrad Russell writes: 'England in 1637 was a country in working order, and was not on the edge of revolution.'[2] However, while, admittedly, the old recipe for civil warfare was no longer there, one might still propose that the very modernity of England (compared to contemporary Europe) made tension grow, especially when Charles I persisted not only in refusing to adapt to change but also in attempting to return to a form of authoritarianism that had provoked rebellion in the medieval past. It is conceivable for tension to mount precisely when a situation is getting better, with an emerging group more confident of itself, rather than when all is chaos and misery. The threat of foreign invasion and of the return to baronial chaos had prevented civil war in the Tudor period; those warning lights were now largely absent and, instead in a new age of major economic and social change, fundamental religious and constitutional norms were challenged by an aloof monarch. There may well have been more tension than revisionists admit.[3] However, consensus now exists that there was no party of 'conscious revolutionaries' eager for war; nobody positively wanted confrontation with the king, not even the Puritans. Everyone thought in terms of past precedent, and there was no conscious wish to change society. Nevertheless the logic of social and economic development may well have made the opponents of the Court into 'unconscious revolutionaries', desiring more change than they were prepared to admit; there was thus a very real possibility of confrontation at some time in the seventeenth century.

Revisionists Russell and Morrill agree that, apart from the archaic and inadequate financing of the monarchy, the one structural problem which predated Charles's accession was the quite recent – and accidental – situation of the personal union of the three crowns within the British Isles, occasioned by the Stuart succession. For the first time ever the British Isles were united under the same ruler; it was now a multiple kingdom. If keeping Catholic Ireland subdued had proved a major problem for England in the past, keeping Presbyterian Scotland happy in the seventeenth century would require much tact. But tact was a virtue completely lacking in Charles I, who was to fan the dying flames of religious controversy in England with his support for 'Arminianism' and also to attempt to impose religious uniformity on all three of his socially, economically and religiously very different kingdoms. As Morrill puts it: 'The stability of early Stuart *England* made civil war unlikely; it was the instability of early modern *Britain* that first made the war of 1642 possible.'[4] And the most inflammable issue which divided the three realms was that of religion. The lack of any discernible social issues dividing the two sides in the war has led to a return to an essentially religious interpretation of the conflict, although not a return to S. R. Gardiner's 'Puritan revolution' thesis because the revisionists stress that, far from being revolutionary and aiming to seize power, as Gardiner believed, the Puritan opponents of the Court were innately conservative and eager to reach an accommodation with the king.

John Morrill regards the Civil Wars as 'England's Wars of Religion', with religious tensions at their core.[5] On his accession King Charles found himself presiding over four variants of Christianity: Anglicanism in England, Presbyterianism in Scotland and a *de facto* toleration of Roman Catholicism for the vast majority of his Irish subjects, as well as a more Calvinist form of Anglicanism for the colonial rulers there (in the Church of Ireland). The contemporary European norm was for subjects to follow the religion of the ruler, and while there were some states that allowed more than one religion (such as France and Brandenburg) few people agreed that this was a good thing in itself, rather a sign of weakness. Conrad Russell states that 'Louis XIII, Philip II, and the Emperor Ferdinand, insisted without a moment's hesitation that neither their authority nor their consciences would permit them to preside over different religions at the same time.'[6] While this is true of the last two, it is not true of Louis XIII, because until 1685 the Huguenots were allowed civic equality and religious toleration. Charles had actually made a study of Cardinal Richelieu's regime in France in the 1630s, and he would have been wise to have followed Richelieu's lead in not insisting on religious uniformity. But Charles was stubbornly imposing Laudianism on both England and Ireland, and now in 1639 he was determined to extend religious uniformity to Scotland also.

Charles I's Personal Rule came to a crashing halt with the so-called 'Bishops Wars' of 1639–40. These resulted from the attempt begun in 1637 by the king, Laud and the Scottish 'Arminian' bishops to impose the Anglican Prayer Book (in a special Scottish edition) on the Presbyterian Scots by royal proclamation, ignoring both the General Assembly of the Church of Scotland and the Scottish Parliament. Charles tried to push through major change using only his prerogative powers. When the Anglican liturgy was first used at St Giles, Edinburgh, on 23 July 1637 a riot ensued because people believed they were attending the hated Catholic mass, with a stool being hurled at the celebrant by one 'Gutter Jennie', a vegetable and herb seller, whose action was imitated by others present. Similar popular disturbances erupted in other churches in the city. These mass protests had been made possible by the advance publicity that the government had given to the introduction of the new Prayer Book: a foolish policy was thus compounded by incompetent application. The result was a storm of protest and abuse which the authorities could not handle. Although the government quickly backed down and surrendered to the demonstrators, nothing could stop the groundswell of national religious feeling against Charles. Scotland had long been tense under the rule of its absentee king, ever since the Scottish Act of Revocation of 1625, which had threatened the property rights of the landowning class there by trying to confiscate all church lands acquired since the Reformation, but it was the 'alteration of religion' that galvanised the Scots into rebellion. Scottish Presbyterians of all classes signed the National Covenant (28–29 February 1638) in Edinburgh to protect their religion; and this was followed by the raising of an army of some 22 000 men under the leadership of General Alexander Leslie.

How was King Charles to respond to this act of popular disobedience by his Scottish subjects? As he had largely united the Scots against him in a popular crusade, Charles's only real hope lay in using an English army to invade Scotland to break it to his will. This resort to force against his Scottish subjects in 1639 would not be forgotten by his English critics, and would steel them a few years later to demand control of the army lest it be used against them. In 1639 Charles drew up a plan for a four-pronged attack on the country, but the problem was how to finance it. He refused to go to Parliament for financial help, so an army had to be recruited on the feudal base of the duty of the nobility to furnish troops and on loans from prominent supporters. Some nobles gave generously of their money, notably Worcester and Winchester (both of whom were Catholics, which thus further alienated the Scots and their English Puritan sympathisers), others promised to come but in the event did not, while two Puritan peers, Lord Brooke and Lord Saye and Sele, refused outright to help the king. An army was assembled in the north of England, and the king joined it at York on 30 March 1639, but it was badly led and riven by the mutual jealousy of its commanders, and this feudal levy was no match for the religious fervour of the Covenanters, who had overcome any remaining centres of support for the king within Scotland. Charles's situation was very grave, and without any fighting the king abandoned his immediate plans for invading Scotland and instead made peace with the

Covenanters at Berwick (19 June 1639). Charles had not forgiven his Scottish rebels, and was merely waiting for the right time to enforce his will on them.

Charles's final, desperate hope of finding a solution to the Scottish crisis on his own terms lay in recalling Wentworth from Ireland in August 1639. Wentworth for his part revelled in the chance being offered him to take full control of the king's government. From September 1639 he was the leading force in the king's government, and in recognition of his supremacy he was elevated in January 1640 to the earldom of Strafford.

Strafford now persuaded Charles to call a Parliament to gain supply for continuing the war against the Scots. He was convinced that the traditional English hatred for the Scots would weigh more heavily with the MPs than any sympathy for their Presbyterianism. This Parliament, known to history as the 'Short Parliament' (13 April–5 May), was a failure because it refused to vote any money for the war until the Members' grievances had been met. There had indeed been much political campaigning before the Short Parliament, and the candidates' attitude to the Court seems to have been the most important consideration in the minds of many of the electors. Political issues, rather than simply local concerns, assumed a much greater importance than was customary in the seventeenth century. Traditionally, parliamentary elections were a means by which the gentry in the counties and merchant oligarchies in the cities and boroughs could manifest their local supremacy; ordinary voters were not generally involved in decison-making, but merely expected to voice their assent in a display of unanimity, and thus elections were not political as they are in the modern world. Furthermore, who exactly was to be returned to Westminster was almost always in the past decided by the local bigwigs well in advance of the official formal election. Thus genuine election contests, when more than one candidate for a seat turned up, were rare and meant that the traditional local system of power had broken down. In the elections of 1604 only about 13 constituencies had seen contests; later elections were to see more, the highest number being contests in about 33 constituencies in 1628. However, there was something different about the elections to the Short Parliament, when contests occurred in at least 55 constituencies, and possibly in as many as 61; this certainly signifies a much greater politicisation of the polls.

It seems clear that grievances about ship money, recruitment for the army and religious innovations, especially the fear of popery at Court, were all being hotly debated. The importance of religious ideology in particular urged more candidates to come forward. The lawyer Bulstrode Whitelocke was persuaded to contest (unsuccessfully) a seat 'by my friends here [in London] upon the argument of doing public good, and chiefly by divers of the contrary faction to the Court, and who favoured the Scots Covenanters'. It has been argued that the expansion of the electorate, especially in the counties where because of simple inflation there were more and more 40-shilling freeholders, helped politicise elections; in the larger, more open electorates, candidates had to be more responsive to the attitudes of their electors. This is true, although it must be made clear that the electorate could wield influence only when there was rift among the elite.[7] Windebank bewailed that 'the elections have been very tumultuary and with much opposition to all that have relation to the Court', while a foreign observer reported home that 'not only Puritans but those who in the past have shown much boldness in opposing the King's decrees' had been returned. These 'political' candidates were only a small minority, of course, in a fairly traditional House of Commons, but their entry marked an important development in the political history of seventeenth-century England, especially as they seem to have been involved in the drafting of petitions relating to grievances.

In the Short Parliament John Pym emerged as the power-hungry leader of a genuine opposition to the Court, and in a long speech he catalogued all the grievances of the country from the 1630s, ranging from the disregard of parliamentary liberties back in 1629 through ship money, the forest laws, illegal tunnage and poundage and such like, but he put religious innovations at the top of his agenda for emphasis because he saw Arminian practices as introducing his *bête noire* of popery by the back door. Charles was foolish, to say the least, if he expected Parliament to grant him money for war without major concessions in return. Eventually he offered to abolish ship money in return for 12 subsidies – which the Commons thought was too high a price to pay. It is clear that Pym was still in contact with the Scots, and he was about to raise in the House the urgent need for reconciliation with them. On discovering this development, Charles, who wanted not reconciliation but war, quickly dissolved the Short Parliament, with Strafford's reluctant compliance. The king seems to have been hoping for Spanish military aid and papal money to defeat the Scots without recourse to Parliament.

Convocation, the Church's own parliament, continued sitting despite the dissolution of the Short Parliament, and was urged by the king to produce new canons (or laws) to maintain the unity of the Church of England. Above all, these new canons reaffirmed the royal supremacy and set out a new oath to prevent changes in the doctrines and to maintain the hierarchical government of the Church 'by archbishops, bishops, deans and archdeacons etc.'. The canons were to be directed at nonconforming Papists and Puritans, but in themselves could be seen as reasonable laws, in no way specifically Arminian. Yet this moderation was not appreciated by the Puritans, who denounced them bitterly. One MP thundered that these canons aimed 'to blow up the Protestant religion'! The use of the term 'etc.' in the oath of allegiance also upset many men of tender conscience, who claimed that this was an open door to abuse because they could not be sure what they were affirming. These canons were meant in part as a reply to the Scots' use of the Covenant as the basis of their unity. The big difference was that in England convinced Protestants no longer trusted the king as supreme governor, and a large minority were eager for further reformation rather than the continuation of the existing system, so that the canons inflamed the situation rather than appeased the king's critics.

The failure of the Short Parliament convinced Strafford of the pointlessness of invoking 'constitutional' support; instead, using the royal prerogative the government was now to pursue an aggressive policy towards the Scots, claiming that Parliament had let the English people down. Strafford advised Charles that in this emergency situation the king should not be held back by any restraints but be 'loosed and absolved from all rules of government'. In the next few months Charles and Strafford pursued a policy of doing 'everything that power might admit'; these were emergency wartime powers, just like those invoked in 1626–8. Back then, of course, Strafford had been an opponent of those emergency measures; now he was their chief protagonist and turned on his critics. The homes of Warwick, Saye, Brooke, Pym and Hampden were searched for evidence of treasonable contacts with the Scots, and those individuals harassed. Four aldermen of the City of London were gaoled in May for refusing to pay a forced loan. These measures were very unpopular, and the government found itself universally vilified. London was especially tense, with riots breaking out after the dissolution of the Short Parliament. Over 1000 sailors and apprentices attacked Lambeth Palace because they blamed Laud for the crisis – with the result that the archbishop had secretly to escape over to Whitehall by boat. There were many disturbances throughout the country, and there was much violence and resistance associated with the impressment of men for the army. There was a widespread refusal to pay ship money or 'coat and conduct' money,[8] and much popular discontent, with impressed men involved in violence (such as attacking altar rails in churches) and even mutinying against their officers. This popular disquiet was what alarmed the governing class most.

The government's only chance of salvation lay in a military defeat of the Scots. Strafford was hoping for support from Spain, France, Holland, Venice and even the papacy. The exciting spectre of a fat pension of 4 million ducats from Spain in return for guarding Spanish convoys in the English Channel, which would enable the king to rule unimpeded by his subjects' protests, evaporated on Dutch threats of immediate warfare with England: Charles certainly could not afford to take on the Dutch and the Scots at the same time. Humiliation soon followed when the Scots marched over the border. The flight of the poorly armed, unpaid and dispirited English army at the rout of Newburn (near Newcastle) on 28 August represented the first Scottish victory within England since 1388, and to some English sympathisers this indicated divine approval for the Covenanters. On the same day as the rout, the Petition of the Twelve Peers, drawn up (almost certainly) by John Pym and Oliver St John, was signed at the London home of their patron the fourth Earl of Bedford, by the earl himself and 11 other nobles, including Saye and Sele, Essex and Warwick, calling for the summoning of a Parliament to put an end to the war and to re-establish the true Protestant faith by abolishing innovations in religion and by punishing those responsible for the present sad state of affairs. There seems little doubt that the petitioners (or most of them) were acting in concert with the Scots and could be regarded as committing treason.

Despite defeat on the battlefield and the opposition of a number of his privy councillors, Charles was eager to press on with his quarrel against the Scots, especially since his army was still in existence, and it was bigger than the Scots' force; all he needed was more money, and the Council of Peers had already pledged £200 000. He believed that Parliament would be sensitive to his honour and help repulse the enemy, because it was indeed unprecedented for the English to support the hated Scots against their own sovereign, especially now with the suffering of the northern counties under the invading Scots. Indeed by the Treaty of Ripon Charles had to pay the Scots £25 000 a month and suffer the indignity of their occupation of the counties of Durham and Northumberland until the new Parliament should make a lasting settlement and pay off the armies. The Scottish triumph revealed the king's military and financial bankruptcy and led to the collapse of his government. As in 1628, Charles was taught the hard lesson that he could not afford war without the support of the traditional ruling class. The contemporary observer James Harrington, speaking of this collapse, wrote that 'the dissolution of this Government caused the War [that is, the Civil War], not the War the dissolution of this Government'. It is certainly true that the collapse of the Personal Rule in the face of the Scottish crisis was the essential prelude to the outbreak of civil war in England, but it is not true to suggest that the dissolution led inexorably to civil war: far from it, much had to happen between 1640 and 1642 to bring on the war; much would depend on personalities, especially on the attitude and the political and religious agenda of the king.

The Long Parliament

On 3 November 1640 the first session of that fateful Parliament known as the 'Long Parliament' opened. It was to last in various forms down to April 1653, and would be recalled in 1660 preparatory to the restoration of Charles II. Nobody coming to the precincts of Westminster that very first day could have imagined the huge changes to English life that would unfold in the next few years. Certainly no one was thinking in terms of any kind of civil war at this stage. A civil war was, in any case, impossible in 1640 because to have a civil war one needs two fairly equal parties, and that is just what did not exist in 1640: the king was almost friendless. There had been even greater interest in the calling of this Parliament than in the one in the spring, if one is to judge by the increased number of contested elections: at least 74 constituencies had witnessed a confrontation of candidates in the autumn. There was evidently a greater eagerness on the part of members of the ruling class to be present at Westminster. The courtier group had largely collapsed and many, like Laud, made no attempt to get their nominees returned. Bulstrode Whitelocke this time got a seat, by defeating a courtier. However, apart from opposition to the king's recent policies and the wish to return to an imaginary golden age of harmony from the (Elizabethan) past, there was no general positive political programme being advanced, and certainly the display of local supremacy still remained the predominant factor in a man's wish for election. The only Members who might have harboured more definite ideas for change were the group centred on Pym and Bedford.

The Long Parliament would prove a very different assembly from all previous Parliaments, if only in the first instance because, with the Scots breathing down his neck and demanding a parliamentary solution, the king no longer had the practical option to dissolve Parliament whenever he wished. It has been the general wisdom that the House of Commons which met in November 1640 was a fairly united body led by John Pym in opposition to the Court. This traditional view has been restated recently in a number of works, but the idea of unanimity and of the paramount role of Pym has also been attacked. It has been argued that the notion of unanimity is belied by the many examples of close voting on a number of issues, while Pym's pre-eminence is not borne out by the surviving parliamentary records. Sheila Lambert has contended that Pym became the 'hero-scapegoat' for those who later regretted their earlier rebelliousness.[9] John Morrill has recently painted Pym as a visible activist and 'team member' rather than the undisputed leader.[10] However, whatever qualifications need to be made from the division-lists about these early days of the Long Parliament, a general unity appears evident in that both future royalists and future parliamentarians voted for reforming legislation in the first session. The Lords, too, were amazingly of one mind, reaffirming the Petition of Right and condemning ship money unreservedly. Much obscurity remains about the opening manoeuvres of the Long Parliament, and certainly in the past historians were too Whiggish in their eagerness to portray the Commons as the great originators of the struggle with the king to the virtual exclusion of any role being assigned to the Lords. The later abolition of the House of Lords in 1649 did much to colour historians' preconceptions of the primacy of the Commons in 1640. Revisionists have been eager to redress the balance and show the importance of the Lords in this still very aristocratic society; and some have even attempted to portray the Lords – notably Bedford and Essex – as the true leaders of the struggle against the king, with the Commons-men as their docile clients, merely acting on the instructions of their patrons in the House of Lords.[11]

The primary aim of the parliamentary leaders was to remove 'evil ministers', and accordingly both Strafford and Laud were imprisoned in the Tower. The Scots too were adamant for them both to be punished, and Parliament decided to impeach them. Thirteen Arminian bishops were also arrested and detained in the Tower. Secondly came the need for a financial settlement and a programme of reform to avoid a recurrence of recent evils. There was at this early stage no thought of Parliament's wishing to gain sovereignty or to impugn the royal prerogative. No attack was made on the king personally: John Pym claimed that evil advisers had influenced the innocent Charles to 'alter the kingdom both in religion and government'. He repeated the idea of a great Catholic conspiracy to submerge England under the tyranny of the pope. In his speech of 7 November Pym reminded the House of the military danger of 'putting Papists or suspected persons into command of armies'; and he saw the direct threat posed by Strafford in the latter's creation of the 'Irish army to bring us to a better order'. Far more than his patron Bedford, who was a moderate episcopalian Puritan, Pym was religiously an extremist, obsessed with the spectre of Catholicism, and always intertwining the religious issue with the constitutional.

At first the reforming activists attempted to maintain unity by focusing attention on the universally hated Strafford. In the impeachment brought against him the unusual procedure was adopted of arguing that all his actions together constituted treason, rather than specifying individual crimes which he had committed against the king – which was indeed hard to prove, and Strafford himself was confident of answering the specific charges. Pym was also worried that the Lords were divided on the impeachment of Strafford, and many there thought that he was being unfairly treated.

After the removal of Parliament's enemies came the Commons' reform proposals to guarantee good royal conduct in future. Early in 1641 Charles agreed to reforms because at long last he realised that, far from helping him to fight the Scots, the MPs actually sympathised with them; and some appeasement of his critics was attempted by making Oliver St John solicitor-general on 29 January, and by appointing his patron, Bedford, along with Essex, Warwick and Saye and Sele, to the privy council in February.

The first parliamentary reform was the Triennial Act (15 February 1641) which made mandatory a Parliament every three years, each to last at least 50 days. This certainly impinged on the royal prerogative by preventing any long period of personal rule, but it hardly made Parliament into the government, and its passing now was designed as a security for loans to pay the army rather than as stage one of a constitutional revolution. The crisis then escalated owing to a number of developments. First, the removal of Laud and his machinery of censorship led to Puritan fanatics coming out of the woodwork and labelling the government as satanic and AntiChrist. Second, the mob started to appear at Westminster in January 1641 to influence events from outside of the two Houses. This mob was partly orchestrated by Pym and Alderman Isaac Pennington, and partly spontaneous, especially in the harsh economic conditions of the time. The mob had been active in the City since November when some 1500 Londoners had signed the Root and Branch petition to eradicate episcopacy and replace bishops with committees of laymen to govern the Church. This Root and Branch petition was brought into Parliament in December 1640 by Pennington, but with little support it was not discussed before February 1641. Third, a royalist counter-offensive took place, signified by Strafford's secret negotiations with Spain from the Tower, and the queen's attempts to get help from her brother Louis XIII and to intrigue with the army (in the First Army Plot of May 1641). Charles on three occasions refused to disband the royal army in Ireland, while plots devised by Sir John Suckling and others to seize the Tower and rescue Strafford were uncovered. All this helped to raise the political temperature dramatically. The discovery of plots to rescue Strafford, and Pym's revelation of the First Army Plot to dissolve Parliament by force led to the heated atmosphere of the month of May 1641.

On 3 May the Commons 'Protestation' (an oath of association) asserted that conspiracies were afoot 'to introduce the exercise of an arbitary and tyrannical government'. This 'Protestation' was indeed 'a unilateral appeal to the country against King and Lords'.[12] On the same day the Self-Perpetuating bill was passed by the Commons, which prevented the dissolution of the present Parliament without its own agreement. Generally seen by historians as a pledge that reform was not to be cut off by a royal guillotine and thus as the first real attack on the royal prerogative, it was originally introduced to guarantee more loans to pay the armies. The measure was later referred to by the king as the 'act for the securing of moneys'. Thus too much revolutionary fervour, or even a clear determination on reform, should not be read into the early history of the Long Parliament. But there is no gainsaying the fact that mob passions were so high in London in the first two weeks of May that the Lords were forced to agree to this Self-Perpetuation measure without amendment, as well as to the death of Strafford through a bill of attainder, rather than through impeachment. The attainder bill passed the Commons on 21 April by 204 votes to 59, with some 200 abstentions. From the start the force of neutralism, signified by these absences, was to prove very strong. Then on 8 May the attainder passed the Lords (in the absence of the bishops) with 51 for and 9 against, but the exact figures are not certain. Some 10 000 Londoners had stormed through the streets and called for Strafford's death, while threatening those Members who intended to vote against the attainder. The king was forced to sign the death warrant out of fear for the safety of the royal family, though the fact that Strafford's life was in jeopardy was precisely because the king had refused to dismiss or abandon him; this had signalled that Charles was standing by the policies associated with the minister.

Signing the death warrant was a deed which Charles never forgave himself for, having personally guaranteed Strafford's safety. The earl's execution on Tower Hill on 12 May was a major public event, with large seating-stands erected for about 100 000 spectators.

Strafford's death might have acted as a safety-valve, as a means of bloodletting: the most hated man in England was no more. Nobody publicly blamed the king for what had transpired; a fresh start could be contemplated. If only Charles had shown some sense! But the real problem, of course, had not been Strafford, but the king. The prosecution of Strafford had been undertaken to press home to the king that he needed to be reconciled with the leaders of the ruling class; Strafford's death merely confirmed the king's intention to do no such thing. Nevertheless, for the time being reforms continued to be passed. Both Houses were united in support of constitutional reform to make personal rule again impossible. Customs duties were made legal for only two months at a time. The conciliar courts (Star Chamber, the Court of High Commission, the Council in the Marches and the Council of the North) were abolished. Ship money was declared illegal, as were knighthood fines. The judgement against John Hampden was overturned. The royal forests now had their limits set. For the time being wardship was still allowed (down to 1646, mainly because Lord Saye and Sele was master of wards). But while the Lords wanted harmony, there was a strident Puritan group in the Commons, led by Pym and St John, who wanted further church reform, and they were able to command a slight majority in the Lower House, whereas the religious reformers in the Lords were always an impotent minority.

These constitutional reforms, to which the king assented, were significant improvements, but they really solved very little because there was no confidence that Charles would keep his word; there was a general feeling that at an opportune moment they would be cancelled, despite the royal signature on the acts. The achievements of 1641 would be meaningless unless Parliament achieved greater control of the executive; that is, unless the king could be induced to accept some members of the parliamentary leadership into his government. Of course, forcing individuals on the king would be a clear violation of the prerogative, but there were medieval precedents for it in times of weak monarchy. Charles had (in secret talks) already refused to include Pym and Hampden in his government. This confirmed in the minds of his opponents that Charles was not serious in his attachment to permanent reform. The demand for control of the executive was first voiced officially by Pym in the 'Ten Propositions' of June 1641 – a document passed by both Lords and Commons, and thus indicative of the isolation of the king. These 'Ten Propositions' had been drafted in reply to Charles's decision to go to Scotland, which was a move that alarmed the parliamentarians because they suspected that the king would avail himself of the English army in the north against them. The 'Ten Propositions' requested the king not to leave England until all armies had been disbanded; furthermore, all Catholics had to leave the Court, especially those around the queen; the royal children had to be educated by sound Protestants; the militia should be placed only under lords-lieutenant in whom Parliament had confidence; and, above all, evil ministers had to be removed and the king had to accept 'officers and counsellors as his people and Parliament may have just cause to confide in'. Thus in May and June 1641 Charles was effectively isolated. How then can one explain the outbreak of civil war, in which two fairly even sides fought against each other?

The answer to that crucial question is that a split was to develop within the House of Commons which would give the king a party of supporters. This split came about over the interrelated issues of religion and the social order. It came down to the point that James I had expressed so succinctly in 1604: 'No Bishop, No King.' Indeed James's dictum could be extended to read: 'No Bishop, No King, No Gentleman.' Those who attacked hierarchy in the Church were seen by many as undermining the privileged position of the gentry in society. A group of religious reformers had emerged in the Commons who advocated the abolition of bishops. The whole House had certainly been eager to get rid of Arminian bishops, and a bill to confine bishops to spiritual work only and to exclude them from the House of Lords was easily passed in the Commons (11 March). However, to suggest the complete eradication of bishops smacked of social revolution, and the Root and Branch bill had a much tougher time, with debates on this and other religious measures showing up the first serious divisions within the House of Commons. While Members like Denzil Holles and Oliver St John spoke in favour of abolition, episcopacy found defenders in John Culpepper and Edward Hyde, two emerging royalists. Religion was also a divisive issue between the Commons and the Lords.

Despite Parliament's pleas, King Charles left for Scotland on 10 August 1641. In October he announced from there that he aimed to stand firm in his adherence to the Elizabethan Church Settlement. This was one of the very few really clever manoeuvres Charles ever made. He was shrewdly exploiting the evident divisions within Parliament that had been growing during the first session and were clearly manifest at the beginning of its second session. Charles was thus announcing that he had abandoned Laudianism. Calvinist social conservatives now began to look more favourably on the king, especially because many had been alienated by the extremist language of some Members during the closing weeks of the first session of Parliament (which had ended in September). The second session opened on 20 October, and it was now that parties formed which would make the Civil War possible. Before the end of 1641 between 55 and 57 former anti-Court Members would go over to the king, and a clear part of their motivation was the king's agreement to reform. Two in particular of those who changed over and who were to make a great contribution to the royalist propaganda cause were the intellectuals Hyde and Falkland.

In November the question of control of the executive became an urgent issue when news came of a great Catholic rebellion in Ulster in which between 2000 and 3000 Protestant settlers (or about 20 per cent of the newcomers) were massacred. What more timely event was needed to prove the existence of the great Catholic conspiracy that Pym had been warning about for so many years? Pym's prophecy of the dangers presented by Papists was largely a self-fulfilling one as far as Ireland was concerned because of the appalling treatment meted out to the native Irish by the new Protestant settlers. In the state of panic in which Pym and his colleagues found themselves the king could easily be viewed as a fellow-conspirator with the Irish, especially as the rebels themselves were employing the king's name. The timing of the rebellion was indeed the worst imaginable for the king, and brought all suspicions about royal policy to a head. There was, of course, no logic in these denunciations, especially as Charles had appointed the Irish Protestant Earl of Ormond to raise some forces to suppress the uprising. Nevertheless, a new army would now be needed to crush the revolt, but the major question was: who was to command this army – the king or Parliament?

If Parliament agreed to this traditional royal role of military commander, there seemed a great risk that Charles would use the recruited army against the Parliament and all internal opposition. This situation, together with Pym's revelation of a Second Army Plot to use the Portsmouth garrison to bring Parliament to heel, led to an ultimatum being presented to the king (who was still in Scotland) that unless he changed his policies and councillors it would give him no help in quelling the Irish rebellion. Moreover, it would take measures of its own against the rebels. This threat by Parliament was both unprecedented and revolutionary. In the event over 1000 parliamentary soldiers were raised by voluntary subscriptions and dispatched to Ireland.

Besides the urgent question of Ireland, the other great issue of November 1641 was the debate on the 'Grand Remonstrance', which was a document produced by the reforming group in the Commons representing a lengthy and formidable indictment of the king and his policies over many years. There was no attempt to involve the House of Lords in the drafting of the document, and it appears in its original form to have been designed as an appeal to the people against both the king and the conservative majority in the Lords. It was a very controversial measure which created parties within the House of Commons itself: it was passed by only 159 votes to 148, with some 190 abstentions. Neutrality, or the wish to avoid involvement, was thus the attitude of the largest party there, but the substantial numbers of those who were prepared to show their hand for or against the king at this critical juncture were very evenly balanced. The 'Grand Remonstrance' included a long catalogue of over 200 religious and political grievances going back to the beginning of Charles's reign, and claimed that 'malignant parties' (that is, those involved in what Pym saw as the great Catholic conspiracy) had corrupted so many of the bishops and royal councillors and had sown such discord between the king and his subjects. To counter all this an 'effectual course' was now proposed, which included removing all bishops from Parliament and curbing their power in the Church, removing 'some oppressive and unnecessary cere- monies' within the Church and having a general reform of the Church through a synod of divines. Furthermore, evil advisers were to be removed from the privy council and replaced by such men 'as your Parliament may have cause to confide in'.

Almost half the Members present in the House thought that such measures were going too far in invading the royal preroga- tive and in challenging hierarchy: although the 'Remonstrance' does not explicitly mention the eradication of bishops this seems to have been its import. Furthermore, the social conservatives hated the idea of having the 'Remonstrance' printed after it was passed, thus turning it into a direct appeal to the people. The advocates of the measure were trying to get the despised masses on to their side. On the issue of printing the measure, and thus breaking the code of secrecy in relation to parliamentary matters, swords were first drawn within the House of Commons. Many former opponents of the Court now came over to the king: one such was Sir Edward Dering, a man whose religious views are hard to categorise but who appeared at one time to be a root and brancher; nevertheless his social conservatism made him hate the spectre of printing the 'Remonstrance' and thereby to 'tell stories to the people and talk of the king as of a third person'. Although it was agreed initially only to make manuscript copies, this deci- sion was changed in December to allow it to be fully published. Dering also hated the sight and sound of unlearned preachers taking over the pulpits, because this undermined the privileges of the educated. Thus the previous general unity within the Commons was now shattered when many innately conservative men thought that these attacks on the existing order had gone far enough; hence they crossed over to the king's camp because they saw in the monarch the best defence of their own privileged status against 'the many-headed monster' of the mass of English people. These social conservatives defended 'their own interests upon the preservation of your rights', as Hyde later told Charles. Thus when the king returned to London from Scotland on 25 November 1641, he was pleased to find the nucleus of a royalist party. His moderate reply in December to the printing of the 'Grand Remonstrance' by the Commons played to the middle ground with its promise to maintain the 'ancient constitution', and its denouncing the Irish rebels as the king's enemies.

This platform of moderation was a winning one, but Charles never displayed consistency of purpose, and he swung beween the advice of the moderates and the exhortations of the hard-liners, including the queen. Charles's growing resentment at his financial plight and his feeling of being threatened – by the presence of angry mobs around Westminster and by Parliament's challenge to his accustomed sole right to recruit soldiers – led to an atmosphere of severe crisis by Christmas-time 1641. When Parliament resumed on 27 December, most bishops could not make their way through to the Lords for fear of the crowds. By the end of December 1641 Charles seemed to be planning a military solution to the parliamentary problem. The king ordered the peers to recruit 10 000 men to serve in Ireland; he wanted all courtiers to wear swords, and he entertained the army commanders at Whitehall. Charles decided to recover his author-ity by impeaching five leading Members of the Commons (and Lord Kimbolton[13] in the Lords) on charges of undermining legitimate royal authority and of encouraging the Scots to invade; and on 4 January 1642 he flouted parliamentary privilege by entering the House of Commons in person, along with his nephew the Elector Palatine, in order to arrest the accused, leaving a threatening contingent of some 80 soldiers (the esti-mates vary) in the lobby.

However, the Five Members (as they became known) – namely Pym, Hampden, Haselrig, Holles and William Strode, as well as Lord Kimbolton – had been warned in advance by the French ambassador and were able to escape to the City of London. 'All the birds have flown', cried King Charles in frustration. This invasion of the Commons was a foolish act on the king's part because he put himself in the wrong and undid much of the good work he had recently accomplished. It also gave the Commons' leadership some justification for resistance measures against the king in future. The event was a public-relations disaster, with his own lord keeper refusing to issue a proclamation for their arrest, and with his most prominent supporters in the Commons, such as Hyde, Culpepper and Falkland, horrified. Despite all the soothing words of moderation, Charles now seemed to be show-ing his true hand. Moreover, the imprisonment, or indeed execution, of these Members would have solved nothing – which suggests that the king did not want anything solved short of a military crushing. The whole House of Commons fled to the City for refuge and took over the militia.

This month of January was a very tempestuous one in London, with mass demonstrations in support of Parliament; both the militia and the navy helped escort the Members back to Westminster. On 10 January Charles and the royal family fled from London to Hampton Court, and then on to Windsor and Greenwich. The next time he would see Whitehall would be for his execution in the same month of January seven years later. His flight from London was probably due to his fears for the safety of the royal family, but it was a major blunder because it allowed his capital to fall into the hands of Parliament, whose Members might now be swayed more easily by Pym's aggressive oratory. On 17 January Pym proposed that a new privy council should be chosen in Parliament. This was fighting talk, but what prevented an immediate outbreak of hostilities was the fact that England was an extremely demilitarised society by this date, with no standing army or large private baronial armies, and with no one having enough funds to hire mercenaries straightaway.

The king's party needed to repair the situation by returning to studied moderation, and eventually Charles would apologise for his attack on parliamentary privilege by entering the House. Meanwhile, Hyde and Falkland presented the king as the upholder of the old constitution against the extremist innovations of Pym and his 'junto', but they were losing out in the Commons to Pym's increasingly strident propaganda. The absence of the king led to a weakening of his cause at Westminster, and this was especially true of the House of Lords, which had been prepared to vote with the Commons to impose some political restrictions on the king but had not sanctioned further religious change or tried to make the king into a cipher. Now the peers were being threatened by both Pym and the crowds outside, which led to absences by those who disliked what was transpiring in the Commons. A large number of peers went to attend on the king at Windsor, so that the solidly conservative majority in the Lords was whittled away. Accordingly on 1 February the reduced House of Lords agreed to the Commons'

Militia bill, which represented a major assault on the royal prerogative. On 5 February the Lords passed the Bishops' Exclusion
bill, which amazingly, on Culpepper's urging, Charles agreed to,
thus removing a solid phalanx of royal supporters from the
Upper House. For the moment the bishops were expendable in
a new burst of conciliation, which also included the promised
enforcement of the recusancy laws and a parliamentary settlement of the Church. However, he refused to compromise on the
long-term command of the army.

On 3 March the king decided that the best course of action
would be to leave Greenwich for York and try to gather support
in the provinces, or even possibly in his other two kingdoms. In
reply Parliament took measures to defend itself, including a
direction to the governor of Kingston upon Hull not to admit
the king to the town, because it contained arms and ammunition
for the royal army in the north. On 23 April King Charles, who
had appeared in person outside its walls, was accordingly denied
entry there by the governor – a major proof of rebelliousness
on the part of the parliamentarians. A propaganda war was
underway with both sides urging those in authority locally to
publicise their cause and condemn their opponents.

At first the king had only a small following in the north, but by
late May a steady stream of royalist peers and MPs were making
their way to York, while back in Westminster it was announced
that 'the King intends to make war against the Parliament'. By
early June Parliament began recruiting forces under the Militia
Ordinance, while the king on 11 June resurrected the medieval
Commission of Array to call men to arms. Each side condemned
the other's recruiting instrument as illegal: the Militia Ordinance
because it did not have royal support, and the Commission of
Array because it had been superseded by the Militia Act of 1558.
Indeed the very unmilitary nature of England in the mid-seventeenth century is well borne out by the confusion over the legal
right to recruit soldiery. The king's reliance on a well-forgotten
late-medieval custom threatened to lose him much support, so
reminiscent was it of those medieval fiscal devices he had
employed in the 1630s.

Parliament's 'Nineteen Propositions' of 3 June, which emanated from a committee of 12 peers, with modifications from the
Commons, included the demands that the king must accept

Parliament's Militia bill and that Parliament must approve all privy councillors and great officers of state and the three leading judges. On 6 June in a 'Declaration in Defence of the Militia Ordinance' Parliament also distinguished between the office of the monarch, which was sacrosanct, and the person of the monarch, who might require correction – a distinction used previously against Edward II. However, the 'Declaration' went beyond the traditional medieval understanding of the the king's 'two bodies' by clarifying the role of Parliament as the location of ultimate power in the state.

The opening of the Civil Wars had a superficially very medieval air to it, which some revisionists have emphasised to show the aristocratic nature of the initial rebellion. When the king later set up his banner calling his supporters to arms, he claimed to be resisting not Parliament but the 'late rebellion of the Earl of Essex'.[14] John Adamson argues that the 'Nineteen Propositions' really demanded a medieval-type baronial council, wherein the leading officers of state were to be the lord high steward, lord high constable, lord chancellor, lord treasurer, lord privy seal and so on. The nobles were reasserting their ancient right to counsel the king. All together there were to be 13 noble officers of state approved by Parliament who would numerically dominate any privy council of no more than 25 members. Adamson argues that in the months preceding the official outbreak of hostilities in August, England saw the nobles contending for arms, men and territory in a manner reminiscent of the opening of the Wars of the Roses. The opposition peers are represented as seeing themselves as continuing the late-medieval struggle of responsible barons trying to bring irresponsible kings to order. Adamson points to the spate of books dealing with the fifteenth-century upheaval and the links between the writers and the opposition peers. However, the argument that the Lords were the real driving force with men in the Commons simply as obedient clients mouthing what their noble masters told them to say is a major *ultra-revision* which seems not to have been generally accepted by historians. Conrad Russell, a more moderate revisionist, has shown that John Pym, for example, was no tame lap-dog of Bedford's, and argues for a much greater earnestness in religion among the Commons leaders than among the reformers in the Lords.[15] One should speak more of a common purpose between

Lords and Commons rather than accept too easily the predominance of either House at the start.

The royal reply to the 'Nineteen Propositions', drafted by
Hyde and Falkland, made some telling points against what
appeared to be parliamentary intransigence: there was no need,
it was argued, for a new rule for the removal of unpopular
ministers because they could be removed by impeachment, a
procedure now far easier to invoke after the Triennial Act and
the Self-Perpetuating Act because a royal dissolution was no
longer possible. Altogether the royal 'Answer' was a brilliant
defence of the concept of the 'Ancient Constitution'. The rival
recruiting campaigns provoked agony in the minds of many
confused men over whose instructions to follow, and there were
many armed scuffles and skirmishes. Within the City of London
the conservative lord mayor opted for the royal Commission of
Array against the wishes of the radical common council which
had triumphed in the elections of the previous December; and
his imprisonment, and replacement by Alderman Pennington,
led to the complete radical take-over of the City of London (July).
Parliament set up a Committee of Defence with five Lords and
ten Members of the Commons to overcome any attack from the
king, and on 6 July gave instructions for an army of 10 000 men
to be recruited. Major conflict was now just on the horizon.

10 The British Civil Wars, 1642–51

'This war without an enemy'

The traditional title of 'The English Civil War' has lost favour among historians of late because it suggests a homogeneous conflict within one kingdom, whereas it is clear that more than one civil war was fought, more than one country was involved and that events unfolded in a quite startling and unforeseen way, with the various players competing for completely different prizes. The belated recognition by English historians of the crucial role played by both Scotland and Ireland has led to a general preference for the term 'British Civil Wars' or 'Wars of the Three Kingdoms'. While one certainly must bear in mind the different course and impact of the fighting in each of the three kingdoms, the crucial point is that it was their fusing together that ignited the flames of protracted warfare. The Scottish crisis of 1637 was the opening page of the drama, whose later scenes turned heavily on the preparedness of the Scots to help either Parliament or the king. As for Ireland, its role was surely necessary to buttress the notion of a great Catholic conspiracy which so obsessed men like Pym; the rebellion there in October 1641 lit the spark that flamed up into civil war in England less than a year later.

The very idea of civil war was anathema to English people of the seventeenth century, and the devastation in Europe occasioned by the Thirty Years War was a salutary reminder of what might happen at home. Nevertheless the common perception was that both sides simply drifted into war. 'It is strange to note', Bulstrode Whitelocke commented,

> how we have insensibly slid into this beginning of a civil war, by one unexpected incident after another as waves of the sea...

On a rainy 22 August at Nottingham, in the very centre of England, the king unfurled his banner, calling his subjects to render him assistance 'against the late rebellion of the Earl of Essex'. It was an important symbolic ceremony, but in truth the war had already begun, with skirmishes and sieges and with many towns having taken measures to defend themselves by building up supplies of ammunition and strengthening their walls.

The early expectation was that the war would be a short one, to be ended by one decisive battle. The parliamentary forces were placed under the command of the third Earl of Essex, who had seen service during the Thirty Years War. He was a melancholy Puritan, who would take his coffin with him on to the battlefield. He may well have felt alienated from the king by being over-looked so often for important appointments. Now it was his high social status and general popularity that commended Essex to the parliamentary leaders, and he was appointed lord general of the army and high constable of England, a position of quasi-regal status, and indeed dictatorial powers. The Puritan Earl of War-wick was put in command of the navy because of his great experience with a private fleet he had maintained for colonising ventures and anti-Spanish piracy.

King Charles himself commanded the royalist forces, with the support of his dashing young nephew, Prince Rupert of the Rhine, who was aged only 23 but who had already seen military service in Europe. The major drawback about Rupert's appoint-ment was his inability to get on with many of the king's native-born supporters, both civilians and soldiers, as well as his being prone to rashness on the battlefield. He and his younger brother Prince Maurice had just brought over a consignment of weapons and ammunition from the Dutch Republic.

One of the major historical problems of the opening of the first Civil War is to explain how large armies were collected at all in a short space of time in a country that was effectively demilitarised. The nobles had been civilianised, with only about 20 per cent having seen active military service. We are indeed far away from the age of the Wars of the Roses. The king had no standing army, and could immediately depend only on the Yeomen of the Tower and the royal bodyguard known as the Gentlemen Pensioners. There were no permanent regiments with any sense of tradition, and British professional soldiers had to be prepared to sell their services to many masters in Europe throughout their careers.

The only sense of a permanent military force in England was supplied by the trained bands (or militia) in the counties under the lords lieutenant, but these were really only an amateur 'home guard'. While many militia units (such as at Great Yarmouth and Manchester) were keeping up their drill and were indeed to supply many serviceable soldiers for the war, most had inadequate training, and some were almost completely non-operational. The poet Dryden expresses the general feeling about 'the rude militia', that they were

> In peace a charge, in war a weak defence;
> Stout once a month they march, a blustering band,
> And ever, but in times of need, at hand.

Only the six regiments of the London trained bands could be described as a serious military force.

In terms of numbers of men under arms at the beginning of the war, Parliament had the upper hand with some 15 000 men to the king's 13 500. At first the royalist cavalry were superior to their parliamentarian counterparts in numbers, training and equipment, simply because those who volunteered were from the class where horse riding was a normal activity. The parliamentary army may have been recruited more quickly than the king's – at least in terms of voluntary infantrymen. This might have been because Charles was unpopular with the lower classes, especially the 'middling sort',[1] or alternatively simply because of the geographical problem posed by the king's recruiting ground in the north.[2] However, it was a major achievement for such large numbers to have been collected so quickly on both sides. Little is known about the composition of these armies because of the absence of muster lists, but many men may have enlisted for the pay being offered: this was after all a period of economic depression, and as today many entered the army to avoid unemployment. The majority of soldiers at first seem to have been volunteers – certainly this was true of parliamentarians; and those who enlisted were probably those without a secure place in society. However, some landlords on both sides seem to have marched their tenants to battle with the threat of evicting them if they refused; indeed the royalist Earl of Derby threatened reluctant men with death. Leading protagonists raised and equipped soldiers, and sometimes, as with John Hampden, whole regiments. The rates of pay were low, and were to be the cause of trouble later; and when it became clear that the war would be a long one, there was much desertion among the ordinary soldiery. The infantryman's rate of four to six shillings a week made him no better off than an agricultural labourer, but food rations, especially when in winter quarters or in garrisons, were more reliable. Another possible attraction for enlistment was the hope of plunder. The cavalry, at about 17s. 6d. a week, were paid much better than the infantry, but for all soldiers the biggest problem was getting their pay in full or at all. These mostly raw recruits had to be drilled into shape, and here the core of professionals, both natives and foreign mercenaries, who had seen service in Europe were especially valuable to both sides. Indeed one must assume that many of the thousands of Englishmen serving abroad returned to England to give a professional heart to both armies. It is also important to remember that, with only a few exceptions, the commanders were already well battle-tested in Europe: those exceptions with no military experience were the king, the Earl of Newcastle, the Earl of Manchester and, the greatest natural soldier of them all, Oliver Cromwell.

When it came to fighting neither side had an advantage in terms of weaponry or tactics. Both sides had absorbed the new tactics employed by the Dutch and Swedes in the course of the Thirty Years War. Generally, tactics were employed only at the start of an engagement (choice of time and location and so on), but once the battle began it soon became a bloody, smoky mess where no overall plan was of much use. As Lord Eythin told Prince Rupert of the latter's plan at Marston Moor in 1644: 'By God Sir, it is very fine on paper, but there is no such thing in the field.' Also, until the formation of the New Model Army in 1645 there were no general uniforms, only regimental ones, so that each army had a variety of colours on display, which made it difficult to know in the haze who one's enemy was. At the battle of Edgehill, royalists wore red scarves to distinguish themselves from the parliamentarians who wore orange scarves. When some parliamentarians went over to the king's side they forgot to change the colour of their scarves and got killed by the royalists.

The majority of people were horrified at the prospect of war, especially against the king, the Lord's Anointed, and at all times the sentiment of neutralism was to be the strongest one of all: only a small minority on both sides relished a conflict – young cavaliers (derived from the Spanish *caballeros*, a form of abuse that compared the royalists to the bloodthirsty Spaniards) for adventure, and radical Puritans yearning for the chance to remove popish images and altar rails from churches. The term 'roundhead' to denote a parliamentarian derived from the lower-class fashion for short hair and was used by royalists as a term of social snobbery equivalent to 'tradesman', although parliamentary commanders in fact wore their hair long as befitted their class.

The first Civil War (1642–6)

It was a major blow to Charles that the fleet had decided to support Parliament: already in January 1642 some 2000 sailors had appeared at Westminster to offer their assistance to the parliamentarians. Reasons for such naval partisanship seem to have been both hatred of Catholicism (linked to hatred of Spain) and the king's poor record of payment of wages to his seamen. If the fleet had remained under his command Charles could easily have blockaded London and reduced Parliament to an early submission. However, even without the fleet Charles had the better chance of victory at first, but he needed to regain possession of his capital. The Earl of Essex left London on 9 September with the intention of going to Nottingham to make the king see sense and persuade him to return to London. But Charles had left Nottingham and was moving south towards the capital in order to retake it.

When news reached the king that the Earl of Essex was only seven miles away, Charles established his army at Edgehill, an elevated position overlooking the Warwickshire plain. The royal force of some 24 000 men was slightly larger than Essex's, and by pure luck Charles found himself intercepting the earl's route home to London. Charles, occupying the high ground in all senses, waited in the hope that Essex would foolishly try to launch an attack uphill. However, the earl had better judgement than this and was probably loath to commence hostilities against his monarch – indeed officially Essex was fighting only 'cavaliers...and evil persons' – and so waited, thus forcing the king to attack downhill (23 October). After an exchange of cannon fire, Charles's men swept down into the plain, with Prince Rupert's cavalry routing their opponents, whose morale was low because of the earlier defection of their cavalry leader, the nicely, if inappropriately, named Sir Faithful Fortescue. However, Rupert failed to exploit this initial success by leading his cavalry off in search of plunder rather than regrouping and recommencing the attack. Many of the parliamentary infantry fled, but those who remained fought stoutly, as did the two parliamentary cavalry regiments who had taken no part as yet but who now joined in the attack on the royalist infantry. Prince Rupert, on his return from plundering, was amazed to find that there was no complete royalist victory but that his men were needed to fend off defeat. The day ended with both sides exhausted; it could be described technically as a royalist victory, but not a decisive one, and both sides retreated. The heavy casualties (of over 1000 on each side) had revealed the grim reality of civil war. Among the fallen were both Charles's standard-bearer and his general-in-chief.

The king still had a chance to defeat Parliament quickly if he were to march on London straightaway; Prince Rupert advised this, but Charles refused, partly because of the shock of so many casualties at Edgehill, and partly because he feared that such an action would engender too much hatred against him in London. Accordingly on 29 October, Charles moved to the university city of Oxford, which he made his military headquarters and the residence of his court. A belated attempt was made by Rupert to march on London in November 1642, but the real chance had already been lost, and the advance was stopped at Turnham Green (Middlesex) by Essex's force of 24 000 men, including the city trained bands that had been organised by Pym. Rupert's earlier ruthless plundering of nearby Brentford had ensured that Londoners would resist his approach to the capital. Nevertheless, the king's fortunes soon improved with the formation of two new royalist armies, in addition to the king's own army based around Oxford: one in the north under Newcastle, and one recruited in Cornwall by the Puritan royalist, Sir Ralph Hopton.

Parliament was better organised than was the king's side. Parliamentary finance, as arranged in 1643, was sounder, coming from loans in the City of London and a property tax (of about 5 per cent) on the counties in its control (the 'assessment') as well as a Dutch-style excise (or sales tax). Confiscated royalist lands also contributed to the parliamentary purse. As for Charles, he too levied similar taxes in the areas which he controlled, but because these areas were poorer than those under Parliament, he had to depend more on voluntary loans, gifts from supporters and money borrowed in the Dutch Netherlands by the queen. Yet no matter which side was levying money, taxation was much heavier than anything known previously, and some areas that changed hands might find themselves paying taxes to both sides.

Although Parliament had better access to funds on a continuing basis, its political philosophy (with the fiction that it was fighting not the king but only his wicked advisers) and its war aims were poorer. Charles, on the other hand, knew exactly what he wanted: namely, to defeat the rebels, to execute the leaders and to stamp his authority indelibly on the realm. However, the strategy to gain these ends was less well defined, and the king's policies were hampered by his own vacillation and his honourable desire to avoid carnage. He was also the recipient of conflicting advice.

Parliament's strategy was better coordinated, but its long-term plans were the subject of discord. Three broad groups have been discerned among the parliamentarians at the start of the war: an extremist (or win-the-war) party, a conservative (or peace) party and a 'middle group'. The extremists, who included men like Arthur Haselrig, Henry Marten and Henry Vane, wanted a decisive victory and a dictated peace with the king. The conservative peace party, with Simonds D'Ewes, John Maynard and Denzil Holles prominent among them, hated radicalism and the use of the military, opposed the excise and the weekly 'assessment', and earnestly sought an accommodation with the king. In the historiography of the Civil War the dialectic of the war and peace parties had been long established, but the notion of a third party, a 'middle group', was first introduced in 1941 by J. H. Hexter in his influential *The Reign of King Pym*. It is now agreed that this 'middle group' was led by Pym and Oliver St John in the Commons, and supporters in the Lords included Lord Saye and Sele, Lord Wharton and the new fifth Earl of Bedford. Their wish was to secure a negotiated peace with the king rather than a dictated one, although they were certainly prepared to use military force to persuade him. Thus clarity of aim was shared by only a minority of the parliamentary leaders at first. Many of the back-benchers who had remained at Westminster were fearful and hesitant, and 44 of these were to move over to the king's camp during the early stages of the war, mostly during 1643 when the royalists seemed to be gaining the upper hand. The Earl of Manchester summed up this typical hesitancy in November 1644:

> If we beat the King ninety-nine times yet he is King still, and his posterity, and we subjects still; but if the King beat us once we should all be hanged and our posterity undone.

Cromwell's retort to such an attitude was: 'My Lord, if this be so, why then did we take up arms at first?'

One of the major early problems for the parliamentarians, as for the royalists, was the reluctance of their recruits to fight outside their native counties because they did not want to leave their homes unguarded. To overcome this, Parliament through the Committee of Safety (set up in July 1642) began forming associations of counties in 1643 to coordinate military planning; the most famous and effective of these new groupings were the Eastern Association army (some 14 000 strong) under Manchester (which brought together men from Essex, Norfolk, Cambridgeshire, Suffolk, Hertfordshire, Huntingdonshire and Lincolnshire), and the smaller South-Eastern Association army (of some 4700 men from Surrey, Sussex, Kent and Hampshire) under Sir William Waller. Later in 1643 Waller would be given command of the Western Association army (incorporating Somerset, Gloucester, Wiltshire, Shropshire and Worcester). In the north, ranged against the Earl of Newcastle, was the Northern Association army under Ferdinando Lord Fairfax and with his son Sir Thomas Fairfax second in command. The main parliamentary force, however, remained that under the commmand of Essex, and this force alone was free from the pressures of localism.

In the north the Earl of Newcastle had managed to establish a garrison at Newark, strategically important for the area and for allowing communications with Queen Henrietta Maria in

Holland. The queen, on her return, with arms and cannon, was met at Bridlington (Yorkshire) by the Earl of Newcastle, and after a stay at York she made her way to Oxford at the head of her own force, calling herself 'Her She Majesty Generalissima'. Meanwhile, Parliament's main force under the Earl of Essex was making its way towards Oxford to pressure the king into negotiation. Prince Rupert attacked a parliamentary force under John Hampden, who was mortally wounded in the engagement at Chalgrove Field in Oxfordshire (18 June). At the moment of his death Hampden was wearing a silver locket with the inscription that summed up his political views: 'Against my King I never fight/But for my King and country's right.' Thereupon Essex abandoned his march on Oxford and offered his resignation to Parliament, which refused to accept it. On 30 June at Adwalton Moor (near Bradford) the Earl of Newcastle decisively beat Lord Fairfax, rendering the king supreme in Yorkshire. Then – more bad news for the parliamentarians – at Lansdown Hill (in the west, near Bath), Hopton, with the aid of Prince Maurice, defeated Waller (5 July 1643), who was forced to retreat. Waller and Hopton were old friends, and Waller's reply underlines the fact that for most of the landowning class this was indeed a 'war without an enemy':

> my affections to you are so unchangeable, that hostility itself cannot violate my friendship to your person, but I must now be true to the cause wherein I serve.... That great God which is the searcher of my heart, knows with what sad sense I go upon this service, and with what a perfect hatred I detest this war without an enemy....

Such successes as these encouraged assaults on the cities of Gloucester and Bristol. Bristol fell to Prince Rupert (26 July) with heavy loss of life. This was a major prize indeed, the second largest city in the kingdom, with a major arsenal, port and a fleet of ships, although the royalists had to pay a heavy price in casualties to win it. Gloucester, however, was holding out, so that Charles himself was forced to appear outside its walls. But he did not have the stomach for a full assault, with the inevitable slaughter involved, and he hung around outside hoping to starve it into capitulating. This laxity allowed the parliamentary forces under Essex, including the London trained bands, to make it all the way from the capital to Gloucester, which they entered on 8 September, just in time to ensure that it remained a parliamentary stronghold. Charles had been overconfident and under-aggressive, and paid the price. Missing the chance to take Gloucester, which in parliamentary hands impeded direct access to royalist Wales, was the first major setback to the royalists: but worse was yet to come.

On his march home to London, Essex was caught by Prince Rupert at Newbury and was forced to do battle. The two sides were fairly equal in numbers, except that the royalists had the advantage on horse, but this would prove an unusual battle in that, owing to the obstacles in the form of hedges and trees, there was little that the cavalry could do; the outcome of this long battle, unlike most, did not depend on the cavalry. It was an infantry affair, and both sides fought until exhausted and most of their powder spent. The king returned to Oxford, while Essex made his way back to London. The first battle of Newbury (20 September) was very significant and proved that the war would now be a long one. No single battle had decided the issue either way, and there was no possibility that the king could now march on London. As the year 1643 came to a close, the king was in control of most of the north of England, the west and south-west, while Parliament held sway in the home counties, the south-east, East Anglia and Lincolnshire. However, away fom the turmoil of the battlefield an agreement had been forged that would change the course of the war and render the term 'English Civil Wars' a very misleading one.

In September 1643 an alliance was forged between Parliament and the Scottish Presbyterians: the Solemn League and Covenant. This was Pym's final contribution to his beloved parliamentary cause before dying in December 1643. Pym's 'middle group' would not long survive his death. There can be no doubt about the close links between the Scots and the parliamentary activists going back to 1640. The Scots felt that they needed a guarantee against a future attempt to impose episcopacy on them, and all negotiations with Charles had so far failed. They also felt a missionary zeal to spread Presbyterianism in England; Parliament, for its part, urgently needed Scotland's military assistance. The basis of the new agreement was to reform the religion of both

England and Ireland on the Scottish model, that is to establish Presbyterianism throughout the British Isles, to uphold 'the rights and liberties of Parliaments' and 'to preserve and defend the King's Majesty's person and authority'. They still did not see themselves as rebels. The Committee of Both Kingdoms was established (February 1644) to replace the Committee of Safety and to coordinate planning between the two nations, but the two Houses of Parliament were to remain in overall control. The price of such help was Parliament's agreement to accept Presbyterianism as the new state religion. However, Scottish-style Presbyterianism was generally disliked in England (as being too clerical), and the religious deal with the Scots was softened by the loophole that the final religious settlement would be 'according to the Word of God', which gave the parliamentarians some scope for prevarication. The task of reaching a religious formula was entrusted to the Westminster Assembly of divines, but Parliament was determined to have the guiding hand by having 20 MPs and 10 Lords appointed to it. Later the Scots and their English allies were to fall out on religious issues because the vast majority of MPs were adamant not to follow the intransigent Scottish model of Presbyterianism.

This deal with the Scots was essentially the work of the middle group and the war party, with the peace-party men being opposed to it because they believed that militarily it would merely exacerbate the situation. John Adamson has argued that the creation of the Committee of Both Kingdoms in 1644 was a device to reduce the quasi-regal powers of Essex, who had become an 'over-mighty subject' and too eager to make peace with the king.[3] Pym had always supported Essex, but after Pym's death Oliver St John of the middle group combined with Sir Henry Vane of the war party against the earl.

In January 1644 a Scottish army of some 21 000 men under the very experienced Earl of Leven entered England to support the Parliament. Meanwhile, King Charles had also been looking for Celtic allies: in Scotland he gained the backing of the Calvinist royalist Earl of Montrose, who disliked the radicalism of the Covenanters; and in Ireland the royalist Marquis of Ormond made peace with the Irish rebels (in September 1643) so that English troops could return to England to fight for the king.

The first success of the allied Scots–parliamentary army was at Marston Moor in the north of England on 2 July 1644, an evening battle fought in a thunderstorm between 7 pm and 9 pm, which was inaugurated by the parliamentarians on the urging of Leven, and to the amazement of the royalists who were preoccupied with their supper at the moment of attack. The royalist army of some 18 000 under Newcastle and Prince Rupert was defeated by a much larger combination (about 28 000) of the Scots, the Yorkshire army under Lord Fairfax, and the Eastern Association army led by Manchester. The fighting went badly for both sides, and both Leven and Lord Fairfax believed that the allies had lost and so actually left the battlefield; only Manchester remained at his post. However, the parliamentary cavalry commanded by Cromwell were re-formed to menace the royalist infantry, and later to rout the royalist cavalry. This last action was what gave the battle to Parliament. Some 4500 men on both sides fell at Marston Moor, with bodies strewn over a wide area. The battle, soon to be confirmed by the loss of the city of York on 16 July, symbolised the king's loss of the whole north of England. Newcastle felt so ashamed over the destruction of his own regiment of 'Whitecoats' that he went into exile, whereas this was the battle where Oliver Cromwell made a great name for himself with his cavalry, known as the 'Ironsides'.

Despite this success at Marston Moor, Parliament was unable to force the king to the negotiating table because of two major setbacks. First, Essex was humiliatingly forced to surrender in Cornwall at Lostwithiel (1 September), although the earl himself for the sake of honour was allowed to escape in disguise to Plymouth in a fishing boat. The second setback came after the second battle of Newbury (27 October), which although technically a parliamentary victory for Waller and Manchester was ruined by the king's escape to Oxford. These failures drove home to many parliamentarians that a new will to win and a new army leadership were both needed.

Self-denial and the New Model Army

Lack of clear parliamentary war aims led to both Manchester and Essex being verbally attacked by Cromwell and Waller for their half-heartedness, while Essex in return sought Cromwell's impeachment. The religious meaning of Essex's humiliating defeat was debated by the Westminster Assembly of divines,[4] and there was a general feeling that sinfulness and self-seeking were at the root of Parliament's failure. These tensions led to a further splintering of the parliamentary cause, and to the decision to revamp the army to settle the issue with the king once and for all. The indecisive aristocratic generals were to be jettisoned, and command was to be given to more determined men. This was all to be achieved by Parliament's acceptance of the Self-Denying Ordinance (April 1645), which deprived Members of Parliament of their army commands. The Ordinance had originally been introduced into the Commons on 9 December 1644 by the vehement Presbyterian Zouch Tate as a measure of spiritual self-denial, and on the same day in the Lords by Lord Saye and Sele.[5] However, it had been thrown out of the Lords in order to protect Essex and Manchester, against whom it was primarily directed. While Members of the Commons could resign their seats and remain in the army, no such choice was possible to the peers, who were automatically Members of Parliament; it was thus an essentially anti-aristocratic device, with profound social implications. Finally, faced with the pressing need to choose new officers, the Lords agreed to it, especially as they had already assented to the formation of the New Model Army under a new leader on 27 January 1645. The new commander-in-chief was the 33-year-old Sir Thomas Fairfax, chosen because of his eligibility and competence, because he was politically inoffensive and had been a loyal supporter in the north of England of the war party's Earl of Northumberland. Fairfax was to have charge of an amalgamated army of some 22 000 men, comprising the forces of Essex, Waller and Manchester, and financed by the monthly 'assessment' tax – at first fixed at £53 000 a month, but climbing to £120 000 a month by 1649. The New Model comprised 11 cavalry regiments, 12 of infantry and one of dragoons. The cavalry came mainly from the Eastern Association army, where they had been drilled by Cromwell. Despite the Self-Denying Ordinance, Cromwell would be reinstated in his military commission; the Lords tried to prevent this but were frustrated by Cromwell's military success at Naseby in June. Cromwell wanted an army with promotion based on merit, not on sectarian religious allegiance, and he pointed to evidence of Presbyterian persecution and discrimination against radicals. Two other MPs who kept their commissions despite the Ordinance were John Alured and Sir William Brereton. An important innovation of the New Model was its use of a red uniform for all its members (red being chosen especially to disguise bloodstains), whereas previously only different regimental uniforms had been known – and they were not always donned, making it difficult for soldiers to distinguish enemies on the basis of the colours being worn. Instead passwords had been used to tell friend from foe.

The creation of the New Model Army has traditionally been seen as a major turning-point in the history of the war. Clarendon in the seventeenth century believed this, as did S. R. Gardiner in the nineteenth. Indeed most historians have followed this approach until the revisionist attack by Mark Kishlansky in the late 1970s. Certainly no one any longer believes the old legend of the army as being filled with psalm-singing idealists and revolutionaries. However, the revisionist attempt of Kishlansky to downplay the importance of the changes involved has not been widely followed. Kishlansky pointed to the fact that the New Model was organised on the same lines as Essex's army, with the same rates of pay, and that therefore the New Model 'was an amalgamation, not a fresh beginning'. He sees its creation as a conservative response to a military problem and not a plan by the war faction to oust the peace party: quite the contrary, Self-Denial was designed by Tate to heal the differences between the commanders. Religious differences between the various groups were not important in the event: 'military necessity rather than ... religious zeal' was the mainspring of action. Thus the creation of the New Model, according to Kishlansky, was 'the final achievement of consensus decision making'.[6] The great majority of the parliamentary soldiers were mercenaries, impressed men (over one-third were conscripts) and also captured royalists who had thereupon decided to change sides, with no particular religious axe to grind. Promotion based on merit in the New Model (without the use of patronage and favouritism) was not new either, for that had been a characteristic of Manchester's Eastern Association army. Kishlansky's arguments, although an important corrective to the legend, have failed to dislodge the older tradition that the military reorganisation was indeed a politically inspired attempt by the win-the-war party to wrest control from the lukewarm aristocrats and the peace party. Ian Gentles has recently reasserted the primacy of political antagonism and religious contention over simple military necessity, important though that last element was.[7] Zouch Tate, who was a Presbyterian in religion, nevertheless belonged to the war party, and his motion for Self-Denial was seconded by Sir Henry Vane and supported by Cromwell, fellow members of the war party. Also, one should not forget that cashiering the nobility, the traditional military leaders since time immemorial, was a great innovation in itself, and pregnant with enormous social consequences. Religious zeal was once again imperilling the old principle of hierarchy. John Adamson argues that the demotion of Essex and the revamping of the army were the result of a 'palace coup' organised by Saye, Northumberland and other members of the war party: 'a conservative aristocratic reaction against the phenomenon of Essex'.[8] But whether one regards the Puritan peers or the Puritan House of Commons men as the instigators, the results were the same: namely, the end of the military domination of the aristocracy. Furthermore, the aristocratic Saye–Northumberland clique were later themselves to be swept from power by the army.

Despite all the reservations about the majority of New Model soldiers being mercenaries, the overwhelming impression is still one of a great religious enthusiasm welling up. The army command was certainly imbued with religious fervour. As for the rank and file, while evidence for scepticism, blasphemy and irreligion can be found (especially later), there seems little doubt of much genuine religious inspiration during the first Civil War, and large crowds are known to have assembled for sermons. Ian Gentles argues that 'the evidence for devoutness and piety in the New Model Army is at all times far more voluminous than that for irreligion. This piety extended from the highest to the lowest ranks.' Many ordinary soldiers were 'mechanic preachers', and the army fostered debates about religious and political issues. A sense of spiritual equality pervaded the army, and all this 'made a palpable difference to its fortunes on the battlefield'.[9] Army debates, and the sense of freedom which they engendered, were a logical development of the removal of bishops and nobles from their official functions. All this made the New Model a most unusual animal from the very start, and very different from any other army in seventeenth-century Europe.

There were now two groups in the revamped parliamentary side: the Presbyterians and the Independents. These were the contemporary terms, but historians today refer to the Presbyterians as political Presbyterians, because they were not religious supporters of true Presbyterianism. The political Presbyterians were essentially social conservatives: they had agreed to the Scottish alliance and the price of Presbyterianism, but they really wanted to find an accommodation with the king and restore peace. The political Presbyterians, led by Denzil Holles, were the peace party; they had formerly been antagonistic to the Scots, but now saw them as friends. Religiously, they wanted to maintain a uniform state Church because they saw religious conformity as a pillar of the social order. Ranged against these political Presbyterians were the Independents, who comprised the old 'war party' plus some former adherents of the 'middle group' (such as Oliver St John), desiring the defeat of the king and a dictated peace which would guarantee religious freedom (within limits). The war party had previously been supporters of the Scots, but had now fallen out with them because of Scottish demands for religious uniformity. The middle group as such had long disappeared.

Victories were soon forthcoming for Parliament. King Charles had become overconfident after successfully sacking the town of Leicester, and this emboldened him to attack a much larger force than his own at Naseby (Northamptonshire) in June 1645, where the royalists suffered a painful defeat, as well as the capture of the king's correspondence with Henrietta Maria that revealed plans both to bring over the army from Ireland for use against Parliament and to concede toleration for Catholics. At Naseby Prince Rupert's cavalry at first easily defeated the parliamentary cavalry under Henry Ireton, and the parliamentary infantrymen seemed doomed as well. However, Cromwell and Fairfax saved the day. Cromwell's disciplined cavalry charge against the royalist infantry was successful, and when Rupert's men returned from their expedition in search of booty they found that they had missed their chance to undo Cromwell's victorious tactics. Rupert had repeated the mistake he had made at Edgehill. So despite initial hopes that day, the royalists ended up losing 1000 men killed and 4000 taken prisoner, whereas the New Model's losses were very low at about 150. Cromwell had gained great renown with his new commission of lieutenant-general of horse.

The battle of Langport, the following month, when Lord Goring's army was scattered by parliamentary cavalry under Fairfax and Edward Whalley, was another major royalist defeat, after which Prince Rupert advised Charles to sue for peace. In Cromwell's eyes the deity had shown his approval at Langport: 'to see this, is it not to see the face of God?' he gloated. The thundering guns of the New Model soon brought various troublesome sieges to a successful conclusion (as at Bridgwater, Devizes, Basing House and Tiverton), while on 11 September 1645 Prince Rupert surrendered Bristol to Fairfax – much to the disgust of the king, who unfairly blamed Rupert and ordered him to leave the country; however, the situation there had in truth been hopeless. Two days later the royalist Earl of Montrose, who was hugely outnumbered, went down to the Scottish Covenanters in heavy fog at Philiphaugh. Prince Charles fled to France to join his mother, and the royalists in the west under Sir Ralph Hopton surrendered to Fairfax on 14 March 1646. King Charles was now in a corner, and he decided to escape from Oxford in disguise, surrendering to the Scottish army near Newark, Nottingham-shire, on 6 May. He was then taken to Newcastle upon Tyne. The first Civil War was over.

However, the fact that Charles had surrendered to the Scots and not to the parliamentarians showed clearly that he had not accepted final defeat. In July 1646 the 'Newcastle Propositions' were presented to the captive king, a set of conditions which included the abolition of episcopacy, the acceptance of Presbyter-ianism and the placing of the militia in parliamentary hands for 20 years. The king refused to make a decision on them and played for time: had he accepted these terms he would have been restored to the throne very soon. The king remained in the hands of the Scots until the end of January 1647, when after receiving the first downpayment of their arrears from Parlia-ment, they went home and left Charles at Newcastle in the hands of conservative Presbyterian soldiers.

Split between Parliament and the army, 1647

During the first Civil War Parliament at Westminster had become increasingly unpopular, and its membership had dwindled to about 25 in the Lords and 150 in the Commons. Although what were termed 'recruiter elections' in 1645 added some 240 MPs to the House, attendance remained thin. From 1645 onwards the main issues dividing the House of Commons were the same as those at the end of 1641, namely the interrelated questions of religion and the social order. Episcopacy had been abolished since 1643, and the debate now turned on whether or not to maintain a state Church. Those MPs desirous of a state Church (and thus religious uniformity and control) were the social conservatives, or political Presbyterians. They were opposed by the Independents, who wanted religious toleration and thus less social control, but more stringent controls on the king. The political Presbyterians, on the other hand, prominent among whom was Denzil Holles, urgently wanted an agreement with the king in order to preserve social order and hierarchy. Indeed the conservative reaction against the war (especially against high taxes and a standing army) was playing into the king's hands. The political Presbyterians had been forced to accept the Scottish religious system, and in January 1645 the Presbyterian *Directory of Worship* for use in all English churches appeared. However, they made sure that the English Parliament would remain in overall control of the new Presbyterian Church: there would be a lay supremacy, not a clerical one as the Scots wished – 'a lame Erastian presbytery' in the critical eyes of the Scots.

The political Presbyterians feared the army and wanted to get rid of it in the winter of 1646–7. With the restoration of peace it was certainly more difficult to collect the taxes needed to maintain the army, and because of lack of money soldiers resorted to free quarter, especially the taking of horses and other livestock, which increasingly alienated ordinary people from the army. Denzil Holles led a campaign to demobilise the army, getting rid of all the top brass apart from the commander-in-chief, Sir Thomas Fairfax (and even he just survived), while sending some troops to Ireland and purging Independents from the army and the London militia. Only Presbyterians were to remain as officers. Holles branded those soldiers who petitioned for their arrears of pay as 'enemies of the state'. The Presbyterian programme for an agreement with the king and for the dissolution of the army was not, of course, what the Independents in the army had fought for. Nor did they take kindly to being demobilised without their arrears of pay or a guarantee against prosecution for actions undertaken in the war (although this indemnity would come in June). Even when Parliament agreed to eight weeks' back pay (25 May 1647), this appeared only as an insult because money for about the past year was still owing. There was now in truth an insurmountable barrier between the army and the Presbyterians at Westminster.

The month of May 1647 saw the final break between Parliament and the army. Parliament thought that the king was prepared to negotiate with it on the basis of the 'Newcastle Propositions', and so the army could safely be dispensed with. Indeed there were rumours that the Presbyterians were planning to whisk the king away to Scotland. In reaction to Parliament's attitude, on 29 May 1647 Sir Thomas Fairfax ordered the army to camp at Newmarket to discuss the situation. Then on 2 June Cornet George Joyce, together with some 500 cavalrymen, seized the king from the Presbyterian soldiers who were holding him at Holdenby House, Northamptonshire, and brought him to Newmarket. If Joyce's seizure of the king had been off his own bat, this would have meant that all traditional authority had collapsed. However, this seems highly doubtful despite the protestations of Cromwell and Fairfax that they had not sanctioned it. The most likely explanation is that the army command had given orders to prevent the removal of the king from Holdenby House by the Presbyterians, but had not endorsed the transfer of the king to Newmarket. Joyce may well have panicked and feared a Presbyterian counter-attack at Holdenby. Whatever the exact truth, the New Model Army now held King Charles.

The army during 1647 had become a political army – something unique in seventeenth-century Europe, and indeed in the history of the world before the French Revolution. This idea of ideological radicalism as a special mark of the New Model Army seemed to be under a cloud among historians for a time in the late 1970s and 1980s, with the argument that all they cared about was lack of pay and little about politics – a part of the process of 'functional radicalism' that revisionists seemed to have detected to explain unforeseen developments during the course of the wars. However, it now looks once more as though, besides its material concerns, the army 'was already thoroughly politicized' by 1647,[10] influenced in particular by a radical London group, the Levellers. Although the radicals in the army remained a minority they wielded great influence in 1647, especially by being elected 'agitators' (or adjutators or agents) by the different regiments. The more conservative officers found themselves forced to follow the lead of these agitators, who had succeeded in radicalising most of the rank and file; moreover, about one-quarter of the conservative officers decided, or were forced, to resign. On 5 June the army at Newmarket vowed not to disperse until its grievances had been met (by the 'Solemn Engagement'), and later claimed in the 'Declaration of the Army' (15 June) that it was 'not a mere mercenary army hired to serve any arbitrary power of a state', but self-consciously political and dedicated to preserving 'the people's just rights and liberties'. The army was thus implying that it was more representative of the general will than was Parliament.

The army's immediate aims were to purge Parliament of political Presbyterians and to gain religious liberty. On 8 June the army had called for the impeachment of Holles and ten other Presbyterians, and in early August 1647 the army, with the support of the trained bands in Southwark, invaded Westminster and the City of London in order to establish what they considered to be a free Parliament. Denzil Holles and ten others were accordingly removed from Parliament. Thus in the summer of 1647 the Independents defeated the Presbyterians. In the next stage the army was to become split between the conservative Independents and the social and political radicals.

This split within the army showed up clearly in the Putney debates, taken down in shorthand in Putney parish church between 28 October and 1 November 1647, which record the variety of opinions among the soldiers at the time. The army had retired to Putney after the purge of Parliament: far enough away to allow calm to reign at Westminster, but close enough to move in again if necessary. It was also close enough for the Levellers to influence wide sections of the New Model. The army leaders (dubbed 'Grandees' by the Levellers), such as Cromwell, Ireton and John Lambert, threw their weight behind some kind of limited monarchy in order to preserve the old social order. They wanted really two quite incompatible things: social conservatism and religious liberty – two things which could not mix, as James I had so astutely pointed out. The Grandees had earlier put before the king (*c.* 23 July) the 'Heads of the Proposals', an agreement drawn up with the support of Lord Saye and Sele, the Earl of Northumberland, Lord Wharton, Oliver St John and others,[11] which included a Parliament every two years, religious toleration except for Catholics (the Prayer Book could still be used, and even bishops might return so long as they had no judicial power), the council of state commanding the army for ten years (compared to 20 years as in the 'Newcastle Propositions') and – as a concession to army radicals – the abolition of tithes and a promise to reform the law. On balance these terms were more generous than what the Presbyterian-dominated Parliament was offering and indicate the Grandees' sincere wish for a settlement with Charles.

Ranged against the Grandees at Putney were the Leveller-inspired radicals. They had already stated their views in *The Case of the Army Truly Stated* of October 1647, which had attacked the Grandees for making the army generally unpopular with ordinary people and for their lukewarm attitude towards significant reform, and they now demanded religious freedom and manhood suffrage (with only supporters of the king excepted). The basis of their political philosophy was that 'all power is originally and essentially [vested] in the whole body of the people of this nation'. This assumed that the interests of the people and the interests of the army were one and the same, but the very unpopularity of the army at the time belied it. These ideas were also embodied in the first *Agreement of the People*, which envisaged a written constitution, and was far more democratic than anything imaginable by the Grandees. Although in the first draft discussed at Putney no mention is made of the king or voting rights, the tenor of the document implies a republic with manhood suffrage. These advanced views were hateful to the Grandees, with the notable exception of the less well-born Colonel Thomas Rainsborough, who pleaded that:

> the poorest he that is in England hath a life to live as the greatest he; and...that every man that is to live under a

government ought first by his own consent to put himself under that government.

But most of the army leaders agreed with Ireton's view that these notions were a threat to the rights of property and that those who ruled should be only those who had 'a permanent fixed interest in this kingdom . . . that is, the persons in whom all land lies, and those in corporations in whom all trading lies'. Cromwell was not sure that a majority of the common people would actually endorse popular sovereignty, and his doubts were justified. In the debate in the General Council of the army it seemed that the radicals were getting their way, and Leveller ideas, such as having biennial Parliaments with manhood suffrage (with the exception of servants, who were deemed dependent on others), were being prepared for presentation to Parliament. Although the Grandees appeared to be making many concessions, they were in fact plotting to frustrate such radical demands. At a showdown at Corkbush Field (Hertfordshire) in November, Colonel Rainsborough begged Fairfax to accept the *Agreement*, copies of which were being worn in the hats of many radical cavalrymen. A scuffle ensued, but it was put down by Cromwell and other officers, and the *Agreement* was torn from its supporters' hats. One agitator was shot in the aftermath as an example.

In the meantime the king's escape on 11 November 1647 from military custody at Hampton Court and his flight to the Isle of Wight – in an attempt to get to France – sparked off the second Civil War. Charles agreed to go to Carisbrooke Castle on the island because its governor was a moderate soldier out of sympathy with the New Model's radicalism, one who took his orders directly from Parliament. Thus essentially Charles became a prisoner of Parliament again, not of the New Model. He immediately wrote to Parliament offering to make concessions, including allowing Presbyterianism for three years if episcopacy could also remain, but Parliament proved intransigent in its demand for the abolition of bishops. Nevertheless, the king was given freedom to receive visitors, including a Scottish delegation of moderate Covenanters, and at Christmas-time a new agreement was hammered out with them. The Scots had become very disillusioned with their parliamentary confederates and their lukewarm support of true Presbyterianism. By the 'Engagement' of 26 December 1647 Charles agreed to accept Presbyterianism for three years (although he and his household were exempt from taking the Covenant) and to extirpate the Independents and other religious radicals, while the Scots pledged military support to put him back on his three British thrones. Conservative Presbyterians in Scotland under the Duke of Hamilton now veered back to the king, although there was a split in the Covenanting movement with more radical Presbyterians, including the Marquis of Argyle, wanting nothing to do with this agreement because Charles had refused to take the Covenant. For his part it was a reluctant Charles who had signed this agreement, solely because he had been frustrated in his goal of getting away to France.

The second Civil War (1648)

The second Civil War may appear with hindsight not to have represented much of a military threat to the New Model Army (or officially 'the Standing Army' as it became known in February 1648), but no one knew that at the time; and until the danger was past the army command was distinctly worried, with much soul-searching, as well as prayer meetings, to decide how best to respond. Politically, there can be no doubt, the second Civil War raised the temperature quite dramatically, and the army treated its enemies more ferociously and vindictively. The king's attempted escape convinced the Grandees that Charles was completely unreliable and that all negotiations with him were pointless. In Parliament Cromwell and Ireton denounced the king as a hypocrite with whom there could be no further dealings. At an army prayer gathering at Windsor Castle in April a resolution was passed 'to call Charles Stuart, that man of blood, to an account for that blood he had shed'; these were the first rumours of the need to put the king on trial.

The major worry for the Grandees was that Charles's flight would provoke outbreaks of royalist sympathy and plotting; in this they were correct. Demonstrations of popular royalism were soon forthcoming, provoked by Parliament's intrusiveness into local affairs through the county committees, and hatred of the army among ordinary people, especially because of the assessment and excise taxes (which were levied on very poor people for the first time) and the free quarter that the soldiers often resorted to (despite its official prohibition by Parliament). It is important to realise that the county committees did not feel bound by the common law, but could override it in the emergency situation of civil strife – the same arguments previously used by the king. Indeed, parliamentary tyranny seemed worse than the king's, because of more extensive powers of search and imprisonment without trial, all of which helped the swing back to nostalgia for the past. This popular royalism was manifested in support for traditional customs, such as the keeping of Christmas, which the Puritans had tried to suppress. A riot at Canterbury at the very end of 1647 had been directed against the banning of Christmas and the enforcement of normal shopping hours. Similar sentiments were also voiced in London, and on 13 January 1648 crowds had cried out 'for the King and no plunder'; and the Commons had to call on the army for protection from this traditionalist mob. In May some 2000 men from Essex marched on Westminster to demand the return of the king and the 'known laws'. Resentment at the army was being displayed in a number of ways and places, and Cromwell's point at Putney about whether ordinary people would actually support the notion of popular sovereignty was well made.

Despite popular rioting, and despite the activities of cavaliers and the king's secret negotiations with the Scots, the real outbreak of the second Civil War began with discontented parliamentary soldiery. While most of those soldiers marked for demobilisation took their pay and went home quietly, in south Wales this was not the case. In late March the governor of Pembroke Castle, who was disgruntled for a number of reasons, including that of back pay, turned royalist and rose in revolt and defeated near Carmarthen the force of parliamentarians sent against him, thereupon causing a flurry of royalist activity in south Wales. In the far north Sir Marmaduke Langdale captured Berwick-upon-Tweed and Carlisle (28–29 April). Even more worrying was the fact that part of the navy had rebelled against their vice-admiral, Thomas Rainsborough, and Leveller control and in favour of conservatism; the docks at Rochester and Sandwich were in the hands of these rebels, and even the reappointment of Warwick as lord high admiral did not ease the situation. The

Earl of Holland, Warwick's brother, turned royalist and was appointed commander-in-chief by Prince Charles.

However, the biggest danger was still on the horizon, resulting from the agreement that had been concluded by King Charles with the Scots the previous December. The Scottish Engager army of some 10 000–14 000 men was assembled by Hamilton and crossed the border on 8 July 1648 and was joined by northern royalists under Sir Marmaduke Langdale, greatly outnumbering the forces under Lambert in the north. Had the Scottish army remained together they would have presented an enormous danger to the English Standing Army, but Hamilton foolishly kept his troops dispersed. At Preston on 17 August Cromwell, having returned from south Wales where he had been involved in a mopping-up campaign against royalist intransigence, now caught up with Langdale's royalist rearguard. Langdale requested urgent assistance from his Scottish allies, and although Hamilton himself was prepared to come to relieve Langdale, the Scots' second-in-command, the Earl of Callander, thought it wiser for them to continue moving south, leaving Langdale to look after himself. Cromwell emerged the victor after a difficult four-hour struggle against Langdale; and the Scots themselves after much harassment were forced to surrender their infantry near Warrington, while Hamilton and the cavalry gave up at Uttoxeter. The very wet weather had drenched the Scottish soldiers and completely demoralised them. Cromwell followed up this victory in October by making an agreement with the Marquis of Argyle, who had given no support to Hamilton's invasion, and this deal robbed Charles of any further Scottish help for the moment. In Scotland there was a purge of Engagers and royalists from all public offices as radical Presbyterians took power.

Whether one regards these revolts of 1648 as signs of positive royalism or, more probably, as signs of exasperation with the Independents and the unpopularity of the army, it is clear that in 1648 general opinion in the country was very much on the side of a conservative settlement with the king. Indeed, many of those who had backed the army in 1647 now followed the Presbyterian line for a settlement with Charles I. Parliamentary negotiators on the Isle of Wight drew up the Treaty of Newport (October), which Charles partially assented to: he agreed to allow

Parliament control of the army for 20 years but refused a permanent Presbyterian settlement, instead agreeing only to a three-year trial of Presbyterianism, after which time a permanent settlement would be made by a conference of 60 theologians. Although neither side was happy, this represented a basis for negotiation and the end to immediate conflict, as both sides feared the violence of the army. The published *Declaration of Peace* (14 October) boasted their 'unanimous resolutions for an Agreement with both Houses of Parliament' on the basis of the king's 'gracious and final answer to the paper of Ireland, presented to the Commissioners on Friday last, with their happy and joyful Agreement therein'. Given such conservatism among the political nation and probably among the country at large, a revolution was simply not on the cards. But the joy felt by the parliamentary commissioners was not to last long. Instead revolution was soon to occur because power was seized by the radicals in the army and their civilian allies – a small group of men quite untypical of the majority.

The political revolution and the execution of the king, 1649

King Charles was removed by the army from Carisbrooke Castle to the mainland in November 1648, a move understandably condemned by Parliament. The army had acted to prevent the Treaty of Newport being finalised and the king being taken to London on a wave of popular royalism. Differences of opinion between the Grandees and the radicals in the army were for the moment swept aside, priority being given to getting rid of the king and the monarchy. On 18 November Henry Ireton's remonstrance which demanded that the king be put on trial was accepted by the army's Council of Officers. The radical newspaper *The Moderate* belied its name by campaigning for the removal of the king, whom it dubbed in its 14–21 November number 'the great Delinquent of the Kingdom and Author of England's ruin', descended from a line of tyrants. Indeed radical opinion in the country, although undoubtedly a minority point of view, was being rallied to demand the king's execution, and the Levellers were exerting considerable influence on the junior officers. On 2 December 1648 the army entered Whitehall for the second time, and the Parliament, which was discussing terms of peace with the king, was purged on 6 December by the low-born Colonel Pride. The two criteria used by the army for demanding the removal of any Members were voiced support for the Treaty of Newport and opposition to the Scottish invaders being branded as enemies. William Prynne asked by what authority Colonel Pride was interfering with Parliament, and Pride pointed to his soldiers' swords; in 'Pride's Purge' 80–90 MPs were ousted, of whom 41 were personally taken away and imprisoned, while many others left of their own volition. What was left of the Long Parliament, those 40–50 Members prepared to do business with the army, became known as 'The Rump' and annulled recent conservative resolutions for an agreement with the king. A seemingly modern-style military *coup d'état* had taken place.

With Parliament purged and power in the hands of the army and doctrinaire republicans (like Henry Marten, Thomas Scott, Thomas Challoner and Edmund Ludlow), and with a radical take-over in the City of London on 21 December, the true revolution could begin. 'What is clear', writes Brian Manning, 'is that the driving force for the *coup d'état*, both inside and outside the army, was provided by the religious radicals.' [12] Many historians have of late been anxious to emphasise that the events of late 1648 into early 1649 constitute a genuine political revolution only indirectly connected with the 'constitutional revolution' of 1641–2. The first Civil War had been fought to bring the king to his senses; the total abolition of monarchy was the result of a new and unforeseen set of circumstances, which the vast majority of the original critics of the king now abhorred. Indeed back in 1643 Henry Marten had been suspended from the House for suggesting the abolition of monarchy. Historians who believe in the reality of the 'constitutional revolution' of 1641–2 can speak of two distinct revolutions: 1640–2 and 1648–9. But the most recent general attitude has been to regard the first upheaval as a rebellion and only the second as a true revolution. One of the few historians opposed to such distinctions is Brian Manning, who interprets the events of the 1640s as a unity, as 'successive stages of a single revolution' which began with the collapse of traditional authority and control of the political elite over the common people back in 1640. [13] He regards the radical 'middle sort' and their bold aspirations as a major force to be reckoned with all the way through.

On 20 January 1649 Charles Stuart was put on trial in the name of the people of England: a revolutionary event indeed, unparalleled in English history and unique in seventeenth-century Europe. Like so many great events before it, the trial was held in Westminster Hall. The king refused to acknowledge the validity of the court and challenged the assertion of its president, John Bradshaw, that the English monarchy was elective. Despite much popular clamour for the king the result was, of course, a foregone conclusion, and on 27 January Charles I was found guilty of 'high treason and other high crimes', but he was not given the right of reply to the sentence. He was brought to execution by the axe on 30 January, on a platform raised outside the Banqueting House in Whitehall, his father's great architectural legacy, inside which the painted ceilings of Rubens portrayed James I, as a representative of kings in general, entering into Heaven. To judge by the brave way he met his end Charles evidently believed he would soon join his father there. Previous kings, like Edward II, Richard II, Henry VI and Edward V had been murdered in secret, not executed before a crowd in the capital after a public trial. 'It was not a thing done in a corner', as Colonel Thomas Harrison proudly put it.

The execution was the work of a minority of a minority. Fairfax had agreed with Ireton's remonstrance, but he disliked the proceedings and stayed away from the trial, although his wife attended and protested against it as being illegal with no popular sanction. The name of Thomas Fairfax is thus not to be found among the 59 signatories on the king's death certificate; other officers with cold feet included Skippon and Lambert. Not a single member of the House of Lords signed, and the only aristocratic heir to sign was the radical Thomas Grey, son of the Earl of Stamford; Grey's name appears second on the certificate because of his high social position, directly after that of the court's president, John Bradshaw. Among the other signatories were 18 serving army officers, as well as radical parliamentarians and some classical republicans like Marten, Challoner and Bradshaw, men not at all representative of the landowning class or the people at large. The execution of Charles I was the most important political event of seventeenth-century England. This remains true whether one supports a traditionalist or a revisionist interpretation of the period: traditionalists have depicted later Stuart kings as essentially limited monarchs because of the severe lesson given in 1649, while revisionists emphasise the feeling of shame felt among the conservative majority of the realm which impelled the return of monarchy in 1660 and, indeed, the return of authoritarian, not limited, monarchy then.

There was no clear ideology behind the execution of Charles I. True, there were some ideological, 'classical', republicans (inspired by the ancient Roman Republic) among the regicides, but not all those who voted for the death of Charles I were against monarchy as such. Charles I was not put to death because he was a king, but because he was untrustworthy. The fact that Charles had refused to plead at all had made his enemies' job so much easier. Had the king pleaded not guilty that would have forced his accusers to prove their case, giving him time perhaps to win support from abroad.

The revolution of 1649 was a limited one. It consisted of the abolition of the monarchy and the House of Lords, and the replacement of a uniform state Church with liberty of conscience and religious pluralism (within limits). But beyond this, nothing. The social system remained essentially the same. This is why the Republic was doomed to failure from the start. Monarchy had gone, but not the social system based on landownership, or the political power that went along with it. The Levellers wanted popular sovereignty, and now that monarchy had been repudiated and Parliament tamed, army radicals campaigned for democratising the army. John Lilburne lashed the army leadership for their conservatism and broken promises. The situation was likened by the radicals to that in the 1630s: it was now the turn of the generals to be stigmatised as 'jesuits and traitors' and the radicals' suffering to be compared to that of Prynne, Burton and Bastwick. Lilburne's two-part pamphlet, *England's New Chains Discovered*, led the attack on the Grandees and their 'vile apostasy'. Lilburne and three supporters were sent to the Tower in consequence. The Levellers, exploiting the severe economic conditions of 1649 after three bad harvests in a row, tried to inspire militancy and resistance to authority among both the soldiery and ordinary people, especially in London, where a number of marches and demonstrations by hundreds of women were held outside Parliament. These women were rudely told to get back home 'and meddle with your housewifery'.

One of the continuing major sources of discontent within the army was the question of arrears of pay and the harsh conditions which the ordinary soldiers had to endure, but whereas previously the blame for the army's woes could be put on Parliament, now the army leadership was getting the lash. There were political demands too. The Levellers had influenced the junior officers, and a new version of the *Agreement of the People* had been presented to the Rump on 20 January 1649. But the Grandees would have nothing of this and turned on the Levellers and their supporters in the army, with the execution of a radical trooper in London; and a Leveller mutiny involving some 900 soldiers was crushed at Burford (Oxfordshire), with three ringleaders being executed in the churchyard there (May 1649). The City of London expressed its relief at the lower orders being kept under control by putting on a banquet in honour of the generals, while the University of Oxford gave Fairfax and Cromwell honorary doctorates in law. Dr Fairfax and Dr Cromwell had made the world safe for the traditional landed elite. Thus any notion of democracy or simply widening the franchise was stillborn. The Republic was established on too narrow a base of support, that base itself being made even narrower by the crushing of the Levellers. The problem which had to be faced by governments of the Interregnum was how to keep the old social order going without the king, while keeping the radicals happy with some concessions in their direction. This was to prove an impossible task. Neither the old order nor the new radicals liked what they got. The military coup was based on the notion of 'godly rule' with the army as the instrument of the Lord; but beyond this the protagonists were grappling in the dark not knowing which direction to take. What the army leaders did not want were Leveller attacks on the legality of the Rump, and a number of religious radicals agreed with them that radical social experiments could imperil the religious gains of the coup by endangering the very existence of the new Commonwealth. The Leveller call for free elections, given the mood of the times, would almost certainly have resulted in a conservative, royalist assembly. The Leveller reply to this forecast was their belief that if fundamental social and political reforms were instituted to improve the lot of the common people a very different and favourable outcome could be expected at the elections. But this was a leap of faith that the Grandees were not prepared to take. Indeed the lack of genuine social revolution and political reform opened up a huge chasm between the new regime and many radicals, while the conservative political nation was already alienated by the death of the king. Really the execution of Charles I far from heralding the abolition of the old social and ruling system actually reinforced it, because the execution led to a great feeling of shame and disgrace among the propertied class. Unless the propertied class were to be removed the revolution of 1649 was doomed to failure. The Grandees were members of the landowning class in a very uneasy alliance with the radicals. When the Leveller mutiny of May 1649 was crushed, it was only a matter of time before monarchy, although not necessarily that of the Stuarts, was restored.

The third Civil War (1649–51)

The death of the king led to the abolition of two institutions: the monarchy and the House of Lords. England was now a republic. Despite being in exile in Holland, Prince Charles was proclaimed in Scotland almost immediately as King Charles II (5 February 1649), mainly because the Scots took umbrage at the English executing the King of Scotland without their permission. If Charles II was hoping for support from European rulers to regain the throne, his hopes were soon to be dashed. More hopeful in royalist eyes would be an invasion of England from Ireland or Scotland.

In Ireland the Marquis of Ormond forged the Treaty of Kilkenny between Protestant royalist and Catholic confederate elements at the price of religious freedom for Catholics, and headed an army of some 13 000 men, but with few supplies. Thus with most of Ireland in royalist hands Charles II hoped to land there and make it a springboard for an invasion of England. Charles procrastinated about going to Ireland himself, but sent Prince Rupert with some ships. However, Charles's tardiness meant that he had lost the initiative in Ireland to his enemies, and on 30 March 1649 Parliament placed Cromwell in charge of a military assault on Ireland to clear it of royalists; a savage, quick series of victories would be needed to reduce the menace posed there, as well as to gain revenge for the massacre of Protestants back in 1641.

Cromwell landed in Dublin with a well-supplied army of 12 000 men in August 1649. This was to be a campaign of sieges rather than set battles. The infamous massacres of the garrisons of Drogheda and Wexford in September and October were savage even by seventeenth-century standards, although at Drogheda it was within the rules of contemporary warfare because the commander of the town had been given the chance to surrender but refused. Here some 3500 soldiers, townspeople and priests were killed, while the English lost only about 150. Cromwell, who had given the order for slaughter, said that he was 'persuaded that this is a righteous judgement of God upon these barbarous wretches'. At Wexford, on the other hand, Cromwell gave no order for a general massacre, but it happened none the less while negotiations were under way for surrender. Some 2000 people perished there, mainly as a spontaneous reprisal for the deaths of Protestants at the hands of Catholics back in 1641. The Irish coalition forces now started breaking up, with Protestants going over to the parliamentary side. Because of the growing danger emanating from Scotland, Cromwell returned to England in May 1650, leaving his son-in-law Ireton in control of Ireland.

On 1 May 1650 Charles II signed the Treaty of Breda with the Scots Covenanters, by which he agreed (unlike his father) to take the Covenant himself and to reintroduce Presbyterianism into England in return for Scottish help to repossess his throne. It is unlikely that the Scots would have precipitated conflict so soon, but battle was forced on them by the English Council of State, which decided to nip the threat in the bud. Because Fairfax refused to make war on Presbyterians (especially as his wife was one) Cromwell was appointed commander-in-chief of the army, with John Lambert second-in-command and General Monck in charge of infantry.

Now with a force of about 16 000 men Cromwell marched into Scotland on 22 July and got to within a mile of Edinburgh, but then withdrew to Dunbar, on the coast, in order to guarantee his supplies by sea. After a number of weeks of vacillation battle was joined at Dunbar when Cromwell's troops almost miraculously defeated a much larger Scottish force of some 23 000 men under Sir David Leslie. It had first seemed that the English were cornered at Dunbar and ready only to take to the sea, and indeed some officers advised such an evacuation. Despite this, Lambert and Cromwell thought in terms of attack once they had espied the Scots coming down from the impregnable position of Doon Hill, which overlooked Dunbar. The Scots saw themselves as moving in for the kill, but the English struck first before the Scots could fully assemble, with an infantry attack under cover of darkness at around 4 am on 3 September which scattered them, to be followed by a cavalry assault at daybreak. Between 3000 and 6000 Scots soldiers perished that day, and some 10 000 were taken prisoner, whereas English losses were incredibly low – less than 40. It was an amazing outcome, but the 'miracle' had been helped along by the Scottish Presbyterian divines who had persuaded Leslie against his own better judgement to attack the invaders, instead of wearing them down and cutting off their supplies, a policy which had been working well up to that point.

The defeat of the Presbyterian Covenanters at Dunbar still had not made Charles II's cause an impossible one. Now he rallied the alternative Scottish allies, the royalists and the Engagers. Charles was crowned King of Scotland at Scone on 1 January 1651 and made commander-in-chief of the army, with the Duke of Hamilton as lieutenant-general and Sir David Leslie as major-general. The war in Scotland against Cromwell's invading force continued. The capture of Perth (2 August) was a major blow to the Scots, severing their lines of communication. Thus Charles decided to take the war into England against the advice of both Hamilton and Leslie and to link up with English royalists, but it was an unwise move because the Scots began to desert, and the English still regarded the Scots as their natural enemies. Furthermore, recruits to the invading force were required to subscribe to the Presbyterian Covenant, a commitment thoroughly opposed by Charles, but there was little he could do as he was dependent on Presbyterian support. The demand to sign the Covenant certainly helped sabotage his English campaign, and partly because of this there was no popular rising in his support.

If the majority of the English people had favoured a deal with Charles I at the end of 1648, then by 1651 there was little sign left of enthusiastic royalism for Charles II. Only small numbers of Englishmen answered his call. Charles's army marched south and reached Worcester on 22 August. Cromwell, with a force more than double that of Charles and much more skilled, attacked the city on 3 September, exactly one year after the great victory at Dunbar. Despite individual examples of bravery, the royalists were overwhelmed and fled the city, Charles among them, escaping in disguise and hiding out for 45 days before embarking for France. Up to 3000 royalists perished at Worcester, compared to less than 200 parliamentary soldiers, and more than 6000 prisoners were taken. Thus ended the English (or British) Civil Wars. Indeed, with the subjugation of Dundee by General Monck on 1 September 1651 Scotland became firmly subject to the English republican government, and the Civil Wars were to force a union of the two countries that James I, in very different circumstances, had only dreamed of.

The Civil Wars and society

Although not on the scale of the terrible devastation of the Thirty Years War in Germany, where at the siege of Magdeburg in 1631, for example, nearly 20 000 people were massacred, there can be no doubt that the British Civil Wars were fierce and destructive, with a large loss of human life and considerable destruction of property. It has been reckoned that all the events of the Civil War in England, large and small, total something approaching 635 incidents; there were some 18 major pitched battles, and over 300 sieges. Some 10 per cent of all men were involved in armies between 1643 and 1645, and between 20 and 25 per cent experienced military service at some stage of the wars. Figures for loss of life in England are uncertain, but the most recent estimate is that 84 700 people in England and Wales died in combat, and that 117 500 were taken prisoner. Most of the deaths did not take place in the big battles. The nine bloodiest battles, where over 1000 men apiece died, account for the loss of only 17 per cent of parliamentarians and 12 per cent of royalists; it was rather the small skirmishes that killed the largest number, about 47 per cent of soldiers on both sides. There were many examples of savagery, such as the massacre of male villagers at Nantwich on Christmas

Eve 1644, or Prince Rupert's attack on Liverpool. The largest number of casualties in general did not result directly from any fighting, but indirectly from the worse conditions of wartime, including the outbreak of disease, especially the plague, accidents with firearms and such like. Altogether more than 180 000 Englishmen may have died between 1639 and 1651 out of a population of about 5 million. If correct, this would mean that the proportion of the population affected by the upheaval was greater than the percentage of British casualties in the First World War (3.6 per cent compared to 2.6 per cent).

Destruction of property could also be severe in those areas where fighting occurred: in the towns and cities this was the result not only of bombardment by the enemy (punitive damage) but also of the need for protective clearance (defensive damage). As soon as it was realised that the war would be a prolonged one both sides sought to strengthen their grip on the regions they controlled by fortifying their bases. This entailed, for example, reinforcing existing town walls with the more recent system of earthworks and *bastions* (otherwise known as *sconces*, which were arrow-like projecting parts of an earthwork that allowed the defenders to shoot sideways at invaders); these had been originally devised in Europe to combat the emergence of mobile cannon-power which rendered medieval town walls easily demolishable targets. Thickening existing walls with earth and turf or building new earthworks around a town necessitated much demolition of existing structures in the suburbs outside the old town walls; had such extra-mural buildings been allowed to remain they could have afforded the besieging enemy shelter for shooting or laying mines. Structures outside town walls were also levelled to allow the defenders an unobstructed panorama of the enemy's movements. Outlying villages might also be razed to the ground to prevent their being used as bases by the enemy.

The question of allegiance

Who exactly fought for each side? What was the pattern of allegiance in the wars? This is a difficult subject over which much ink has been spilt, mainly because of lack of clear evidence of who exactly composed the bulk of the armies, compounded by the ideological presuppositions of the historians. It is also very hard to know whether men fought voluntarily out of conviction or simply because they were impressed. Some historians have attempted to argue that the country was divided socially, with the great nobility and gentry and their slavish tenants supporting the king, and on the other side the lesser gentry, the yeomanry and the more independently minded common people taking up the cause of Parliament. This notion of a socio-economic cleavage, argued in recent times by the Marxist historians Christopher Hill and Brian Manning, receives some support from contemporary opinions. The cleric Richard Baxter left this analysis:

> A very great part of the knights and gentlemen...adhered to the King...Most of the tenants of these gentlemen, and also most of the poorest of the people, whom the other call the rabble, did follow the gentry and were for the King. On the Parliament's side were...the smaller part (as some thought) of the gentry in most of the counties, and the greatest part of the tradesmen and freeholders and the middle sort of men, especially in those corporations and counties which depend on clothing and such manufactures.

Mrs Lucy Hutchinson, wife of a regicide, echoed the same theme of social division when she wrote that:

> most of the Gentry of the country [the county of Nottingham] were disaffected to the Parliament. Most of the middle sort, the able substantial freeholders, and the other Commons who had not their dependence on the malignant nobility and gentry, adhered to the Parliament.

However, the gentry were certainly more evenly divided at the beginning of the wars than these two writers supposed. The fracture within the gentry sitting in House of Commons in 1641–2 gave a majority to the parliamentarians (albeit a slight one), and the noteworthy thing about the gentry is that families were split down the middle with fathers fighting sons, brother against brother and cousin against cousin. Among Members of the Long Parliament themselves, some brothers chose different sides: Henry Cholmley supported Parliament while Sir Hugh Cholmley stayed loyal to the king; Sir John Coke was a parliamentarian and sat in the Westminster Assembly, but his younger brother Thomas supported the king. Among other relationships between MPs, Thomas Arundell fought for Parliament, but his young nephew John Arundell was a king's man. Denzil Holles had a royalist cousin Gervase Holles. Hugh Rogers followed Parliament, but his uncle Thomas was a royalist. Lord Robert Rich in the Commons broke with his father in the Lords, the second Earl of Warwick, and obeyed the king's summons to York. Outside of Parliament Sir Edmund Verney, a royalist, and indeed the king's standard-bearer at Edgehill, saw his son Sir Ralph Verney take up the Parliament's cause. The parliamentarians Sir Henry Vane and Charles Fleetwood each had a brother, Walter Vane and Sir William Fleetwood, who fought for the king. The Earl of Manchester had a zealous royalist brother, Wat Montagu. The regicide Sir Thomas Mauleverer had a royalist son, Richard. The royalist earls of Denbigh and Dover had sons who fought against them on the very same field at Edgehill. Oliver Cromwell had six royalist cousins. Thus gentry families were split down the middle, and it is impossible to discover social or economic factors to account for the differences in allegiance. Motivation seems to boil down to the old-fashioned principles of religion and liberty (however that word might be interpreted). It is also now clearly recognised that the largest group of gentry wanted to avoid all involvement and stay neutral. Men of principle ready to act on their beliefs were always in a minority; for most it was a heart-rending choice. The only county in England that contained MPs all of one persuasion was Middlesex (which included London). If the activist gentry were fairly evenly balanced, the majority of nobles remained loyal to King Charles. They had favoured constitutional safeguards, such as those in the Petition of Right, but had remained cold towards major religious reform. The parliamentary Lords were those with profound religious scruples or else deeply suspicious of Charles I. The rift between them and the majority was equally painful. The Earl of Essex, for example, had shared a home in the Strand with his sister and her husband, the Earl of Hertford, until the war made them go their opposing ways.[14] The analysis of Baxter and Mrs Hutchinson in regards to the gentry, interpreting the greater gentry as royalist and the lesser gentry as parliamentarian, makes better sense for the later stages of the war, from 1646 onwards, when under pressure of events and of army radicalism the greater 'county' gentry veered back towards a conservative settlement with the king; they abstained from collaboration with the army and their places in local affairs and on the county committees were taken by the lower 'parish gentry'.

As for the allegiance of the common people, this is very hard to gauge. The traditional sociological interpretation was to follow the Reverend Baxter and Mrs Hutchinson in equating parliamentarians in the localities with the 'middle sort' of industrious Puritans. Christopher Hill has argued that the war did not begin in the House of Commons but in the country at large: 'the real strength even of Pym's party came from outside the House'.[15] Hill cites the Earl of Clarendon's opinion that the common people were fully involved in the upheaval on the side of Parliament out of sheer jealousy of the rich. Clarendon's impression of general popular support for Parliament cannot be taken at face value, and anyway flies in the face of Baxter and Mrs Hutchinson, but to Hill it is proof of widespread popular participation.

Opposed to the thesis of widespread popular interest in the upheaval is the view that the vast majority of ordinary folk wanted to be left alone, and were intensely neutral. They participated only out of compulsion. The activities of the 'Clubmen' are pointed to in proof of the pervasive notion of neutralism. The 'Clubmen' were neutrals of various social grades who took up arms (clubs and pitchforks) in defence of their neutralism, to keep all armies out of their local areas, and they even issued manifestos in defence of their stance. From December 1644 through 1645 they were active in many counties of southern and western England. They were activists in protecting their homes against all outsiders, but they were eventually forced into fighting. The situation was clearly complex, as one might expect in a society that was becoming modern. One should expect from the people of the time a wide range of reactions and opinions; and that is what is evident in the records, though it is hard to make complete sense of it all; and historians differ greatly in their use and interpretation of them.

On the point of allegiance being based on one's socio-economic status, much used to be made of the fact that in the early stages of the war the more developed south-east of England and London, as well as the ports, were parliamentarian while the more backward rural north of England and Wales were royalist. The parliamentary cause was viewed as progressive and bourgeois capitalist, whereas the royalists were seen as standing for the old agrarian regime. The royalist gentry were jealous of their old privileges, and their followers were their poor unthinking dependants. In this interpretation, towns, even in royalist areas, were seen as really inclined towards Parliament, and showed their support for Parliament unless prevented from doing so by the royalist oligarchy in power. The rift in the gentry at Westminster simply took the lid off a boiling cauldron of popular discontent with the monarchy of Charles I. Ordinary people are regarded as being antipathetic to King Charles, who apparently encountered difficulties in recruiting them. However, this sort of interpretation no longer commands the general acceptance it once did. The split between the advanced south-east, supportive of Parliament, and the backward north, loyal to the king, is, according to the revisionists, more easily explicable by reference to the position of the opposing armies in the early stages of the war. Because the king foolishly left London to recruit in the north, this meant that the north would become royalist, because this was where the royalists were. Had the king stayed in London and forced Parliament to flee, then London would have been royalist. At least this is the argument, but (because it did not happen) it sounds hard to swallow. After all, one reason for the king's flight was that London had grown so hostile. But a crucial point raised is that the proximity of armies tended to overwhelm genuine feelings of loyalty, at least for a time, making it very hard for the historian to make a judgement on where people's hearts really lay. It looks as though the real picture is complex and we are nowhere near coming to any kind of general agreement on the role of ordinary people and their loyalties.

As for the towns, for example, the late J. P. Kenyon rather baldly stated that he regarded all the towns as having been naturally parliamentarian; and it is quite true that even royalist Oxford was initially hostile and had to be browbeaten into supporting the king and constructing earthwork defences for the city.[16] On the other hand, John Morrill has written that 'it is just not true that most towns were Parliamentarian'.[17] Morrill is also sceptical about the innate parliamentarianism of the ports, and regards their allegiance as being due to trade dependency on London rather than to political radicalism. If, on the other hand, one accepts that a Puritan agenda was a major reason for opposing the king, then the force of 'Puritanism' in the towns may be the real motivation, rather than economic reasons, for their proclivity towards Parliament. However, revisionists are not prepared to concede that towns were 'solidly for Parliament', as Kenyon put it: indeed the late Roger Howell argued for the force of popular royalism in many towns.[18]

A different version of social cleavage has been outlined by David Underdown in what has been dubbed 'the ecological interpretation', as opposed to the economic, where different patterns of popular culture dictated allegiance. In his *Revel, Riot and Rebellion* (1985) Underdown suggests that those areas of England which were subject to arable farming and organised into nucleated villages with resident squires and parsons tended to be traditionalist and royalist, whereas the upland areas with isolated homesteads, and often inhabited by those who had fled there, tended to be more independent-minded and parliamentarian. It was a clash of popular culture rather than of class that decided allegiance. His area of research was based only on Wiltshire and Dorset, and other historians have shown scepticism about the possibility of extending the criteria to explain allegiance over a wider area.[19] On Underdown's criteria, upland Wales should have been parliamentarian rather than royalist. Nevertheless, this seems an avenue well worth exploring, but it looks as though no single factor, or even set of factors, will be found to account for allegiance.

11 The English Republic

England's new status as a republic was partly cloaked by use of the old familiar Tudor word 'Commonwealth', with its associations of policies for the common good. But nothing could disguise the hatred felt by the majority of the political nation for what had been done to the king. The Republic was the creation of a minority within a minority and its chances of succeeding were only very slim. What needs to be understood are the reasons why the republican experiment lasted as long as it did, rather than why it eventually collapsed. The main answer to that lies in the charisma of Oliver Cromwell and the power of the army.

The Rump Parliament, 1649–53

If the Civil Wars were originally a struggle between Parliament and the king, the chaos ended with a defeat for both of them. Parliament had been purged in August 1647 and in December 1648 (and would be purged again later) by the army. Nevertheless the Rump Parliament that ruled England from the death of the king to April 1653 gave the superficial impression of parliamentary supremacy, so that for the first time Parliament could claim to be governing. Treason was defined in July 1649 as involving offences against 'the Commons in Parliament' rather than as previously against the king. The executive was vested in a 40-man Council of State, which was to be elected annually by Parliament and which was initially composed of 31 MPs and nine army officers. The legislature was the Rump House of Commons, comprising those who had survived Pride's Purge plus those 50 or so moderates who decided to accept the 'Engagement' of loyalty to the Republic of February 1649 and were readmitted – making a small House of about 200 Members. But attendance was always poor, with only about 60 active Members. And, of course, so many constituencies remained unrepresented. Parliamentary supremacy was really a sham.

The rule of the Rump has received a very bad press indeed from historians and was certainly unpopular at the time in the country at large – but not because of any extremism. It was to prove itself a very conservative body, and the return in February of some former victims of Pride's Purge confirmed this fact. Cromwell, amazingly, can be partly blamed for this development because he sought an accommodation with conservatives as soon as Charles I was dead in order to induce them to work with the new regime. He tried to win over the Presbyterians; he had even tried to prevent the abolition of the House of Lords. Cromwell also helped draw up an acceptable councillor's oath of loyalty to the new regime which did not require the swearer to accept the legality of Pride's Purge or the king's execution. All that was necessary by the 'Engagement' oath of 22 February was to swear allegiance 'to this present Parliament' and 'for the future in way of a Republic without King or House of Lords'. Significantly 22 members of the Council of State had refused the original oath specifying the legality of the king's execution. But if Cromwell was accommodating towards the conservatives he was to prove ruthlessly opposed to the social radicals. The political revolution would therefore not expand into a social one. The gentry would remain in charge, even if the activists generally came from a lower rung within the gentry – the more numerous 'parish gentry' rather than the elite county gentry. The shift in power would be one within the same class, with outsiders being regarded with the highest suspicion. And as the elite gentry largely abstained and stayed at home on their estates, so too did most nobles, with only very few of their number being prepared to participate in the new order – notably the Earl of Denbigh and Viscount Lisle, as well as two who took seats in the Commons – the Earl of Salisbury and the Earl of Pembroke.

The Rump began well, declaring that the people under God were sovereign, but it soon emerged as a conservative force, which Cromwell would come to dislike for betraying the godly cause. The Rump inherited a bankrupt treasury from the war years, but still had to finance military operations against the Irish and the Scots. Furthermore, the Rump frightened off creditors by threatening to declare a state bankruptcy. Its dislike of the army led it to reduce the monthly assessment for its main-tenance, which of course merely exacerbated the problem because the army and its operations still had to be paid for. The Rumpers could expect no existence without the army but they stubbornly refused to recognise this fact. Instead they tried to make ends meet by taking over royalist estates and the recovery fines from the care of the county committees, and selling off the lands of royalist delinquents. Also sold were the church lands of the former deans and chapters, which brought in money but at the cost of losing assets. More long-sighted was the Rump's support of trade by the Navigation Act of 1651, which insisted on the use of English vessels for trade with England and her colonies. This was directed at the flourishing Netherlands carrying trade, and was part of an attempt to force the Netherlands into a religious and economic union with England. The war against the Dutch from 1652 to 1654 was essentially ideological, the result of the combination of apocalyptic Protestantism and classical republicanism against the Netherlanders' seeming lukewarmness on such ideals.[1] Religiously, the Rumpers showed themselves less tolerant than the army would have liked. The official Presbyterian state Church inherited from 1645 to 1648 was overturned by only one vote in August 1649. A more pluralist system was allowed by the Toleration Act of 1650, which officially rescinded the Act of Uniformity of 1559 and other Elizabethan statutes that enforced attendance at the parish church on Sundays. Now 'pious and peaceably-minded people' could have their own services where they wished; but everybody was still expected to be at some form of divine service on Sundays. Irreligion was to be curbed by the Blasphemy Act and the Adultery Act. The construction of a 'godly commonwealth' inspired the formation of the Committees for the Propagation of the Gospel in Wales, the north of England, Ireland and New England. Only the first two committees were to have many achievements to their name, and the Welsh one was especially active in expelling lax ministers both to foster godly reform and to undermine the royalist cause there.

When the army had vanquished all its enemies and made the Rumpers safe by the battle of Worcester in September 1651, the Parliament then found itself threatened by the army, which wanted godly reforms to match its great triumphs on the battlefield. However, the Rump showed less and less enthusiasm for major reforms, despite receiving many suggestions for change. There were many demands for reforming the law, but these were blocked by lawyer MPs, while the Rumpers were half-hearted about religious toleration. Once again Parliament and army were to fall out.

The Rump has traditionally, and unfairly, been painted as a selfish and corrupt minority. True, there was a degree of corruption – but no worse than was usual – partly because some Members could not afford to pay their own parliamentary expenses, and the Long Parliament had sat on and off since November 1640. The problem lay not so much in the Rump's vices as in the unrealistic expectations of it from the radicals.

Historians have generally thought that Cromwell dissolved the Rump by military force in April 1653 because it desired to perpetuate its own existence by holding recruiter elections. This old idea has been challenged by Blair Worden.[2] Certainly Parliament's selfish wish to perpetuate itself was what Cromwell and the army alleged in their propaganda. But it is now known that the Rump, on the very day it was dissolved, was in the middle of debating an election bill – which no longer exists because Cromwell took it away with him – to hold fresh elections for a new Parliament to meet the following November. The army had been consistently calling for a new assembly to be elected, so why did it oppose this particular bill? The full truth of this episode will never be revealed because of the loss of the contentious bill.[3] It is known that Parliament proposed to narrow the franchise to the well-off, but it is doubtful if this was the cause of complaint because such was also to be Cromwell's aim later in the Instrument of Government. It is just conceivable that Cromwell was temporarily converted to having a wider electorate, but this seems on balance unlikely, and it is more probable that the final bill contained some clause that ensured sufficient continuity of membership from the existing Parliament to the next to make the new start demanded by the army impossible to achieve. What Cromwell wanted above all was a new untrammelled godly beginning commensurate with his military glories. He was thoroughly disillusioned by the slowness of the Rump and its poor legislative and attendance record, and it now looked as though Parliament was not going to renew the commissions for the Propagation of the Gospel in Wales and the north of England. Indeed the Rump's lack of a religious agenda seems quite to have upset Cromwell. In November 1652 he remarked to Bulstrode

Whitelocke: 'We all forget God, and God will forget us, and render us up to confusion.' Yet confusion was the keynote of Cromwell's reforming impulse, because on the same occasion he mused: 'What if a man should take upon himself to be King?' Cromwell's religious impulses were always blunted by his craving for the traditional political and social system, including the value of monarchy. His sudden dissolution of the Rump Parliament, which was technically illegal under the Self-Perpetuating Act of 1641, was preceded by a period of withdrawal from public life and by prayer meetings in the army council. As a well-known Dutch cartoon of the time depicting the expulsion of the Members put it: 'This House is to let.' The next set of tenants were to be more saintly, perhaps, but equally disappointing to Cromwell.

The rise of Oliver Cromwell

From a minor gentry family but inheriting considerable wealth on the death of a childless uncle, Oliver Cromwell underwent a serious religious conversion in the 1630s. Before this, in his first Parliament of 1628 as Member for Huntingdon, he had already attacked Arminianism, but his profound religiosity was acquired only during the Personal Rule. He was elected for Cambridge to both Parliaments of 1640. Eleven Members of the Long Parliament were his cousins, but although Cromwell was an industrious committee man and moved the second reading of Strode's bill for annual Parliaments, he hardly cut much of a figure in the House. The royalist Philip Warwick recorded in his 'Memoirs' the first visual impression which Cromwell made on him in the Commons: he

> wore a plain cloth suit which seemed to have been made by an ill country tailor; his linen was plain and not very clean, and I remember a speck or two of blood upon his little band . . . his countenance [was] swollen and reddish; his voice sharp and untunable and his eloquence full of fervour.

No one could have predicted from such an inauspicious beginning the role that Cromwell would come to play in the Civil War.

He had had no practical experience of warfare at all before the 1640s, when he discovered his own military genius on the battle-field. In the Civil Wars he picked his own men to serve under him: 'I think that he who prays and preaches best will fight best.' When Fairfax became disillusioned with politics, Cromwell succeeded him as commander-in-chief of the army in 1650.

Cromwell was a man of amazing apparent contradictions. The soldier of the 1640s seemed all set to abandon his class and sympathise with the common people, at least the godly people: 'I had rather have a plain russet-coated captain that knows what he fights for, and loves what he knows, than that which you call a gentleman and is nothing else.' 'It [would have] been well that men of honour and birth had entered into these employments, but why do they not appear?...better plain men than none.' According to the Earl of Manchester, Cromwell had said that he hoped to 'live to see never a nobleman in England'; and that 'God would have no lording over his people'. But these slighting remarks against the well-born during the Civil Wars and his appreciation of the religiously motivated common people never developed into sympathy for giving the common people political power. Despite his eagerness to defeat the king decisively, Crom-well never became a theoretical republican. In 1647 he thought that a 'settlement with somewhat of monarchical power in it would be very effectual'. Cromwell wavered in his allegiance to his class only because his first considerations were religious. His religious radicalism made him dream of annihilating the papacy: 'Were I as young as you,' he said to John Lambert, 'I should no doubt ere I died to knock at the gates of Rome.' His greatest belief was in religious freedom for all those Christians who had 'the root of the matter in them'. He believed that God was guid-ing his and the revolution's destiny, and that the political events revealed the workings of God. Cromwell thought that '[r]eligion was not the thing first contested for, but God brought it to that issue at last'. What had begun as a clash over political rights grew into a manifestation of God's will. Cromwell had few preconcep-tions, but was always seeking God's revelation – 'waiting on the Lord'; this lack of planning is why the Republic lurched from crisis to crisis.

After Charles I's execution, Cromwell then made a name for himself in Ireland; and his Irish experiences made him more determined to create a godly society in England. He described Ireland as 'a clean paper' after his successes there, to be inscribed with an experiment in godliness that would serve as a model for England; there is a parallel here with Strafford's rule in Ireland in the 1630s.[4] The great difference between Cromwell and most of his class was his deep belief in wide religious toleration, a belief well ahead of his time and doomed to failure, without social revolution to accompany it. His dislike of intolerant and persecuting churches was that they stifled free expression and thus the search for God's truth. Cromwell was not a modern religious pluralist; he believed that God's will would be revealed in history, but until then the godly, and in theory only they, should be free to seek it.

Barebone's Parliament, 1653

The very fact of the dissolution of the Rump meant that something novel would have to be tried. The army could not summon a traditional Parliament because it had no authority to do so, and because it would inevitably encounter a hostile and unforgiving assembly. Instead an experiment in divine guidance was undertaken in the calling of a nominated assembly, otherwise known as the 'Parliament of the Saints', or 'Barebone's Parliament' after one of its Members, Praise-God Barebone. It used to be thought that at this juncture power was given over to the Puritan Congregational churches throughout the land who were allowed to nominate the membership. However, despite some contemporary allegations to that effect, it is now clear that it was the Council of Officers that made the final selection, with some individual officers consulting local churches and some congregations sending in their own unsolicited nominations. Of the 139 chosen Members only 15 were nominated by the gathered churches; with the assembly co-opting Cromwell, Lambert and three other army officers to join them the total nominal membership ended up at 144 – much smaller than a traditional Parliament, and even theoretically the Rump. The aim of the Council of Officers was to have an assembly that would undertake godly reform, 'a just and righteous reformation', but what exactly this entailed remained vague. There was a general feeling among enthusiastic Puritans that they were living in 'the last days'; and the Fifth Monarchists, including Colonel Harrison, stressed the imminence of Christ's return to earth and the view that traditional Parliaments were now finished. Cromwell, however, never committed himself to this as an immediate possibility but remained more bound to the old system, seeing the new assembly rather as a means of acclimatising the old ruling class to the need for godly reform. God had given him victory on the battlefield; surely God would now lead the nation through an incorrupt Parliament. The assembly was opened by Cromwell on 4 July in the council chamber at Whitehall, but it soon decided to meet in the old venue of St Stephen's, Westminster, and espouse the name of Parliament, choosing a Speaker in the figure of the old parliamentarian Francis Rous, as well as appointing as its clerk the previous clerk to the Rump. The Members thus did not wish to emphasise any great break with parliamentary tradition; and to judge by Cromwell's opening remarks, he was envisaging two nominated assemblies down to 1655 and then probably the return of a traditionally elected one. Cromwell was not creating a military dictatorship or a cowed assembly because Barebone's Parliament was given the power to decide the composition of the Council of State.

The assembly that finally met was composed overwhelmingly of the gentry, with some exceptions just a rung below the traditional parliamentary kind. Despite Clarendon's famous jibe that 'much the major part of them consisted of inferior persons . . . artificers of the meanest trades', the majority can be legitimately classed as some kind of gentry. Indeed 39 out of the 144 belonged to the county gentry. One was a peer, Viscount Lisle, while four Members would later be made peers by Charles II: Charles Howard, Edward Montagu, Anthony Ashley Cooper and George Monck. Four others would be knighted by Charles II. Well over one-third had been to a university, and a similar proportion had had some legal training at an inn of court. They were therefore not a bunch of wild-eyed fanatics. The overwhelming majority of Members were indeed moderates; only about 47 can be classed as radicals, and only some 12 or 13 were Fifth Monarchists. One important fact of the Barebone's Parliament is that it was the first Parliament to which Scottish and Irish Members were returned: it was thus the first Parliament of

Great Britain, although not the ideal one because the representatives were only of the colonising party in those countries. Scotland returned just four MPs, while Ireland elected six.

Barebone's Parliament was not destined to succeed. Despite its industry in passing more than 30 statutes, including measures allowing civil marriage, new means of registering births, marriages and deaths and of proving wills after the demise of the church courts, the Barebone's would come to grief on the irreparable split between the majority of moderates, who valued property rights, and the minority of radicals, who had less of a vested interest in property. There were not many radicals among the substantial gentry MPs, but many among the lesser gentry and merchants. The minority of millenarian zealots wanted major reforms to the law, especially the codification of law, the abolition both of tithes and of the court of Chancery, and the ending of lay patronage in the Church. Despite the majority of moderates and their landslide victory in the elections to the Council of State in November, the zealots actually succeeded on 17 November in passing an Act by 61 votes to 43 to stop lay patrons choosing clergy. This was a warning to the moderate majority, to whom lay patronage was both a form of property and a way of spreading the Gospel, that the assembly was getting nowhere. The end came on 10 December when the radicals defeated by 56 votes to 54 a clause of a parliamentary report to remove unfit church ministers. The moderates then walked out and surrendered power back to Cromwell, with some 80 Members eventually signing the petition for dissolution. Cromwell had become altogether disillusioned with this Parliament because it had not contributed to reconciling the traditional social elite to the new system and also because a minority had shown intolerance to other Christians of a Puritan bent. It has been argued that Cromwell's refusal to manage his Parliaments in the old Elizabethan way, leaving them instead to their own devices, was a recipe for disaster. True, this negligence did not help, but Cromwell tried to maintain his belief in free Parliaments, and in any case no amount of management would have papered over the gaps of profound disagreement between the various interest groups. The failure of the Saints proved to Cromwell the need for a stronger executive and led to the experiment of the protectorate, based on a document drafted by John Lambert known as the 'Instrument of Government'. Many radicals, especially the millenarians, were thoroughly despairing over the demise of the Barebone's Parliament and became avowed enemies of Cromwell, whose assassination they now planned.

The Instrument of Government and the protectorate, 1653–9

On 16 December 1653 Oliver Cromwell officially became lord protector of England in a ceremony in Westminster Hall, and would remain so till his death in 1658. This period has been dubbed the personal rule of Oliver Cromwell, to be compared to the personal rule of Charles I in the 1630s. Certainly at times it did amount to this and could seem equally authoritarian, with some people believing that little had changed from the days of the king. In 1655, for example, Lord Chief Justice Henry Rolle resigned his position in support of a merchant who refused to pay customs duties not sanctioned by Parliament: it had been Henry's brother John Rolle who had refused to pay Charles I's non-parliamentary customs back in 1628.

Many historians have indeed labelled Cromwell as a military dictator in these years, and superficially it can seem this way. But the notions of both personal rule and military dictatorship are misleading and inaccurate, simply because these were not what Cromwell aimed at, and constitutionally did not achieve. Had he wanted a military dictatorship the best opportunity had already been missed – on the dissolution of the Rump.[5] His use of authoritarian means was an admission of defeat because he had been unable to gain the cooperation and consent for a godly reformation, which all along had been his main priority. Despite dictatorial aspects to his rule, especially in 1655–6, he had no true desire to be a dictator or to seek power for himself. Moreover, his authoritarian rule was accompanied by a new attempt to achieve cooperation with the social conservatives – a trend that makes his policy confusing to follow.

The new system of government was embodied in a written constitution of 42 clauses, the 'Instrument of Government', the work of John Lambert and the army council. As with the term 'Commonwealth', the term 'lord protector' had a familiar ring to it; it was a quasi-regal term – again showing a hankering after tradition. The aim was to have a strengthened executive, but answerable to both Council and Parliament, and harked back to the various solutions put to Charles I between 1641 and 1647. Sovereignty was to reside 'in one person and the people assembled in Parliament: the style of which person shall be the Lord Protector of the Commonwealth of England, Scotland and Ireland'. Oliver Cromwell was declared to be the first lord protector for life, with his successors to be elected by the Council. The leading officers of state were to be chosen with Parliament's support. The executive was vested in the lord protector and a Council of State of 13–21 members. New members were to be chosen by the lord protector from a shortlist of names submitted by the Council from an original list of nominations emanating from Parliament. For every Council vacancy Parliament started the ball rolling by proffering six candidates. Thus all councillors needed parliamentary confidence, but a wide latitude was given to the protector and council for the final decision. Control of the army would be vested in the lord protector and Parliament. Cromwell could never constitutionally be a dictator because of his reliance on the Council and on Parliament.

The legislature was a single-chamber Parliament consisting of 460 Members, including 30 for Ireland and 30 for Scotland. Fewer boroughs were enfranchised now than in the old system and they were allocated only one seat each: so to make up for the loss in borough seats extra county seats were created (depending on the wealth of the county concerned, with for example Essex being allocated 13 seats, and Kent, Somerset and Devon 11 each). Voters became more of an elite group: instead of the old 40-shilling freeholders, county voters now consisted of men who were assessed at £200 in lands or moveable goods. This clause aimed at keeping the poor out of politics. Royalists were also excluded from the vote. Members were to be 'of known integrity, fearing God, and of good conversation'. Parliament was to meet every three years, was to be of five months' duration and could not be dissolved without its own permission. However, truly free Parliaments were now impossible under the provision that the Council would scrutinise the returns and be allowed to exclude unwelcome Members – officially those who had 'abetted in any way against the Parliament'. Between parliamentary sessions, it seems, the lord protector and Council would rule by ordinances, later to be confirmed by Parliament; however, this is not clearly spelled out in the Instrument, which allows for rule by ordinance only up to the very first Parliament. Ordinary government would be carried on with an annual supply of £200 000 (which was less than than what Charles was receiving in the 1630s), and provision was also to be made to finance a normal army of 30 000 men as well as the larger forces currently being employed. Parliamentary legislation could not be vetoed or repealed by the Protector; the most he could do would be to delay it by 20 days, unless the bills aimed to overthrow or change the provisions of the Instrument.

The Instrument of Government also outlined a remarkable religious experiment in religious toleration by forbidding a compulsory confession of faith and allowing toleration of all who professed a basic Christianity, with the exception of Catholics, Anglicans and licentious sectaries. By two ordinances of March and August 1654, the parish churches were given over to Presbyterians, Baptists and Congregationalists. The new ministers, of any one of these persuasions, could expect to be supported still by the parishioners through the continuation of tithes. However, despite compulsory financial support, parishioners were not forced to attend the parish church, although it was expected that they would attend some form of religious meeting. Under an ordinance of March 1654 for the promotion of a godly clergy the suitability of candidates for the Puritan ministry was to be investigated by 38 commissioners called 'triers', and in August another ordinance subjected incumbent ministers to investigation of their competence by county commissioners called 'ejectors'. In practice, the vast majority of ministers conformed and remained in their posts. With ordinary Anglicans and Catholics often left to their own devices, there would never be such wide religious freedom again in England until the nineteenth century. Indeed Catholics were treated better by Cromwell than they had been by Charles I. Furthermore, Jews were to be unofficially invited back into England at the end of 1655, for two reasons: their economic benefit, and above all the need to convert them to Christianity before the millennium and the return of Christ to earth. Cromwell viewed Spanish Catholicism as the great enemy, and he embarked on a neo-Elizabethan foreign policy; he ended the Rump's war against the Dutch and launched a defensive war at sea against Spain.[6]

First Parliament of the protectorate (September 1654 to January 1655)

The new electoral system of the protectorate was designed to create a Parliament of genuine Independents, that is country squires like Cromwell himself – essentially a Parliament of back-benchers. More seats were given to the counties and fewer to the boroughs in order to reduce clientage and patronage by both individuals and the government. The Instrument enormously increased the penalties for a sheriff making a false return from £20 to 2000 marks (about £1350) to show how seriously Cromwell wanted to eliminate corruption. Cromwell seems to have sincerely wished for a free House of Commons (despite the reserve power of the Council to debar unwelcome Members), but Parliament had also to be committed to a godly reformation on the basis of a wide toleration. The problem, of course, was that Cromwell seemingly forgot about the art of parliamentary management. What government could simply expect cooperation and agreement? A part of Cromwell's enigma is that he expected this to happen. More probably he decided not to use management, preferring God's guidance instead. One new possible source of government support and patronage came from the newly conquered and enfranchised Ireland and Scotland, whose seats were kept exclusively for nominees of the English colonising government there. But apart from these 60 nominees the House was composed mainly of independent country gentlemen. Before Parliament met, the Council had objected to the return of eight Members, but as a concession to the House it now cut the army's assessment tax by one-third.

Cromwell's opening speech to Parliament made much about the task of 'healing and settling' the nation, but he then withdrew and left the Members to their deliberations, and waited in hope at Whitehall. He simply assumed agreement – an amazingly naïve attitude in view of the lack of agreement that Cromwell had witnessed over the previous decade or more. He saw himself as a 'good constable to keep the peace of the parish'. A political vacuum was created, into which strode the doctrinaire or classical republicans who detested the Protectorate for its quasi-monarchical constitution. Sir Arthur Haselrig and Thomas Scott returned, and such republicans almost got their nominee John

Bradshaw made Speaker of the House. A week after the opening Cromwell himself came and used force to purge the Parliament of its doctrinaire republicans; about 70–80 Members who refused to acknowledge the legitimacy of the new constitution and sign the 'Recognition' were ousted (in the third purge since 1647). Nevertheless, the House remained uncooperative because it was now dominated by Presbyterians, who hated both Cromwell and the army for the death of the king and for allowing social subversion. They detested the very idea of a standing army as well as such great powers being conferred on Cromwell as lord protector. They abhorred the treason and taxation ordinances and the wide religious freedom of the Instrument, as well as the triers and ejectors. They wished to reduce drastically the monthly army assessment tax. But it was their dislike of religious freedom that drove the biggest wedge between them and the Protector: their refusal to grant 'a just liberty to godly men of differing judgements'. 'What greater hypocrisy', Cromwell charged the MPs, 'than for those who were oppressed by the bishops to become the greatest oppressors themselves'. Cromwell was forced to dissolve this uncooperative Parliament on 22 January 1655 just before the end of its statutory five-month duration, justifying the act by using the lunar rather than the normal calendar, and before it had passed his ordinances and validated the continued collection of the assessment tax.

The early dissolution of the first protectorate Parliament was followed in March 1655 by a small-scale royalist rebellion beginning at Salisbury (Wiltshire) led by John Penruddock, the whole affair being easily suppressed by Major-General Desborough. Some 39 men were condemned either to death or to transportation to Barbados. God seemed to be still on the side of the 'Good Old Cause' of republicanism and religious toleration.

The failure to gain parliamentary support and the anxiety over possible resurgent royalism led to a bold experiment in godly reformation in August 1655. Cromwell and Lambert now believed that the entire country should be pacified and made godly by military means. Thus was instituted the rule of the major-generals, with the whole country being divided up into 11 districts. Cromwell was conscious of the nation's sins: had not God rebuked England by allowing her to be defeated at San Domingo in Hispaniola? The failure of the 'western design' to defeat Spain in the Caribbean and to strike at the economic foundations of Spanish Catholicism was taken as a very grievous blow, and the occupation of Jamaica was not regarded as much of a consolation. Hence the need was discerned for a sweeping godly reformation in order to make the republic prosper in the sight of God. The major-generals would root out the last vestiges of sinful royalism and 'promote godliness and virtue and discourage all profaneness and ungodliness'. Local militias would be set up, to be financed by a 'decimation' tax (a 10 per cent tax on land worth £100 p.a. and goods worth £1500) to be levied on former active royalists (that is, those who had fought for the king in the 1640s; active royalists of the 1650s, of course, would be subject to imprisonment, exile and confiscation). It seemed sensible to make those of a royalist persuasion pay this tax, but besides its dubious legality – that is, could the lord protector govern by ordinance between Parliaments? – it contradicted the Act of Oblivion of 1650, opening up old wounds and alienating the very conservatives whose support Cromwell badly needed to win.

In their campaign to foster godliness the major-generals took action against blasphemy, drunkenness and swearing, as well as against plays and entertainments. The government also banned all newspapers apart from its own two, *Mercurius Politicus* and the *Public Intelligencer*. Cromwell tried to cloak the military essence of the new system by putting the major-generals on the revived commission of the peace, with godly JPs to support them. But the traditional county gentry were not involved and remained hostile to such military rule. The rule of the major-generals came to an end when Parliament undermined them financially by refusing to legalise the 'decimation' tax in January 1657; amazingly, Cromwell had stood idly by while others engineered their demise.[7]

Second Parliament of the protectorate (September 1656–May 1657; January–February 1658)

The need for money for the war against Spain impelled the government to call another Parliament. The major-generals persuaded a rather doubtful Cromwell that they could secure a cooperative House; and this time a full electioneering campaign was undertaken to gain the return of reliable Members. However, this proved a failure, thanks partly to the effective slogan 'No Swordsman! No Decimator!', and partly to the alliance of Presbyterians and republicans to block the election of official candidates. Once again a Parliament of true independent country gentlemen was elected. The doctrinaire republicans returned, but were again purged, this time by the Council of State without Cromwell's apparent support. Over 100 MPs left in this the fourth purge since 1647. However, one ray of sunshine for Cromwell appeared in the large number of monarchists (as distinct from royalists who supported the Stuarts) being elected; and these monarchists now wanted to make Cromwell into a king, partly because the dark day of succession was fast approaching in view of Cromwell's bad health, and they wanted to avoid further upheaval. The 'kingship men' were led by Lord Broghill, a former royalist who had suggested that Cromwell's daughter Frances should marry Charles II; and they were behind Parliament's request of 23 February 1657 that Cromwell should take the title of king. They aimed at civilianising the government: as Cromwell was apparently exercising the powers of a king it seemed sensible to give him the title of one too. Cromwell took the suggestion proposed by a majority of MPs very seriously, but by early May had decided against becoming king, partly because of objections from the army, partly because of fears for the safety of his family should the Stuarts succeed in retaking the throne, but mostly because by this time he had convinced himself that God had turned against monarchy (at least in England) and that it would be seen by the Almighty only as personal pride and ambition for him to revive it. Nevertheless Cromwell agreed to constitutional modifications in the 'Humble Petition and Advice' of 25 May: the lord protector could now name his own successor; an Upper House was restored to Parliament ('the Other House' to consist of 40–70 nominees); councillors had to be approved and dismissed with parliamentary approval; and in order to guarantee 'a free election of the people', MPs could be removed only by vote of the House, not by the lord protector or his Council. Also, supply was increased to £1 300 000 p.a. Cromwell's acceptance of the Humble Petition now led to his breaking with the army, which had protested against it, and with John Lambert who resigned over it and retired to his garden. Lambert seems to have coveted the top job for himself in the event of Cromwell's death, but also suspiciousness of Cromwell's growing moderation was behind his opposition. It appeared to him to be yet another attempt to inch back to the traditional system and to abandon the 'Good Old Cause'. The army's budget was reduced, and Cromwell went over to the civilians; he had long since abandoned wearing an army uniform. A feared army backlash did not occur, and Cromwell was able to imprint his authority on the situation. Although Cromwell had a group of ready-made supporters in the 'kinglings', as some called them, he did not exploit this possibility to manage Parliament, and so wasted a golden opportunity.

When the second session of the Parliament opened in January 1658, the formerly excluded republicans were readmitted by the new Commons committee that could judge the eligibility of men to sit. Accordingly the troublemakers Scott and Haselrig were readmitted. There was also a new Upper House in this second session, for which nominees had to be found. Cromwell's former partisans of the 1640s – Saye and Sele, Lord Wharton and Oliver St John – coldly refused his offer of a seat in the new House. So army officers and House of Commons men had to be moved upstairs to make a total of 63, among them Broghill, Whitelocke, Monck and Richard Cromwell. With his best men upstairs Cromwell was forced to watch his republican opponents take over the Commons and render it useless to the government. Finally he personally dissolved Parliament and dismissed some junior officers in his own regiment whom he suspected of disaffection at a critical time of a feared Spanish invasion. Cromwell was obeyed, but only grudgingly. The future was still unknown. There was no vast support for the Stuarts, and it may well be that Cromwell made a big mistake in rejecting the Crown. An ensconced Cromwellian dynasty was at least an equal match for the exiled Stuarts. But Cromwell was not a king, and he was not to live much longer. Cromwell's rule had enlarged England's prestige abroad; his 'gun-boat diplomacy' had overawed Europeans. The capture of Dunkirk in 1658 seemed a recompense for the loss of Calais in 1558. Yet the Spanish war was not popular at home, involving loss of trade and appearing anachronistic; opponents pointed to the greater danger to national interests emanating from Sweden and France.

Cromwell's death on 3 September 1658 led to the Protectorate continuing under his designated successor, his son Richard Cromwell. However, Richard had hitherto led a quiet life and had in no way been trained by his father to take over until 1657, when he became a privy councillor and was nominated to the Upper House. He was a true moderate country squire, who had never seen active military service and who therefore had no standing within the army. Perhaps Oliver consciously desired to continue with civilianising the government. But the army leaders were soon dissatisfied and demanded a new commander-in-chief separate from the head of state. Richard was now propelled to the front of the political stage without any necessary experience or aptitude. His chances of success were therefore slim.

In this final period of the Republic all the different political groups tried to find a solution to the problem of England's government, but all failed. Richard Cromwell relied on civilians rather than on the army leaders, even on some conservatives outside the Council, such as his brother-in-law Lord Fauconberg. General Monck advised Richard to root out 'insolent spirits' from the army and to win over conservatives. Because of the desperate need for money and also to take decisions on foreign policy, Richard called his only Parliament (January–April 1659). The majority of country squires in the House were supportive of Richard and the protectorate, but antagonistic to the political powers of the army and to the current wide religious freedom. The minority of parliamentary radicals desperately made common cause with dissidents outside, such as disgruntled junior officers and sectaries, and called for an end to the protectorate and the return of the 'Good Old Cause'. The Grandees, such as Desborough and Fleetwood, not to be left isolated, joined republicans like Haselrig and Vane and forced Richard to dissolve Parliament without supply being granted (22 April). The Grandees would have liked to have kept Richard as a figurehead, but their political and army allies were set against the Protectorate in any form. However, the army had no real solution of its own to put forward: its bankruptcy of ideas was proved by its decision to recall the Members of the old (single-chamber) Rump Parliament, whereupon in May 1659 Richard resigned as protector. He was succeeded as commander-in-chief of the army by Charles Fleetwood. The Rumpers, of course, were no happier with the army than they had been originally between 1649 and 1653; and the Rump was dissolved – for a second time – on 13 October 1659. Slightly earlier, a royalist rebellion in Lancashire and Cheshire led by Sir George Booth (a Presbyterian) was easily quashed by Lambert at Nantwich. At this stage there was still no overwhelming support for the Stuart cause, and even Booth was more of a champion of free Parliaments than of the Stuart dynasty, and his proclamation had not actually mentioned Charles II at all. It would indeed take more chaos over the next few months in order for the Stuarts to be seen as the essential saviours of the realm.

A short-lived Committee of Safety under Major-General Charles Fleetwood was then set up by the army to rule, but it also failed because it received no wider support. The conservative generals Monck and Fairfax, together with the navy, declared for the second return of the Rump, whose Members traipsed back to Westminster in December 1659. Monck was a realist, as well as an ex-royalist, and having bought no lands during the upheaval had less of a vested interest in the Republic, but at this stage he had no clear plan. The Scottish army under Monck marched south and occupied London on 3 February 1660. Despite his earlier promises to be faithful to the Rump, Monck could see how unpopular that small assembly really was. Therefore, with no solution forthcoming from the Rump or from the army, Monck decided to recall the old Members who had been purged by Colonel Pride back in 1648. The overwhelming majority of the restored Long Parliament were non-republican conservatives, so that all was now set for the return of the Stuarts. On 16 March 1660 the Long Parliament declared itself legally dissolved, but had arranged for free elections under the old franchise to a Convention of Lords and Commons – not a Parliament, which only a true king could summon. The Convention had a majority in favour of the Stuarts, and Monck agreed with their request. In May 1660 Charles II returned to England and was met by Monck at Dover. Charles II was not restored to the throne by the people – although probably had there been a referendum he would have won – but by the landowning class. They had finally grasped the fact that a legitimate monarch was necessary to maintain the whole fabric of inherited land and wealth. The Puritan diarist Ralph Josselin saw clearly that the men of power recalled Charles Stuart 'out of love to themselves not him'. The crisis of authority was finally resolved.

The radical sects

The period of the Civil Wars and the Republic also witnessed an amazing outburst of plebeian thought in both the spoken and the written word on a scale previously unknown in the whole history of the world. Radical religious and political ideas proliferated because the blanket of censorship was for a time lifted in the years after 1641. Christianity had often been used by the ruling class in its own interests to keep the lower orders down. But, of course, the New Testament is a revolutionary document, which says that there is no difference between the rich and poor, male and female, that the meek shall inherit the earth and the rich find it almost impossible to enter the kingdom of heaven. The Bible in the hands of ordinary people was explosive material, leading them to conclusions not sanctioned by the ruling landowning class.

What collapsed in mid-seventeenth-century England was the concept of authority, in both religion and the state. Authority had been challenged before, of course, but never so comprehensively or with such seeming success. We know so little about the thoughts of ordinary people before 1642 because of the government's heavy censorship of ideas. Heterodox thought before that date comes to the surface mainly because of the campaign to stifle it, normally in the law courts. Yet there seems no reason to doubt that people thought for themselves in ways not congenial to the Establishment. Christopher Hill has emphasised the disruptive effects of the growth of capitalism and unemployment on the land, with the increase in the numbers of rootless people or 'masterless men'. The Civil Wars intensified geographical mobility, and the New Model Army provided a perfect environment for the spread of radical ideas.[8]

The aim of the radicals in the 1640s and 1650s was to 'turn the world upside down', an expression they obtained from the Bible (Psalm 146; Isaiah 24: 1–2, 20–1; Acts of the Apostles 17: 6) to indicate the inverting of normality when traditional authority is overthrown and the poor inherit the earth. Of the main radical sects that grew up in these years all of them combined political and religious thought; there were no purely political or secular groups in the modern sense because the religious idiom was all-pervasive. But two were more political than religious: the 'democratic' Levellers and the agrarian–communist Diggers. Of the overtly religious sects the most important were the Quakers, Baptists, Fifth Monarchy Men and Muggletonians. All of these sects were opposed to a comprehensive state Church. Most of the above reacted against Calvinist predestination and in favour of free will, with the exception of the Fifth Monarchists and the Particular Baptists, who retained a Calvinist theology, while the Muggletonians had their own strange version of predestination. All the sects took the Protestant notion of the priesthood of all believers to its logical conclusion, with chaotic results. Many of the sects were millenarian, awaiting the second coming of Christ who would rule the earth for a thousand years with his saints. The Muggletonians had a variation on this, believing that the damned would inherit a desolate earth, while the elect went to heaven.

The importance of the radical sects lay not in their numbers, for they were always a small minority – the majority of English people appear to have remained loyal to the ideal of parish Anglicanism.[9] The Prayer Book would triumph again in 1660, but because of the experience of a wide toleration under the Republic and the organisation which the sects had built up, there could be no return to a comprehensive state Church after 1660.

Epilogue: the Restoration and beyond

The Stuart monarchy was restored in 1660. What does this tell us about the nature of the mid-century upheaval? Can one speak of a 'revolution' having taken place at all in view of the return of monarchy? Alternatively, had the nature of the monarchy after 1660 now changed so significantly for one to be able to use the word 'revolution' even in a monarchic context? Were its consequences made clear and permanent in the reigns of the later Stuart kings, Charles II (1660–85) and his brother James II (1685–8)?

Historians are divided over the nature of later Stuart England. Those of a Marxist persuasion might still see the Civil War period as constituting the decisive break, as the world's first 'bourgeois revolution', defeating feudalism and absolutism. Whig–Liberals accept the significance of the Civil Wars, along with the Glorious Revolution of 1688–9, in preventing absolutism. But modern revisionist sceptics, on the other hand, see little significance in such 'petulant outbursts' that hardly disturbed England's Old Regime.[1] Indeed revisionists claim that after 1660 royal policy was moving, whether intentionally or not, towards authoritarianism or even absolutism in England, which thus negated the whole idea that a genuine revolution had taken place.[2] It can be claimed that '[i]n some ways English government in the early 1680s approximated more closely to French "absolutism" than ever before'.[3]

The modern debate between traditionalists and revisionists on the causation and impact of the wars can be traced to the seventeenth century itself. Much has been made in modern times of the Civil Wars as the inevitable result of the rise of the gentry class, who demanded political power commensurate with their new economic wealth gained from the capitalist exploitation of their estates.[4] This idea of political change consequent on economic and social change was held by James Harrington, who in his *Oceana* (1656) claimed that the acquisition of land by 'the people' – by whom he meant the monied sort, the gentry and merchants – enriched them at the expense of the monarch and nobles, who were thus destined to lose power in the political 'superstructure' (he uses the very word that Marxism was to make famous). This was similar to what Marx and Engels believed in the late nineteenth century, and was taken up by historians in the twentieth century to popularise the view of the English Civil War as a 'bourgeois revolution' in which the great capitalist gentry are viewed as a rural bourgeoisie. In contrast, the modern-day revisionist view of the Civil Wars as only the result of short-term errors of judgement, and in no way destined, was propagated by Edward Hyde, Earl of Clarendon in his *History of the Rebellion* (1702).

Had England experienced a genuine, permanent revolution or only a failed rebellion? A 'rebellion' is considered as having fewer long-term causes, as being less 'inevitable' and more the result of short-term mistakes by those at the top. A 'revolution', on the other hand, is seen as probably the result of a long build-up of discontent, more predictably as the result of social and economic change, more drastic in its consequences and more likely to be permanent. A wider variety of social groups are presumably involved in a revolution than in a rebellion.

One criterion for 'revolution' is revolutionary motivation and self-consciousness, but this idea that once seemed clear about the English Civil War must now be abandoned: in no way were the leading opponents of the Court before 1640 a self-conscious revolutionary opposition. Thanks to revisionism we now know that no one thought in such terms; there was no revolutionary model for them to follow, and almost everyone looked for consensus. The Civil Wars were fought between different members of the same gentry class. One of the old arguments of the 'bourgeois revolution' thesis was that the line of demarcation between the different sides in the war was an economic one, that the progressive capitalist gentry fought for Parliament while the backward feudal types fought for the king. However, this notion will no longer stand up: it is false to see the king's side as uncomplicatedly feudal and his opponents as brash capitalists. Lawrence Stone, for example, has demonstrated that in a sample of wicked capitalist-style depopulating enclosers an overwhelming majority actually fought for the king, and even the Marxist

Robert Brenner has traced the emergence of the nobility into a neo-capitalist class that desired absolute property ownership and a contractual relationship with capitalist tenants.[5] Nowadays those historians who see the Civil War period as constituting a revolution place the emphasis on the quite unforeseen consequences of opposition to the Crown and on more impersonal trends.

No matter how much one might make of the medieval-style opening of the first Civil War under aristocratic leadership, there can be no doubt that events escalated out of the nobles' control and that they were soon put on the sidelines. More than a 'rebellion' occurred. The execution of the king after a public trial, the abolition of the monarchy and of the House of Lords, the proclamation of the Republic, the great degree of religious freedom accorded to ordinary people in this decade as well as their ability to express radical political and religious views all bear out that a genuine revolution occurred between 1649 and 1660, of an unprecedented kind. Of course, such revolutionary fervour was soon to be quashed and religious freedom curtailed. A revolution does not necessarily have to be permanent. Was this period, therefore, just an amazing interlude, whose significance had to be suppressed by the ruling elite, or had major structural changes occurred that would make England a different sort of state after 1660 from what it had been prior to 1640?

Christopher Hill has emphasised the great differences between the England of 1700 and the England of 1600 – changes which he attributes to the 'bourgeois revolution' of the mid-century.[6] The revolution, he believes, established new economic conditions in which capitalism could flourish and bloom. Above all, the abolition of feudal tenures and and the institution of wardship in favour of true freehold allowed landowners to develop their estates without royal intrusion, allowing long-term investment in a capitalist agriculture, and also weakening the monarchy as against the landowners. However, the greater security which the big landowners obtained they were not prepared to share with others beneath them, whose security thus decreased. Furthermore, the abolition of monopolies and non-parliamentary taxation meant that the king could no longer directly intervene in the economic system. Lawrence Stone agrees with Hill that the consequences of all this were good for capitalism: 1642 and 1689 'made possible the seizure of political power by landed, mercantile and banking elites'.[7] There is certainly no doubt that economically England's position improved remarkably between 1600 and 1700, but it has proved difficult to link those improvements specifically with the political revolution. England's capitalism and sense of individualism had been developing well before. Nevertheless, there is no gainsaying the economic benefits to the gentry of the freeing up of the land market with the abolition of the vestiges of feudal law, or the benefits that merchants derived from the abolition of monopolies and purveyance. Whether this is enough to constitute a 'bourgeois revolution' must remain a matter of opinion.

Had there been a political revolution which left its mark on the post-1660 period? This remains a contentious issue, between those who regard the reigns of Charles II and James II as developing towards an inevitable absolutism that was frustrated only by James II's foolishness and those historians who regard any attempt at absolutism as doomed to failure because of the real changes to English politics that flowed from the mid-century upheaval. What both sides can agree on is that the Restoration Settlement of 1660 was extremely vague.

The return of Charles II in May 1660 was technically *unconditional*. This is a crucial point: the new king was not forced to accept any limitations placed on him by Parliament. On 8 May Charles Stuart was declared by the Convention to be the rightful King of England. Of course, the reasonableness of Charles's recent offer made from his exiled court in the Netherlands in the Declaration of Breda (4 April 1660) helped smooth his path home. This Declaration offered to heal the wounds of civil war with a 'free and generous pardon' to all except those specified by Parliament, a 'liberty to tender consciences', the confirmation of titles to lands, and the payment of arrears in wages to the army. All these offers were to be subject to Parliament's approval. But Charles undertook nothing specific either before or immediately after his accession. Nevertheless, his references to Parliament in the Declaration and letters to Monck led to the assumption that he would support the authority of Parliament. The unconditional nature of the Restoration was not to be taken as a blank cheque for the future monarchy; it was just that the fear of anarchy goaded the landowning class into a quick acceptance of Charles's offer. Charles went on voluntarily to accept the reforming legislation which his father had conceded in 1641–2, including the abolition of non-parliamentary taxation and the prerogative courts, but not the exclusion of bishops from the House of Lords. Does the situation after 1660, with the acceptance of the reforms of 1641, now mean that a significant and permanent change had occurred?

First of all, what exactly was restored? The monarch returned to his lands, he was head of the executive, commander-in-chief of the army, supreme governor of the Church of England; he appointed ministers, bishops and judges; all legislation had to be approved by him and he could veto what he disliked. He could also dispense individuals from the provisions of Acts of Parliament. Foreign affairs were still his sole province. However, he could no longer raise non-parliamentary taxes as his father had done and, it seemed, had to rule with Parliament, which was meant to meet every three years. However, the Triennial Act of 1641 which had included machinery for calling the Parliament automatically with or without the king's permission was replaced by a new Act in 1664 which merely requested its calling without any procedure for doing so without the king. Nevertheless, cooperation with regular Parliaments was assumed, and the Cavalier Parliament set a precedent by being in session from 1661 to 1679 on a fairly regular annual basis; there was thus a new political atmosphere. The prerogative courts were gone, apart from the council in the Marches which had been given a reprieve. The privy council lost its judicial functions, and all legal appeals now went to the House of Lords. The king was no longer expected to 'live of his own' but received £1 200 000 a year from Parliament, drawn from customs and excise and also later from a hearth tax: this amount could be topped up if necessary by additional taxes voted in Parliament. In many ways this scheme resembled the 'Great Contract' of 1610, except that now the great landowners won, with the merchant sector footing the bill – and also the poor drinkers through the beer excise. The traditional Parliament was restored with both Lords and Commons, as well as the traditional franchise. The Anglican Church once more was established as the state Church, but after the defection of Nonconformists in 1662 it could no longer pretend to be comprehensive.

What kind of monarchy existed after 1660? This is a difficult question to answer because the Settlement was pragmatic and based on not asking too many questions but on being hopeful of cooperation. Essentially the monarchy was restored to the position it had found itself in at the beginning of 1642, but that had been an unstable situation which had led to war; the king had been reduced in his prerogatives, but he was still powerful, and Parliament had not trusted him. Now in 1660 the arrangement could work only if both sides trusted each other; there was nothing in the Settlement itself that guaranteed success. Charles II said that he did not want to go on his travels again, while the gentry in Parliament urgently needed the king as a defence against the mob.

The constitutional situation after 1660 was thus ambiguous. It has been usual to argue that the monarchy of Charles II was weaker than that of his father. J. P. Kenyon in 1985 claimed that 'its [the monarchy's] authority was now defined and confined'.[8] Christopher Hill and Lawrence Stone believe that only the trappings of monarchy were restored, not its essential inner power.[9] The confirmation of the abolition of feudal tenures can be seen as putting the king on a new footing with his leading subjects – more of a first among equals than feudal overlord. The restored monarchy can also be viewed as suffering psychologically from the public trial and execution of Charles I. However, this traditionalist approach was challenged in 1982 by Angus McInnes, who claimed that royal powers were hardly, if at all, curtailed after 1660.[10] Indeed, he writes, '[i]n so far as the civil war had been fought to place further tangible limits on the crown, it had proved a dismal failure'. McInnes denies that Parliament after 1660 was as powerful as historians have generally assumed. Because the Triennial Act of 1641 was modified in 1664 to make three-year Parliaments merely desirable rather than mandatory, there was nothing to stop Charles II ruling without Parliaments – as he did for the last four years of his life. Historians have usually emphasised Charles II's unwillingness to antagonise Parliament, yet on some crucial points he was adamant – notably on the succession of his Catholic brother James Duke of York to the throne, against the wishes of many Protestants. During the Exclusion Crisis of 1678–81 when political parties were born, the Whig party led by the Earl of Shaftesbury tried to bar the succession of the Duke of York, and the country underwent another period of religious upheaval with allegations of a 'Polish Plot'. But on this occasion Charles would not budge, and finally smashed the Whigs, purging them from public office and ending up as a Tory Anglican 'absolutist'. One of McInnes's major points is that the influence of the Civil Wars was not all one-way, that is to say not all in the direction of reducing the powers of the Crown. The Civil Wars had unleashed the power of the the masses, 'the many-headed monster', and this had instilled fears in the hearts of the landowning class, whose aim was now to clamp down on the lower orders. One reason why Charles II triumphed over the Whigs was that they had appealed directly to the common people for support, and indeed had initiated the practice of widespread political canvassing, which in the end undermined them in the eyes of the majority of the squirearchy. By 1681 the landowners put class domination before their religious principles, but Charles was required to pay their price and support the Anglican Church. Thus because they feared the masses, many former critics of Charles I now veered back to support the restored monarchy, William Prynne among them.

Moreover, the reforms of 1641, argues McInnes, did not radically reduce the king's powers after 1660; and the really crucial demands of the opposition in 1641–2 – parliamentary control of the privy council and of the army – were never conceded. A standing army was accumulated, which by the time of James II stood at 40 000 men. Thus what had been one of the most sensitive points in the early Stuart period and the technical justification for going to war in 1642 – the gentry's worry over being cowed by a standing army – was now resolved decisively in the king's favour.

Charles II died in his bed, a convert to Catholicism, and was succeeded by the openly Catholic James II – the worst nightmare of English Protestants. Yet the common people were held in such fear by the ruling elite that James was initially welcomed with open arms and given an income of £2 million a year. It was only because he made some fundamental mistakes – in reality the most foolish imaginable, including his instigation of social revolution to help along the Catholicisation of the country – that he was to be swept from power at the end of 1688. While the squires could tolerate Charles II's 'absolutism' based on Anglicanism and their own entrenched supremacy, they could not abide being replaced as local governors under James by lower-born Dissenters to whom the king was forced to appeal in order to obtain support for his Catholicism. Had James II, like his brother, forged an alliance with the Anglican elite his 'absolutism' might have gone on for some considerable time rather than being cut short. Certainly the royalist revival of the 1680s was completely out of harmony with the trends of the mid-century. But it would be foolish to conclude that this royalist trend could go on indefinitely or that 'by the 1680s England was once more approaching the condition of an absolute monarchy, a country different in detail [only] from the classic absolutist states of continental Europe'.[11] Not only were the details very important – no absolutist bureaucracy in England – but also the whole trend of English history was against it. Lord Saye and Sele had declared that the nobles traditionally

> have preserved the just rights and liberties against the tyrannical usurpation of kings, and . . . upheld the Crown from falling and being cast down upon the floor by the insolency of the multitude.

The insolence of the multitude had been curbed by the Restoration; it was now the turn of tyrannical kings to be tamed. Hence the aristocratic coup that overthrew James II.

A more far-reaching settlement than that of 1660 could then be achieved. The Bill of Rights (1689) prevented the king keeping a standing army in peacetime without parliamentary sanction; it banned the use of the king's power to dispense individuals from parliamentary legislation, and the levying of non-parliamentary taxes. It also called for frequent Parliaments, which in fact had annual sessions because of the need to confirm the Mutiny Act, which allowed the keeping of a standing army that was now vital for England's new role in the world. The new coronation oath reflected the new contractual monarchy and the demise of divine-right kingship. The monarch was to rule henceforth with 'the statutes in Parliament agreed on'. A genuine constitutional monarchy had emerged. By the Act of Settlement of 1701 royal powers were further limited by ensuring that judges could not be dismissed at the royal will but only with parliamentary approval.

There seems little reason to doubt the profound changes wrought by the English Civil Wars, even if there was an urgent need to cloak them in 1660. One cannot imagine the swiftness and completeness of the Glorious Revolution without the execution of Charles I and the experience of the Republic. There had undoubtedly been a significant political shift, and although English capitalism had been under way for some time one must not undervalue the death of fiscal feudalism in assessing the growth of capitalist agriculture, or the abolition of monopolies and purveyance in the success of the 'commercial revolution' of the second half of the seventeenth century.

Perhaps the best indicator of the change in the monarchy's situation is in regards to religion. All the Tudor monarchs and the first two Stuarts were in a meaningful sense in control of the Church, imposing their will to a large extent on that institution and its beliefs. Although Charles II was supreme governor of the Church of England, he did not exercise the power that his father had wielded. After 1660 Anglicanism was defended by Parliament: the reality henceforth was parliamentary control of the Church. When Charles II tried to use his authority in order to give toleration to Nonconformists and Catholics by his Declaration of Indulgence of 1672, he had to back down in the face of the hostile Anglican Cavalier Parliament and accept the Test Act of 1673 to ensure that only true Anglicans received public employment. It was now the Anglican Parliament that persecuted Nonconformists. In opposition to those historians who emphasised England's rapid rise to modernity after 1660 a sceptical revisionist attitude has grown up in recent years which portrays England from 1660 to 1832 as an Old Regime confessional state. Perhaps the truth lies in between these two extremes: England may not have been a modern capitalist state hurtling towards industrialisation after 1660, but with colonies and a 'commercial revolution' in the offing, England in 1660 looked very different from the way it had in 1460 – an England about to make its mark, for good or ill, on the world stage.

Notes

Prologue

1. P. Laslett, *The World We Have Lost* (2nd edn, London, 1971), p. 127.
2. All figures are vague: see S. M. Jack, *Towns in Tudor and Stuart Britain* (Basingstoke, 1996), p. 173.
3. E. Kerridge, *The Agricultural Revolution* (London, 1967); *The Farmers of Old England* (London, 1973).
4. J. V. Beckett, *The Agricultural Revolution* (London, 1991), p. 40.
5. First proven use was in Dorset in 1608: M. Overton, *Agricultural Revolution in England* (Cambridge, 1996), p. 112.
6. A. Macfarlane, *The Origins of English Individualism* (Oxford, 1978), pp. 165ff.

1 The Wars of the Roses

1. S. B. Chrimes, *Lancastrians, Yorkists and Henry VII* (London, 1966), p. xiv. R. L. Storey, *The End of the House of Lancaster* (1st edn, London, 1966), p. 6.
2. K. Dockray, 'The Origins of the Wars of the Roses', in A. J. Pollard (ed.), *The Wars of the Roses* (New York, 1995), p. 82.
3. Dockray, 'The Origins of the Wars of the Roses', pp. 76–8.
4. Storey, *End*, p. 162.
5. R. A. Griffiths, *The Reign of King Henry VI* (London, 1981), p. 772.
6. The emblems refer to York, Norfolk, Salisbury and Warwick.
7. Griffiths, *Henry VI*, p. 822.
8. *The Times* (London, 17 Oct. 1997).
9. From 'readept' to recover.
10. F. Hepburn, *Portraits of the Later Plantagenets* (Woodbridge, 1986), pp. 56ff and plates 41, 44.
11. C. Ross, *The Wars of the Roses*, (London, 1976), p. 43.
12. J. R. Lander, *Crown and Nobility, 1450–1509* (London, 1976), p. 62.
13. A. Goodman, *Wars of the Roses* (London, 1981), pp. 227–8.
14. A. J. Pollard, *The Wars of the Roses* (New York, 1988), pp. 74–5.
15. R. H. Britnell, 'The Economic Context' in A. J. Pollard (ed.), *The Wars of the Roses* (New York, 1995), p. 46.
16. J. Gillingham, *The Wars of the Roses* (London, 1981), p. 1.
17. Goodman, *Wars of the Roses*, p. 209.
18. K. B. McFarlane, 'Extinction and Recruitment', in his *The Nobility of Later Medieval England* (Oxford, 1973), p. 147.

19. The third Duke of Buckingham and the fifth Earl of Northumberland.
20. K. B. McFarlane, 'The Wars of the Roses', *Proceedings of the British Academy*, 1 (1964), p. 115.

2 The Restored Monarchy, 1461–1509: Edward IV, Richard III and Henry VII

1. R. A. Griffiths, in K. Morgan (ed.), *The Oxford History of Britain* (Oxford, 1988), p. 236.
2. A. Goodman, *The New Monarchy: England, 1471–1534* (Oxford, 1988).
3. J. Watts, '"A newe ffundacion of is crowne": Monarchy in the Age of Henry VII', in B. Thompson (ed.), *The Reign of Henry VII* (Stamford, 1995), pp. 31–53.
4. C. Ross, *Edward IV* (London, 1974), pp. 306–7.
5. C. Carpenter, *The Wars of the Roses* (Cambridge, 1997), p. 187.
6. Ross, *Edward IV*, pp. 331–41.
7. Ross, *Edward IV*, p. 334.
8. Carpenter, *Wars of the Roses*, pp. 182–95.
9. R. Horrox, *Richard III: a Study of Service* (Cambridge, 1989), pp. 92–3; C. Richmond, '1483: the Year of Decision', in J. Gillingham (ed.), *Richard III. A Medieval Kingship* (London, 1993), pp. 44–7.
10. Horrox, *Richard III*, pp. 111–12.
11. C. T. Wood, 'Richard III, William Lord Hastings and Friday the Thirteenth', in R.A. Griffiths and J. Sherborne (eds), *Kings and Nobles in the Later Middle Ages* (Gloucester, 1986), pp. 157ff.
12. J. Potter, *Good King Richard?* (London, 1983), pp. 41–4.
13. M. O'Regan, 'The Pre-contract and its Effect on the Succession in 1483', in J. Petre (ed.), *Richard III Crown and People* (London, 1985), pp. 51–6.
14. A. Weir, *The Princes in the Tower* (London, 1992), p. 253.
15. Horrox, *Richard III*, pp. 166–77; C. Ross, *Richard III* (London, 1981), pp. 105ff., esp. 111–12.
16. Horrox, *Richard III*, pp. 282–3.
17. C. Richmond, 'The Battle of Bosworth', *History Today*, 35 (August 1985), pp. 17–22; P. J. Foss, 'The Battle of Bosworth: Towards a Reassessment', *Midland History*, 13 (1988), 21–33.
18. Bacon did criticise Henry's avariciousness.
19. For an unpersuasive revisionist view of Henry VII and a caricature of Tudor historiography, see Carpenter, *Wars of the Roses*, pp. 219ff.
20. S. B. Chrimes, *Henry VII* (London, 1972), p. 183.
21. M. Condon, 'Ruling Elites in the Reign of Henry VII', in C. Ross (ed.), *Patronage, Pedigree and Power in Late Medieval England* (Gloucester, 1979), p. 130.

22. J. Currin, 'Henry VII and the Treaty of Redon (1489): Plantagenet Ambitions and Early Tudor Foreign Policy', *History*, 81 (1996), 343–58.
23. T. B. Pugh, 'Henry VII and the English Nobility', in G.W. Bernard (ed.), *The Tudor Nobility* (Manchester, 1992), pp. 77, 82.
24. C. Carpenter, 'Henry VII and the English Polity', in Thompson, *Reign of Henry VII*, p. 22.
25. Pugh, 'Henry VII', p. 78.
26. Storey, *Henry VII*, p. 213; Carpenter, *Wars of the Roses*, p. 248.

3 The Reign of Henry VIII, 1509–47

1. L. Baldwin Smith, *Henry VIII. The Mask of Royalty* (London, 1971), p. 23.
2. P. Gwyn, *The King's Cardinal: the Rise and Fall of Thomas Wolsey* (London, 1990), p. 23; S. M. Jack, 'Henry VIII's Attitude Towards Royal Finance: Penny Wise and Pound Foolish?', in C. Giry-Deloison (ed.), *François I et Henri VIII. Deux Princes de la Renaissance* (Lille, 1996), pp. 145–63.
3. Gwyn, *King's Cardinal*, pp. 11–12.
4. D. Starkey, *The Reign of Henry VIII* (London, 1985), pp. 76–81.
5. G. Walker, 'The "expulsion of the minions" of 1519 reconsidered', *Historical Journal*, 32 (1989), pp. 1–16; Gwyn, *King's Cardinal*, pp. 555–61.
6. G. R. Elton, *Reform and Reformation* (London, 1977), p. 49.
7. J. J. Scarisbrick, *Henry VIII* (London, 1968), p. 240.
8. J. Guy, *The Cardinal's Court: the Impact of Wolsey in Star Chamber* (Hassocks, 1977).
9. J. J. Scarisbrick, 'Cardinal Wolsey and the Common Weal', in E. W. Ives *et al.* (eds), *Wealth and Power in Tudor England* (London, 1978), pp. 45–67.
10. With personal meetings between Henry and the Emperor in England (May 1520), and with Francis at the Field of Cloth of Gold, near Calais (June 1520).
11. A. F. Pollard, *Wolsey* (London, 1965 reprint), pp. 121, 124.
12. D. S. Chambers, 'Cardinal Wolsey and the Papal Tiara', *Bulletin of the Institute of Historical Research*, 38 (1965), pp. 20–30.
13. Scarisbrick, *Henry VIII*, p. 139.
14. P. Gwyn, 'Wolsey's Foreign Policy: the Conferences of Calais and Bruges Reconsidered', *Historical Journal*, 23 (1980), pp. 755–72. Gwyn, *King's Cardinal*, pp. 147ff.
15. G. W. Bernard, *War, Taxation and Rebellion in Tudor England: Henry VIII, Wolsey and the Amicable Grant of 1525* (Brighton, 1986), p. 24.
16. Gwyn, *King's Cardinal*, p. 399.
17. Scarisbrick, *Henry VIII*, p. 229.
18. Starkey, *Reign of Henry VIII*, pp. 99–100.

19. E. Ives, 'The Fall of Wolsey', in S. J. Gunn and P. G. Lindley (eds), *Cardinal Wolsey: Church, State and Art* (Cambridge, 1991), p. 288.
20. Gwyn, *King's Cardinal*, pp. 633ff; G. W. Bernard, 'The Fall of Wolsey Reconsidered', *Journal of British Studies*, 35 (1996), pp. 277–310.
21. Gwyn, *King's Cardinal*, pp. 599–639.
22. G. R. Elton, *England under the Tudors* (3rd edn, London, 1991), p. 127.
23. G. W. Bernard, 'Elton's Cromwell', *History*, 83 (1998), pp. 587–607.
24. J. Guy, 'Wolsey, Cromwell and the Reform of Government', in D. MacCulloch (ed.), *The Reign of Henry VIII* (Basingstoke, 1995), pp. 48–53.
25. P. R. Roberts, 'The English Crown, the Principality of Wales and the Council in the Marches', in B. Bradshaw and J. Morrill (eds), *The British Problem, c.1534–1707* (Basingstoke, 1996), pp. 123–9.
26. For the debate see: G. Bernard, 'The Fall of Anne Boleyn' *English Historical Review*, 106 (1991), pp. 584–610; E. Ives, 'The Fall of Anne Boleyn Reconsidered', *English Historical Review*, 107 (1992), pp. 561–4; G. Bernard's 'Rejoinder', *English Historical Review*, 107, (1992), pp. 665–74.
27. E. Ives, 'Faction at the Court of Henry VIII: the Fall of Anne Boleyn', *History*, 57 (1972), pp. 169–88; *Anne Boleyn* (Oxford, 1986).
28. R. Warnicke, 'The Fall of Anne Boleyn', *History*, 70 (1985), pp. 1–15, esp. p. 3.
29. Starkey, *Reign of Henry VIII*, pp. 108–15.
30. Retha Warnicke, *The Rise and Fall of Anne Boleyn* (Cambridge, 1989), pp. 191–204, 246.
31. Elton, *Reform and Reformation*, p. 297.
32. Smith, *Henry VIII*, p. 23.
33. E. A. Bonner, 'The Genesis of Henry VIII's "Rough Wooing" of the Scots', *Northern History*, 33 (1997), pp. 11–14.
34. A. F. Pollard, *England under the Protector Somerset* (London, 1900), pp. 1–38.
35. L. B. Smith, 'The Last Will and Testament of Henry VIII: a Question of Perspective', *Journal of British Studies*, 2 (1962), pp. 14–27; Smith, *Henry VIII*, Ch. 12.
36. Scarisbrick, *Henry VIII*, pp. 487–95.
37. Starkey, *Reign of Henry VIII*, p. 167.
38. E. Ives, 'Henry VIII's Will – a Forensic Conundrum', *Historical Journal*, 35 (1992), pp. 779–804. Debate with R. Houlbrooke, *Historical Journal*, 37 (1994), pp. 891–914.

4 The Henrician Reformation

1. A. G. Dickens, *The English Reformation* (London, 1964), p. 107.

2. This statute attempted to curb the power of the church courts *vis-à-vis* the royal courts, and was a product of the tensions between Church and state in the later Middle Ages. It was not normally invoked when Church and state were in harmony.

3. C. Haigh, *English Reformations* (Oxford, 1993), p. 42.

4. Dickens, *English Reformation*, pp. 30–1.

5. J. F. Davis, 'Lollardy and the Reformation in England,' in P. Marshall (ed.), *The Impact of the English Reformation* (London, 1997), pp. 17–37.

6. C. Harper-Bill, *The Pre-Reformation Church in England, 1400–1530* (London, 1996), pp. 82–3; J. A. F. Thomson, *The Early Tudor Church and Society, 1485–1529* (London, 1993), pp. 352–6.

7. J. A. F. Thomson, *The Later Lollards, 1414–1520* (London, 1965), pp. 198–201.

8. J. J. Scarisbrick, *The Reformation and the English People* (Oxford, 1984), p. 1.

9. S. Brigden, *London and the Reformation* (Oxford, 1989), pp. 30, 43.

10. Haigh, *English Reformations*, p. 37.

11. Scarisbrick, *Reformation*, p. 8.

12. E. Duffy, *The Stripping of the Altars* (Newhaven, Conn., 1993), p. 4.

13. A. F. Pollard, *Henry VIII* (London, 1951 reprint), p. 352.

14. G. Redworth, 'Whatever Happened to the English Reformation?,' *History Today*, 37 (Oct. 1987), pp. 29–36; G. Bernard, 'The Pardon of the Clergy Reconsidered,' *Journal of Ecclesiastical History*, 37 (1986), p. 262.

15. P. Gwyn, *The King's Cardinal* (London, 1990), p. 595.

16. R. W. Hoyle, 'The Origins of the Dissolution of the Monasteries,' *Historical Journal*, 38 (1995), esp. pp. 284–90.

17. Erastianism means lay domination of the Church.

18. J. J. Scarisbrick, *Henry VIII* (London, 1968), p. 279.

19. G. Nicholson, 'The Act of Appeals and the English Reformation,' in C. Cross *et al.* (eds), *Law and Government under the Tudors* (Cambridge, 1988), pp. 19–30.

20. J. Guy, 'Thomas Cromwell and the Intellectual Origins of the Henrician Revolution,' in A. Fox and J. Guy, *Reassessing the Henrician Age: Humanism, Politics and Reform, 1500–1550* (Oxford, 1986), p. 159.

21. As argued by C. Russell, 'Henry VIII and Religion,' in J. Morrill (ed.), *The Oxford Illustrated History of Tudor and Stuart Britain* (Cambridge, 1996), pp. 272–3. However, this seems false because Cranmer received no forewarning, but was in Germany at the time and had recently married.

22. Scarisbrick, *Henry VIII*, p. 403.

23. Scarisbrick, *Henry VIII*, pp. 340–1; Scarisbrick, *Reformation*, p. 82.

24. Dickens, *English Reformation*, pp. 124–5.

25. G. R. Elton, 'Politics and the Pilgrimage of Grace,' in B. C. Malament (ed.), *After the Reformation. Essays in Honour of J. H. Hexter* (Manchester, 1982), pp. 25–56.

26. M. Bush, *The Pilgrimage of Grace* (Manchester, 1996).
27. Bush, *Pilgrimage*, pp. 416–17.

5 Mid-Tudor Turbulence, 1547–58: Edward VI and Mary I

1. A. F. Pollard, *England under Protector Somerset* (London, 1900).
2. W. K. Jordan, *Edward VI: the Young King* (London, 1968); W. K. Jordan, *Edward VI: the Threshold of Power* (London, 1970).
3. Jordan, *Threshold of Power*, p. 210.
4. Jordan, *Threshold of Power*, p. 517.
5. E. Russell, 'Mary Tudor and Mr Jorkins', *Historical Research*, 63 (1990), pp. 263–76.
6. S. T. Bindoff (ed.), *The House of Commons, 1509–1558* (London, 1982), App. xi, 16.
7. C. Haigh, *English Reformations* (Oxford, 1993), pp. 206–16.

6 The Reign of Elizabeth, 1558–1603

1. From Edmund Spenser's poem *Prothalamion* (*c*. 1596).
2. J. E. Neale, 'The Elizabethan Age', in his *Essays in Elizabethan History* (London, 1958), p. 22.
3. C. Haigh, *Elizabeth I* (London, 1988), p. 7.
4. Haigh, *Elizabeth I*, p. 18.
5. S. Doran, *Monarchy and Matrimony. The Courtships of Elizabeth I* (London, 1996).
6. W. MacCaffrey, 'Elizabethan Politics: the First Decade, 1558–1568', *Past and Present*, 24 (1963), pp. 25–26.
7. S. Adams, 'Faction, Clientage and Party. English Politics, 1550–1603', *History Today*, 32 (Dec. 1982); S. Adams, 'Eliza Enthroned? The Court and its Politics', in C. Haigh (ed.), *The Reign of Elizabeth I* (Athens, Ga, 1985), pp. 55–77.
8. Haigh, *Elizabeth I*, pp. 99–101.
9. P. W. Hasler, *The House of Commons, 1558–1603* (London, 1981), vol.1, p. 63.
10. A. L. Rowse, *William Shakespeare* (London, 1963), pp. 220–7.
11. P. Croft, 'The Reputation of Robert Cecil', *History Today*, 43 (Nov. 1993), p. 44.
12. Haigh, *Elizabeth I*, p. 103.
13. Parliaments were called in 1559, 1563 (with a second session in 1566–7), 1571, 1572 (with two later sessions in 1576 and 1581), 1584, 1586, 1589, 1593, 1597 and 1601.
14. Neale, *Elizabeth and her Parliaments, 1559–1581*, p. 134.
15. J. S. Roskell, 'Perspectives in English Parliamentary history', *Bulletin of John Rylands Library*, 46 (1963–4), pp. 448–75.

16. G. R. Elton, '"The Body of the Whole Realm": Parliament and Representation in Medieval England', in his *Studies in Tudor and Stuart Politics and Government*, vol. 2 (Cambridge, 1974), pp. 19–61.

17. G. R. Elton, *The Parliament of England, 1559–1581* (Cambridge, 1986), pp. 350–5.

18. N. Jones, *Faith by Statute* (London, 1982).

19. 'The body of our Lord Jesus Christ which was given for thee preserve thy body and soul unto everlasting life; and take and eat this in remembrance that Christ died for thee, and feed on him in thine heart by faith with thanksgiving.'

20. P. Collinson, *English Puritanism* (London, 1983), pp. 7–11.

21. R. T. Kendall, *Calvin and English Calvinism to 1649* (Oxford, 1979), esp. pp. 13–76. Whereas Calvin taught that Christ had died for all men but interceded only for the elect, Perkins claimed that Christ had died only for the elect.

22. C. Haigh. 'The Continuity of Catholicism in the English Reformation', *Past and Present*, 93 (1981), pp. 36–69; 'From Monopoly to Minority: Catholicism in Early Modern England', *Transactions of the Royal Historical Society* 5th series, 31 (1981), pp. 131–2.

23. M. L. Carrafiello, 'English Catholicism and the Jesuit Mission of 1580–81', *Historical Journal*, 37 (1994), pp. 761–74, who argues for Parsons' political aims since 1575.

24. Haigh, *English Reformations*, pp. 264–7; 'From Monopoly to Minority', pp. 129–47; P. McGrath, 'Elizabethan Catholicism: a Reconsideration', *Journal of Ecclesiastical History*, 35 (1984), pp. 414–28; debate, 36 (1985), 394–406.

25. Francis Duke of Anjou, previously known as the Duke of Alençon, was the brother of Henry Duke of Anjou, now King Henry III of France.

26. Notably the 'sieve portraits' of 1579–83. See R. Strong, *Gloriana: the Portraits of Queen Elizabeth I* (New York, 1987), pp. 94–107.

27. For the growth of Elizabethan trade, see R. Brenner, *Merchants and Revolution: Commercial Change, Political Conflict and London's Overseas Traders, 1550–1653* (Cambridge, 1993), pp. 4–22.

28. J. Thirsk, *Economic Policy and Projects. The Development of a Consumer Society in Early Modern England* (Oxford, 1986).

7   The Coming of the Stuarts: James I, 1603–25

1. The House of Richmond, to be less anachronistic. The link between Tudors and Stewarts came from the marriage of Margaret Tudor, Henry VII's daughter, to James IV.

2. During the early sixteenth century it became more usual to spell the family name as Stuart, mainly because of the French influence in Scotland and the lack of the letter *w* in the French alphabet.

3. Great-grandaughter of Margaret Tudor by her second husband the Earl of Angus.
4. L. Stone, *The Causes of the English Revolution, 1529–1642* (London, 1972), p. 91.
5. C. Russell, 'Parliamentary History in Perspective, 1604–1629', *History*, 61 (1976), p. 1.
6. J. Sommerville, *Politics and Ideology in England, 1603–1640* (London, 1986); 'The Ancient Constitution Reassessed', in R. M. Smuts, *The Stuart Court and Europe* (Cambridge, 1996), pp. 39–64, esp. 58ff. G. Burgess, 'The Divine Right of Kings Reconsidered', *English Historical Review*, 107 (1992), pp. 837–61; *The Politics of the Ancient Constitution* (London, 1992); *Absolute Monarchy and the Stuart Constitution* (New Haven, 1996).
7. R. Lockyer, *Buckingham. The Life and Political Career of George Villiers* (London, 1981), p. 22.
8. Russell, 'Parliamentary History', p. 9.
9. Russell, 'Parliamentary History', pp. 2–3.
10. W. Notestein, *The Winning of the Initiative by the House of Commons* (London, 1924), pp. 26, 32–40.
11. S. Lambert, 'Procedure in the House of Commons in the Early Stuart period', *English Historical Review*, 95 (1980), p. 762.
12. C. Russell, *Parliaments and English Politics, 1621–1629* (Oxford, 1979), p. 134; R. Lockyer, *The Early Stuarts* (London, 1989), pp. 202–4.
13. Russell, 'Parliamentary History', p. 18.
14. Sommerville, *Politics and Ideology*, p. 174.
15. L. Levy Peck, *Northampton. Patronage and Policy at the Court of James I* (London, 1982), pp. 208–10; C. Russell, *The Addled Parliament* (Reading, 1992), p. 17.
16. Sommerville, *Politics and Ideology*, pp. 121–7, 131. This can be compared to Charles I's banning of *Apello Caesarem* by Richard Montagu and Filmer's *Patriarcha* despite their pro-regal stance.
17. P. Collinson, 'The Jacobean Religious Settlement: the Hampton Court Conference', in H. Tomlinson (ed.), *Before the English Civil War* (London, 1983), pp. 27–51.

8 The Reign of Charles I to 1640

1. C. Russell, *Parliaments and English Politics, 1621–1629* (Oxford, 1979), pp. 227–9.
2. R. Cust, *The Forced Loan* (Oxford, 1987), pp. 91–2.
3. It has been argued that the Crown stooped to tampering with the written-up judgement in King's Bench: J. Guy, 'The Origins of the Petition of Right Reconsidered', *Historical Journal*, 25 (1982), pp. 289–312. However, this now seems insecure: M. Kishlansky,

'Tyranny Denied: Charles I, Attorney General Heath, and the Five Knights Case', *Historical Journal*, 42 (1999), pp. 53–83.

4. P. Christianson, 'Arguments on Billeting and Martial Law in the Parliament of 1628', *Historical Journal*, 37 (1994), pp. 539–67.

5. M. Smuts, 'The Puritan Followers of Henrietta Maria in the 1630s', *English Historical Review*, 93 (1978), p. 26.

6. Julian Davies argues for the pivotal role of the king, *The Caroline Captivity of the Church. Charles I and the Remoulding of Anglicanism* (Oxford, 1992). N. Tyacke emphasises Laud's role, while Peter Lake and Kenneth Fincham find it difficult to disentangle the two. These conflicting views can be sampled in K. Fincham (ed.), *The Early Stuart Church, 1603–1642* (Basingstoke, 1993), pp. 44–5, 53.

7. J. Morrill, *The Revolt of the Provinces* (London, 1980), pp. 24, 28.

8. P. Zagorin, 'Did Strafford Change Sides?', *English Historical Review*, 101 (1986), pp. 149–63.

9. P. Collinson, *The Religion of Protestants: the Church in English Society, 1559–1625* (Oxford, 1982), p. 90.

10. R. Ashton, *Reformation and Revolution* (London, 1984), p. 294.

11. N. Tyacke, *The Anti-Calvinists: the Rise of English Arminianism, c.1590–1640* (Oxford, 1987).

12. P. G. Lake, 'Calvinism and the English Church 1570–1635', *Past and Present*, 114 (1989), p. 32.

13. G. Bernard, 'The Church of England c.1529–c.1642', *History*, 75 (1990), pp. 183–206.

14. P. White, *Predestination, Policy and Polemic* (Cambridge, 1992), pp. 287ff.

15. Davies, *Caroline Captivity*, p. 90.

16. H. Kearney, 'On Second Thoughts... Strafford in Ireland', *History Today*, 39 (July 1989), p. 24.

17. T. Ranger, 'Strafford in Ireland: a Revaluation', *Past and Present*, 19 (1960–1), pp. 26–45.

9 The Coming of War, 1640–2

1. J. Morrill, *The Nature of the English Revolution: Essays* (London, 1993), ch. 1.

2. C. Russell, *The Fall of the British Monarchies* (Oxford, 1991), p. 1.

3. For the notion of underlying tension and polarisation, see C. Hill, 'Political Discourse in Early Seventeenth-century England', in C. Jones *et al.* (eds), *Politics and People in Revolutionary England* (Oxford, 1986), pp. 41–64; T. Cogswell, 'Underground Verse and the Transformation of Early Stuart Political Culture', in S. D. Amussen and M. A. Kishlansky (eds), *Political Culture and Cultural Politics in Early Modern England* (Manchester, 1995), pp. 277–300; R. Cust, 'News and Politics in Early Seventeenth-century England', *Past and Present*, 112 (1986), pp. 60–90.

4. Morrill, *Nature*, p. 5.
5. Morrill, *Nature*, pp. 33ff.
6. Russell, *Fall*, p. 28.
7. M. Kishlansky, *Parliamentary Selection, Social and Political Choice in Early Modern England* (Cambridge, 1986), p. 229.
8. Payment to maintain soldiers on their journey to join up with the main army.
9. S. Lambert, 'The Opening of the Long Parliament', *Historical Journal*, 27 (1984), pp. 265–87.
10. J. Morrill, 'The Unweariableness of Mr Pym: Influence and Eloquence in the Long Parliament', in Amussen, *Political Culture*, pp. 19–54.
11. J. Adamson, 'The Baronial Context of the English Civil War', *Transactions of the Royal Historical Society* 5th ser., 40 (1990), pp. 93–120; Lambert, 'Long Parliament', pp. 283–4.
12. J. P. Kenyon, *Stuart England* (London, 1985), p. 136.
13. Later known as second Earl of Manchester.
14. Adamson, 'The Baronial Context', p. 94.
15. C. Russell, 'The Parliamentary Career of John Pym' in P. Clark *et al.* (eds), *The English Commonwealth, 1547–1640* (Leicester, 1979), p. 151; Russell, *Fall*, p. 473.

10 The British Civil Wars, 1642–51

1. J. Malcolm, 'The King in Search of Soldiers: Charles I in 1642', *Historical Journal*, 21 (1978), pp. 257–68.
2. M. D. G. Wanklyn and P. Young, 'A King in Search of Soldiers: Charles I in 1642: a Rejoinder', *Historical Journal*, 24 (1981), pp. 147–54.
3. J. Adamson, 'The Baronial Context of the English Civil War', *Transactions of the Royal Historical Society* 5th ser., 40 (1990), pp. 110ff.
4. M. Kishlansky, *The Rise of the New Model Army* (Cambridge, 1979), p. 26.
5. Adamson, 'The Baronial Context', p. 113.
6. Kishlansky, *Rise*, pp. 27, 45, 50.
7. I. Gentles, *The New Model Army in England, Ireland and Scotland, 1645–1653* (Oxford, 1992), p. 5.
8. Adamson, 'The Baronial Context', pp. 115–16.
9. Gentles, *New Model Army*, pp. 91, 115.
10. Gentles, *New Model Army*, pp. 149–50.
11. J. Adamson, 'The English Nobility and the Projected Settlement of 1647', *Historical Journal*, 30 (1987), pp. 567–602. Cf. M. Kishlansky, 'Saye What?' *Historical Journal*, 33 (1990), pp. 917–37; 34 (1991), pp. 231–55.
12. B. Manning, *1649. The Crisis of the English Revolution* (London, 1992), p. 43.

13. Manning, *1649*, p. 14.
14. J. P. Kenyon, *The Civil Wars of England* (New York, 1988), p. 33.
15. C. Hill, *The Century of Revolution* (1991 reprint), p. 102.
16. Kenyon, *Civil Wars*, p. 38.
17. J. Morrill (ed.), *Reactions to the English Civil War, 1642–1649* (London, 1982), p. 14.
18. R. Howell, 'Neutralism, Conservatism and Political Alignment in the English Revolution: the Case of the Towns, 1642–9' in Morrill, *Reactions*, pp. 67–88.
19. J. Morrill, 'The Ecology of Allegiance in the English Revolution', *Journal of British Studies*, 26 (1987), pp. 45–67; Underdown's reply, pp. 468–79.

11 The English Republic

1. S. C. A. Pincus, *Protestantism and Patriotism* (Cambridge, 1996), pp. 14ff, 190.
2. B. Worden, *The Rump Parliament* (Cambridge, 1974), pp. 345–84.
3. A. Woolrych, *Commonwealth to Protectorate* (Oxford, 1982), ch. 3 for an exhaustive discussion of the possibilities.
4. B. Coward, *Cromwell* (Harlow, 1991), p. 76.
5. A. Woolrych, 'The Cromwellian Protectorate: a Military Dictatorship?', *History*, 75 (1990), p. 209; P. Gaunt, *Oliver Cromwell* (Oxford, 1996), pp. 169ff.
6. Pincus, *Protestantism*, p. 191; B. Capp, *Cromwell's Navy* (Oxford, 1989), pp. 395–6.
7. C. Durston, 'The Fall of Cromwell's Major Generals', *English Historical Review*, 113 (1998), p. 33.
8. C. Hill, *The World Turned Upside Down* (Harmondsworth, 1975), p. 85; B. Reay, B. and J. F. McGregor (eds), *Radical Religion in the English Revolution* (New York, 1984).
9. J. Morrill, 'The Church in England, 1642–9', in J. Morrill (ed.), *Reactions to the English Civil War* (London, 1982), pp. 89–114.

Epilogue: the Restoration and beyond

1. J. C. D. Clark, *Revolution and Rebellion: State and Society in England in the 17th and 18th Centuries* (Cambridge, 1986), p. 130.
2. Notably, A. McInnes, 'When was the English Revolution?', *History*, 67 (1982), pp. 377–92.
3. J. Miller, *Bourbon and Stuart* (New York, 1987), p. 228. However, the differences between English and French political realities are clarified in his 'The Potential for Absolutism in Later Stuart England', *History*, 69 (1984), pp. 187–207.

4. For the old debate see L. Stone, *Social Change and Revolution in England, 1540–1640* (London, 1965).
5. L. Stone, 'The Bourgeois Revolution Revisited', *Past and Present*, 109 (1985), pp. 44–54; R. Brenner, *Merchants and Revolution: Commercial Change, Political Conflict and London's Overseas Traders, 1550–1653* (Cambridge, 1993).
6. C. Hill; 'The Place of the Seventeenth-century Revolution in English History', in S. N. Mukherjee and J. O. Ward (eds), *Revolution as History* (Sydney, 1989), pp. 24–30; idem, 'A Bourgeois Revolution?', in J. Pocock (ed.), *Three British Revolutions* (Princeton, 1980), pp. 109–39.
7. Stone, 'Bourgeois Revolution', p. 53.
8. J. P. Kenyon, *Stuart England* (Harmondsworth, 2nd edn, 1985), p. 195.
9. C. Hill, *The Century of Revolution* (Edinburgh, 1961), pp. 224–5; L. Stone, 'The Results of the English Revolutions of the Seventeenth Century', in Pocock, *Three British Revolutions*, pp. 50–2.
10. McInnes, 'When was the English Revolution?', pp. 377–92.
11. McInnes, 'When was the English Revolution?', p. 387.

Bibliography

1   The Wars of the Roses

Carpenter, C., *The Wars of the Roses: Politics and the Constitution in England, c. 1437– 1509* (Cambridge, 1997).

Kekewich, M. *et al.*, *The Politics of Fifteenth-Century England. John Vale's Book* (Stroud, 1995)

Pollard, A. J. (ed.), *The Wars of the Roses* (New York, 1995).

Watts, J., *Henry VI and the Politics of Kingship* (Cambridge, 1996).

2   The Restored Monarchy, 1461–1509: Edward IV, Richard III and Henry VII

Britnell, R. H., *The Closing of the Middle Ages? England, 1471–1529* (Oxford, 1997).

Gunn, S. J., 'The Courtiers of Henry VII', *English Historical Review*, 108 (1993).

Hicks, M. A., *Richard III and his Rivals* (London, 1991).

Luckett, D. A., 'Crown Patronage and Political Morality: the Case of Giles, Lord Daubeney', *English Historical Review* 101 (1995).

Pollard, A. J., *Richard III and the Princes in the Tower* (Stroud, 1991).

Weir, A., *The Princes in the Tower* (London, 1992).

3   The Reign of Henry VIII, 1509–47

Block, J., *Factional Politics and the English Reformation, 1520–1540* (Woodbridge, 1993).

Elton, G. R., *Thomas Cromwell* (Bangor, 1991).

Loades, D., *The Politics of Marriage. Henry VIII and his Queens* (Stroud, 1994).

For a symposium by various historians on Elton's work, see *Transactions of the Royal Historical Society*, 6th ser., 7 (1997).

4   The Henrician Reformation

Bernard, G. W., 'The Making of Religious Policy, 1533–46; Henry VIII and the Search for the Middle Way,' *Historical Journal*, 41 (1998).

Harper-Bill, C., *The Pre-Reformation Church in England, 1400–1530* (London, 1996).
Loades, D., *Revolution in Religion: 1530–1570* (Cardiff, 1992).
MacCulloch, D. (ed.), *The Reign of Henry VIII* (Basingstoke, 1995).
Rex. R., *Henry VIII and the English Reformation* (Basingstoke, 1993).

5   Mid-Tudor Turbulence, 1547–58: Edward VI and Mary I

Loach, J., 'Mary Tudor and the Re-catholicisation of England', *History Today*, 44 (Nov. 1994).
Loach, J., *Parliament and the Crown in the Reign of Mary Tudor* (Oxford, 1986).
Loades, D., *Essays on the Reign of Edward VI* (Bangor, 1994).
Loades, D., *John Dudley, Duke of Northumberland* (Oxford, 1996).
Loades, D., *The Mid-Tudor Crisis, 1545–1565* (Basingstoke, 1992).
MacCulloch, D., *The Later Reformation in England 1547–1603* (London, 1990).
Pettegree, A., *Marian Protestantism* (Aldershot, 1996).
Shagan, E. H., 'Protector Somerset and the 1549 Rebellions: New Sources and New Perspectives', *English Historical Review*, 14 (Feb. 1999).

6   The Reign of Elizabeth, 1558–1603

Adams, S., 'A Godly peer? Leicester and the Puritans', *History Today*, 40 (Jan. 1990).
Alford, S., *The Early Elizabethan Polity: William Cecil and the British Succession Crisis, 1558–1569* (Cambridge, 1998).
Dean, D. M. and Jones, N. L. (eds), *The Parliaments of Elizabethan England* (Oxford, 1990).
Deane, D., *Law-making and Society in Late Elizabethan England: the Parliament of England* (Cambridge, 1996).
Foster, A., *The Church of England, 1570–1640* (Harlow, 1994).
Guy, J. (ed.), *The Reign of Elizabeth I: Court and Culture in the Last Decade* (Cambridge, 1995).
MacCaffrey, W. T., *Elizabeth I* (London, 1993).
Marsh, C., *Popular Religion in Sixteenth-Century England* (Basingstoke, 1998).
Somerset, A., *Elizabeth I* (London, 1991).

7   The Coming of the Stuarts: James I, 1603–25

Durston, C., *James I* (London, 1993).

Foster, A., *The Church of England, 1570–1640* (Harlow, 1994).
Houston, S. J., *James I* (London, 1995).
Lindley, D., *The Trials of Frances Howard* (London, 1993).
Lockyer, R., *James I* (New York, 1998).
Patterson, W. B., *King James VI and I and the Reunion of Christendom* (Cambridge, 1997).
Peck, L. (ed.), *The Mental World of the Jacobean Court* (Cambridge, 1991).
Smith, D. L., *A History of the Modern British Isles, 1603–1707: the Double Crown* (Oxford, 1998).

8   The Reign of Charles I to 1640

Foster, A., *The Church of England, 1570–1640* (Harlow, 1994).
Merritt, J. F. (ed.), *The Political World of Thomas Wentworth, Earl of Strafford, 1621–1641* (Cambridge, 1996).
Sharpe, K., *The Personal Rule of Charles I* (New Haven, Conn., 1992).
Young, Michael B., *Charles I* (New York, 1997).

9   The Coming of War, 1640–2

Cust, R. and Hughes, A. (eds), *Conflict in Early Stuart England* (London, 1989) .
Donald, P., *An Uncounselled King: Charles I and the Scottish Troubles, 1637–1641* (Cambridge, 1990).
Downing, T. and Millman, M., *Civil War* (London, 1991).
Fissell, M., *The Bishops' Wars: Charles I's Campaigns against Scotland, 1638–1640* (Cambridge, 1994).
Hughes, A., *The Causes of the English Civil War* (Basingstoke, 1991).
Morrill, J. (ed.), *The Impact of the English Civil War* (London, 1991).
Russell, C., *The Causes of the English Civil War* (Oxford, 1990).

10   The British Civil Wars, 1642–51

Adamson, J., 'The English Context of the British Civil Wars', *History Today*, 48 (Nov. 1998).
Ashton, R., *Counter Revolution. The Second Civil War and its Origins* (New Haven, Conn., 1994).
Bennett, M., *The Civil Wars in Britain and Ireland, 1638–1651* (Oxford, 1997).
Carlton, C., *Going to the Wars: the Experience of the British Civil Wars, 1638–1651* (London, 1992).
Donagan, B., 'Prisoners in the English Civil War', *History Today*, 41 (March 1991).

Kenyon, J. and Ohlmeyer, J. (eds), *The Civil Wars* (Oxford, 1998).
Laurence, A., 'Women's Work and the English Civil War', *History Today*, 42 (June 1992).
Manning, B., *Aristocrats, Plebeians and Revolution in England, 1640–1660* (London, 1996).
Morrill, J. (ed.), *The Impact of the English Civil War* (London, 1991).
Morrill, J., *The Nature of the English Revolution* (London, 1993).
Ohlmeyer, J., 'The Wars of the Three Kingdoms', *History Today*, 48 (Nov. 1998)
Porter, R., *Destruction in the English Civil Wars* (Dover, NH, 1994).
Russell, C., *The Fall of the British Monarchies, 1637–42* (Oxford, 1991).
Seel, G., 'Cromwell's Trailblazer? Reinterpreting the Earl of Essex', *History Today*, 45 (April 1995).
Smith, D. L., *Constitutional Royalism and the Search for Settlement, c.1640–1649* (Cambridge, 1994).

11   The English Republic

Hutton, R., *The British Republic, 1649–1660* (Basingstoke, 1990).
Morrill, J. (ed.), *Oliver Cromwell and the English Revolution* (Harlow, 1990).
Morrill, J. (ed.), *Revolution and Restoration. England in the 1650s* (London, 1992).
Smith, D.L., *Oliver Cromwell: Politics and Religion in the English Revolution, 1640–1658* (Cambridge, 1991).
Venning, T., *Cromwellian Foreign Policy* (Basingstoke, 1995).

Index